DATE DUE

OCT 1 3 1999	
Fraser Valley Reg due Mar 2/03	

The Llanos Frontier
in Colombian History
1830–1930

The Llanos Frontier
in Colombian History
1830–1930

Jane M. Rausch

University of New Mexico Press

Albuquerque

Library of Congress Cataloging-in-Publication Data

Rausch, Jane M., 1940–
    The Llanos frontier in Colombian history, 1830–1930 / Jane M.
Rausch.
        p. cm.
    Continues author's: A tropical plains frontier : the Llanos of
Colombia, 1531–1831.
    Includes bibliographical references and index.
    ISBN 0-8263-1396-5
    1. Colombia—History—19th century. 2. Colombia—
History—1903–1946. 3. Llanos—Colombia—History. 4. Frontier and
pioneer life—Colombia—Llanos. I. Rausch, Jane M., 1940–
Tropical plains frontier. II. Title
F2273.R37 1993
986.1—dc20   92-480
                                                                          CIP

Parts of chapters 2 and 8 of the present work appeared in slightly different
versions in "Frontiers in Crisis: The Breakdown of the Missions in Far Northern
Mexico and New Granada, 1821–1849," *Comparative Studies in Society and
History*, 29:2 (April 1987), 340–59, © Cambridge University Press, and
"Rebellion in the Colombian Llanos: The Arauca Affair of 1917," *The Americas*,
34:4 (April 1978), 502–31, © Academy of American Franciscan History.

Contents

Illustrations

Maps

Tables

Preface

$\mathscr{H}$istorians who study the impact of the frontier on the development of the United States are accustomed to thinking of a line of settlement that moved rapidly westward across the North American continent. Since the publication in 1893 of Frederick Jackson Turner's paper, "The Significance of the Frontier in American History," they have come to associate the concept of *frontier* with territorial expansion, freedom from restraints, and limitless opportunities. Today they reject many aspects of Turner's thesis, but most still concede that a series of moving frontier zones influenced the course of American history, and that as a result of the constant surge of settlers to the west, the frontier defined by Turner as the "hither edge of free land" had largely disappeared by 1890.[1]

By contrast, one of the remarkable features of South American life is the persistence of frontier zones through the centuries since the conquest. Writing in 1931, geographer Isaiah Bowman pointed out that the first burst of European settlement into South America was "one of the most extraordinary human events this earth has ever witnessed."[2] The Spanish quickly incorporated the Indians in the high Andes and along the coasts into their New World empire, but when they reached the inhospitable jungles and valleys of the Amazon basin, their impetus was checked. Blocked by geographic obstacles, deadly climate, native resistance, and lack of material incentives, they contented themselves with extending nominal rule over thousands of miles of unexplored wilderness. The frontier line established by the seventeenth century expanded eastward only slightly despite improved health conditions and technology that made these marginal lands potentially more accessible in the twentieth century. As a result, Bowman and other geographers have suggested that Colombia, Ecuador, Peru, and Bolivia, unlike the United States, are characterized by "permanent" frontiers and that the people who live in these eastern frontier regions are essentially "pioneers" even though they may live on farms or in villages occupied by their families for generations.[3]

One segment of this "permanent" eastern frontier is formed by the Llanos Orientales of Colombia, the tropical plains that extend east and south of the Eastern Andean Cordillera to the Venezuelan border

ix

and comprise 253,000 square kilometers. Cut by fast-flowing rivers which join the Orinoco to the east, the Llanos are subjected to annual cycles of severe flooding and drought. Strips of rain forest stand along the rivers, but the predominant vegetation is tall, tropical bunch grass. The region, which includes the Department of Meta, the Intendancy of Casanare, and the Comisarías of Arauca and Vichada, accounts for one-fifth of Colombia's national domain but only 1.7 percent of its population.[4]

By 1830 the Llanos frontier was already old. Ten years before, the patriot victory in the War of Independence (1810–21) ended three centuries of Spanish rule and a devastating conflict that had reduced the once flourishing province of Casanare to a few thousand inhabitants. South of the Meta River lay the Llanos of San Martín, a wilderness little altered by the presence of some fifteen hundred whites, while beyond the line of settlement lived the Guahibo Indians, increasingly determined to protect their ancestral territory from further encroachment.

Throughout the nineteenth century the governments of Colombia sporadically attempted to develop the eastern portion of the republic. Their strategies included reviving the missions, promoting steam navigation on the Meta River, building roads, encouraging immigration, and fostering economic growth by introducing new crops, improved pasture, and better cattle breeds. By the beginning of the twentieth century these policies had little impact on Casanare, which remained as isolated geographically, economically, and politically as in colonial times. On the other hand, Arauca registered modest growth due to its close contacts with Venezuela; while the Llanos of San Martín, now organized as the National Intendancy of Meta with a population of nearly twelve thousand, a viable highway to Bogotá, and an economy bolstered by rice cultivation and improved cattle breeding, had emerged as the region with the highest development potential. Yet, even in Meta, the *colonos* (settlers) clung close to the Andean Cordillera. The frontier exhibited little tendency to move rapidly across the endless grasslands as had occurred in the western United States, southern Argentina, northern Mexico, or more recently in the Brazilian Amazon. As geographers Raymond Crist and Ernesto Guhl observed in 1956, "The tragedy of the Llanos is the tragedy of a frontier zone that by its very nature is not yet able to live a life of its own."[5]

In 1984 the University of New Mexico Press published *A Tropical Plains Frontier: The Llanos of Colombia 1531–1831*, in which I traced the history of the Llanos of San Martín, Casanare, and Arauca, and their interaction with the Colombian highlands from the sixteenth century to the breakup of Gran Colombia. The study which follows continues that history from the founding of the independent nation of New Granada to the election of Enrique Olaya Herrera as president, in 1930. My objectives remain the same: to illuminate an unexplored theme in Colombian historiography and to provide data for scholars concerned with comparative world frontiers. The research demonstrates that the Llanos as a region and as a tropical frontier have played a far greater role in the national evolution of Colombia than heretofore acknowledged, and that the problems the Llanos pose for future development have much in common with other Amazonian frontiers that have remained outside modern exploitation and settlement. The monograph is based on a review of manuscripts and published documents at the Archivo Histórico Nacional, Archivo del Congreso, Biblioteca Nacional, Biblioteca del Ministerio de Gobierno, and the Biblioteca Luís Angel Arango in Bogotá; the Archivo Departmental de Boyacá in Tunja; and the University of Massachusetts Library in Amherst. In addition, visits were made to the Llanos cities of Villavicencio, San Martín, Puerto López, Yopal, and Arauca.

For a definition of the elusive concept of *frontier,* I have resorted to the model proposed by Howard Lamar and Leonard Thompson, which asserts that a "frontier" is a geographic area where the edge of Hispanic settlement meets the wilderness. Since the wilderness is not empty but inhabited by native Americans, the frontier is also a zone of interpenetration between two previously distinct societies, and the geographic characteristics of the area set the limits for human activity there. The Colombians intrude into the area from their base of operations, or "metropolis," in the Andean highlands. They establish institutions designed to incorporate the land and people into the republic. Over the course of centuries the interplay of cultures with the environment produces a regional identity that has an impact on the metropolis.[6] The Indian contribution is an integral part of the story, but because of the nature of my sources, my primary concern is with the Colombian side of the frontier.[7]

The country known since 1886 as the Republic of Colombia has had many names during its long history. Under Spanish rule it was first the Presidency and later the Viceroyalty of the New Kingdom of Granada. Between 1819 and 1830 it united with Ecuador and Venezuela to form the short-lived nation of Colombia, which modern historians refer to as Gran Colombia. On achieving independence, it became New Granada (1832–57), the Granadan Confederation (1857–63), the

United States of Colombia (1863–86), and finally the Republic of Colombia. To minimize confusion, I refer to New Granada and New Granadans in the chapters dealing with the years before 1863 and to Colombia and Colombians in those dealing with the years after. I have also taken the liberty of calling the towns of Arauca and San Martín Arauca City and San Martín City to distinguish them from the regions with the same names.

Many institutions and people have contributed to this project since its inception in 1973. Generous grants from the National Geographic Society, the American Philosophical Society, the Fulbright Program, and the University of Massachusetts Graduate Research Council facilitated the research. In all the archives and libraries where I studied, I received unfailing courtesy and much assistance. Among directors and staffs of those institutions, a special word of thanks goes to Alberto Lee López and Pilar Moreno de Angel of the Archivo Histórico Nacional; Jaime Duarte French of the Biblioteca Luís Angel Arango; Conrado Zuluaga Osorio of the Biblioteca Nacional; and Pauline P. Collins of the University of Massachusetts Library.

I want to acknowledge the help of María Eugenia Romero Moreno, who has devoted her career to recovering the history of the Llanos. Through the organization of Orinoquia Siglo XXI, she has coordinated the efforts of scholars from many different academic disciplines who are studying the region; and the success of the First Simposio de Historia de los Llanos Colombo–Venezolanos in Villavicencio, August 11–13, 1988, was a tribute to her dedication. David Weber provided encouragement and direction at a critical point in my work, and Catherine LeGrande shared with me unpublished data collected during her own research in Bogotá. Rogerio Guáqueta Gallardo, J. Noé Herrera, Miguel Izard, Audrey Kieras, Susan Berglund, Erika Brieke, and Gerald and Dorothy McFarland all gave generously of their time and wisdom. Frank Safford and Marco Palacios read the text and made many helpful suggestions. I am indebted to Patricia Cutts for her fine maps and to Karen Thatcher for her careful preparation of the manuscript. Finally, I am grateful for the unflagging support of my husband, Marvin D. Rausch, whose patience and understanding made the completion of this work possible. For its errors and shortcomings, I alone am responsible.

Amherst, Massachusetts
June 1991

1. New Granada and the Llanos Frontier

*W*hen New Granada embarked upon an independent existence after the breakup of Gran Colombia, one of the most difficult tasks its leaders confronted was to mold a conglomeration of disparate regions into an integrated nation. Rugged topography divided the country into two distinct parts: the western third dominated by the Andean Cordillera, with its three high ranges running north and south and separated by the deep longitudinal valleys of the Cauca and Magdalena rivers, while fringed on the north and west by coastal lowlands; and the two-thirds lying to the east of the Andes and made up of the Amazon rain forest south of the Guaviare River and the Llanos Orientales, or tropical plains, to the north of it. Throughout the colonial era the bulk of the population lived in isolated clusters in the western part of the country, set apart from each other by mountains, jungles, and rivers and dependent on the Magdalena River for access to the Caribbean Sea and the world beyond. The eastern two-thirds formed a remote frontier, first settled in the sixteenth century but never effectively exploited or developed.[1] An understanding of the constraints imposed by geography on both parts is vital for an analysis of the development of civilization in the Llanos between 1830 and 1930. The Colombians expelled the Spanish after nine years of fighting, but they could not so easily conquer the challenges posed by topography nor alter the historical relationship of the eastern frontier to the western heartland—a relationship that had crystalized during three hundred years of Spanish rule.

The Colombian Heartland

Since all of Colombia lies within tropical latitudes, the Spanish, like the Indians before them, preferred to live in the cool highlands created by the Andes. By 1830 approximately 60 percent of the population of one and one-half million lived in or around Bogotá, Tunja, and Socorro at altitudes of more than seven thousand feet in the altiplano of the Eastern Cordillera or along its western slope. Another

1

15 percent, including a high proportion of black slaves, inhabited the agricultural and pastoral areas of Popayán and the Cauca Valley to the south and west or lived in the mining zone on the Pacific slopes of the Western Cordillera. The northern coastal region, including Panama and the seaports of Cartagena, Santa Marta, and Barranquilla, accounted for 15 percent of the people, while 9 percent lived in Antioquia, which was rich in minerals but poor in agriculture and formed a closely knit, dynamic society nestled between the coast and the Cauca Valley.[2]

Transportation between these regions was uncertain and hazardous. Little more than mule trails, the roads pitched off down the sides of steep mountain slopes at gradients only animals could negotiate. During the rainy season, torrential storms frequently washed out whatever paths had been cut through the Andes, and on even the most important highway linking Bogotá to Honda on the Magdalena, "mules sank to their girths in mud holes or skittered over slippery clay slopes."[3] Communication from the highland interior to the Caribbean coast depended on the Magdalena River. Boats poled by black slaves or freedmen took several weeks to make their way up six hundred miles of shifting channels to reach Honda, where passengers and freight were transferred to mules for the long haul up the Eastern Cordillera to Bogotá or across the even more treacherous Western Cordillera to the Cauca Valley. By the 1850s the introduction of steamships greatly expedited travel along this route, but the trip remained costly and arduous throughout the nineteenth century.[4]

Geographic isolation fostered the regional self-sufficiency that characterized the New Granadan economy. Almost every region enjoyed variations in altitude within a closely circumscribed area and produced many foods for a diversified diet. Each was more or less self-sufficient in agriculture, but some had assets that could be shared with the others—manufactures, flour, and textiles in the Eastern Cordillera; silver and gold mining in Cauca and Antioquia; and livestock in the coastal plains and the upper Magdalena. During Spanish rule, the costs of goods moving into the interior of the country via the Magdalena were high enough to protect domestic producers and to provide some leeway for overland freight charges. This national market survived the War of Independence but began to break down in the 1840s, when the adoption of free-trade policies and the use of steamboats on the Magdalena lowered the cost of foreign goods arriving in the interior. In the second half of the nineteenth century, British manufactures and North American agriculture usurped the regional markets, reducing Colombian wheat growers and textile weavers in the highlands to production on a local subsistence basis.[5]

Regionalism also dominated politics in the national period. New Granada's eighteen provinces, which made up the republic in 1831, had increased to thirty-six provinces in 1855, some of which were much more powerful than others. The dominant elites hailed from Bogotá in the altiplano; Medellín and Manizales in the mid-Cauca Valley; Cali and Popayán in the upper Cauca Valley; and Cartagena, Santa Marta, and the new city of Barranquilla on the Caribbean Coast. They were landowners and merchants, who along with the middle-class professional men, government officials, clergy, and intellectuals made up the ruling element in the country; and in 1831 they were loosely allied in two ideological groups. Those fanatically devoted to the Liberator Simón Bolívar and those who took a more moderate stance on his behalf were called the Bolivarians. Their opponents were the Santanderistas, followers of Francisco Paula de Santander, who objected to the authoritarianism and militarism associated with Bolívar's personal rule. After the death of Bolívar in 1830 the Santanderistas gained the upper hand and elected their leader president two years later. In 1836 the candidate of the moderate Bolivarians, Ignacio Márquez, succeeded Santander to the highest office. By the 1850s the Bolivarians and the Santanderistas coalesced into the Conservative and Liberal parties and adopted distinctive strategies to deal with the major political issues of the time—the relations between church and state, the role of the individual, federalism, and the reform of the colonial economic structure.[6] Absorbed by these pressing concerns, neither party devoted much thought to the Llanos, which, along with the Amazon jungle, formed a little-known frontier. Then, as now, highland politicians tended to dismiss this part of the nation as a worthless tropical desert or to extoll it unrealistically as a fabulous "eastern land of promise" destined to become the Colombian heartland in the not-too-distant future.

The Llanos of Colombia and Venezuela

The vast grasslands that spread across north central South America are no less imposing than the Andean mountains. The region that extends from the Eastern Cordillera to the Atlantic Ocean, bounded by

the Coastal Range to the north and by the Orinoco River and its Guaviare tributary on the south, covers some 300,000 square kilometers of
Venezuela and 253,000 square kilometers of Colombia. Sloping gently
from a few hundred feet in elevation at the base of the mountains
toward the Orinoco, the plains are broken here and there by low mesas
and are drained by numerous tributaries of that great river, the largest
being the Apure, Arauca, and Meta rivers. Although they are hot
throughout the year, the Llanos are alternately flooded and dry in response to changing conditions of weather and terrain. The rainy season, or "winter," begins in May and intensifies between June and
October, when much of the land becomes flooded. During the dry
season, or "summer," from December to March the swollen rivers re-
cede; the land becomes parched while the grass turns brown and
brittle for lack of moisture. Dense forests line the stream beds and
cover the base of the mountains, but the typical vegetation is tall,
coarse grass with some dry, scrubby forest and scattered palms. In this
difficult environment characterized by clouds of noxious insects, a bru-
tally hot climate, and unappetizing pasturage, cattle and horses introduced by the Spanish in the sixteenth century managed to adapt and
thrive, grazing freely in large numbers over the open grassland and
forming the basis for the distinctive Llanero subculture that had
evolved by the eighteenth century.

The Andes, which dominate Colombia, are likewise a key geographic feature of Venezuela, creating a mountainous barrier between
the Caribbean and the plains. In Venezuela, the Eastern Cordillera
divides around the Maracaibo Basin to form the Guajira Peninsula to
the left and the Sierra Nevada de Mérida to the right. The Sierra
Nevada has many peaks above the snowline and reaches its highest
point of 5,003 meters at Pico Bolívar, near the city of Mérida. Farther
to the east it joins the Coastal Range, a mountain system of similar
length and breadth but with fewer elevations. Here the crests reach
only 2,134 meters to 2,743 meters, and there are many passes running
north and south through the cordillera. At its base are the Llanos,
which run the length of the country from east to west and form substantial portions of the states of Anzoátegui, Monagas, Guárico,
Apure, Barinas, Portuguesa, and Cojedes.[7]

Unlike the Colombian llanos, however, the Venezuelan plains
are the geographical if not the historical heartland of the republic,
comprising 35 percent of its territory. While most of the population
have preferred to live in Caracas and in other highland cities, access to

the plains is relatively easy, and the Orinoco River to the south provides a direct entry way from the Atlantic. Beginning in the sixteenth
century, black slaves escaping from plantations and cities on the coast
and in the highlands found refuge in the Llanos, where they lived by
hunting the wild cattle. Some worked as vaqueros on the *hatos*
(ranches), while others formed *palenques* (fortified hamlets of runaway
slaves) called *puntas de monte*. By the eighteenth century a boom in
ranching had sparked a wave of creole migration so that by 1810 over
one-quarter of the 785,000 inhabitants of the Capitancy General lived
in the plains.[8] The black Llaneros, branded as outlaws by the creoles,
formed the nuclei of both the royalist and patriot armies during the
War of Independence, and despite the devastation wrought by this
bloody struggle, the Llanos continued to play a significant role in the
economy and politics of republican Venezuela. Cattle increased from
2.5 million head in 1833 to 12 million in 1858. In that same year,
390,000 persons, or 40 percent of the population, lived in the plains.[9]
Llanero armies were active participants in the civil wars that wracked
Venezuela throughout the nineteenth century.

Because of the acknowledged importance of the Llanos in the
historical formation of Venezuela, most studies have concentrated on
the Venezuelan portion, obscuring the fact that the Colombian side of
the border exhibits marked contrasts.[10] In Colombia, where the passes
through the formidable Eastern Cordillera lie above 3,200 meters (ten
thousand feet), only the most determined colonists, escaped slaves,
and outlaws found their way out to the plains. The Llanero cowboys
who emerged there were overwhelmingly mestizo, as opposed to the
mulattos and blacks in neighboring Venezuela; and in spite of the fact
that the Spanish began settlements on the western edge of the Llanos
as early as in Venezuela, the Colombian plains, with the exception of
the Jesuit missions in Casanare, did not become a significant cattle-
producing region within the viceroyalty. During the War of Independence, defeated patriot armies from the highlands fled to Casanare,
and Simón Bolívar and Francisco Paula de Santander organized there
the famous Liberation Campaign that dealt a deathblow to Spanish
rule in New Granada; but unlike the Llanos of Venezuela, the Colombian plains failed to recover demographically or economically after
the war. While the above generalizations apply to all three subregions
of the Colombian Llanos, a review of their geography and history will
show that there were also striking differences between them.
Throughout the colonial era, Casanare was populated by Spaniards,

missionaries, and Indians, and formed the core of the eastern frontier; while Arauca was settled almost exclusively by Venezuelans, and San Martín, except for some Franciscan missions, remained largely unexplored and lacking a white population.

The Llanos of Casanare

The Llanos of Casanare are a triangular-shaped area covering 67,790 square kilometers bordered by the Eastern Cordillera and by the Meta and Casanare rivers. They consist of two sections—the piedmont, or lower slopes, of the Andes, which was dominated by the highland Province of Tunja in colonial times and by the Department of Boyacá during the national period; and the open grasslands that extend to the Meta River and blend imperceptibly into the Llanos of Arauca. The geologically complex piedmont contains eight *ramales* (mountain spurs) separated by rivers that plunge down from the altiplano to make their way through the plains to the Meta. Moving from south to north, the first *ramal* is the Páramo of Las Alfombras that ends at the confluence of the Langupá and Upía rivers. The second is the Páramo of Toquillo, which begins east of Lake Tota and rises up between the valleys formed by the Upía to the west and the Cusiana River to the east. Containing rich salt deposits and fertile land, this spur was the site of the colonial towns of Chámeza and La Sal and the modern towns of Pajarito and Recetor. The third ramal originates from the Páramo of Puchicavo to the northeast of Tota Lake and separates the valley of the Cusiana on the west from that of the Cravo Sur on the east. The fourth is born in the Páramo of Pisba, near the Laguna of Socha, and divides the Cravo Sur on the southeast from the Tocaría River on the northeast. Here are located the towns of Labranzagrande and Marroquín. The fifth leaves the Alto del Perro. It separates the Tocaría on the southeast and the Pauto River to the northeast, and is the location of Paya, Pisba, and Nunchía. The sixth begins near the Laguna Ocubies and separates the Pauto to the south and the Ariporo River to the north. Here are found Támara and Pore, and descending into the plains, Trinidad and Moreno. The seventh ramal also leaves the Laguna Ocubies and separates the Ariporo to the south from the Casanare River to the north. On its southern slopes are Sácama, Chire, and Manare. Finally, there is the ramal that leaves from the Sierra Nevada del Cocuy (also known as the Sierra Nevada de

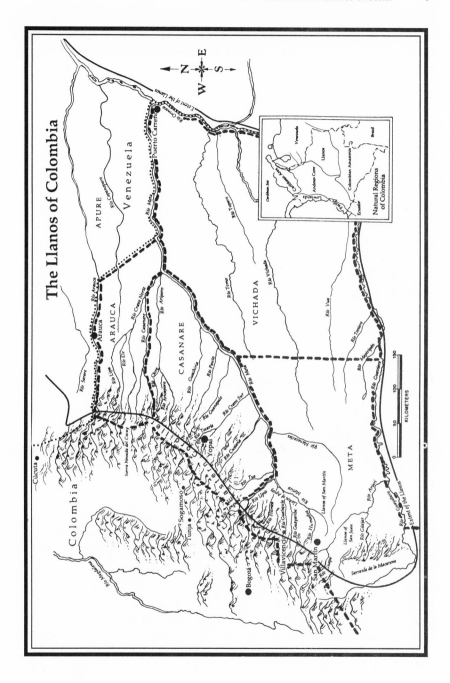

The Llanos of Colombia

Natural Regions of Colombia

Chita or Güicán), a mountain range that extends for twenty kilometers and contains the highest peaks in the Eastern Cordillera; it continues in a northeasterly direction to form the piedmont zone of the Llanos of Arauca.[11]

Spanish settlers from the highland valleys of Boyacá who moved into Casanare settled in the piedmont zone because of the healthier climate afforded by the higher altitudes. While the northern ramales are quite angular and present few opportunities for agriculture, those farther south offered better possibilities. On those slopes, creoles and Indians raised cotton to be spun into thread and woven into cloth. They grew subsistence crops of plátano, corn, and yuca. They made cheese, mined the salt deposits, and kept herds of cattle. Tobacco became an important crop by the eighteenth century, succeeded in the nineteenth century by coffee. Communication with the interior depended on perilous roads, the most important of which connected Pore and Labranzagrande with Sogamoso.

The true Llanos emerge from the forested lower level of the piedmont at about 350 meters of altitude. They are bordered by the Upía River on the west and the Casanare on the north, and are dissected by the Cusiana, Cravo Sur, Tocaría, Pauto, and Airiporo rivers—all tributaries of the Meta. Structurally speaking, there are two zones. The first zone is a strip of plains fifty to five hundred meters wide and lying next to the piedmont; they are relatively high in altitude and are made up of alluvial fans and slackwater areas called locally *bancos* and *bajos*. The soil is infertile, and the land is suitable only for grazing. The second zone, called the *plano eólico*, includes the plains that extend to the gallery forests lining the Meta River. This zone also will support cattle, although it has even poorer drainage than the alluvial section.[12]

The landscape presented by the true Llanos is grassland and sky. The temperature is always very hot. In summer the plains give off a melancholic sensation, with their arid savannas, dry grasses and rivers, and *caños* (narrow waterways, originating in the Llanos, that move with little velocity) reduced to tiny streams. In winter the land is covered with water, which forms large lakes in some places. Nevertheless, there is some fertile soil along the forested banks of the rivers. During the colonial era, creoles began to settle between the Cusiana and Pauto rivers, while the Jesuits established missions and haciendas along the Meta, between the Cusiana and the Cravo.

In precontact time, the Indians of Casanare accommodated so

well to the conditions imposed by the environment that anthropologists postulate that the region was occupied to the limits of its potential, given the exploitative techniques that were available.[13] Arawak-speaking Achagua, Sáliva, Tunebo, and other groups of cultivators lived in kinship-based hamlets in the piedmont and along the banks of the rivers. Employing slash-and-burn agriculture, they raised food crops and supplemented this diet by hunting and fishing. Some of them traded and fought with the Chibchas in the highlands, while others maintained commercial relations, via the Meta River, with people who lived as far away as the island of Trinidad, the Atlantic Coast, and the Guiana highlands.[14]

Scattered through the open plains were the Guahibos (also called Chiricoas), foragers who depended on hunting and gathering. Originally, they may have practiced agriculture, but on being forced out of choice riverine areas by stronger Indian groups, they adopted a mode of subsistence more suited to the grasslands. The Guahibos were true nomads. They had no dwellings of any kind. They travelled in kinship-related bands from place to place, hunting animals, gathering the fruit of palm trees, trapping fish and turtles in the rivers, and trading with the sedentary cultivators. Their mobility made them excellent fighters. After the arrival of the Europeans, they vigorously pursued the Achaguas and Sálivas, capturing their children and selling them to Spanish slavers and to the Dutch and their Carib allies in Guiana.[15]

The Spanish conquest of the Chibchas on the altiplano in 1538 began a new era as well in the history of Casanare. The conquerors quickly divided up the Indian villages around Bogotá and Tunja and assigned them to Spanish encomenderos. By 1544 these grants included Indians in the piedmont of the Cordillera Oriental, who had formerly paid allegiance to the Chibchas. Pauto and Támara, the two oldest towns in Casanare, were established as *doctrinas* (curacies) in that year, and in 1551 Chita and La Sal were added. Augustinians were administering doctrinas of Labranzagrande, Paya, Pisba, Morcote, and Chámeza by 1630. The residents of these towns were mostly encomienda Indians who raised cotton and wove cloth for the markets in Tunja and Bogotá.[16]

In 1588 Captain Pedro Daza founded the first Spanish city in Casanare, Santiago de las Atalayas, located near the Cuisana River at the foot of the Cordillera southeast of Tunja; and he divided up the surrounding Achagua villages in encomiendas. By 1620 the crown had designated the city as the capital of the Provincia de los Llanos, an immense, largely unknown area extending to the Orinoco and encompassing both banks of the Meta River. By the midseventeenth century, Santiago was sending twelve thousand *varas* of cotton cloth back to Tunja as well as six thousand pigs and five thousand head of cattle.[17]

In 1649, the governor of the Llanos, Don Adrian de Vargas founded two other Spanish cities, San José de Pore and Santa Bárbara de Cravo. Santa Rosa de Chire was begun in 1672 and Zapatosa in 1688, while Barroblanco and Nunchía were founded in the eighteenth century. All of these settlements were in the piedmont, and the Spanish who came here were administrators, slavers, encomenderos, or ranchers who periodically ventured out to the plains to round up wild cattle, which they slaughtered for meat and hides. Few dared to reside permanently in the open grasslands, where heat, lack of wood and food, and Guahibo attacks made life hazardous at best. To gain control of this region, the crown relied on missionaries.

In 1662 the missionary crusade got under way. While Augustinians remained in charge of the old textile-producing towns in the mountains, the Jesuits established a base in Pauto. Soon, they "reduced," or brought into submission, the Achaguas in Tame, Patute, Macaguane, San Salvador, and Betoyes—all missions located in the foothills and plains along the Casanare River. Between 1732 and 1746 they expanded operations along the Meta River, founding Guanapalo, Surimena, Jiramena, and Casimena between the Cusiana and Cravo Sur tributaries. The Jesuits supported their missions by creating eight large cattle haciendas, which in 1767 had a combined herd of 44,066 cattle and 3,634 horses.[18]

The expulsion of the Jesuits from the Spanish empire in 1767 disrupted the missions in Casanare, but it did not trigger their complete collapse, as historians have sometimes asserted. The Dominicans took over their operations in the north, and although the Junta de Temporalidades sold the haciendas to private individuals, under their rule five ex-Jesuit missions of Tame, Patute, San Salvador del Puerto, Macaguane, and Betoyes survived into the nineteenth century with a population of 5,425. The Recoletos, who received the ex-Jesuit missions along the Meta, were more aggressive. Between 1773 and 1805 they founded six new towns, each with its own cattle hacienda. By 1810 these Missions of Meta included nine towns with 8,070 Indians and nine haciendas, known as the Haciendas of Meta, with 104,400 cattle, 2,981 stallions, and 6,044 mares.[19]

By this time, largely due to the work of the missionaries, the

Provincia de los Llanos had become an integrated administrative unit within the Viceroyalty of New Granada. In 1778 its population of 20,892 included 1,535 whites (7 percent), 15,189 Indians (73 percent), 4,025 mestizos (10 percent), and 119 black slaves (less than 1 percent).[20] Pore had replaced Santiago de las Atalayas as the capital, and in spite of competition from Socorro, the creole inhabitants maintained a vigorous trade with Tunja in textiles, pottery, articles of wood and straw, and cattle. On the other hand, three hundred years of European subjugation had ravaged the Indian cultures. Spanish demand for slaves, encomienda workers, and Christian converts devastated the Achaguas, Sálivas, and Tunebos, forcing them to sacrifice much of their original way of life to survive within the new system. Entire villages were relocated, and some groups simply disappeared before the end of the seventeenth century. More fortunate were the Guahibos, who as foragers proved to have more flexibility in countering the Spanish threat. Learning to ride the wild horses, they attacked missions and haciendas and, in general, waged a fierce resistance against the white intruders. Joined by remnants of the Achaguas and Sálivas who escaped from Spanish rule, the Guahibos adopted some of their customs and began to plant cotton and bitter manioc. By the nineteenth century, the once powerful cultivators had dwindled to a handful of different tribes while the Guahibos roamed the plains with impunity, outside the line of Spanish control.[21]

On the Spanish side of the frontier, mestizaje was producing a regional subculture that blended European and native American traits. The whites imposed their political organization, language, forms of labor, and religion on the Indians, but to survive in the Llanos they had to adopt native techniques. The Indians showed them how to build houses out of palm leaves, fashion tree trunks into boats, and fish in the rivers. They taught them how to grow yuca, plátanos, and corn. Both the Indians and Spanish hunted deer, tigers, and tapirs with pointed sticks, lances, and bows and arrows. Achagua and Guahibo words became part of the regional dialect, and Indian religious beliefs made their way into Catholicism. The blend of the two traditions was especially evident in the life-style of the mestizo vaqueros who worked on the hatos and gained fame as patriot soldiers during the wars of independence.[22]

Throughout the colonial era, the crown's principal objectives in Casanare were to convert the Indians and defend the eastern border. The presidents and viceroys in Bogotá relied on missionaries to achieve these aims, and they did not regard the participation of several Casanare towns in the Comunero revolt of 1781 or the aborted insurrection of José María Rosillo and Vicente Cadena in 1809 as sufficiently alarming to warrant the stationing of militia in Pore. As a result, with the call for independence in 1810, rebel sympathizers quickly seized control of the Provincia de los Llanos, and in Arauca, Llaneros fought bravely to repel an invasion by Venezuelan royalists.

After the collapse of the First Republic in Bogotá in 1816, highland patriots retreated to the Llanos and made Casanare the base of their resistance movement against the Spanish reconquest. In August 1818, Simón Bolívar, who had installed his headquarters at Angostura and formed an alliance with José Antonio Páez in Apure, decided to send Francisco de Paula Santander to Pore to organize the disparate Llanero guerrilla factions into a new army. The following year, he led this army in a historic march across Casanare and up the Eastern Cordillera to deal the Spanish a stunning defeat at the Battle of Boyacá on August 7, 1819.

The long war was traumatic for Casanare. It disrupted the population, decimated the livestock, and depleted the economy. Some of the mission Indians were impressed into the army. Others fled to the wilderness, so that only three missions remained in 1819. When they were dismissed from the army, the Llaneros, lacking opportunities for gainful employment, joined bands of rustlers who plundered the few remaining hatos. The halfhearted efforts by Gran Colombian leaders in Bogotá to redress these conditions were not reassuring. In 1830, General Juan Nepomuceno Moreno, patriot hero and powerful caudillo, overthrew the provincial government and declared that Casanare would secede from New Granada and join Venezuela. A year later, Moreno led a Llanero army over the cordillera to help overthrow a dictatorship imposed by Rafael Urdaneta. Once they were in command, the highland leaders who had first welcomed Moreno's assistance firmly insisted that he return with his "barbarous" horde to the Llanos. In December 1831, Casanare, rebuffed by Venezuela, officially rejoined the Republic of New Granada.[23]

In 1821, the Congress of Cúcuta divided Gran Colombia into seven departments: Orinoco, Venezuela, Zulia, Boyacá, Cundinamarca, Cauca, and Magdalena, and incorporated Casanare as a province within the Department of Boyacá. With the creation of New Granada, the Fundamental Law of November 21, 1831, suppressed the former departments and established a federation of thirteen provinces, one of which was Casanare. With its capital at Pore, Casanare was subdivided into six cantons: Pore, Chire, Macuco, Nunchía, Taguana, and Arauca. The president of New Granada appointed the governor, who, in turn, chose the *jefe políticos*, or chief administrative officers, of the cantons. Each canton elected representatives to the provincial legislature, which met annually in Pore, for several weeks beginning on September 15, to consider any business brought before it by the governor. *Consejos municipales* in each town handled local matters, but they were not as powerful as the colonial cabildos.[24]

The census of 1835 set the population of Casanare at 15,948 (including 3,599 inhabitants of the canton of Arauca)—a dramatic decline of nearly 25 percent from the estimated 1810 population of 22,000 attributable to disease, war casualties, and the flight of mission Indians.[25] Neither the 1810 nor the 1835 figures counted Indians living outside white control, but in a separate report dated May 22, 1835, Governor M. Arenas estimated that there were 6,625 Indians (3,235 males and 3,390 females) living independently in tribes and *capitanías* (units ranging from 100 to 700 members loyal to a single chief). He added that the eight capitanías of Achaguas along the Vichada River interacted peacefully with the colonists, but others such as the ten Guahibo capitanías along the Casanare and Meta rivers were "indominable, treacherous murderers," who preyed upon nearby hatos and river commerce.[26] In 1836, Arenas submitted a detailed statistical summary of provincial economic activity. If Arauca is omitted, there were 15,823 cattle, 466 goats, 811 horses, 402 mules, 79 burros, and 190 sheep in the other five cantons. Casanare produced cacao, coffee, honey, cheese, salt, cotton, corn, rice, straw hats, and pottery, and sent hides and live animals to highland Boyacá and Venezuela.[27]

It is clear that in 1831 Casanare had regained political autonomy, but it had yet to recover from the damage caused by the wars. As the second smallest of the thirteen provinces (only Riohacha with a population of 14,514 had fewer people), it had little national influence, being limited to one senator in the twenty-six-member upper house of congress and one representative in the eighty-four-member lower house. Throughout the nineteenth century the region was dominated by its more populous neighbor, Boyacá, with which it maintained close political, demographic, and economic ties. When modernization, propelled by export booms in tobacco, quinine, and coffee, transformed western Colombia into the economic heartland of the nation, Casanare shared the catastrophic decline of Boyacá, which by 1870 had become the poorest state in the Colombian federation.[28]

The Llanos of Arauca

In 1831, Arauca was the most prosperous canton in Casanare. As part of the Provincia de los Llanos, under the Spanish and variously ruled by Casanare and Boyacá in the nineteenth century, this portion of the Llanos—which covers 23,490 square kilometers and extends east from the Eastern Cordillera to Apure and north from the Casanare River to the Arauca River—had, in many respects, the same historical experiences as the larger territory; but Arauca's location next to Venezuela made it seem more like a southwestern frontier of that country than the eastern limit of New Granada. Settled by Venezuelans and linked economically to the Llanos of Apure and Guárico, Arauca's ties to Bogotá, Tunja, and Pore were tenuous, and the border was a scene of constant tension and unrest. As we shall see in later chapters, the problems of governing Arauca as part of Casanare were evident throughout the nineteenth century, but it was not until 1911 that Bogotá created for it a special territorial government, in a belated effort to prevent this isolated corner of the republic from being absorbed by an ever more aggressive Venezuela.

Arauca shares with Casanare the piedmont zone formed by the Eastern Cordillera, and the ramal that extends between the Casanare and Arauca rivers contains the highest peak in the entire range, the Sierra Nevada del Cocuy (also called Sierra Nevada de Chita). At 5,527 meters, this mountain is snowcapped the year round and forms a continental divide: rivers to its north flow to the Arauca, while those to its south go down to the Meta. There are no fertile valleys on its lower slopes, so that in contrast to Casanare, the Arauca piedmont supported no major Indian or Spanish settlements.[29]

Beyond the piedmont and moving west to east, the plains of Arauca divide into two zones. The first, lying between the Casanare and Lipa rivers, is heavily forested. Its inaccessibility made it a favorite base for Guahibos, cattle rustlers, and other outlaws. The second, lying between the Lipa and Arauca rivers, consists of open grasslands readily adaptable to cattle ranching. Most of the hatos in these so-called *savanas cautivas* lay along the banks of the Arauca River, which can be navigated between June and August by ships coming up from the Orinoco. The huge lake, or *estero*, of Cachicamo is a permanent feature of this low-lying zone, and during the winter, constant rains flood a still larger area.[30] Captain Alberto Santos, who visited Arauca for the first time in January 1917, described the seasonal contrast with the astonishment of a man from the highlands:

All of this plain is covered with coarse grass higher than a man on horseback. . . . Imagine this plain without roads, so that one may get lost at any moment, flooded in winter so that rivers cannot be distinguished because all is a lake, and in summer covered with a dry straw that makes walking on foot impossible! Here are wild animals and snakes. Add to this picture the suffocating heat, the mosquitoes and other insects more or less fearful and you will have the Llanos of Arauca.[31]

The natives of Arauca, a region the Spanish called the Airico de Macaguane, were the Betoy, Jirara, and Tunebo, cultivators like the Achaguas, who lived in the foothills and along the riverbanks, and the Guahibos, who roamed the open plains. In 1662, the Jesuits began the first missions of Patute, Macaguame, and Tame on tributaries of the Casanare River. After their expulsion, the crown handed these reductions over to the Dominicans, who sustained them at a modest level. In 1785, the Capuchins accepted a mission field farther to the east, along the Ele, Lipa, and Cravo rivers. They founded five small towns, which they turned over to the Recoletos in 1796. The Cuiloto missions, as they were called, suffered from isolation, a chronic lack of material resources, and attacks by Guahibos. Although the Recoletos administered these towns until the War of Independence, they had only 642 neophytes in 1800 and lacked the vitality of their missions along the Meta.[32]

More critical to the development of Arauca than the missions was the arrival in 1780 of two men from Barinas, Venezuela, Juan Isidro Daboin, a secular priest, and Antonio Useche, a laborer, who crossed the Arauca River and founded Santa Bárbara de Arauca (which I will call Arauca City in order to distinguish it from the region Arauca) by settling down with some partially Christianized Guahibos. Soon other Venezuelans joined them, bringing their black slaves and cattle to found hatos near the town. By 1793 Arauca City, with more than one hundred white vecinos, had earned the status of *vice-parroquía* of Chire, which meant that the priest in Chire served its chapel on a regular basis and that the town was reserved exclusively for the residence of Spaniards.[33]

Arauca flourished at the turn of the eighteenth century because of its vigorous trade with Venezuela and along the Orinoco River, but with the outbreak of the War of Independence, its border location became a liability. Between 1812 and 1816, royalist armies from Venezuela attempted repeatedly to invade New Granada via Arauca, only to be beaten back by the fiercely patriotic Llaneros. As the conflict intensified, both sides confiscated cattle and horses from the hatos. In 1816, Fray Ignacio Mariño, Dominican superior of Tame, Macaguane, and Betoyes, transformed his Indian neophytes into guerrilla fighters and led them against Spanish garrisons at Cuiloto, Pore, and Chire.[34] In June 1819, Bolívar passed through Arauca City on his march across the Llanos to the Battle of Boyacá.

Despite its key role in the war, Arauca recovered much more quickly once peace was restored than did the rest of Casanare. Most of the missions of Cuiloto and Casanare had disappeared, but the hatos were soon reestablished. In 1820, Governor Juan Nepomuceno Moreno complained to Santander that Arauca was the only place in Casanare where one could still find cattle. By 1835 the herds had grown to 29,787 head, or nearly double the number in the other five cantons taken together; and there were 425 horses and 1,515 pigs.[35] Venezuelans continued to move into the territory, founding the town of Arauquita near Caño Agua Limón on the Arauca River in the early 1820s. In 1835, the canton of Arauca had 3,599 inhabitants, including 10 of the 20 black slaves registered in Casanare Province.[36]

Throughout the nineteenth century, Arauca City remained New Granada's chief port on a waterway leading to the Orinoco. Its border location and large Venezuelan population inevitably embroiled it in the turbulent politics of that neighboring country. The constant civil wars that beset Venezuela produced a stream of refugees and deposed caudillos seeking asylum in New Granada. Some made new lives for themselves in Arauca, but others plotted to return to their homeland, mounting armed incursions from Colombian soil. The canton's isolation from Bogotá and Tunja enabled such individuals to carry out their schemes without fear of punishment. Contraband trade, political unrest, and roving outlaw bands were chronic problems besetting New Granadan officials unlucky enough to have accepted a post on the Araucan frontier.

The Llanos of San Martín

In contrast to Casanare and Arauca, in 1830 there were few white inhabitants in the Llanos of San Martín south of the Meta River. Extending from the Eastern Cordillera eastward to the Orinoco and south to the Guaviare River, this region, also known as Meta, encompassed the modern Department of Meta, 83,770 square kilometers, and the Comisaría of Vichada, 98,970 square kilometers, to total 182,740 square kilometers. When one considers that these Llanos are within 145 kilometers of Bogotá and that the first permanent settlement east of the Andes was founded here at San Juan de los Llanos in 1555, their lack of development prior to the midnineteenth century is all the more remarkable. The explanation lies in the rugged topography of the Eastern Cordillera south of Bogotá and the historical orientation of that city toward the Magdalena River.

The portion of the Eastern Cordillera to the south of Bogotá is one of the least-known parts of the Andean chain. It has none of the high valleys that, with their rich soil and dense population, characterize the Cordillera to the north, and it still has not been explored for mineral resources. The range is narrower here than farther north, so that the Magdalena and Orinoco river systems are closer together. Southward, from the Páramo of Sumapaz at 4,000 meters, the Cordillera lowers until at Paz de las Cruces, at the headwaters of the Papamene branch of the Río Guayabero, its elevation is only 1,874 meters—the lowest pass in the Cordillera south of Bogotá and considerably lower than any pass farther north. On the eastern side of the Cordillera, the Río Negro flows in a longitudinal valley until it breaks through to the Llanos, but the Ariari, Guape, and Güejar flow in transversal valleys that further inhibit transportation and communication.[37]

Unlike the Spanish in Tunja, who subdued the Indian villages scattered throughout the Casanare piedmont, Bogotá's dominion was limited to the Chibchas living in the valleys of the high sierra. Cáqueza and Quetame, the principal towns to the southeast on the road to San Martín, are part of the highland department of Cundinamarca rather than of the piedmont section of the plains. The geographical obstacles presented by this road, which follows the course of the Río Negro as it meanders precipitously down the mountain, were only slightly less terrifying than those presented by the alternate route, a trail that went from Gachetá via Guasca to Medina; and they deterred all but the most intrepid individuals from sallying forth to explore the potential resources of the Llanos. Ever since the arrival of Gónzalo Jiménez de Quesada, who reached the sabana in 1538 by traveling up the Magdalena and over the western slope of the Cordillera Oriental, the orientation of Bogotá was toward the west.

The Llanos of San Martín have a second mountain range, the Serranía de la Macarena, which is detached from the Andes and distinct in its formation. La Macarena is an extensive sandstone plateau, stratigraphically related to the Guiana highland complex, which rises to an altitude of over two thousand meters. These mountains have been weathered into fantastic forms, leading early explorers to believe that they could see spires and turrets of old cities. Once these explorers assured themselves that La Macarena was not El Dorado, they were content to leave it alone, and so it remained a rugged, virgin wilderness until the twentieth century.[38]

The Llanos of San Martín divide into two zones, the Meta Cercano and the Meta Lejano. The Meta Cercano includes the plains lying between the Eastern Cordillera, La Macarena, and the Metica River, which stretch from west to east for fifty to eighty kilometers. Built up by alluviation from the Humadea, Guayaribe, Guatiquía, and Humeo tributaries to the Meta, this zone is relatively high. From the air, the rivers look like small streams cutting through the forests at the base of the cordillera, but farther out their beds become so wide that it is the forests that appear as green streams outlining the savanna rivers. During the rainy season there is constant shifting of channels and extensive flooding. Near the mountains annual rainfall is as high as 406 centimeters a year, but it decreases to the east so that the town of Cabuyaro, at the edge of the Meta Cercano, averages annually 223 centimeters. The rivers divide the zone into three sections: between the Upía and the Humadea is the Savana of Apiay; between the Humadea and the Ariari are the Llanos of San Martín; and between the Ariari and the Güejar are the Llanos of San Juan. Heavy gallery forests along the Guayabero and the Guaviare marked the dividing line between the plains and the Amazon Basin. A fourth section, called the Serranía or the Meta Medio-lejano, continues from the right of the Metica River to the Manacacías River. This "little ridge" country is a minutely dissected alluvial plain. Gallery forests, with moriche palms dominating, outline the valley floors with their permanently high groundwater tables. The hills of the Serranía often have unusual shapes, and grass protects their very steep slopes from obvious erosion.[39]

East and south of the Manacacías and the Serranía is the Meta Lejano, a zone of plains sloping gently toward the Orinoco and the Guaviare. Although certain sections resemble the Serranía, there are large expanses of perfectly level terrain. Natural grass covers all the higher surfaces, but on the poorly drained valley floors and along the rivers, there are denser stands of forest. In colonial times this region was called the Gran Airico. Today, it takes its name from the major river that flows through it, the Vichada. The plains in the Meta Lejano have a generally cooler climate, more luxuriant grass, and less protracted periods of drought. More suited for cattle than the better-known Llanos of San Martín, San Juan, and Apiay, their distance from the Eastern Cordillera and from navigable tributaries of the Orinoco delayed their development.[40] Even in the post–World War II era, the Comisaría of Vichada has played a minimal role in the evolution of the Llanos frontier south of the Meta.

That story began when Juan de Avellaneda, a former companion of the German conquistador Nicolás Federmann, set out from Santa Fe de Bogotá in 1555 to look for gold in the land east of the Andes. On the banks of the Ariari, he discovered a significant amount of alluvial gold and founded his city, San Juan de los Llanos, at the site now occupied by San Juan de Arama. On a second trip from Bogotá, Avellaneda brought cattle and settlers. For a while, the little outpost thrived by extracting a modest amount of gold and supplying expeditions that stopped on their way to search for El Dorado, but by the end of the century both the mines and the Indians captured to work them had been depleted.[41] As San Juan declined, Captain Juan de Zarate began the town of San Martín in 1641 (which I will call San Martín City to distinguish it from the region); but the settlement showed little prospect of expansion. Nominally under the jurisdiction of Santiago de las Atalayas in the Provincia de los Llanos, the two towns survived into the eighteenth century, each with fewer than one hundred white vecinos.

Along with geographic isolation, the unhealthy climate was a major obstacle to population growth. Padre Basilio Vicente de Oviedo, who surveyed all the three hundred parishes in the Archbishopric of Santa Fe in 1761, wrote that in the Llanos of San Juan and San Martín nearly everyone suffered from chills and fever. To reach Bogotá, trav-

elers had to ford deep rivers and cross the mountains on a trail so rough
that the journey was feasible only during January and February, at the
height of the dry season; "and for being today so poor and unfortunate
and without people or trade, the two cities of San Martín and San Juan
have very little communication and commerce with Santafé and other
parts." [42] An anonymous explorer of the Ariari River in the 1760s confirmed Oviedo's observations, writing:

The condition of the country and that of the inhabitants in the Christian towns is
unhappy, poor and with no hope for better ideas; all flee from future wealth preferring present misery, and even to equip the ordinary pack trains [that go] from
San Martín to San Juan, there is no one who has enough animals, pack saddles
and harnesses. They all pool together to outfit a single animal, and none of these
are mules . . . [43]

A major function of San Juan and San Martín City in the seventeenth and eighteenth centuries was to provide a base for missionaries.
In 1620, Dominicans began the campaign to proselytize the natives
when Fr. Alonso Ronquillo founded Medina at the end of the trail that
began in Gachetá, Cundinamarca. Medina remained a Dominican parish throughout the colonial era, but the priests made little effort to
convert natives in the surrounding forests. [44] Oviedo reported that by
1761 the town had "a competent number" of Indians and mestizo vecinos known as "whites," who gathered wild cacao and produced salt
from the mines in nearby Upín and Cumaral to supply the demands
of ranchers in the plains. [45] The Franciscans, who came to San Juan
and San Martín City in 1662, were more energetic. By the early eighteenth century they ruled six small missions, whose populations fluctuated daily from a handful of Sálivas and Achaguas to as many as sixty
in each village. The leading missionary enterprise in the territory was
the Jesuit Hacienda of Apiay, an estate located in the headwaters of
the Guatiquía, consisting of 11,498 hectares and 1,693 cattle divided
into three hatos—Apiay, Cumaral, and Patire. [46]

When the crown expelled the Jesuits in 1767, it sold the Hacienda of Apiay to Nicolás Bernal for 4,200 pesos and turned over three
of their missions in Casanare to the Franciscans. The Franciscans relocated one of these, Jiramena, to the Meta River, where in 1806 it
had 140 neophytes. At that time, they ruled 1,542 Indians in six other
reductions in the Llanos of San Martín—Túa, Mayoral, Cabuyaro,
Campo del Arrojo, Concepción de Arama, and Maricuare. [47] After the
War of Independence, only Jiramena remained.

In sum, before 1810 the population of the Llanos of San Martín, including mission Indians, never exceeded two thousand, in sharp contrast to the twenty-two thousand people in Casanare and Arauca. Moreover, the War of Independence, fought primarily in Casanare, had less devastating consequences. During the reconquest, a Spanish army, on orders from Pablo Morillo, seized Medina and San Martín City but did not advance farther out into the plains. In 1818, patriot chieftain Ramón Nonato Pérez retook both positions, expelling the royalists forever.[48]

The war did not drastically alter the political administration of the Llanos of San Martín. At some point in the eighteenth century, the crown detached them from the Provincia de los Llanos and placed them under the direct jurisdiction of Santa Fe de Bogotá. This arrangement continued during the Republic of Gran Colombia, with San Martín forming one of eleven cantons in the Province of Bogotá, which along with the provinces of Neiva, Mariquita, and Antioquia made up the Department of Cundinamarca. The Fundamental Law of November 21, 1831, which organized New Granada, abolished the departments, but it left the provinces intact so that San Martín continued as a canton in the Province of Bogotá. This district, which included San Martín City and the city of Medina and the parishes of Cabuyaro, Concepción de Arama, and Jiramena, was authorized to send one delegate to the provincial assembly that met each September in Bogotá. Since, in 1832, San Martín was the only canton in the province that failed to hold a presidential election, it is unlikely that a delegate was ever selected.[49]

The principal problem continued to be the lack of population. Writing in 1832, geographer Feliciano Montenegro Colón asserted that the canton had no more than 421 houses and 1,530 inhabitants. A census conducted in 1835 failed to give a population figure, but it listed 453 houses in the canton. Farmland was valued at 19,223 pesos and grazing land at 20,500 pesos. The census revealed that there were 12,127 head of cattle, 499 horses, 50 mules, 39 pigs, and 21 riverboats. Economic activities included cultivation of cacao and coffee; production of honey, cheese and salt; and manufacture of straw hats and pottery.[50] Governor Rufino Cuervo was impressed by the potential wealth of the canton. In his annual message of 1832, he noted that San Martín had rich deposits of salt and was extremely fertile. "It has a navigable river and is so extensive that its limits are lost in countries where civilization has not penetrated, but it is almost completely un-

populated . . ."⁵¹ The following year, Cuervo proposed a law to permit
people convicted of vagrancy and other crimes to serve out their sentences in the Llanos. As he explained:

The vast and meritorious canton of San Martín calls for people; to it can be sent
the men who have been lost in the larger society in order that at the side of
innocent and hard working citizens, in the midst of fertile and uncultivated fields
and without temptation to dissipate themselves, they can dedicate themselves to
work, forget their bad habits, make their own fortune, augment the population
and contribute to the prosperity of the state.⁵²

The legislature did not approve this measure, but the scheme to transport criminals from the highlands to populate the Llanos was periodically revived until, in 1907, the government began the first federal
prison at the town of Acacías, near Villavicencio.

An Old Frontier

By 1830 three hundred years of European contact had transformed the ecology of the Llanos. Cattle and horses grazed on plains
that had previously supported no animals larger than the jaguar. On
the western side of the frontier, the Achaguas, Sálivas and Tunebos,
once powerful cultivators, had been decimated or absorbed into Spanish society by missionaries and encomenderos; while to the east, the
Guahibos, no longer peaceful foragers, dominated large portions of
Casanare, Arauca, and almost all of San Martín, and were determined
to resist further encroachment. Both whites and Indians cut down the
gallery forests in the piedmont and along the rivers to plant crops, and
they systematically burned the dry savanna grass to produce better
pasturage for the cattle; but surprisingly enough, as geographer John
Blydenstein has pointed out, man's direct influence on the landscape
was slight because of low population density. Even in a place like
Tame, Casanare, where records show that cultivation occurred for
more than four hundred years, the forest was able to maintain itself.
It was not until the massive influx of *colonos* (settlers who farm or graze
cattle on public land without legal title to the territory) into the Department of Meta after World War II that the piedmont forest began
to disappear, leaving chronic erosion and scarred mountain slopes.⁵³

The tropical climate, which had deterred the Spanish from occupying the Llanos in large numbers, continued to discourage coloni-

zation throughout the nineteenth century. Agustín Codazzi, the Italian geographer who surveyed Casanare in 1855, concluded flatly that immigrants from highland New Granada could not survive in the plains. Besides the dangers posed by Indians, tigers, snakes, crocodiles, and mosquitoes, the heat in some sections was so intense that a thermometer registering 30°C (87°F) at 8:00 P.M. dipped only to 29°C (84°F) by 11:00 P.M. The merciless sun caused rivers to evaporate quickly and converted them into stagnant pools filled with rotting fish and plants emitting fever-causing poisonous fumes. The grass itself also gave off fumes that caused epidemics similar to cholera. Temperatures were lower near the cordillera, where cool breezes blew down from the mountains; but these early morning drafts chilled the lightly clothed inhabitants, causing typhoid fever. Codazzi concluded that given such perils, the only people who could survive in the Llanos were Africans or Venezuelan Llaneros who were already acclimated to similar conditions.[54] The continued high mortality rate in the Llanos bore out Codazzi's warning that diseases posed great dangers to Europeans, even though his explanation of their causes had little basis in scientific fact.[55] It was not until the twentieth century that public-health officials realized that malaria, yellow fever, cholera, and tropical anemia could be controlled by mosquito eradication, proper sanitation, medication, and diet, and colonists could move into the Llanos without fear of expiring within a few months or years.

The leaders of New Granada inherited from the Spanish an old frontier that was characterized by a unique cowboy subculture and deeply rooted Hispanic institutions—towns, missions, and ranches. Like the viceroys before them, they neglected the Llanos in order to develop the western heartland of the republic, where economic resources were indisputable albeit dependent on efficient transportation along the Magdalena River. Yet they did not ignore the east completely. As we shall see in the following chapters, efforts to Christianize, defend, and populate the Llanos formed an integral part of the political strategies of the various nineteenth-century governments; though rare indeed was the individual who, in 1830, could have predicted the disintegration of Casanare into a no-man's-land or the emergence by the beginning of the twentieth century of the Llanos of San Martín as one of Colombia's most active regions of colonization.

2. The Missionary Reprise: 1821–49

*S*cholars are still pondering the effect of the War of Independence on Colombian institutions as they had evolved under the Bourbon rulers of the eighteenth century. In his classic work, *Industría y protección en Colombia 1810–1930* (Medellín, 1955), Luis Ospina Vásquez wrote that "in the opinion of many, the colony lasted in our country until 1850."[1] While David Bushnell, among other historians, has shown that the war did influence political institutions, political behavior, and social relations in a significant way, some colonial traditions remained extraordinarily vital. For example, Frank Safford, in *The Ideal of the Practical: Colombia's Struggle to Form a Technical Elite* (August 1976), describes the republican leaders as "neo-bourbons" who were linked intellectually and spiritually to their Spanish predecessors in their efforts to direct the upper class and the poor toward technological enterprise.[2] Likewise, in developing a policy for governing the Llanos frontier, these same individuals resorted to viceregal strategies. Between 1821 and 1849, regardless of other differences in their political ideologies, decision makers in Bogotá agreed that maintaining a strong mission system was the most effective way to rule Casanare, Arauca, and San Martín. Each administration promoted the evangelization of the Indians in the Llanos, but with varying degrees of success. An analysis of their efforts offers an important key to the history of the Llanos frontier in the early years of independence, provides a new perspective on the bitter struggle between church and state in the highlands, and reveals the durability of one Spanish colonial institution—the mission.

Drawing the Battle Lines: Church and State in Gran Colombia

In the succinct words of Robert Gilmore, the New Granada born out of the wreckage of Gran Colombia was a centralized state "characterized by a nineteenth century political superstructure, a colonial economy, and an eighteenth-century society living according to tradition."[3] Its economic base was an agrarian–commercial complex dominated by the great landowners and merchants who constituted the upper class. These individuals, along with middle-class professionals, government officials, clergy, and intellectuals, formed the ruling elite; and "the profound divisions between them influenced the ideals, political forms, and rationales that they provided for New Granadan society."[4]

One of the issues that split the ruling class was the role of the Roman Catholic church in the new nation. Until the impact of the Enlightenment, New Granadan culture had been rigorously religious, and even in the second half of the eighteenth century the Catholic hierarchy and viceregal authorities remained closely knit. The hierarchy used all of its influence to reinforce the imperial system that had permitted the church to acquire great economic power and prestige, but the creole rebellion in 1810 soon revealed that the church was not a monolith. When Pius VII, in 1816, and Leo XII, in 1824, called on the bishops of America to preach to the people that the revolt was a crime against obedience owed to Ferdinand VII, they overestimated the influence of their pronouncements. In New Granada, the Spanish-born hierarchy and priests loyally supported the crown, but the creole members of the ordinary clergy joined wholeheartedly in the patriot cause and brought with them many of the faithful. Since the people remained profoundly Catholic, their disobedience and that of the lower clergy presented an enormous crisis for the church.[5]

In the war's aftermath, the crown-dominated church had to be adjusted to a republican government. The leaders of Gran Colombia wanted to build a society different from the colonial one, but they were reluctant to allow the popular sector broader participation in the economy and in politics. Imbued with philosophic rationalism, they wanted to free themselves from clerical influence, but they did not dare to reject religion completely since it formed the principal tie of national unity. Thus, they found no contradiction in supporting the French *Declaration of the Rights of Man* and stoutly defending the Catholic faith. However much Bolívar and Santander might have wished to restrict the institutional power of the church, they and their followers recognized the need for a modus vivendi with the clerical party. In general, they tried to reduce religious influence by limiting the church's sources of wealth and its role in education. The hierarchy, with its Catholic supporters, fought steadfastly to preserve its prerogatives. Its strength derived from its control over the people, through the pulpit and confessions, and its economic activities; but it was vexed by the decline of religious vocations, the lack of bishops, and the relaxation of monastic discipline.[6]

The anticlericals dominated for most of the Gran Colombian era (1819–30). In 1821, the Congress of Cúcuta abolished the Inquisition. Charging that monastic life was obsolete and parasitic, it closed all convents with less than eight members (*conventos menores*, or minor convents), and a law passed in 1826 required that novices be at least twenty-five years old before taking religious vows. The government headed by Vice President Santander exempted Indians from paying parish fees and stated that the public treasury would no longer remit the stipends that the priests had received under the Spanish.[7] Most importantly, over strong objections from the hierarchy, Santander adopted in 1824 the Law of Patronage (*patronato*), which reserved for the state, among other powers, the authority to nominate the principal religious officials of the country; to grant the exequátur to papal briefs on matters of grace; to watch over the proper supervision of the dioceses by the prelates; and to enact legislation for establishment, rule, and support of missions for the Indians. The Law of Patronage, if endorsed by the pope, would have given Santander more control over the church than that previously exercised by the Spanish kings; but since the Vatican did not recognize his government, all of Santander's actions in religious matters were provisional.[8]

Despite their excoriation of the regular clergy, the anticlericals believed that the monks were obligated to play a key role on the Llanos frontier. In 1824, Secretary of the Interior José Manuel Restrepo estimated that there were at least 200,000 Indians living in the unexplored regions of Gran Colombia, some so remote that their tribal names were unknown. Noting that the missions which had flourished along the Orinoco, Meta, and Apure rivers before the war had all disappeared for lack of priests, Restrepo urged Congress to send religious out to the frontier and to pass laws to promote the civilization of the Indians.[9] The legislators responded with the Law of June 30, 1824, "Methods of Civilizing the Savage Indians," which promised land and tools to any tribe that agreed to settle down and pledged to supply them with secular priests if regular clergy could not be found. In 1826, they passed a second law exempting Indians in Casanare from military service if they would renounce their pagan ways.[10] To implement both laws, the government repeatedly petitioned the superiors of the Franciscan, Dominican, and Recoleto orders in Bogotá to appoint missionaries to the vacated posts in the Llanos. Their failure to comply prompted Santander to complain:

The clergy in general, show in the capital and great cities, much zeal for religion, but on demanding from them some sacrifice as in missions to the gentile Indians in which their apostolic zeal might have a vast field, they withdraw and do not want to leave their comforts; most of them desire nearby parishes which produce two or three thousand pesos of income. There are very few who want to go to the missions in which they cannot become rich.[11]

The desire for the good life in Bogotá undoubtedly contributed to the reluctance of the monks to return to their prewar missions. Already in the eighteenth century discipline had begun to decay, as is attested by the frequent censoring of the orders by the Bourbon viceroys. In addition, proliferation of liberal political and social ideas and the endless controversy over Jansenism had weakened the regular orders in Europe, where the number of religious vocations declined steadily.[12] The Napoleonic War paralyzed the Vatican, and once it was over, the papacy had to negotiate agreements with new regimes. In the meantime, hundreds of Spanish-born clergy returned to Europe during the Spanish American struggle for independence, leaving the New World church crippled and badly understaffed. By 1826 only five of thirty-eight bishoprics were being actively administered, and the missions from Mexico to Argentina were in a lamentable state of collapse.[13]

In Gran Colombia, the laws suppressing minor convents and requiring novices to be twenty-five-years old compounded the woes of the regular clergy. The intent of the measures was to combat lax discipline and immoral practices, but their effect was to diminish further the capacity of the orders to attract new recruits. As a result, the Dominicans lost eighteen convents in the 1820s, and the Recoletos were reduced to a single monastery in Bogotá. Conditions in the Llanos were made even worse when Santander seized the cattle haciendas attached to the Missions of Meta administered by the Recoletos. The vice president leased these so-called Haciendas of Meta to private citizens on the condition that they allot a portion of their profits to cover the missionaries' expenses. The new arrangement proved to be a source of constant irritation. In 1826, Fr. Francisco Forrero reported that the Missions of Meta were "absolutely abandoned, surrounded everywhere by misery and lacking even elemental resources for subsistence."[14] As Recoleto historian Marcelino Ganuza observed, with some missionaries dead, others sick, and "all nervous and upset" about the new laws, the order could not convert Indians in the Llanos with its former zeal.[15]

Assuming dictatorial power in June 1828, Simón Bolívar appeared to be more sympathetic to the plight of the clergy. On July 11, he suspended the law setting twenty-five as the minimum age for making religious vows and, soon after, revoked the law suppressing minor convents. Yet Bolívar continued Santander's program of ecclesiastical reform in other respects and "easily sacrificed the interest of the church to those of the landed elite."[16] He insisted on the right to exercise the patronato; he banned burials within churches and exempted from payment of tithes grain crops cultivated on coffee, cacao, or indigo plantations. In Casanare, he followed Santander's precedent by leasing the Haciendas of Meta to his close associate, General Rafael Urdaneta. Urdaneta appointed Lucas Carvajal and Francisco Segovia to administer the estates. The new *mayordomos* promptly antagonized their neighbors by claiming for themselves all cattle and horses that strayed to hacienda lands and by treating roughly those who protested. Juan Nepomuceno Moreno, caudillo of Casanare, capitalized on the resulting animosity when he ordered Caravajal and Segovia to be murdered in April 1830, seized control of the province, and attempted to secede from New Granada.[17] Throughout this crisis, the haciendas yielded little income for the missions. On December 17, 1829, the Recoletos notified Archbishop Caycedo y Flórez that because there were no longer any cattle along the Meta River, one priest had starved to death and others were deserting their posts to search for food.[18]

When Gran Colombia broke apart in 1830, little progress had been made in reviving the missions. Nevertheless, the leaders of New Granada steadfastly maintained that their restoration was a precondition for civilizing the Llanos. Generally regarded as more friendly to the aspirations of the church and its supporters, they continued the contradictory policy, already firmly established, of attacking the prerogatives of the regulars in the highlands and simultaneously insisting that they redouble their efforts in the evangelization of the Indians of Casanare, Arauca, and San Martín.

Church and State in New Granada

The new republic, centralist and conservative, retained a government similar to that designed by the Congress of Cúcuta. The Constitution of 1832 preserved slavery and restricted nationality, citizenship, and suffrage. It declared Roman Catholicism the only religion of the republic, prohibited the worship of other faiths, and gave the government the full right to exercise the patronato.[19] Santander was elected president, with Joaquín Mosquera as his vice president. Mosquera, who had served briefly as chief executive in 1830, was a member of one of the most influential families in the country. One brother, Manuel José, was archbishop of Bogotá between 1835 and 1853, while another was Tomás Cipriano Mosquera, the victorious general in the Guerra de los Supremos (War of the Supreme Chiefs 1839–42) who succeeded to the presidency in 1845. Pedro Alcántara Herrán, president from 1841 to 1845, was a son-in-law of T. C. Mosquera. His brother, Antonio Herrán, became archbishop in 1853.[20]

Santander, in his second term of office, was a stern figure, legal-minded and inflexible. He had his own favorites and most of his enemies were Bolívar's former followers. He regarded the Law of Patronage as being in full force, even though it still had not been recognized by the pope. He exercised the right of "presentation" by authorizing the election of Manuel José Mosquera as archbishop of Bogotá in April 1834, and by creating an auxiliary bishop of the Metropolitan See of Bogotá to serve in Casanare. He asserted the right of *pase*, or exequátur, over pontifical communications, bestowing approval on a papal brief of March 28, 1835, which reduced the number of feast days. Another brief reforming the regular orders issued in 1835 did not receive government approval until May 8, 1840, and only then with the following reservation: "The *pase* is conceded without prejudice to the sovereignty and the prerogatives of the nation."[21] With the Law of April 16, 1836, Santander mandated the supremacy of civil over ecclesiastical tribunals in many matters formerly regarded as the exclusive domain of the religious orders. In 1832 and 1835, he reactivated the laws suppressing minor convents and requiring novices to be twenty-five-years old. He sponsored a bill permitting non-Catholics to be buried in cemeteries, and proposed but did not institute toleration of other cults.[22]

These policies alarmed many religious and lay people and encouraged them to join the "Bolivarianos," who constituted the opposition and in the 1840s emerged as the Conservative party; yet despite Santander's anticlericalism, Pope Gregory XVI agreed to recognize his government. Since 1824, Dr. Ignacio Sánchez de Tejada had been lobbying in Rome for restoration of normal relations, and on November 26, 1835, the pope rewarded his discretion, energy, and patience by acknowledging New Granada's independence, making it the first Spanish American republic to be legitimized by the Holy See. Complete restoration of the hierarchy followed. On January 16, 1837, Msgr. Cayetano Baluffi arrived in Bogotá as internuncio extraordinary, where he was accepted as the diplomatic representative of the pope, but he was not permitted to exercise his functions relative to ecclesiastical government until the Vatican recognized the right of the New Granadan president to accord the *pase* to papal briefs on June 12, 1840.[23]

The Missions in Casanare

One aspect of Santander's religious policies that is frequently overlooked was his determination to revitalize the missions—a decision prompted, in part, by constant demands from the Llanos. As soon as Casanare rejoined New Granada, Governor M. Arenas asked the executive power to send priests to Taguana, Santiago, Trinidad, and Arauca and to the Missions of Casanare, Meta, and Cuiloto because the clergy were "indispensable" to the development of the province.[24] In 1834, Juan Nepomuceno Moreno warned that Casanare was going daily to its ultimate extermination because savage Indians were killing and robbing the settlers. He urged Santander to send priests to encourage the Indians to accept social life and to persuade the whites to adopt practices that would ensure their happiness.[25] Throughout the decade, similar requests were a regular feature of dispatches coming from Casanare.

To get the missions under way, civilian *pobladores* offered to resettle Indians who had deserted the reductions if the national government would guarantee financial support and priests. One such *poblador* was Ciriaco de Córdoba, a vecino of Chire, who in 1826 founded two Indian towns on the northern bank of the Meta, San Simón, and San Francisco.[26] Another was Juan José Melgarejo, who wrote Governor Arenas on July 20, 1832, that Indians who had formerly resided in the Cuiloto missions were roaming through the plains harassing settlers and travelers. Melgarejo offered to reestablish the reductions of Lipa, Cuiloto, and Arauquita if the government would send him axes, machetes, knives, cloth, salt, tobacco, cattle, and priests; pay him the salary of a captain; and forbid the local *jefe político* from interfering in his activities. Melgarejo recommended that whites who desired to live in the reductions be exempted from taxes and the draft for ten years

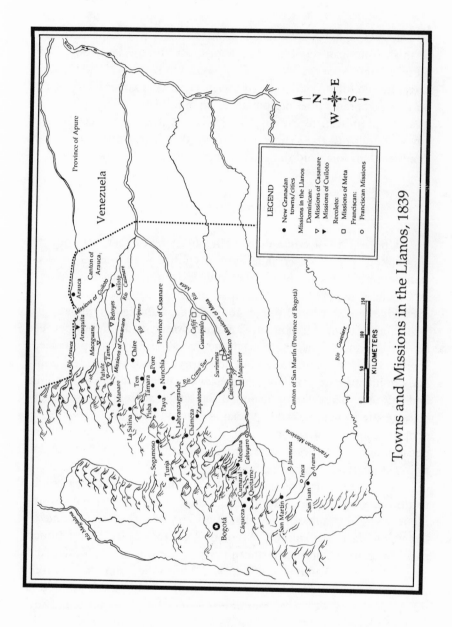

Towns and Missions in the Llanos, 1839

LEGEND

- New Granadan towns/cities

Missions in the Llanos
Dominican:
▽ Missions of Casanare
▼ Missions of Cuiloto

Recoleto:
□ Missions of Meta

Franciscan:
○ Franciscan Missions

and that they be allowed to claim land formerly reserved for the Indians. Finally, he requested the assistance of an *escolta* (squadron) of six armed horsemen to subjugate the Indians, "without which nothing can be accomplished."[27]

Arenas endorsed Melgarejo's proposal and, with the proviso that the province could not supply any of the material goods he demanded, sent it on to José Francisco Pereira, secretary of state for interior and foreign relations, in Bogotá. Pereira approved the plan on August 12, refusing to give whites Indian land or to suspend the jefe político's jurisdiction, but accepting the rest of Melgarejo's stipulations. Pereira awarded to each new reduction two hundred pesos annually from the profits of the Haciendas of Meta, and he approved at the same time a similar project by Antonio María Gallardo to reestablish Santa Rosalia, Guascavía, Caviuna, and Buenavista—towns formerly part of the Missions of Meta.[28]

The secretary had already asked Archbishop Caycedo y Flórez to urge the religious orders to send missionaries to the Llanos. By July the Recoletos appointed Nepomuceno Ordóñez and Domingo Correo for Macuco and Guanapalo, and the Dominicans had assigned Nepomuceno Rojas, Eduardo Vásquez, and Gabriel Rodríguez to Macaguane, Tame, and Betoyes.[29] Six months later, Melgarejo reported that 200 Indians were living in Lipa, and another 160 Indians and three whites had resettled Cuiloto. They had built houses and planted gardens, yet there were still no priests, without whom future progress was limited.[30] A disgruntled Secretary Pereira explained:

Many and repeated times the government has asked the Recoleto prelate to send missionaries to the missions of Meta and Cuiloto. The requests have been ineffective—sometimes because the religious refuse to go and sometimes because the prelate has not taken a personal interest in the matter.[31]

To break this impasse, President Santander embarked on a three-step campaign. First, he created by the Decree of May 3, 1833, an auxiliary bishop of the Metropolitan See of Bogotá with an annual income of six thousand pesos, and saw to it that José Antonio Chaves y Vargas, a Franciscan, was elected bishop *in partibus* of Calidonia and auxiliary to the archbishop with responsibility for the missions in Casanare and the parishes of Pamplona (a newly formed diocese including Pamplona, Cúcuta, Limoncito, and San Faustino de los Ríos, which formerly had been administered by the Bishop of Mérida). Since the pope had yet to acknowledge his right to exercise the patronato, Santander's action was a bold move, but the gamble paid off when Gregory XVI confirmed Chaves's election in January 1834, and the bishop was consecrated in Popayán the following July.[32]

Santander's second step was to gain congressional approval of the Law of May 15, 1833, which reorganized the missions of Casanare and placed them under the care, direction, and instruction of the auxiliary bishop. The law stipulated that Recoletos were to appoint priests for the Missions of Meta (Macuco, Surinema, Casimena, and Maquivor) and the Dominicans for the Missions of Casanare (Tame, Macaguane, and Betoyes) and Cuiloto. The government would pay each missionary an annual stipend of two hundred pesos plus travel funds. The priests were expected to manage the haciendas attached to their missions and to deposit any profits from the sale of cattle in the provincial treasury to create a fund for paying stipends and other expenses. Reduced Indians, New Granadans, and foreigners who lived in the missions were exempted from personal, civil, and ecclesiastical taxes for twenty years.[33]

Santander's third step was to reorganize the Haciendas of Meta. In 1832, the Convention of New Granada ruled that the profits from these estates should be used exclusively to support the missions, thus reversing the Gran Colombian policy of leasing them to private citizens.[34] On October 6, 1835, Santander placed the administration of the haciendas under the direction of the auxiliary bishop. Under the new arrangement, each missionary was responsible for the hacienda attached to his reduction. He was expected to hire the mayordomo and peons, to make sure the cattle were rounded up, to protect the female cows from being slaughtered, and to submit his accounts to the bishop three times a year. Income from the estates was to be used to buy materials; to pay the salaries of the peons, a schoolteacher, and the sacristan; and to meet other mission expenses. Each priest was entitled to a monthly allotment of one steer, one *millar* of cacao, eight *libras* of sugar, and one *arroba* of salt. Every month, a steer and an arroba of salt was to be given to the schoolteacher and his students, while the meat from another steer was to be divided among the peons. On the feast day of the mission's patron saint, two steers and two arrobas of salt were to be awarded to the cabildo members, the *alférez*, sacristan, *cantores*, and musicians. Sixty pesos worth of cloth, salt, and tools taken from the hacienda's profits were to be distributed among the Indians annually. Finally, the decree required the bishop to inspect the haciendas and missions once a year and the governor of Casanare to report on their progress annually.[35]

The creation of an auxiliary bishop and the reorganization of the missions and haciendas promised to invigorate evangelization in the Llanos, but unfortunately three insuperable difficulties quickly emerged: the lackluster performance of Bishop Chaves; a steady decline in the number of cattle; and the failure of the religious orders to staff the missions adequately.

José Antonio Chaves y Vargas went out to Casanare with great enthusiasm. On the eve of his departure on November 26, 1834, from Sogamoso, he wrote Santander of his pleasure at the prospect of working in "the bosom of a province heroic for its liberalism, immaculate for its opinions, and invincible in its courage"; and when he reached Labranzagrande in early January, he dashed off another letter urging that missionaries be sent as soon as possible "before the rains begin" since their absence was causing the ruin of the province.[36] Arriving in Pore, the bishop began to implement the Law of May 15, 1833, but almost immediately he was incapacitated by the torrid heat and malarial humidity. At his urgent request, Santander transferred the seat of the episcopacy on June 28, 1835, to Paya, which at a higher elevation offered a better climate. Even there, Chaves's health did not improve. In September, he asked permission to move to Tame or Támara, but this petition was denied on the grounds that he would be too far away from the missions to make his annual inspections.[37] By February 8, 1836, Chaves was too ill to attend Congress as a senator representing Vélez Province. On October 6, he relinquished responsibility for the Pamplona diocese, affirming that it was public and notorious knowledge "that for more than a year in which I have resided in the province of Casanare, I have not enjoyed a single day of good health, because that hot and humid climate is so notably contrary to my existence that more than once I saw myself on the edge of the grave."[38] At this time, he requested and received permission to go to Bogotá to consult with doctors. After a nightmarish journey that took six weeks because the bishop had to be protected from the sun and rain so devastating to his health, he reached Bogotá and spent the next twenty-five days prostrated in bed. In February, Santander relieved him from his duties in Llanos. No successor was named to the post, and Chaves was eventually reassigned to the parish of Guatavita in Cundinamarca.[39]

It is conceivable that given the powers granted to the bishop, an energetic, determined, and innovative individual might have accomplished much in Casanare. Beset by illness from the beginning,

Chaves was clearly not such a person. Defeatism permeates his letters to Bogotá, for he quickly came to the conclusion that in most of the parishes, the vecinos were too few and too poor to support priests. During his brief administration, the Recoletos started a mission at Cafifi on the tributaries of the Pauto River and the Dominicans revived Arauquita; but there was little improvement elsewhere, and Chaves took no interest in managing the Haciendas of Meta, the key to mission development.[40] Governor Moreno reported in May 1837 that since the bishop had taken charge, the haciendas had decayed considerably due to neglect. Moreover, *renguera*—a fatal rabies transmitted by vampire bats (*Desmosus rotundus,* or *D. rufus*) which attached themselves to the necks of cattle and horses in order to suck their blood—was decimating the herds. So many horses had died that there were not enough for the peons to use as mounts to round up the cattle to pay the tithes and fees required by law.[41] Chaves, like the other missionaries, was simply too inexperienced to know how to improve the cattle and make the estates more profitable.

Realizing that the Law of May 15, 1833, erred in making the bishop responsible for the haciendas, President José Ignacio Márquez, who succeeded Santander in April 1837, decided on November 17 of that year to appoint mayordomos recommended by the governor of Casanare to run the estates; but it is unclear whether he ever implemented this arrangement.[42] In 1839, Governor Julian Beltrán reported that the cattle were still diminishing. He complained that the priests did not know how to manage the haciendas, but as long as they received their monthly ration of meat they remained unconcerned by the loss of steers. The system of keeping a separate hato for each mission was costly, since each herd required a mayordomo and peons. Profits were not sufficient to pay all these salaries, and due to the negligence of the missionaries the peons were stealing cattle at will. Beltrán suggested that these abuses might be minimized if the cattle from all the missions were consolidated into a single herd under the direction of a competent administrator, who might still distribute the profits among the various missions.[43] This idea was incorporated into a law passed on May 28, 1840, which gave the governor responsibility for the haciendas and authorized him to reserve for the Indians one hundred cattle from each of the herds attached to Tame, Macaguane, and Betoyes, and consolidate the rest at an appropriate place to be managed as a single estate. The measure came too late. In September, Governor Joaquín Concepción Melgarejo wrote:

The state of the haciendas of the missions is deplorable. The disease commonly known as *renguera* has killed all the horses so not any remain, and without them, it can be said that the haciendas no longer exist, because it is physically impossible to round up and reduce the few cattle that remain . . . consequently and very quickly the famed Missions of Meta will disappear.[44]

The third problem besetting evangelism in Casanare was the failure of the religious orders to staff the reductions with trained and dedicated priests. Prodded on by the government in Bogotá, the superiors appointed men to serve in the Llanos, but many failed to take up their duties and others stayed only a short time. In 1834 Secretary Lino de Pombo urged the Senate to pass a law compelling religious to honor their assignments because all of his efforts in cajoling and ordering them to go had failed, even after the treasury had paid their stipends and travel expenses. Some refused to go out of patriotism, claiming that they were being exiled to Casanare in retaliation for their religious beliefs or political activism. One excused himself because he was too old, another because he was too young, and a third because he had to support his impoverished family. All feared the deadly climate of Casanare, and as Pombo remarked, no one was willing to go out to the Llanos because of a great desire to convert the heathen.[45]

Father Pedro Achurín, the Recoleto superior, vigorously refuted these allegations. Urging senators to defeat Pombo's bill, he asserted that nothing in Holy Writ required monks to convert Indians. For 114 years Recoletos had worked in Casanare, but up until 1810 the order had six convents, three novitiates, and more than a hundred members. Now the community had shrunk to thirty monks, six of whom had recently left the cloister to become secularized while two others were too old or too ill for mission assignment. The law requiring novices to be twenty-five-years old made it impossible to attract recruits because the personalities of men were already hardened at twenty-five and they could not be transformed into missionaries. Finally, Achurín argued that Pombo's bill was unconstitutional. Regulars, like other citizens, had the right to exercise their chosen profession freely. The government could not tear them out of the convent and force them to go to the "burning plains along the Meta River . . . a fatal grave that has already claimed the lives of more than one hundred victims."[46]

The Dominican priors offered similar excuses. Since the government had suppressed their monasteries in Chiquinquirá, Tunja, and Bogotá, their membership had dropped to sixty-eight priests and lay brothers. If more missionaries were sent to the Llanos, other houses would have to close for lack of enough residents. In the end, the Senate voted down Pombo's proposal.[47] Five years later, President Márquez publicly conceded that the regular orders had suffered grievous personnel losses and that many of the monks who remained were unsuited for the rigors of mission life. In his annual message of 1839, he warned that if the trend continued, "all convents may disappear because monastic rules were the creation of another era, and today they are not reinforced by public opinion or favored by dominant ideas."[48]

While most regulars may have regarded Casanare with horror, some did toil there with a zeal reminiscent of the previous century. In 1835 four Recoletos—Frs. Francisco Monrroy, Pedro Cuervo de la Trinidad, Esteban Olmena, and Benito Martínez—accompanied Bishop Chaves on his trip to Pore. The first three took up posts in the Missions of Meta, while the latter served as the *párroco* (parish priest) of Chire. In 1837, Chaves sent Martínez to Cafifi to take over as superior of the Missions of Meta, which had 1,396 inhabitants, according to the census of 1835. Martínez remained in Cafifi for two years before illness forced him to return to the highlands. In his final report to the prior, dated February 8, 1840, he stated that of the five prewar reductions—San Salvador, Guanapalo, Casimena, Surimena, and Macuco— San Salvador, Guanapalo, and Casimena had disappeared with their few remaining Indians relocating to Maquivor and Cafifi, founded in 1836. The Indians in Macuco had moved their town to a new site called Guayabal, and they were looked after by the missionary in Surimena. The jefe político and the vecinos of the canton of Macuto did not help the missionaries, and the administrator of the haciendas wrongfully deprived them of their monthly ration of chocolate and sugar. The Recoletos had neither tools nor food to give to the Indians, who complained constantly that they did not have enough to eat. Only at the missionaries' insistence did the administrator occasionally cut up for them an old steer, and the jefe político forced them to work for entire weeks on public projects. Given these difficulties, Martínez concluded that it was impossible to win new converts, for when unreduced Indians visited the towns they correctly perceived that there was no advantage to settling down and left after a few days.[49]

On February 12, 1838, Fray Francisco Granados, *cura* (priest) of Tame, wrote to Governor Juan Nepomuceno Gómez to urge him to help the Dominicans working in the Missions of Casanare. His long letter presents a rare picture of mission life in the early nineteenth century, for it describes not only the reductions and the Indians but also the problems besetting the priests.[50] Of the four missions, Tame was the largest, with 624 Indians and 176 whites. There were 400 residents in Macaguane, less than 100 in Betoyes, and about 60 in Patute. Before the war Macaguane and Betoyes had been larger than Tame, but the fighting, a smallpox epidemic in 1819, and the tendency of the mission Indians to return to the wilderness had diminished their populations. Even in Granados's time the Indians continued to leave. Some fled because they had been discovered committing a crime; others because they wanted to improve their fortunes. Children ran away to avoid having to go to school, and in Macaguane and Betoyes they left to escape forced labor on public projects and having to pay taxes. Such fugitives frequently became a menace, hiding in the forests along the rivers to attack travelers and ranchers.

The reductions were organized in accordance with eighteenth-century patterns. In Tame, the public buildings included a church, chapel, cabildo house, jail, and residence for the priest; and there were 163 rude, straw houses for the Indians. The latter planted gardens of plátano, yuca, and corn, and fished in the rivers. They fashioned sombreros, baskets, and *petacas* (trunks) from moriche palms, and made hammocks out of cloth. In Patute the Indians made hammocks; in Macaguane they made hats of straw and cloth; but in Betoyes they had no crafts. Income from the sale of these items as well as from daily wages went to buy salt, cloth, clothing, and tools.

Pitifully few were the cattle and horses belonging to the Missions of Casanare. According to Granados, on December 20, 1834, the national government had ordered that the herd attached to Betoyes be shared with Tame and Macaguane and that Indians rather than hired peons tend the cattle in order to reduce expenses. The Dominicans had convoked the native authorities in each town and requested that they name four individuals every week to look after the cattle; but the system had not worked because the haciendas had no corrals, there was no way to brand the calves, and the Indians refused to work for nothing. By 1838 Tame's herd had been reduced to sixty-eight steers and one horse; at Betoyes there were sixty-four steers; at Macaguane, eighty steers and two wild mares; while at Patute the cattle had completely disappeared. Seven Indians owned their own cattle; the largest private herd was fifteen animals belonging to an Indian in Macaguane. The mission herds had become so small that they cost nothing to maintain (except in Macaguane, where the mayordomo earned four reales a month), but they continued to diminish because each priest received a steer every month as his food allowance.

Spanish was spoken in all the towns, and the Indians professed

Christianity, although they retained elements of their former beliefs. They still practiced witchcraft and resorted to native *curanderos* when they were sick. On Sundays, the Dominicans taught Christian dogma to the adults. Four days a week they held catechism classes for the children, but only about one-third of the youngsters attended. Primary schools had functioned in Tame and Macaguane between 1822 and 1836, until the cabildos stopped paying the teachers' salaries.

From Granados's account it is evident that the hardships besetting the missionaries grew out of their utter poverty and isolation. The Indians paid their priest three pesos on the feast days of their patron saint and Corpus Christi. They brought him a chicken and a hen for performing a marriage, and a chicken for a baptism. They paid nothing for three monthly masses, Holy Week services, or funerals. In the past, they had brought him a daily ration of plátano, but recently that practice had been stopped by the jefe político. Granados admitted that in the eighteenth century the missionaries had not grumbled about their privations, but he pointed out that in those days they had well-run haciendas to pay for fiestas, double rations of meat, and rations of sugar, cacao, and salt for the Indians. Moreover, they ruled like despots, virtually enslaving the Indians. In 1838, the Dominicans could not force the Indians to work if they did not so choose, and they could not prevent them from robbing the whites. The reductions lacked tools and food, and the roads were so treacherous that it was difficult to get supplies from outside. For months on end the missionary had no company other than the savages, who only came to him when they wanted something. Given these conditions, Granados asked, was it no wonder that one priest left his post after three days and another after three months? He himself had served in Tame for four years and three months without rest, while Fr. Gabriel Rodríguez, who had been in Casanare for twelve years, was looking forward to spending his retirement in a convent somewhere in the highlands, "taking with him old age, illness and misery without the hope of a greater reward than life in the cloister and that he will be permitted to cover his gray hair with a black cap."

Granados's letter ends with some concrete recommendations for reform. He argued that it was imperative to pass laws forcing the Indians to work and to appoint a judge who would make sure that they complied with their civic, political, moral, and religious duties. The government should give the Indians tools and provide the churches with the holy objects necessary for religious services. It should raise the stipends of the priests and supply them with books for keeping parish records. It should hire schoolteachers, and it should renew the haciendas. Above all, the government should give the priests money to import food and stop the practice of awarding them a steer every month from the mission cattle. Only in this way was there hope that the herds would reproduce themselves and with time become large enough to support the reductions. After thanking the governor for his consideration, he closed, "If you doubt my honesty, you can order other reports, and if some authority challenges what I have said, I will prove and sustain my word with evidence."

Governor Gómez did not doubt Granados's veracity. With good reason, he sent his letter to the secretary of state and urged him to dictate the reforms the missionary requested, for Granados's statistics confirmed the catastrophic decline of Indians, cattle, and horses. In 1800 there had been 5,425 Indians in the Missions of Casanare, 642 in the Missions of Cuiloto, and 8,070 in the Missions of Meta, for a total of 18 reductions and 14,137 Indians (table 1); while in 1839 there were 1,184 Indians in the Missions of Casanare, an unknown number in the Missions of Cuiloto, and 1,396 in the Missions of Meta for a total of 12 towns and 2,580 Indians (table 2)—a decline of nearly 80 percent. In 1800 the nine haciendas attached to the Missions of Meta had 104,400 cattle and 6,044 horses. By 1839 none of these still existed, and even though Granados reported that there were 209 cattle and three horses in the Missions of Casanare, the decline of the animal population was nearly 100 percent.

The Missions in the Llanos of San Martín

The situation in the Llanos of San Martín, historically a Franciscan mission field, was perhaps worse than in Casanare since Santander's three-step program did not apply to a canton within the Province of Bogotá. In 1834, after the jefe político of San Martín reported that there were no missions in his jurisdiction, the provincial legislature voted to reestablish missions at Jiramena and San Antonio. Governor Rufino Cuervo sent the resolution to the secretary of state for approval, pointing out that it was consistent with the Law of May 15, 1833, regarding Casanare, and that evangelization would be easier south of the Meta River because the Indians were more docile and because the jefe político would assist the missionaries.[51]

Table 1
Missions and Haciendas in Casanare, ca. 1800

| Religious Order | Town | Indian Population | Hacienda | |
			Cattle	Horses
Dominicans				
Missions of Casanare	San Salvador	—	—	—
	Tame	—	—	—
	Patute	—	—	—
	Macaguane	—	—	—
	Betoyes	—	—	—
		5,425[a]		
Recoletos				
Missions of Cuiloto	Cravo	141	—	—
	Cuiloto	141	—	—
	Ele	180	—	—
	Lipa	180		
		642[b]		
Recoletos				
Missions of Meta	Macuco	1,800	22,000	1,900
	Surimena	2,068	20,000	2,600
	Casimena	1,932	24,000	2,600
	Guanapalo	766	33,600	1,399
	Guacacía	631	1,200	90
	Caviuna	458	900	100
	Buenavista	450	900	141
	Cabapune	460	900	145
	Arimena	405	900	50
		8,070[b]		
Totals	18 missions	14,137	104,400	6,044[b]

[a]E. Posada and P. M. Ibáñez, *Relaciones de mando*, 2 vols. (Bogotá, 1910), II, 441.
[b]Marcelino Ganuza, *Monografía de las misiones vivas*, 3 vols. (Bogotá, 1921), II, 55:99.

Three years later there were still no Franciscans in San Martín. In February 1837, the jefe político wrote that a measles epidemic was claiming many victims, and since all the parishes lacked priests, there was no one to administer last rites. When he investigated this com-

Table 2
Missions in Casanare, ca. 1839

Religious Order	Priest	Town	Indian Population	Hacienda	
				Cattle	Horses
Dominicans					
Missions of Casanare	1	Tame*	635	65	1
	1	Macaguane	400	80	2
	—	Betoyes	100	64	—
	—	Patute	60	—	—
			1,184*a*	209	3
Missions of Cuiloto	—	Cuiloto	?	—	—
	1	Arauquita	?	—	—
			?	—	—
Recoletos					
Missions of Meta	1	Macuco	321	—	—
	1	Guanapalo	546	—	
	1	Cafifi	?	—	—
	—	Surimena	209	—	—
	—	Casimena	142	—	—
	—	Maquivor	178	—	—
			1,396*b*	—	—
Total	6 priests, 12 missions		2,580	209	3

*There were 176 whites living in Tame in addition to the 624 Indians.
*a*Population figures for the Missions of Casanare were recorded by Francisco Granados on February 10, 1938 (AHN, GC, vol. 16, fols. 792–96).
*b*Population figures for the Missions of Meta are from the Census of 1835, as recorded by Juan Medina R., *Geografía económica de Colombia, III Boyacá* (Bogotá, 1937), 123.
The rest of the information is from Governor J. Beltrán's report dated April 18, 1839 (AHN, GC, vol. 17, fol. 140).

plaint, Archbishop Mosquera discovered that Fr. José María Molano, a Franciscan who was supposed to be serving the parishes of San Martín and San Juan, had deserted his post for unknown reasons.[52] On September 4, 1837, President Márquez officially reestablished the missions at Jiramena and San Martín. In March of the following year, Fr. Gregorio Becerra left Bogotá to take charge of them, but whether he arrived or not is uncertain.[53]

Meanwhile, a new jefe político was working on his own to bring Indians into towns. In 1839, Pablo Enciso met with two bands of Guahibos near Cabuyaro. The first group, led by Captain Eusebio Emancipa, included 24 natives who had left towns in Casanare not because of ill treatment but simply because of their nomadic instincts; and the second group, led by Captain Guillermo N., consisted of 130 men, women, and children. Both captains indicated to Enciso their willingness to settle down, and the jefe político suggested that they build houses in Cabuyaro where 83 whites, mestizos, and Achaguas already resided. In December, he asked the governor for a priest and for forty axes and sixty machetes to give to the new arrivals. He added that Santo Tomás, with 138 Indians, also needed a missionary, as did the 82 inhabitants of Cumaral, who had just built and whitewashed a beautiful chapel and priest's house in the hope that the government would recognize their community as a parish.[54]

Still, no missionaries arrived, for the Franciscans seem to have been even less able than the Recoletos or the Dominicans to find recruits for the Llanos. In his annual report of 1840, Governor Eladio Urisari lamented "that the vast, beautiful, and fertile canton of San Martín finds itself absolutely ignorant and unpopulated when it contains in itself one thousand precious elements of progress and prosperity." The situation was so bad that no elections could be held in any of the parishes or the missions of Concepción de Arama, San Antonio de Iraca, Jiramena, Santo Tomás, and Cabuyaro because no one knew how to write. Urisari called for priests and improved roads, and for populating the canton with prisoners from the highlands; but the outbreak of the Guerra de los Supremos (War of the Supreme Chiefs), New Granada's "most unjust and disastrous" civil conflict, postponed action on these proposals.[55]

The Guerra de los Supremos

The Guerra de los Supremos began in Pasto in 1839 as a popular protest of the anticlerical politics adopted by Santander and Márquez, whose insistence on exercising the patronato, on limiting the jurisdiction of religious courts, and on instituting secular education had generated smoldering resentment among ultra-Catholic sympathizers. When Márquez invoked the Law of June 5, 1839, to suppress some nearly deserted monasteries in Pasto, which previously had been exempted from the "minor convents" prohibition, their animosity burst into flame. Urged on by the local clergy, the *pastusos* rebelled in July, charging that Márquez was trying to destroy religion. The president, backed by the bishop of Pasto and Archbishop Mosquera, resolved to enforce the decree, and he appointed General Pedro Alcántara Herrán as chief of the armed forces in the South, ordering him to put down the protest. By December Herrán had restored order, but conflict broke out anew as Márquez's political enemies in other provinces recognized an opportunity to unseat his government. General José María Obando, whom Márquez had narrowly defeated for the presidency in 1837, challenged Herrán for control of Pasto, while the governors of Socorro, Santa Marta, and Mariquita declared themselves in revolt, with each taking the title of Jefe Supremo of his province.[56] In Casanare, Colonels Calixto Molina, Mariano Acero, and Francisco Farfán pronounced against Márquez on October 4, 1840. Proclaiming himself "Jefe Superior," Molina overthrew Governor Joaquín Barriga in Pore, while Acero and Farfán, both Venezuelans, rode with two hundred Llaneros to join rebels Manuel González and Juan José Reyes Patria in Sogamoso. The beleaguered Barriga did not surrender, however; but he withdrew with his supporters to Labranzagrande. As José Manuel Restrepo recalled:

It is said that all the governors who were so-called Liberals were traitors to the legitimate government of the republic. There was only one honorable exception—that of Lt. Col. Joaquín Barriga who was governor of Casanare. When Molina and Acero made their rebellion in the previous September [*sic*] Barriga could not stop it, but he rejected it and marched to Labranzagrande telling the President what had happened and offering his support.[57]

Manuel González occupied Tunja on November 19, and with an army of three thousand, which included Acero's two hundred Llaneros, he prepared to attack an almost defenseless Bogotá. As President Márquez hurried south to alert Generals Herrán and Tomás C. Mosquera, Colonel Juan José Neira arrived in the capital and organized a resistance force, calling on all able-bodied men to take arms in defense of the city, "especially against the feared two or three hun-

dred *lanceros* from the Llanos who were coming to sack Bogotá."[58]
After a tense week called "La Gran Semana" (November 22–28),
the rebels withdrew without attacking after learning of the arrival of
Herrán and Mosquera's troops, fresh from victory over Obando. At
about the same time, Márquez learned that Colonel José Concepción
Melgarejo had finessed a countercoup in Casanare, taking Molina prisoner and restoring constitutional government in that province.[59]

On January 8, 1841, Herrán and Mosquera defeated the highland
rebels at the battle of Aratoca (Santander), killing 50 and wounding
433. González escaped to die of a sudden illness on March 21; but
some of the vanquished, including Mariano Acero and Francisco Vargas, fled to Casanare, where they were attacked and defeated by Juan
de Díos Escalona and José Concepción Melgarejo. The latter, now
confirmed as governor, spent the rest of the year in subduing pockets
of rebels—skirmishes that further upset the missions and dissipated
the last of the hacienda cattle.[60] By January 1842 Herrán and Mosquera
had restored order throughout the country; Herrán was already president (1841–1845) and Mosquera would succeed him in 1845.

The Guerra de los Supremos was a critical episode in Colombian
history that accelerated major trends in the society and highlighted the
country's weaknesses. The widespread fighting accentuated its economic problems, but a vigorous attack upon them awaited President
Mosquera. In the political arena, the war led to the Constitution of
1843, with its complete subordination of the provincial governments
to the national president and congress.[61] The war helped to define the
growing distinctions in political ideology held by the nascent Conservative and Liberal parties, and although the revolt's failure left the
former firmly in power, their lack of unity during the next decade
permitted the Liberals to recover and take control in 1849 without
resorting to violence. Intellectually, the conflict was "almost exces-
sively stimulating" as Romanticism and Economic Liberalism made
their way into the New Granadan scene, despite the efforts of President Herrán to restore an orthodox Catholic worldview.[62]

The Return of the Jesuits

The guiding spirit of Herrán's administration was his secretary of
interior, Mariano Ospina Rodríguez.[63] A lawyer, educator, and journalist, Ospina collaborated with José Eusebio Caro to write the first Con-

servative party platform in 1848–49. As secretary of interior, his best known project was his Plan of Studies of 1844, which reorganized the universities. Determined to produce graduates who were "mature and stable in their goals, devoted to family, church and economic progress," Ospina tightened discipline, elevated academic standards, and restructured the curriculum to eliminate objectionable and potentially inflammatory Liberal texts.[64] This attempt to mold a new generation ultimately failed, for the older Liberal texts were in school libraries; Liberals remained on the faculties; and the effort to proscribe radical views simply excited intellectual interest. Rather than complacent conservative Catholics, the "reformed" *colegios* and universities produced "one of the most brilliant generations in Colombian history"— men who were widely read, published often, spoke frequently, and took a vigorous role in political and reform activities in the second half of the nineteenth century.[65]

Producing more immediate impact was Ospina's effort to revive the missions in the Llanos. The secretary believed that priests were essential to integrating the Indians into New Granadan life, and he argued that their failure in the past was due to improper training. In the 1820s and 1830s, the clergy sent to the Llanos had been educated in the highlands and were accustomed to a sedentary life in a temperate climate. It was natural that they found the torrid lands along the Meta and the Amazon tributaries to be intolerable. Longing to return to the highlands as soon as possible, they did not bother to learn the native languages and could not effectively convert the Indians. Ospina believed that the solution was to create special colegios to train missionaries for work in the tropics and to invite a religious order from Europe—preferably the Jesuits, with a proven track record in missions—to come to New Granada to administer them. The government could require the graduates of these colegios to spend at least eight years in working with the Indians, and since they would be individuals who had been attracted to this calling from the beginning, they would go out to the Llanos properly prepared and committed to overcoming the obstacles they would face. The other regulars could then be exempted from missionary work and take up tasks more congenial to their temperament and education.[66]

On April 28, 1842, Congress incorporated Ospina's suggestions into a decree authorizing the president to invite a religious order active in Europe to come to New Granada to establish one or more *colegios de misiones* and *casas de escala* to support missions in Casanare, San Martín, Andaquí (Caquetá), Mocoa, Goajira, and Veraguas. On May 3, Vice President Domingo Caicedo instructed the New Granadan chargé d'affaires in London to ask the Jesuits to take up this challenge. He explained that the congressional debate had convinced him that the legislators regarded the Company of Jesus as the order best equipped to lead the savages to Christianity and civilization. New Granadans remembered the success of the Jesuits before their expulsion in the eighteenth century, and they would support their return. The Jesuits continued to train priests in the exact and natural sciences, and since many were currently serving as missionaries in Asia and Africa, they would find it easier to come to New Granada than some other orders.[67]

While Caicedo's rationale was valid, the principal reason for inviting the Jesuits to return to New Granada was the belief on the part of the Conservatives that if the Company took charge of religious and secular education, it would be able to arrest the popularity of the English Radicalism and French Restoration Liberalism that was sweeping the country. The invitation was a political act made possible by the close cooperation between the church and state, sanctioned by the Constitution of 1843.[68] Although officials and settlers in the Llanos probably would have welcomed the Jesuits because of their proven missionary ability, their return was bitterly opposed by Liberals because they took for granted that the Jesuits' loyalty to the pope was a threat to national sovereignty and that the missionaries would become an unofficial army of the Conservative party, placing public liberties in danger.[69]

Oblivious to the controversy swirling around them, the first thirteen Jesuits arrived in Bogotá on June 17, 1844, led by P. Pablo Torroella. In September they began organizing in Bogotá the first missionary college, and by 1845 they had enrolled nine students, who studied, in addition to the usual religious subjects, at least one Indian language, botany, geology, tropical agriculture, and hygiene. In 1847 the Jesuits founded a second colegio in Popayán, and at the request of the archbishop they took over the Colegio de San Bartolomé. Jesuit schools were also begun in Medellín and Pasto.[70]

During the Herrán administration, government support of the Jesuits was unequivocal; but Tomás C. Mosquera, elected to the presidency in 1845, was less committed. The general had been the choice of the militarists, Conservatives, and many of the clergy; but once in office, he displayed alarming Liberal tendencies by abolishing tithes and reducing the fiscal protection enjoyed by the church.[71] Nevertheless, he did encourage the Jesuits in their missionary activities, and in 1846 P. José Segundo Laínez, a thirty-five-year-old Spaniard, set off with two New Granadan novices from Medellín to explore Cáqueta and Putumayo, a remote wilderness encompassing the headwaters of the upper Amazon south of the Llanos of San Martín and the Guaviare River. Passing first through Pasto, the three penetrated the Amazon forest and set up a base at Mocoa. For several months they explored the region and baptized natives. A year later, Laínez returned to Popayán with some of the newly Christianized Indians and samples of cloth woven of fine feathers, necklaces of monkey's teeth, and bows and arrows. Hearing of his return, Mosquera ordered the Jesuit to come to Bogotá, where he was received cordially. With his plans for reducing the Indians approved but backed by little financial support, Laínez went back to Mocoa in September 1847 and soon was evangelizing the Indians along the Putumayo River; but after four months, fatigue, bad food, and the tropical climate undermined his health. Laínez's death on June 27, 1848, brought an end to the mission in Putumayo and to the missionary impulse in general.[72] When Governor Camilo Tavero asked in that year that Jesuits be sent to Casanare, Mosquera's secretary of the interior, Alejandro Osorio, filed the petition without answering it.[73]

Three factors contributed to the Jesuit failure to sustain the missions in Putumayo or to revive them in the Llanos. First, there never were more than two dozen of them in New Granada at any one time, and since most were teaching, few could be spared to travel to the frontier. Second, the Jesuits busied themselves with a myriad of religious and educational activities in Bogotá, bearing out the opposition's fears that they would become the "shock troops" of the Conservative party. For example, to gain the support of the working class, they founded a special congregation for artisans, published a book of devotions called *El artista cristiano*, and for a while in 1846 edited a newspaper called *La Tarde de los Agricultores y Artesanos*. Finally, the Jesuits, in returning to New Granada, had walked into a hornet's nest of ever more hostile enemies. In 1847 and 1848 Congress refused to fund their activities, and with the election of Liberal José Hilario López as president in 1849, the very existence of the order was imperiled. In June 1850, after six short years of residence in New Granada, the Jesuits were again expelled.[74]

The Special Territory of San Martín

Territorial reorganization, a second project proposed by Mariano Ospina, seemed likely to give the missionaries a boost. In March 1844, the secretary unveiled a plan to expand the number of New Granadan provinces from twenty-two to forty-four and to add six "special territories." This arrangement would have equalized the population so that only two provinces would have had as many as forty-eight thousand people and Casanare, as the least populated, would still have nineteen thousand. All cantons would be suppressed, with the governors exercising functions previously assigned to *alcaldes* and jefes políticos. Ospina's object was twofold: to prevent the governors of large provinces from pronouncing at whim against the national government, and to improve public administration at the local level. He argued that his configuration corresponded better to regional interests and would allow for greater economic growth, but the legislators were not convinced. Determined to protect their traditionally dominant power bases, they voted down the proposal after the first debate.[75]

Few objections, however, were raised to the idea of creating special territories. Already in the 1840s, New Granada's elite was beginning to acknowledge the potential resources of the largely unexplored and uninhabited tropical coastlines and lowlands east of the Andes. Exaggerated reports abounded in Bogotá of the fabulous wealth of such areas, yet the provinces to which they were attached lacked the funds to promote their development. Article 167 of the Constitution of 1843 legitimized the concept of special rule for such regions, stating:

Places which because of their isolated position and distances from other towns cannot form part of any Canton or Province, or because of their sparse population cannot be erected into a Canton or Province, shall be governed by special laws; until they are incorporated into some Canton or Province or erected into such, the constitutional regime may be established therein.[76]

On June 2, 1843, Congress created the first special territory under Article 167, of Bocas del Toro, the Caribbean portion of Veragua Province (western Panama). Ospina suggested that five more special territories be created: Darién (eastern Panama), Remedios (Goajira Peninsula), Caquetá, the Island of San Andrés, and San Martín—the latter to include the canton of San Martín in Bogotá Province and the canton of Macuco in Casanare Province. The administration of each territory was to devolve primarily on a powerful official called a prefect. Appointed by the president, the prefect would exercise all the functions which in the provinces were divided between the governors, jefes políticos, alcaldes, *comandantes generales*, and judges of first instance—positions that would not exist in the territories. The prefect would regulate commerce, develop new towns, and control contraband along the international borders. He would encourage the civilization of Indians by supporting the missionaries, attending to their safety, and deciding where they should reside. As is evident, the bureaucratic centralization advocated by Ospina for the provinces was to be even more extreme in the special territories.[77]

Ospina's special-territory proposal was defeated with the rest of his plan, but support for it was forthcoming from the provinces. Toward the end of 1844, for example, Bogotá's governor, Alfonso Acevedo, dispatched documents to the legislature certifying the natural wealth of the canton of San Martín. Pointing out that Bogotá lacked the funds to develop its resources or navigation along the Meta River, he wrote:

One can not look with indifference at the loss of a beautiful and extensive territory in which are found exquisite woods for construction from more than 30 different types of trees, an abundance of good grass, cattle and horses, 26 different kinds of animals, 52 kinds of bees, 3 kinds of silk worms, and although it is true that there are 23 kinds of snakes, 19 kinds of ants and 17 kinds of wasps and some prejudicial insects, it is also certain that in all our lands of cold climate, these are found in abundance.[78]

Acevedo listed twelve steps to be taken to develop San Martín. The first was that it be made a special territory, while the others dealt with awarding land and tax exemptions to settlers, funding missionaries through the public treasury, and improving the roads. He warned that if reforms were not made, white civilization, which had existed in San Martín since the colonial era, would disappear and the region would become the exclusive domain of cannibalistic Indians.[79]

During the administration of T. C. Mosquera, Congress went on to create a series of special territories. The new president was determined to consolidate sovereignty over sparsely settled areas, and his first secretary of the interior, the former president José Ignacio de Márquez, was a man with wide-ranging administrative experience. In his annual report of 1846, Márquez acknowledged that because some governors were handicapped by the size of their provinces, by the lack of adequate means of communication, and by the multiplicity of their functions, he would propose, as Ospina had done two years earlier, a plan for territorial division so that certain areas of the country would be given a special form of government. Caquetá had already been designated a special territory on May 8, 1845, when Márquez presented to Congress a bill organizing the political, military, and judicial government of such territories. Once this bill was adopted, almost without any change, and became a law, Congress proceeded to create the Territories of San Martín (May 6, 1846), Goajira (May 19, 1846), Darién (June 2, 1846), Guanacas (April 28, 1847), San Andrés (April 28, 1847), and Raposo (May 4, 1848).[80] Alejandro Osorio, who succeeded Márquez as secretary of the interior, gave full support to the territorial initiative, urging Congress to empower the prefects to levy taxes on the parishes to generate funds to build churches, schools, jails, and roads, and stressing that the government should develop a firm plan to send well-trained missionaries to the territories. In 1848, he wrote:

The missions are important today not only to civilize the Indians but also because national integrity is identified with the progress of the missions. The Special Territories will be populated by Indians but Indians who are civilized and who practice New Granadan habits, interests and customs.[81]

Since the special territories were reincorporated with their former provinces by José Hilario López on June 22, 1850, the system did not have sufficient time to prove its viability. From the standpoint of promoting missionary activity, it had no apparent effect. Silverio Medina, the first and only prefect of the Territory of San Martín, reported in 1848 that there were 443 settled Indians in his jurisdiction: 168 in San Juan de Arama; 98 in Jiramena ("all gentle and some of whom known how to read and write"); 48 in Cabuyaro; 52 in San Antonio de Iraca; and 77 Guahibos at the old mission of San Miguel, on the northern side of the Meta. Beyond these settlements were 80,000 Indians untouched by civilization, and still no missionaries in the territory, although one Franciscan had been appointed to serve San Miguel and Cabuyaro. Medina urged that priests be sent who could win the natives' friendship by giving them glass beads, salt, and tools. Only with missionaries, schools, and roads would San Martín begin to progress.[82]

Likewise in Casanare, the missions continued to stagnate throughout the 1840s. Governor Melgarejo observed in 1845 that just two of the Meta reductions remained—Guanapalo and Cafifi. Neither had a priest, and their haciendas consisted of a few head of cattle too wild to round up. The missions of Casanare and Cuiloto were deserted, except that the Hacienda of Cuiloto still contained some cattle "having been managed by an intelligent and honorable person."[83] Melgarejo himself was at least partially responsible for the absence of priests. The previous September, the Recoleto provincial, Fr. José Benigno Hurtado, assigned Fr. Santiago Pinilla and Fr. Santiago Venegas to Maquivor on the condition that the government pay their stipends. Venegas left Bogotá for Casanare in December. When he reached Pore, he was detained by Melgarejo on the grounds that he needed a missionary for Cafifi and Guanapalo, not Surimena and Maquivor; and in any case, Bogotá had not sent Venegas's stipend. Archbishop Mosquera complained to Secretary Márquez, who, on April 27, 1846, ordered the governor to comply with his duties and give the missionaries the help they required. When Melgarejo continued to stall, Mosquera again protested to Márquez, adding that Fr. Santiago Pinilla was now ready to take up his post in Surimena, but he had only received enough travel funds to take him as far as Pore. Thoroughly disgusted, Mosquera wrote, "It is not possible to do anything in the Missions of Meta, if the missionaries are not given the necessities; abandoned to their luck, they can not remain in the Llanos."[84]

The Reckoning

By 1848 the frustration of ecclesiastical and civil authorities over their failure to revive the missions was readily apparent. Writing on December 7, 1848, Archbishop Mosquera noted that while three Dominicans were serving the Missions of Casanare, the Missions of Meta had disappeared, with the exception of Cafifi; and he went on to catalogue the problems that had beset the regulars for four decades. First, the clerical mortality rate was extremely high, lending support to the popular belief that the climate was deadlier than in the previous century when the large cattle hatos had kept the wilderness at bay and cut down infectious disease. Second, the Indians were more warlike than in the eighteenth century; the missionaries were no longer dealing with simple, rude savages but with "hordes of depraved men determined to rob and pillage." Finally, weakened by the decline of discipline, the regular orders were not producing priests with a spirit of self-sacrifice sufficient to overcome these difficulties. Unless the national government did more to aid them, it was senseless to continue to send missionaries to Casanare. Mosquera recommended that, at the very least, the government should create an armed guard based in the province that would force the Indians to respect law and order, and that it should raise the stipends of the priests so they could fortify themselves against the climate and purchase gifts to attract converts.[85]

Secretary Osorio agreed with the archbishop. His annual report of 1848 was a veritable obituary for the missions on the Llanos frontier. Recalling that in 1810 the Recoletos alone had administered 8,137 Indians in the Missions of Meta and 104,200 cattle and 9,125 horses in the adjoining haciendas, Osorio confirmed that not one of these missions or estates remained in spite of the fact that every administration since 1821 had appropriated money for their support and conceded them special privileges. Experience had proven, he concluded, that priests by themselves, no matter how dedicated, could no longer reduce Indians unless they were part of a larger plan that would give them the vital material support that they needed.[86]

In summary, reviving the missions was a dominant theme of the history of the Llanos frontier in the early nineteenth century, and perhaps what is most remarkable is the steadfast conviction on the part of all of the governments that missions were essential to frontier life in spite of changing conditions in the Llanos and in the highlands that worked against their perpetuation. The Mexican Liberals who regarded the missions as antiquated institutions and brought about their complete secularization in California, Texas, and New Mexico by the 1840s had no counterparts in New Granada.[87] When the radical Liberals came to power in 1849, they embarked on a sweeping campaign against the church. President José Hilario López expelled the Jesuits, legalized divorce, annulled all tithes, and extinguished the ecclesiastical *fueros*. Yet even his stridently anticlerical administration advocated the expansion of missions in the Llanos, proposing to staff them not with foreigners whose loyalty was manifestly suspect, as Secretary of the Interior Francisco Zaldúa stated in 1850, but with New Granadans who would be deeply committed to national moral and material progress. Zaldúa urged Congress to reorganize the missions, erecting new parishes when necessary, conceding broader powers to the regulars, and granting greater privileges to Indians who accepted Christianity.[88] Except for the ban on foreign priests, his plan was essentially the same as those proposed by previous governments, and it achieved no greater success. As this history will show, revival of the missions awaited the regeneration of European evangelism and the return to power in New Granada of the Conservatives, who after 1886 would revoke most of the anticlerical legislation and sign a new concordat with the Vatican. By the 1890s Europeans and Colombian regulars were again pursuing the elusive quest of converting Indians in the Llanos. The mission—the most characteristic institution of Spanish colonial frontier rule—survived the challenge of nineteenth-century Liberalism to remain an integral part of life even today in contemporary Meta, Casanare, and Arauca.

Watercolors painted in 1856 by Manuel María Paz, a member of the commission led by Agustín Codazzi that surveyed the Llanos of Casanare in that year. These paintings are the oldest and most authentic pictures of the Llanos. They are reproduced in *Album de la comisión corográfico* (Bogotá, 1953) edited by Julio Londoño.

Panorama of the Llanos of Casanare

Plaza of Moreno, capital of Casanare

Town on the banks of the
Meta River

View of the Meta River from Orocué

Llaneros branding cattle

Guahibo Indians

Indians and whites encamped on the Meta River

Mulattoes and an Indian fishing

3. The Liberals and the Llanos, 1849–63

*I*f, in 1849, enormous obstacles faced the restoration of the Llanos missions, it was also evident that new priorities for the eastern frontier were emerging. The Liberals, who came to power in that year, believed that one reason for New Granada's lack of economic growth was that large and potentially rich portions of its territory were virtually unknown. While 90 percent of the population lived in the Andean core, the Magdalena Valley, much of the Pacific and Caribbean coasts and the immense Llanos and Amazonia regions remained nearly empty. Their conviction that New Granada's prosperity—given its rugged terrain; "unskilled, illiterate labor force; and meager capital resources"— lay in the exploitation of tropical agriculture brought home an awareness of the necessity to explore the unknown areas, to ascertain their resources, and to bring them under more effective rule.[1] Thus, along with their dismantlement of the hierarchical and authoritarian state that had survived under the Conservatives, the Liberals concentrated on the improvement of transportation along the Magdalena River and the expansion of tobacco exports. The reforms initiated by José Hilario López and elaborated by his successors, exacerbated Casanare's problems, propelling the extinction of its provincial government in 1857 and its incorporation into Boyacá. In the Llanos of San Martín, however, they were less destructive, as a small but steady stream of peasants left their homes in Cáqueza and Quetame, Cundinamarca, to seek their fortunes in the plains south of the Meta River. The growth of Villavicencio and a second migration of well-to-do pioneers from Bogotá in the 1860s laid the foundation for the reestablishment of the National Territory of San Martín in 1868.

The Liberals at the Helm, 1849–63

Even more than the Guerra de los Supremos, the regime of José Hilario López, which lasted from 1849 to 1853, marks a watershed in Colombian history. Abolition of the state tobacco monopoly and the reduction of tariffs inaugurated an age dominated by Liberals who were linked through their ideological and economic interests to the industrializing nations of Europe and North America.[2] Supporters of López believed that individuals left alone to pursue their intellectual and material interests would contribute to the progress of civilization and the well-being of society in general. Accordingly, they abolished slavery, accelerated the division of Indian lands, expanded civil liberties, instituted unlimited freedom of the press, abolished the death penalty for political crimes, decentralized administration and tax revenues, gave local governments more control over the church, and extinguished special ecclesiastical courts. All these reforms were incorporated into the Constitution of 1853, which broadened suffrage by ending property and literacy requirements; instituted direct, secret elections; and provided for the election of many previously appointed officials.

The extremism that marked the López regime generated a backlash of resistance. Popular protest against low tariffs prompted an artisan-supported military coup that brought General José María Melo to power in April 1854, but the joint military action of oligarchy-led forces of both the Conservative and Liberal parties restored civilian authority the following December. In 1857 a split in the Liberal ranks between radicals and moderates enabled Mariano Ospina Rodríguez to regain the presidency, but during his second administration, Conservatives failed to break the determination of Liberal partisans who again seized power after a vicious civil war that dragged on from 1859 to 1862. Ruling as provisional president, Tomás C. Mosquera, now a committed Liberal, enacted a set of extreme measures that dealt a body blow to the Conservatives. In particular, Mosquera struck at the temporal power of the church, decreeing the disamortization of its property and the extinction of religious communities.[3] The Constitution of 1863 consolidated these libertarian, anticlerical and federalist reforms, which remained in effect until 1885.

The rise of the Liberal party in the late 1840s closely paralleled the growth of export agriculture. Regularization of steamboats on the Magdalena River and release of tobacco cultivation from a state monopoly generated an expansion of foreign trade based on tobacco exports that became New Granada's largest exchange earner.[4] Tobacco income fluctuated between 100,000 and 200,000 pesos annually in the mid 1840s and increased to more than 5 million pesos annually in most years between 1850 and 1875. By 1878 production was on the wane, sapped by the declining quality of the Colombian leaf and competition from Java and Brazil, but not before it had stimulated the economy, stabilized navigation on the Magdalena, and prepared the way for the transition to coffee.[5]

International demand sparked smaller booms in other products. Acknowledgement by European doctors that quinine extracted from the bark and roots of the cinchona tree was useful in treating malaria spurred a frenzied rush to exploit the forests that grew along the slopes of the Andes from New Granada to Peru. Cinchona export earnings became significant in the 1850s, when they averaged about half a million pesos annually. After peaking in 1880–81 at over 5 million pesos, they declined to almost nothing by 1885, due to competition from higher quality cinchona cultivated on British and Dutch plantations in the East Indies.[6] Large-scale indigo exports began in 1864–65 and peaked in 1870–71, at 182,199 kilos, while chance circumstances sparked brief flurries in cotton and cacao; but it was not until the 1880s that a spectacular rise in world demand for coffee launched the production boom that would dwarf all previous export cycles in magnitude and impact.[7]

Just as rebellions interrupted the process of political change, the growth of the export economy was by no means continuous. The expansion begun in 1850 suffered two serious setbacks in the 1870s and was characterized by considerable instability in the marketing of individual commodities. Despite their substantial growth, New Granada's total exports in 1870 were still three times less per capita than Argentina, Chile, and Peru, and the unpredictable boom and bust cycles created an environment of frustration that fostered continuous conflict. The government found it hard to develop and adhere to priorities in building roads. Public works and private projects went forward fitfully. It was not until after 1870, when a commercial banking system was in place, that the elites redoubled their efforts to establish domestic manufacturing and basic industries.[8] Of the various projects begun before 1863, only one had a significant impact on the eastern frontier and that was the Codazzi Corographic Commission, whose survey of Casanare marked a rediscovery of the Llanos and presaged the changes that would come.

The Codazzi Corographic Commission

The desire of New Granadans to know their country in all of its extension, wealth, and topographic components first found legal expression in 1839, when Congress authorized the government to hire surveyors to prepare a map of each province along with a general map and a written description of the republic; yet no action was taken until the first administration of Tomás Cipriano Mosquera (1845–1849).[9] Mosquera zealously supported the development of science in many fields by contracting with professors from Europe and neighboring South American countries to teach in New Granada; and he greatly admired Agustín Codazzi, an Italian military engineer, who, under the sponsorship of José Antonio Páez, completed a map of Venezuela that won praise from Alexander von Humboldt. In 1845, Mosquera invited Codazzi to make a similar map of New Granada, but the engineer was reluctant to leave Venezuela and declined. The situation changed, however, when Páez was overthrown in 1848 and Codazzi was forced to seek asylum in Cúcuta. On January 13, 1849, President López renewed Mosquera's invitation, and a year later the Italian signed a contract agreeing to produce a map of each of the twenty-five provinces, a general map of the republic, and a detailed written account describing "the customs and nature of the population, ancient monuments, natural curiosities, and all other circumstances worthy of mention"— all for the then extraordinary annual salary of 8,500 pesos.[10]

The Codazzi Corographic Commission began its work in 1850 and ceased to exist in all practical ways with the death of its leader on February 7, 1859, near Santa Marta. Its members included Manuel Ancízar, who served as Mosquera's secretary of state; botanist José Triana; and the painter Carmelo Fernández—a nephew of General Páez who, like Codazzi, had sought refuge in New Granada from the implacable persecution of President José Tadeo Monagas. In 1852 a young English artist, Enrique Price, replaced Fernández, and a year later, a Colombian, Manuel María Paz, took over the position. In nine years the commission made ten trips to different parts of the country, and Codazzi was at work on the maps for the last two states, Magdalena and Bolívar, at the time of his death.[11] The data gathered became the basis for innumerable maps, some of which were published by Manuel María Paz in the *Atlas de Colombia* (Paris, 1889). Felipe Pérez and Francisco Javier Vergara y Velasco drew on the commission's descriptions of regions, towns, and roads to write *Geografía general de los estados de la Nueva Granada* (Bogotá, 1883) and *Nueva geografía de Colombia* (Bogotá, 1901–2). José Triana collected nearly four thousand plants, which became the nucleus of his *Nuevos jéneros i especies de plantas para la flora Neo Granadina,* published in Bogotá in 1854 and in Paris in 1862. Manuel Ancízar wrote *Peregrinación de Alpha* (Bogotá, 1853)—a faithful portrait of the customs of the inhabitants of the northern states, as he observed them in 1850–51. Finally, the commission's three artists made thousands of sketches and paintings, some of which were reproduced in the *Albúm de la Comisión Corográfica* (Bogotá, 1953), edited by Julio Londoño.[12]

Codazzi and his associates visited Casanare on their seventh expedition in 1856. While the others were busy mapping this region that had previously defined scientific description, Manuel María Paz set up his easel and began to paint, capturing for the first time on canvas the unique character of the Llanos and its inhabitants. Included in his portfolio are portraits of Guahibo men ready to hunt, Sáliva women preparing *casabe*, and mestizo Llaneros branding cattle. One of the most enchanting portraits is entitled "The Llanos of Casanare"—a panorama showing a group of cattle in the foreground, and behind them an immense ocean of plains blending imperceptibly with the sky, broken here and there by exuberant palm trees and by distant columns of smoke rising from invisible haciendas.[13] Paradoxically, this artistic portrayal of a tropical paradise was sharply contradicted in Codazzi's written report, which focused on Casanare's problems. "A country," he observed, "that nearly in its totality is covered with plains irrigated by many rivers and innumerable *caños* . . . which during the rainy season leave their beds and flood extensive portions of the land is not, certainly, a healthy country." Codazzi argued that the extreme heat; the prevalence of disease; the tigers, snakes, *caimanes* (alligators), and mosquitoes; and bands of roving hostile Indians were enormous obstacles to Casanare's regeneration. He believed that only blacks or Venezuelans acclimated to the tropics could survive there, and he recommended that a special administrative system be devised to protect settlers from the Indians and to promote ranching by raising the value of the now worthless *baldíos* (lands in the public domain). The well-being of Casanare can best be assured, he concluded, by adding the cordillera towns to the provinces of Tunja and ruling the plains as a separate region, with special protective laws administered by enlightened prefects prepared to endure the climate and bring to the rude population the education and morality that they lacked.[14]

The Collapse of the Province of Casanare

Contemporary documents reinforce Codazzi's depiction of Casanare as a province beset by disease. The census of 1851 counted 9,133 men and 9,440 women for a total of 18,573—an increase of

2,625 over the 15,948 registered in 1853, but only 84 more than the 18,489 recorded in 1843 and still significantly below the 22,137 living in Casanare in 1825.[15] A steady influx of Venezuelans had failed to compensate for outmigration to Boyacá and the high mortality due to malaria, dysentery, intestinal parasites, and yellow fever—afflictions intensified by the suffocating heat, stagnant waters, and abrupt changes in temperature.[16] Outbreaks of measles and smallpox appeared in 1836, with cases of smallpox reported again in 1841 and 1852. Three years later, a cholera epidemic that had penetrated Venezuela from La Guaira and Puerto Cabello threatened to engulf Arauca.[17] By this time, according to Felipe Pérez, just thirty families lived on the open plains, and these were "Indians from the old missions, some *socorranos* and many Venezuelans, that is, Llaneros of the plains of that republic who were accustomed to the heat."[18] The rest of the white and mestizo population was concentrated in the piedmont towns, which, because of their slightly higher altitude, were more salubrious.

Disease was a factor in the transfer of Casanare's capital three times in the 1840s. Since 1802 Pore, described by one governor as "that tomb of the living," had been the provincial capital, but by the 1830s its residents began petitioning the national government to allow them to move on the grounds that chronic illness prevented them from attending to their duties.[19] When authorization came on March 23, 1842, provincial officials moved to Támara only to find that the town did not have a sufficient number of buildings to accommodate them. They returned to Pore in 1843, but renewed their requests for a transfer to a healthier spot. Governor Camilo Tavera wrote, in 1847, that his subordinates did not spend much time at their duties "because sickness has reduced them, each day paralyzing more the march of public service." Recently, he added, "several individuals were assigned to the service of the hacienda and although they were careful they could not escape the fevers common in this locality."[20] Finally, in 1849, the national government designated "La Fragua," a mesa overlooking the Muese River twenty kilometers north of Pore, as the new capital. Renamed Moreno, in honor of revolutionary hero and former governor Juan Nepomuceno Moreno, the town grew rapidly in the first year. By November 1850 there were more than one hundred houses on well laid-out streets, and a government house, church, and jail built around the central plaza. Even in Moreno, however, the fevers persisted. In 1852, Governor Antonio J. Benítes reported that while the transfer of the capital had brought material progress, its inhabitants still suffered greatly, being chilled after the heat of the day by the cold night winds blowing off the mountain.[21]

President José Hilario López, who approved the move to Moreno as one of his first official acts, received little backing from voters in Casanare in the election of 1848. Following the lead of Tunja, Casanare cast twenty electoral ballots for the Conservative candidate, Rufino Cuervo, and seven for López, but Liberalism was gaining popular support.[22] In 1849 a Democratic Society was founded in Pore, and in the 1852 election the province cast twenty electoral votes for José María Obando, the "Draconian" Liberal candidate, and one vote for Tómas Herrera, his "Golgotha" opponent. When, on May 11, 1854, Governor Francisco de P. Cuellar received word of José María Melo's April 16 coup, he pledged support to the legitimate government then headed by General Tomás Herrera in Ibagúe. Herrera named Colonel José Concepción Melgarejo as *comandante de armas* of Moreno and ordered him to raise two hundred men to guard the province.[23] After Melo was deposed and peace restored, Casanare gave 2,644 popular votes to Liberal Manuel Morillo Toro, 28 votes to Conservative Manuel Ospina, and 263 votes to T. C. Mosquera, running on the National party ticket in the 1856 election. Nationwide, Ospina won a majority to become the last Conservative president until the accession of Rafael Núñez in 1886.[24]

The López reforms, traumatic throughout New Granada, triggered the collapse of Casanare. While some measures such as the expulsion of the Jesuits and the abolition of slavery had little impact, the adoption of fiscal decentralization and anticlerical measures accelerated financial insolvency and the deterioration of the missions in the Llanos.[25] Neither López nor his successors managed to improve relations with Venezuela, whose control of the Orinoco blocked economic growth while chronic rebellions kept Arauca in a continual state of unrest. In 1857, after 250 years of an independent existence, the province was extinguished and Casanare was incorporated into the sovereign state of Boyacá.

Financial penury had plagued Casanare since the War of Independence disrupted the missions and ranches and left large numbers of veterans demanding their back pay. Until 1849 its principal revenues came from the tobacco and salt monopolies, a tax levied on aguardiente, and *peaje* (road tolls) assessed on cattle and travelers. Income from these sources was meager due to a lack of trained revenue agents, fraud, contraband, and the poverty of the inhabitants. In 1846, for example, none of the cantons had officials to collect taxes, and in Arauca, the jefe político managed the customs receipts because no administrator had been appointed.[26] Even peaje, which should have been paid by Venezuelans driving cattle into New Granada from Apure, produced little money, since Venezuelans avoided the tax by claiming they had used only a part of the road and were therefore exempt.[27]

Liberal efforts to encourage private enterprise and free trade through decentralization of national finances compounded Casanare's problems. The abolition of the tobacco monopoly in 1850 took away one source of income for the province just as it eliminated nearly one-quarter of the central government's revenue. The López regime regarded a number of other taxes to be detrimental to national growth. By the Law of April 20, 1850, it ceded to the provinces the income from the aguardiente monopoly, the tithe, and the *quinto* (the state's 20 percent share, or tax, on precious metals), in the expectation that many provinces would abolish them altogether and that those which were retained would provide on the regional level the few services that Liberals were willing to admit were indeed the responsibility of the government.[28] The severe impact of this reform on Casanare was revealed in its budget of 1852, which registered a deficit of 48,087.45 reales, the difference between its income of 59,838 reales and expenses of 99,925.45 reales. Revenue from the aguardiente tax accounted for one-third of the income. Governor Benítez reported that a national subsidy awarded by the Law of May 24, 1851, had not been forthcoming, and as a result, government employees had not been paid for six months. He lamented that he could not be optimistic about Casanare's future as he completed his term of office, for in spite of his most determined and patriotic efforts, the Law of April 20, 1850, on decentralization of income had left the province without resources.[29]

The empty treasury complicated the administration of justice. Since because of the low salaries, isolation, and deadly fevers, few lawyers would come to the Llanos when appointed as judges, ignorant, corrupt, and unqualified individuals presided over the courts. In 1845, Governor Julian Beltrán observed:

The judgement of the criminal becomes more difficult every time since the processes are so flawed, and the prisoners get so tired of waiting that they escape which is relatively easy because the jails are flimsy and they are confident that the local authorities will not pursue them.

He added that since crimes went unpunished, outlaws from other parts of the country hid in Casanare in the certainty that they would not be prosecuted and would be able to escape capture.[30]

Poverty also crippled public instruction. There was no money to pay teachers, and as the missions disappeared, priests who had served the schools without pay left the province. Of nineteen primary schools providing instruction to 260 boys and 25 girls in 1839, only nine remained in 1850, enrolling 223 boys. On April 20, 1851, the governor ordered the municipalities to fund schools, but Labranzagrande, Támara, Chire, and Zapatosa had neither money nor inclination to comply. In his annual report of 1852, Governor Benítez explained that even when funds were available, the ignorant cabildo members hired inept, corrupt teachers who abandoned the children. He urged President López to centralize primary education as the most expeditious way to improve public instruction in Casanare.[31]

The Liberals' determination to break the power of the Catholic church prevented a revival of the missions long regarded as essential for the control and civilization of the Indians in the Llanos. Throughout the troubled decade of the 1850s, the religious orders were on the defensive. In 1850, López evicted the Jesuits, proclaimed full religious liberty, assigned the appointment of parish priests to municipal authorities, transferred state support for the church from the central government to the provinces, disbanded ecclesiastical courts, outlawed tithes, and legalized divorce. When Bogotá's Archbishop Manuel José Mosquera and three other bishops protested, they were summarily exiled.[32] With the resurgence of Conservative influence in 1855, the situation eased as the government restored the right of churches and congregations to hold property and abrogated the divorce law. In 1858 President Mariano Ospina recalled the Jesuits, and a new constitution guaranteed religious liberty. This truce was brief, for when T. C. Mosquera seized power in 1861 he renewed the anticlerical campaign. The government once again expelled the Jesuits, ruled that no cleric could exercise his religious functions without civil authorization, passed a new law of disamortization, and suppressed all convents, monasteries, and religious houses.[33]

Meanwhile, in Casanare, Indians unchecked by missionaries attacked towns and ranches. The Guahibos along the tributaries of the Cravo, Ele, and Lipa rivers were especially audacious, and in 1844, they actually isolated the canton of Arauca from the rest of the province.[34] Settlers formed vigilante groups to reinforce the military *resguardos* (squadrons of soldiers), which had been stationed in Pore, Nunchía, and Tame in 1838.[35] By 1853 Governor Benítez was forced to disband the resguardos for lack of money to pay the soldiers, even though the Guahibos continued to attack houses near Moreno and ambush travelers on the road between Ten and Támara.[36] Three years later, after the last Recoleto had left the Llanos, the legislature asked Archbishop Antonio Herrán to send missionaries once again to Casanare. Dated November 30, 1856, the petition stated that the Indians were waging a war of extermination against the whites. In three months they had burned down a town, robbed dozens of travelers, murdered entire families, and left at the very gates of Moreno ten corpses of both sexes and of all ages, whom they had killed with lances and arrows. The legislators threatened to invite Protestant missionaries to come to the province if the archbishop did not approve their request. Herrán responded that he was not indifferent to the plight of Casanare, but with so few priests remaining in the diocese, he could spare no one to go to the Llanos.[37]

After annexing Casanare in 1857, the Constituent Assembly of Boyacá took up the challenge. On October 22 of that year, it authorized President Fernández Madrid to sign a contract with the Jesuits, or with some other Catholic order, to convert the Indians in the Llanos. Fernández Madrid and Herrán took up the matter with the Vatican, and in 1859 Misislao Conde Ledochowski, Apostolic Delegate of the Holy See, announced that the Italian order of the Redemptionist Fathers of San Alfonso de Ligori had agreed to accept the assignment. Padre Enrique Tirino and two other Redemptionists arrived in Tunja in August, and soon afterward Tirino was designated superior and prefect apostolic for the missions of Casanare. The three set off for the Llanos in April 1859, but on May 12, just two days after they had been welcomed in Moreno, Padre Tirino was thrown by his horse and killed instantly. The tragedy crippled the work of the Redemptionists, and although the other two remained in Casanare, they accomplished little before being evicted in 1861.[38]

Venezuela and Arauca

The Liberals were unable to resolve a multitude of problems resulting from Casanare's proximity to Apure, Venezuela. A treaty drawn up in 1834 had confirmed that the international boundary would follow the Arauca River, cutting due south to the Brazilian border a few kilometers east of Arauca City.[39] Most of Arauca City's one thousand residents were Venezuelans who made their living by trading with their compatriots in the town of El Amparo, across the river. Ships sailing from Ciudad Bolívar up the Orinoco and the Arauca rivers unloaded their cargos at these two ports, and from there the merchandise was shipped to the interior. In terms of commerce and cattle, Arauca City was by far the wealthiest town in Casanare, but it was subjected to constant political unrest as Venezuela's civil warfare spilled over the border.

In Venezuela, the Llanos—which cover nearly all of the provinces of Apure and Barinas, half of Carabobo, three-quarters of Caracas, four-fifths of Barcelona and Cumaná, and a fraction of Guayana— had been prone to violence since the colonial era. During the War of Independence, Llaneros joined the royalists to protest republican efforts to tie them to the land, but they were won over to the patriot side by the promises and charisma of José Antonio Páez. Whatever their allegiance, sacking, pillage, and plunder characterized their operations, which were only partially restrained by quasi-military discipline. After the battle of Carabobo in 1821, Vice President Santander sent the Llaneros home on indefinite, unpaid leave, and for the next five years, Congress tried to work out a way to honor their claims for back pay and bonuses. In 1823, it passed a special relief measure for the soldiers of Apure and Casanare, awarding them land and cattle; but the land titles were without practical value, and the soldiers sold their promissory notes to their officers. Life for them was difficult, and on the impoverished plains, banditry offered the most secure route toward fortune and respect.[40]

José Antonio Páez dominated Venezuela between 1831 and 1846. A Llanero himself, he could not pacify the plains. Caudillos in all of the subregions threatened his control of Caracas, drawing into their bands hardened outlaws and disillusioned plainsmen, who followed their leaders out of admiration for their military valor and hope of social and economic gain. Rebellions occurred in 1830, 1831, 1835–36, and 1837, and though they failed to unseat Páez, they perpetuated an atmosphere of unrest. In 1836 the government retaliated with the so-called Ley de Azotes, which legalized whipping for minor offenses committed in the Llanos and the death penalty, imprisonment, and forced labor for serious crimes. This harsh measure provoked ever more bitter resistance, and the Liberal party, formed in 1840 to oppose Páez, won over Llanero followers by branding it as barbarous and counterproductive. In 1846–47, Llaneros joined a revolt against Páez's successor, José Tadeo Monagas; they fought in a rebellion, led by Páez himself, against Monagas in 1848–49 and again in the Liberal revolt of 1853–54.[41] These conflicts affected all of Casanare, but especially Arauca as Venezuelans on the losing side evaded capture by crossing the Arauca River. A brief review of the career of Colonel José Francisco Farfán, a caudillo from Apure who dominated the border between 1835 and 1855, illustrates many dimensions of the problem.

José Francisco Farfán and his brother Juan Pablo were valiant *apureños* who fought with the royalist insurgent Agustín Yáñez in 1813–1814 but went over to Páez when he offered to promote to captain every Llanero who brought him forty men. In his *Autobiografía*, Páez described the Farfáns as "the true type of Llanero Bedouin: men of gigantic stature, of athletic physique, of bravery marked by ferocity and only obedient to brute force."[42] He added that the brothers had aided him on more than one occasion, but they often took off on their own with their followers and, after committing crimes, would want to rejoin his army. The Farfáns did not fight in the critical battle of Murcuritas in 1817, but they did contribute to the capture of Puerto Cabello in 1823, and with the restoration of peace, they retired to their hatos in Apure.

In 1836, José Francisco was accused of stealing cattle. He was tried and sentenced to be whipped under the Ley de Azotes. Before the punishment could take place, Farfán escaped, killed his judge, and took up arms against the government, demanding abolition of the hated law and constitutional reforms. He surrendered in response to a direct personal appeal from President Páez, but his contrition was short lived. In January 1837 Farfán revolted again, this time in support of an insurrection that had begun in Guayana and called for abolition of taxes paid by farmers and ranchers, constitutional reform, and the reestablishment of Gran Colombia. The rebels won several quick victories in Apure, forcing Cornelio Muñoz, commander of the government forces, to retreat to San Fernando. Páez dispatched Col. Agustín Codazzi to assist Muñoz and later took command of the operaions himself. On April 26, 1837, he defeated the Farfáns at San Fernando, killing 150 of the rebels, including Juan Pablo, while Francisco fled across the river to Arauca.[43]

On September 5, 1839, Governor Beltrán warned New Granadan

Secretary of State Alejandro Vélez that the resguardo in Arauca City could not keep the peace. The town was infested with apureños accused of crimes in Venezuela, who were only awaiting word of a new rebellion to cross the border. In the meantime, they broke New Granadan laws with impunity, convinced that they would not be punished. When the jefe político threatened to bring them to justice, Domingo Chacón, "one of the closest companions of Farfán and the most famous and accredited murderer known in Venezuela," escaped from jail; and he was now lurking in the plains, threatening to attack the town. The soldiers of the resguardo were without horses and received so little pay that many of them sympathized with the outlaws. In asking Vélez for help, Beltrán pointed out that he could not replace the resguardo with national guardsmen "because there is nothing to feed them and being the same men as those of the resguardo, we would be in the same situation."[44] By the time he received the secretary's unhelpful reply, suggesting that he fill the empty places in the resguardo with the best people available, the crisis was already at hand.

On October 11, Chacón surrounded Arauca City with eighty well-mounted men. He planned to rob and kill its most notable citizens and then ride on to Pore to kill the *juez de hacienda* and Governor Beltrán. Cut off from their horses grazing on the plains outside the town, the Araucanos spent an anxious night. They armed themselves as well as they could, and in the morning Colonel Farfán, who had earlier repudiated his former associate, decided on a bold plan. With ten men mounted on the only horses remaining within the town limits, he charged out, attacking and wounding Chacón before retreating to the safety of the houses. The siege ended two days later, when Colonel José Concepción Melgarejo, with thirty-four horsemen and two canoes full of soldiers, surprised the bandits on the banks of the Arauca River, capturing twenty, including Chacón, and dispersing the rest.[45]

Farfán found another outlet for his talents in the Guerra de los Supremos, which broke out the following year. On October 4, 1840, along with Calixto Molina and Mariano Acero, he pronounced against President José Ignacio de Márquez and seized Pore. Farfán and Acero led two hundred Llaneros over the Cordillera to join the army commanded by Manuel González and Juan José Reyes Patria. Although they occupied Tunja, the rebels abandoned their plans to attack Bogotá in the belief that the loyalist defense of the capital was invulnerable. Farfán fought with Reyes Patria against Generals Herrán and Mosquera in the Battle of Aratoca (Santander) on January 9, 1841.

After this defeat, he returned to Casanare to find that Melgarejo had retaken Pore and imprisoned Molina.[46]

Soon afterward, Farfán went back to Apure, but he continued to cast a long shadow over Arauca. In 1848, he supported President José Tadeo Monagas in his attempt to put down a rebellion led by former president Páez. On the orders of Monagas's chief of operations in Apure, General Cornelio Muñoz, Farfán took charge of the defense of Alto Apure in Guasdualito canton, harassing New Granadans and Venezuelans alike who crossed the border. Bautista Melgarejo, jefe político of Arauca, interned the Venezuelans in his canton, regardless of which side they supported, and sent them to Pore as a preventive measure. On March 11, General Muñoz defeated Páez at Los Araguatos. Páez fled to New Granada, passing through Arauca on March 16, but the revolt continued in his name until December. All that year, Farfán, who moved to El Amparo, blocked commerce across the border and seized cattle from the supporters of Páez.[47]

By the middle of the nineteenth century Arauca was the center of cattle ranching in Casanare. Every year, twelve thousand steers left hatos along the Arauca River and the caños of Cabuyaro, Guatarito, and Bendición for Moreno, Medina, San Martín City, and points west. Venezuelan cattle crossed the Arauca River for sale in New Granada in equally large numbers. Established in 1832, the aduana in Arauca City collected thirty thousand to forty thousand pesos of revenue annually, while the aduana in Naranjito, Moreno's port on the Pauto River, took in twelve thousand to fourteen thousand pesos, usually paid in hides and coffee. Merchants in Arauca City annually shipped four thousand to six thousand hides, straw hats, hammocks made from palms, and wild animal skins to Venezuela and Guayana, in exchange for merchandise, liquor, hardware, china, medicine, and other articles.[48]

Contraband was equally extensive. In the 1840s, rustlers in Apure discovered that it was easier and more profitable to ship the hides of the cattle they stole down the Orinoco than it was to drive the animals alive to northern Venezuelan ports and have to pay peaje. Joined by many prestigious ranchers, who were frequently in collusion with local judges, they developed a complex network along the river to expedite clandestine shipping. As a result, exports in hides increased from 164,000, in 1839–40, to 646,000, in 1854–55.[49] How many Araucanos participated in this activity is uncertain, but in 1848 New Granada opened a consulate in Ciudad Bolívar because of the active commerce between Casanare and Guayana.[50]

The twenty-five policemen stationed in Arauca City were woefully inadequate to patrol the border and control the brisk contraband trade. In 1853, the jefe político asked President López to designate the town as a free port, arguing that its border location left it wide open to illegal trafficking. When ships came up river from Ciudad Bolívar, they unloaded most of their cargo in El Amparo. Araucanos crossed the river to purchase what they wanted. They then smuggled it back, sometimes in canoes, sometimes hidden in water jugs tied to the backs of burros passing openly through the streets. Some people would go out to the ship dressed in rags and return in elegant clothes, and as the jefe político exclaimed with exasperation, "Who can be so brazen (*descarada*) as to undress a man or woman in the street on the pretext that the clothes [he or she] is wearing are contraband?" Another favorite ploy was to purchase something in El Amparo and get a license to bring it back to Arauca City, keeping the license to use for other items.

Eventually, the captain, after spending as much time as he liked in El Amparo, would bring his ship across river to Arauca City and present to officials a manifest attesting that the cargo came from El Amparo and not from Ciudad Bolívar. If officials questioned him about the contents of the crates, he would reply that since he had been selling goods all along the river, he could not swear exactly as to what was in any of them. The jefe político concluded that to stop this chicanery, the authorities would have "to conquer the obstacles of nature and the art and malice of man." Declaring Arauca City as a free port would be far more effective. The government might lose a small amount in revenue, but the town and Casanare would benefit greatly. Ships coming from Venezuela and other nations would pay no national duties. The province could then impose duties on warehousing or peaje. Trade from the interior of New Granada would increase, since merchandise from Bogotá could go directly through El Amparo to Apure, and everyone would benefit.[51]

Governor Francisco Cuellar endorsed the jefe político's request, pointing out that the aduana did not collect enough money to pay the salaries of its employees; that it did not have a state store, a scale to weigh liquor, nor any scale at all, or even a boat so that officials could go out to the ships that pulled into the dock. Despite these arguments, López denied the request, replying that by his calculations the aduana was earning enough profits to more than cover its expenses.[52]

The aduana might have been more prosperous if regular steamships could have operated on the Arauca and Meta rivers, but trade depended on the ships having free access to the Orinoco, a privilege the Venezuelans refused to grant. Even since the breakup of Gran Colombia, Venezuelan and New Granadan diplomats had met regularly to hammer out an agreement for trade and navigation on common rivers and to draw an international boundary, but frequent revolutions in both countries frustrated these efforts. In 1842, they signed in Caracas a treaty of friendship, commerce, and navigation that assured New Granada complete access to the Orinoco, but most of its articles were later voided.

Ten years later, New Granada declared free navigation on all of its rivers, and in 1856 Captains Martin Höhler and Edward G. Steer sailed the first steamboat up the Meta, traveling thirty-three miles above Orocué before running aground at the mouth of the Cravo Sur River. In 1857, Captain Treviranus, director of the Steamship Company of the Orinoco, bettered their effort by sailing the *Barinas* from Ciudad Bolívar, past Orocué, to reach Cabuyaro. Convinced that the route was feasible and profitable, he petitioned President Mariano Ospina for a monopoly on steam navigation on the Meta River, a concession Ospina granted for twenty years. Treviranus's ship *Orinoco* made at least two successful voyages before the project failed for reasons that are not entirely clear.[53] In the 1860s, other entrepreneurs solicited monopolies on the Meta River trade, but the contracts, laws, and decrees tentatively agreed upon foundered on New Granada's inability to work out a viable treaty with Venezuela.[54] As Daniel Valois Arce concludes in *Reseña sobre límites entre Colombia y Venezuela* (Bogotá, 1970), diplomatic negotiations between 1846 and 1880 produced nothing fundamentally constructive and were marked by protests, demands for satisfaction, frustrated attempts to renew boundary talks, and futile efforts to establish normal diplomatic contacts.[55]

The failure of the Liberals after 1849 to halt the erosion of Casanare's population and resources, and their inability to solve its pressing problems, led inevitably to its demotion in political status within the Colombian union. A trend toward larger regional units began in 1855, with the creation of the sovereign state of Panama followed by the sovereign state of Antioquia in 1856. In 1857, the Law of June 17, 1857, consolidated the provinces of Casanare, Tundama, Tunja, and Vélez into the sovereign state of Boyacá. A year later Boyacá joined Panama, Antioquia, Santander, Cauca, Cundinamarca, Bolívar, and Magdalena to form the short-lived Granadan Confederation.[56]

But union with Boyacá, the poorest state in the nation with respect to government revenue and private wealth, was not the answer to Casanare's difficulties. Agricultural production around Tunja focused upon harvesting grains for local consumption, while the manufacturing sector was limited to woolen textiles and *alpargatas* (sisal sandals) also sold in local markets. The federal government controlled two potential sources of income—the salt works at Chita and the Muzo emerald mines—and hazardous roads inhibited the transportation of products to new regions.[57] The *boyacenses* had no surplus capital to invest in Casanare, and in 1868, when they had the opportunity to cede the region to the federal government to be ruled as a national territory, they did so with relief. The Senate commission which considered the transfer noted that Boyacá was giving up Casanare "because it wants that precious jewel under the immediate and powerful support of the nation which is the entity destined to elevate it to the rank that the most beautiful land of Colombia merits." Recommending that Congress accept the territory, the commission warned that in so doing the national government was pledging itself "to destroy the many obstacles that man cannot overcome and to give the world the immense advantages that will spring forth naturally from that privileged land"—a promise that, like so many others made to Casanare, remained unfulfilled.[58]

Colonization in the Llanos of San Martín

As the lifeblood of Casanare seeped away between 1849 and 1863, the Llanos south of the Meta River showed signs of new growth. Spontaneous immigration from Cundinamarca led to the founding of Villavicencio—the city that would become the principal metropolis in the Llanos in the twentieth century. The policies adopted by the Liberals in the 1850s had little direct impact on the canton of San Martín, but the rebellion of 1859–62, which returned Tomás C. Mosquera to power, triggered a second migration of political refugees to Villavicencio—the harbingers of the powerful territorial initiative that would begin at the end of the decade.

In the 1840s, despite three hundred years of continuous Spanish occupation, the canton of San Martín, with its five small towns, was an isolated New Granadan outpost surrounded by tropical wilderness. In 1844, San Martín City had 647 people, Medina had 519, and Jiramena 270, while Cabuyaro and Concepción de Arama were merely collections of huts. The prewar Franciscan missions had disappeared, although groups of Indians occasionally notified the jefe político of their willingness to settle down if he would send them a priest. There were five or six thousand cattle in the canton, with three hundred horses and a few mules and pigs. Trade was mainly with Quetame, Fosca, and Cáqueza, Cundinamarcan towns along the mule path that led to Bogotá—a road virtually impassable during the nine-month rainy season but still better than the only other cordillera trail connecting Medina with Gachetá, Ubalá, and Gachalá.[59]

Yet the lure of open, fertile land could not be denied, and about this time, some adventurous vecinos of Cáqueza and Quetame, weary of living in grinding poverty, decided to seek their fortunes in the Llanos to the east. The first was Esteban Aguirre, who built his house in a place called Gramalote, at the foot of the Cordillera between the Guatiquía and Río Negro rivers. A stopping place for cattle drives between San Martín and Bogotá, Gramalote was also close to the salt mines at Cumaral and Upín. Soon, Aguirre was joined by his wife, Matea Fernández, his son-in-law Libardo Hernández, and fellow *caqueceños* Silvestre Velásquez and Francisco Ardilla. Gramalote's remoteness was also attractive to army deserters, escaped prisoners, and individuals fleeing debts, so that by 1845 there were more than one hundred colonos.[60]

The lawlessness of the new settlement was notorious. In 1845, Bogotá's governor Alfonso Acevedo ordered the jefe político of Cáqueza to go to Gramalote and arrest Vicente Carillo, Jacinto Chaco, and Atanacio Jura, who were seizing baldíos, forcing newcomers to pay illegal taxes, and forbidding them to grow sugar cane and cacao in certain areas. The jefe político was to assure the colonos that baldíos were national property and that they could live on them and cultivate sugar cane and cacao without paying rent. The jefe político was ordered to choose an official site with an abundance of water for the town of Gramalote and design a plan for it that included a plaza, at least eight streets, and locations for the chapel, *casa cural* (priest's residence), school, jail, and *casa municipal* (town hall). Finally, he was to improve the road between Gramalote and Quetame so that it might become the principal route up the cordillera and enabling an alternative trail known as "La Cabuya" to be discontinued.[61]

A year later, Congress declared the canton of San Martín a special territory, to be ruled by a prefect appointed by the president. The

Law of May 10, 1846, which organized the territory, promised sixty *fanegadas* of baldíos to colonos who agreed to cultivate the land, and proclaimed that Indians who accepted "civilized life" were exempted from civil or religious taxes for their lifetimes.[62] Gramalote continued to grow despite the failure of the territorial scheme after four years. Dr. Ignacio Osorio, the cura of San Martín City, consecrated its first church, Nuestra Señora de la Concepción, in 1848, and the town was divided into two *partidos* called Gramalote and Cumaral.[63]

When López abolished all of New Granada's special territories on June 22, 1850, San Martín became once again a canton in Bogotá Province, but it still enjoyed special privileges. The Law of June 22 authorized the national treasury to spend sixty-one thousand reales on its churches and public buildings. It directed the provincial legislature to distribute up to twenty-five thousand fanegadas of baldíos among its parishes and empowered the president to award up to sixty fanegadas to colonos on the condition that they occupy and cultivate the parcels. Finally, the law exempted all the inhabitants of the canton from paying taxes other than those imposed by their parish cabildos.[64]

In September 1850, the provincial legislature elevated the *caserío* of Gramalote to the status of *distrito parroquial*, and in October it approved its new name, Villavicencio—suggested by the local priest, Manuel Santos Martínez, in honor of Independence hero Antonio Villavicencio, who was executed by the Spanish on June 6, 1816.[65] The town now had a population of 349—191 men and 158 women. In 1852, it replaced San Martín City as the capital of the canton, receiving its first jefe político, Nicolas Díaz, and a unit of the national guard. Mail service with Bogotá via Cáqueza was already functioning, and in August the provincial government sent a doctor to vaccinate the inhabitants against a smallpox epidemic that was sweeping through the canton.[66]

Padre Santos Martínez was not the first to say mass in Villavicencio—that distinction belonged to Dr. Osorio—but he performed the first recorded baptism and did much to stabilize the community in its early days. His proposal to populate Jiramena with beggars from Bogotá attracted national attention. In 1851, noting that there were only ten or eleven families remaining of the eighty who had once resided in Jiramena, Santos Martínez offered to expand this number by transporting to the Llanos the poor and sick of the capital and to teach them useful occupations. The legislature endorsed his scheme, and the president, on December 21, 1851, awarded him six hundred fanegadas of land in the district of Villavicencio to support the colony. A sub-scription taken among prominent Bogotanos netted three hundred pesos, including four pesos contributed by President López. Santos Martínez proceeded to round up four hundred destitute people from the Bogotá streets, and, after a two-week journey down the cordillera, settled them in Jiramena. He tried to instruct them in their new life, but the unlikely colonists were quickly dissatisfied. So many deserted that by March 1855 only thirty-six remained. Eventually, Santos Martínez had to abandon the project and devoted his energies instead to founding a hospital in Villavicencio.[67]

Although Villavicencio was the first viable town to appear south of the Meta in the nineteenth century, its existence was precariously dependent on trade with Bogotá, 145 kilometers away, via a rough trail that ascended three thousand meters over the Eastern Cordillera to the capital. Winding up and down mountain slopes as it followed the Río Negro, the road required travelers to ford streams and cross deep *quebradas* (ravines) using flimsy bridges accessible only by mules. For nine months of the year rains and landslides cut off most communication. Repairs on the road fell to the Cundinamarcan towns that depended upon it—Chipaque, Cáqueza, and Quetame.[68] Even when the legislature signed a contract for the construction of a *camino de herradura* (mule path) between Cáqueza and Apiay, as occurred in 1852, the entrepreneur, inhibited by heavy rains and insufficient funds, did little more than make the most obvious repairs.[69]

In 1855, the British firm of Stiebel, Rothschild and Son hired Ramón Guerra Azuola, a Colombian engineer, to survey the Meta River and the road connecting it with Bogotá, in order to ascertain the feasibility of river transport. Joining a party that included nine Englishmen and a French botanist, none of whom spoke Spanish, Guerra Azuola departed from Bogotá on March 10, 1855, reaching Villavicencio five days later and Macuco, on the Meta, on July 14. His wry account of his experiences, in his *Apuntamientos de viajes*, includes a pessimistic report about the development possibilities of the main "highway" to the Llanos.[70]

Guerra Azuola began his narrative by recalling that the group had set off at a gallop from Bogotá on a beautiful morning, and that his companions were in high spirits until they reached the "sad and miserable village" of Yomasa, two leagues south of Bogotá.[71] At the engineer's request, the party stopped to allow him to unpack his instruments and take scientific observations to determine if the trail could be transformed into a cart road, but the Europeans endured the two-hour delay with ill grace. In a more sober mood, they continued along the trail up the mountain rim southeast of the Sabana of Bogotá. They passed through the gloomy Boquerón de Chipaque, at 3,144 meters altitude, and started down the mountain to reach Chipaque at 6:30 P.M. This town, at 2,512 meters, was a regular overnight stopping place for wayfarers from Bogotá, yet it offered neither corral nor inn. There was nothing to eat, and since their pack mules had not yet arrived, the weary travelers had neither bedding nor candles to light the darkness. Ravenously hungry, they spent the night lying on the floor of a hut, surrounded by bundles of yuca and cabbages and tormented by insects. The next day, they followed the Cáqueza River down the mountain to the town of Cáqueza, "where we gave a splendid demonstration of the strength of our mouths and the astonishing capacity of our stomachs." Cáqueza, at 1,600 meters, was "a sad town where there is a jefe político and *juez letrado*, but in all the rest is as miserable, solitary and apathetic as any other Indian town." Already, the sharp, twisting descent of the mule trail from the Boquerón had convinced Guerra Azuola that transforming it into a cart road would be "a colossal project" that would require extending the road bed eight leagues to negotiate the turns.[72]

More encouraging was the next section of the trail from Cáqueza to Quetame, which he described as "one of the best laid out that I have ever seen. Rigid in direction, soft in descent, skillfully taking advantage of the accidents of the terrain—all indicated that the hand which laid it out was expert and knowledgeable." Nevertheless, at Quetame the path was interrupted by a deep quebrada, a gorge cut by the Río Negro. In the dry season travelers climbed down into the quebrada to ford the river, but during the rainy season and without a bridge they were forced to cross it by standing in a basket suspended from a cable and hauled across the chasm. This makeshift arrangement severely restricted commercial use of the trail and was also a sore point for the inhabitants of Quetame, who lived on both sides of the quebrada. Because of the difficulties in crossing the river, those living on the right side demanded that town offices be located on their bank, "so that they could go to Bogotá without wetting their stirrups," while those on the left bank felt the same way. "Today things have reached such a state," wrote Guerra Azuola, "that one side has only to propose some improvement for the other side to oppose it and so they live in eternal war, being themselves the victims of such quarrels. Of course in Quetame there is no school because it can only be built on the river which would be the only neutral site acceptable to both camps. What a pity that a town remains in rusticity (*barbarie*) and tears itself apart for lack of a bridge!"[73]

From Quetame the trail continued in an easterly direction to Villavicencio, but this third section was the worst of all. Careening up and down the mountain, blocked by tree roots and landslides, it passed over dizzy precipices that made work heavy even for mules. Torrents of water poured off the slopes, causing rock and mud slides, and nearly all of the quebradas were unpassable during the rainy season. The bright spot in this difficult journey was the Buenavista outcropping above Villavicencio, where the travelers got their first view of the Llanos, "losing themselves in the horizon like a vast green sea." As Guerra Azuola observed, "On seeing this llanura a man becomes sad to think that he will have to leave it in order to climb once again the high crests of the mountains where cold, fog, and storms reign."[74]

The party made its triumphal entrance into Villavicencio at 4:00 P.M. on March 15, "without further problem than three bruised Englishmen and the loss of two horses that had died on the road." Guerra Azuola's notebook contained pages of calculations, but he was resolved to report to Stiebel, Rothschild, and Sons that transporting goods between the Llanos and Bogotá was technologically unfeasible, a judgment corroborated a year later by Agustín Codazzi.[75] In a report submitted to the national government, Codazzi affirmed that for many more years geographic obstacles would limit commerce between Bogotá and Villavicencio to cattle driven on the hoof up the mountain. The government might profitably spend four or five thousand pesos to improve the road for that purpose, but the building of a full-fledged *camino de rueda* (cart road) was a task that could be better undertaken by future generations.[76]

There was another alternative, however. Assessing the roads of Cundinamarca in 1858, Codazzi suggested that the government might open a new route to the Llanos that would connect the valley of Neiva to San Martín City. The Eastern Cordillera, so towering between Bogotá and Villavicencio, was considerably lower in Neiva Province, where there was a pass through the mountains called Alto del Viento that could be easily crossed at 2,600 meters. There were no *páramos* (high-mountain, treeless plateaus) or rock slides, two causes of suffering for cattle on the Bogotá–Villavicencio trail, and the town of Colombia on the western side of the mountain, at 1,000 meters, had good pastures and would be an excellent resting place for the animals after their trip over the cordillera. The distance between Neiva and San Martín was 350 kilometers, or 150 kilometers shorter than the present route from Neiva to Bogotá, to Villavicencio, to San Martín City; thus, a new road would cut down on the distance that the cattle had to be driven as well as the acclimation problems they currently experienced when crossing the Boquerón de Chipaque.[77] In 1865, the national government commissioned the construction of a road based on Codazzi's recommendations, and the success of Francisco A. Uribe's Compañía de Colombia in using it over the next thirty years proved the logic of the original suggestion.

The Second Wave of Immigration

The spontaneous immigration of colonos from Cáqueza and Quetame in the 1840s had laid the foundation for Villavicencio. In the 1860s there was another wave of immigration, set off by the civil war of 1859–62, which returned Tomás C. Mosquera to power, and by the efforts of merchant families in Bogotá to cash in on the coffee boom by buying lands in the valleys of Cundinamarca and the hot country. Unlike their peasant predecessors, the people who came to Villavicencio in the 1860s had capital to invest and political influence in Bogotá.[78] Their enthusiasm and commitment to their adopted region opened a new era for the Llanos of San Martín.

The Liberal revolt of 1859 broke out in Santander and spread rapidly to Boyacá, Bolívar, Cauca, and Cundinamarca. Although Mosquera proclaimed himself provisional president in 1861, it was not until October 25, 1862, that the last Conservatives surrendered at Yomasa, near Bogotá. The conflict reshuffled the Liberal leadership. Some men like Julian Trujillo, Santos Acosta, and Santos Gutiérrez gained fame and experience for their military exploits, but others lost their lives, the most notable being José María Obando, who was killed after a skirmish near Bogotá on April 29, 1861. After their defeat at El Oratorio on August 16, 1860, virtually the entire Liberal leadership of Santander was captured and imprisoned.[79]

Discouraged by the destruction caused by the fighting in Cundinamarca, many young men decided to seek their fortunes in the Llanos. In 1860, Manuel Fernández arrived in Villavicencio without a real in his pocket. He worked hard, bought two ranches and one thousand cattle, and was able to educate his numerous family in the best colegios of Bogotá. Ricardo Rojas R. arrived equally penniless in 1862 and became one of the leading landowners in the Llanos of San Martín by the end of the century.[80] In 1864, at the age of twenty-eight, Sergio Convers left his store on Bogotá's Calle Real to travel to Villavicencio, where he was enchanted by the beauty and fertility of the land. He had planned to cultivate indigo, but his mother-in-law Araceli Fernández de la Hoz, the wife of Agustín Codazzi, persuaded him to try coffee, a crop she had seen growing in Venezuela. Convers bought land in Apiay in 1865. He cleared the forest from seventy-five hectares to begin his Hacienda El Buque and planted eighty thousand coffee trees. At about the same time, his neighbors Narciso Reyes and Federico Silva were planting seventy thousand coffee trees on their Hacienda Ocoa. Both El Buque and Ocoa had machines to shell and wash the coffee beans, and Ocoa had a drying stove.

Other Bogotanos who settled down near Villavicencio to grow coffee, cacao, or cattle were Santos Gutiérrez, Nicolás and Ciriaco Castro, General Heliodoro Ruíz, Joaquín Piñeres, Celestino Martínez, J. A. Sucre, and José María de Francisco, but the most tireless champion of the region was a Liberal lawyer and journalist from Antioquia, Emiliano Restrepo E.[81] Born in Medellín on September 14, 1832, Restrepo earned a law degree from the Colegio del Rosario in 1853 and was a judge in Antioquia before moving to Bogotá, where he served as secretary of government of Cundinamarca and defended T. C. Mosquera during his trial in 1867.[82] A year later he made his first trip to the Llanos of San Martín, lured by glowing tales of the fertility and natural wealth of the region. Restrepo's three-week trip took him to Villavicencio, the Salina of Upín, and the Sabana of Apiay, where he visited the estates of Nicolás Castro, Narciso Reyes, and Federico Silva. He returned to Bogotá convinced that the Llanos were destined to be "the location of a rich, civilized and populous nation."[83] Restrepo bought several tracts of land around Villavicencio, began the Haciendas La Vanguardia and El Salitre, and later founded a cacao plantation. As a congressman representing Cundinamarca in 1870–1871, he lobbied successfully for improvements on the Bogotá–Villavicencio road. Restrepo was deeply involved in national politics throughout the Federation Era, but he still found time to promote the interests of the Llanos. The publication of his book *Una excursión a los llanos de San Martín* in 1870 anchored within the national psyche, perhaps more than any other event, the conviction that the plains south of the Meta River represented the "future of Colombia."

Meanwhile, in Tolima, Francisco A. Uribe, spurred on by the quinine boom, organized the Compañía de Colombia, in partnership with Nazario Lorenzana and Bernardo Herrera, and began to harvest the cinchona forests on the western slopes of the Eastern Cordillera. Headquartered in the town of Colombia, Tolima, the Compañía's directors began acquiring land on the eastern slopes of the cordillera and in the Llanos of San Martín, where they planned to breed pack mules and cattle for transport and food. Between 1865 and 1870, they built a road connecting Colombia with the town of Uribe in the Llanos of San Martín, following the route suggested by Codazzi. The new road made it possible to bring cattle from the Llanos to Tolima in three or four days. By the end of the century, the Compañía de Colombia had become the largest enterprise south of the Meta, controlling thousands of hectares of forest and grasslands and transforming Uribe into a company town.[84]

In her noteworthy monograph *Frontier Expansion and Peasant Protest in Colombia 1830–1936* (Albuquerque, 1986), Catherine Le-Grand has suggested that Colombia integrated frontier regions into its economy during the nineteenth century in a two-step process. With the exception of Antioquia, the hinterlands were opened first by peasant squatters, who migrated to the wilderness seeking economic opportunity and independence. After a decade or two, profit-seeking entrepreneurs appeared on the scene, extending control over the land itself and the peasants' labor by asserting private ownership to vast areas of public domain.[85] Although this process did not occur in Casanare, which in the last half of the nineteenth century attracted mainly Venezuelan immigrants, the evidence suggests that something of the sort did occur in the Llanos of San Martín. The entrepreneurs who arrived in the 1860s encroached upon the rights and independence of the peasants who had come before, but they also used their influence in Bogotá to stimulate the first concerted national effort to develop the Llanos frontier. The territorial initiative set in motion during the Federation Era foundered in Casanare, but it brought about unprecedented expansion in the Llanos south of the Meta River.

4. The Territorial Initiative, 1863–86

On May 8, 1863, representatives from Antioquia, Bolívar, Boyacá, Cauca, Cundinamarca, Magdalena, Santander, Tolima, and Panama signed the Constitution of Rionegro to create the United States of Colombia. The federation, dominated by the extreme Liberal faction known as the Radicals, survived two coups d'état, the civil war of 1876–77, twelve rebellions, and six years of widespread agitation to fall at last to a victorious Conservative uprising in 1885.[1] While some historians have dismissed this era as a period of hopeless civil warfare that paved the way for Rafael Núñez, Regeneration, and the Constitution of 1886, others have shown that it was also a time of critical transformation. Especially between 1868 and 1874 the economy prospered, bolstered by an unprecedented European demand for tobacco, cinchona, and indigo. State governments stabilized. Federal authorities made conciliatory gestures to the Catholic hierarchy. The Radicals began a national system of obligatory primary lay education, laid a basis for a commercial banking system, and promoted railway construction.[2] In addition, through a system of national territories, they endeavored to develop the two-thirds of the republic's domain that was still wilderness. Chief among the regions targeted for exploitation were the Llanos of San Martín and Casanare, frequently extolled by legislators as "the future of Colombia." Like most other Radical projects, the territorial initiative ultimately failed, but, as this chapter will show, not before it had stimulated significant growth on the Llanos frontier.

A National Territorial System

The Constitution of 1863 carried forward the libertarian, anti-clerical, and federalist reforms instituted after 1849. It prohibited the death penalty, decreed a ten-year maximum of imprisonment, and explicitly sanctioned unrestricted commerce in firearms. It proclaimed absolute separation of church and state, but granted to federal and state governments the right of supreme inspection (*tuición*) of religious cults. The federal government enjoyed exclusive powers over foreign relations, trade, and wars; public credit, control of waterways, the national army, and the adoption of a system of weights and measures. It shared responsibility with the states for fomenting public instruction, postal service, geographical surveys, and civilizing the Indians. The president, known as the executive power, served a two-year term and could not succeed himself. Amendments to the constitution required approval of all nine states—a stipulation that made change virtually impossible.[3]

The Liberal historian Milton Puentes once observed that under the Rionegro Constitution, the unifying concept of a common fatherland was the only limiting factor upon the independence of the "sovereign" states, since Article 16 reserved for the states all matters of government not delegated "expressly, especially and clearly" to the general government.[4] Guaranteed protection from federal interference, each state could study its needs and adopt appropriate solutions. Each was free to compose a constitution, elect a president and assembly, draw up its own law code, and even have its own army.

It is paradoxical that this same constitution that pared down federal government to the barest essentials also awarded it unlimited control over frontier regions. Article 78 declared that those territories "thinly populated or inhabited by tribes of Indians which the State or States to which they belong may cede to the general government for the purpose of promoting colonization or making material improvement shall be governed by a special law." It added that as soon as a territory had a civilized population of 3,000 inhabitants, it could send a commissioner (*comisario*) to the chamber of representatives who would have a voice and a vote in discussions about laws concerning the territory and a voice but no vote in discussions about laws of general interest. When the population reached 20,000, it could elect a deputy (*diputado*) in place of a commissioner with a voice and vote in all discussions. On achieving 100,000 inhabitants, the territory would be eligible for statehood.[5]

Thanks to Article 78, the Federation Era witnessed the emergence of the first national system of territories that reflected the Radicals' admiration for the territorial setup of the United States and stands as the predecessor to the present Colombian *intendencias* and *comisarías*. With their resources sorely overtaxed, the states quickly recognized the advantages of having the federal government take control of unproductive, wilderness regions. Between 1866 and 1872 they turned over six territories to federal rule: San Andrés and Providencia islands (ceded by Bolívar September 28, 1866; accepted by the federal government June 4, 1868); the Llanos of San Martín (ceded by Cundinamarca September 16, 1867; accepted June 4, 1868); Casanare (ceded by Boyacá September 5, 1868; accepted March 29, 1869); Bolívar (ceded by Santander September 30, 1870; accepted November 18, 1870); La Nevada y Motilones (ceded by Magdalena March 24, 1871; accepted August 17, 1871); and Goajira (ceded by Magdalena September 25, 1871; accepted January 24, 1872).[6]

In Law 39 of June 4, 1868, which accepted San Andrés–Providencia and San Martín, Congress outlined the system of territorial rule. In each territory, a prefect appointed by the president for two years was the principal administrative officer, empowered to enforce laws, settle disputes, create towns, civilize Indians, and defend Colombian sovereignty from foreign encroachment. The prefects were to name corregidores to head divisions formerly known as *distritos parroquiales*, but now called *corregimientos*. Municipal councils (*corporaciones*) were to handle town government. Working closely with the corregidores, they could impose direct or indirect taxes to raise money for local needs. The national government pledged to pay the salaries of the prefects, corregidores, priests, missionaries, and schoolteachers. It promised to build a primary school in each corregimiento, to raise a census of the territory, and to maintain mail service and police protection. The law authorized the president to grant up to ten hectares of baldíos to any colonist who would settle in the territory, and it exempted Indians who accepted civilized life from military conscription.[7] President Santos Gutiérrez's Decree of July 6, 1868, executing Law 39, described specifically the duties of the prefects, corregidores, and municipal corporations, and set forth the process for adjudicating baldíos, conducting a census, providing police, and building district jails.[8] The responsibility for overseeing the territories fell to the secretary of the interior and foreign relations (a cabinet post reorganized in 1880 as the secretary of government), who reported to Congress on their progress in his annual *memoria*.

During the administrations of Santos Gutiérrez (1868–69), Eustorgio Salgar (1870–72), Manuel Murillo Toro (1872–74), and Santiago Pérez (1874–76), an enormous amount of official energy and money was invested into the territorial system. These were years of relative peace and economic growth, and the Radicals imbued their initiatives with unbounded optimism. On February 1, 1870, President

Gutiérrez told Congress that the nation had embarked on a new road of regeneration: "Calming political passions are taking a less dangerous direction; public trust has been reestablished; capital is again giving life to industry; men return to work, and an era of peace and prosperity flatteringly presents itself before us." "Attend to the territories with solicitude," he exhorted, "if only because the expenses made on their behalf will be fully returned with considerable wealth, and because being traced through them the line that separates us from other nations, we can stop projects offensive to our sovereignty."[9] In 1873, and again in 1874, Secretary of Interior and Foreign Relations Gil Colunje extolled the redemption of the territories:

The extraordinary fertility of their soil and their frequent communication with the civilized center as well as the perservering action of the government supported throughout by men who are truly interested in the fate of the country, will make those extensive regions, nearly deserts today, come quickly to occupy among the entities that constitute the Colombian Union, the preeminent place to which they are called by the advantageous position and the immense wealth that nature has given them.[10]

From the Islands of San Andrés and Providencia, which were separated from the mainland by 383 kilometers of Caribbean Sea, to Goajira, which was carved out of disputed territory with Venezuela, each of the six territories combined thorny problems with unique potential; but it was the Llanos of San Martín and Casanare that captured the popular imagination. Fully 40 percent of the 455,379.50 pesos appropriated for the territories between 1868 and 1881 was invested in the eastern frontier.[11] Camacho Roldán, secretary of finance and development (*hacienda y fomento*) between 1868 and 1872, had been born in Nunchía, Casanare, and was a tireless proponent of the region he regarded as Colombia's counterpart to the Great Plains of the United States. Several Radicals, including Santos Gutiérrez, bought land near Villavicencio, and a steady stream of travelers published accounts of their adventures in the Territory of San Martín.[12] Congress passed many laws intended to promote the development of the Llanos by building roads, establishing steam navigation on the Meta, encouraging foreign immigration and domestic colonization, civilizing the Indians, making salt more readily available for human and animal consumption, and improving public administration. A review of these efforts shows that while much was attempted, the results were often disappointing.

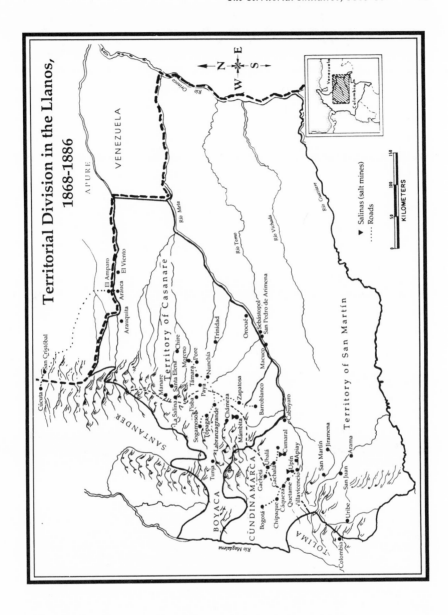

Territorial Division in the Llanos, 1868-1886

Building Roads

Although the Constitution of 1863 limited the responsibility of the national government to "the regulation of interoceanic routes which already exist or may be opened in the territory of the Union," the Radicals interpreted this provision broadly since they were convinced that road construction was a fundamental step in the modernization of the republic. Law 40 of May 28, 1864, "on the development of public works" set forth a master plan for a national transportation system. While most of the fifteen projects enumerated were for cart roads connecting various population centers with the Magdalena, one of them called for "the establishment of steamship navigation on Meta River and a good road between the middle or upper part of that river and the most populated regions of the States of Boyacá and Cundinamarca." [13] Of three possible routes for the so-called Camino del Meta —Bogotá–Villavicencio–Macuto; Gachalá–Medina–Cabuyaro; or Sogamoso–Labranzagrande–Zapatosa—it was the former that received the most support. In December 1868, Santos Gutiérrez personally inspected the route between Bogotá and Villavicencio, becoming the first Colombian president to visit the Territory of San Martín, and Camacho Roldán, as his secretary of finance and development, gave it priority status. "The Llanos Orientales," he wrote in 1870, "have a future for us like the territory west of the Ohio has had for the U.S.A., the pampas for Argentina and the northern tropical region for Australia. . . . The Territory of San Martín lying twenty leagues from the capital of Colombia is the door, and the road to the Meta is the key to that vast region. Our duty is to open them." [14]

In 1869, when construction got under way, engineers divided the 193-kilometer route into three sections: Bogotá to Quetame (50 kilometers), Quetame to Villavicencio (53 kilometers), and Villavicencio to a port on the Meta (90 kilometers); and estimated that the entire project would cost 180,000 pesos. In July, the government appropriated ten thousand pesos to begin work, signed a contract with Nicolás García to widen the Quetame–Villavicencio section, and ordered an iron bridge to be manufactured at a New York City factory to replace the cable and basket that spanned the Río Negro at Quetame. A year later, Camacho Roldán made a careful inspection of the entire route. Dissatisfied with García's progress, he signed a new contract with Juan Nepomueno González Vásquez in December 1870. Congress increased the subsidy to twenty thousand pesos in 1870 and 1871, thanks to the intense lobbying by the deputy from Cundinamarca, Emiliano Restrepo.[15]

González Várgas stayed on the job until 1876, struggling against daunting obstacles. The road that skirted around jagged mountain peaks offered little shelter for the workers at night or sources of food. Torrential rains complicated all efforts, and it was difficult to find peons willing to do such dangerous labor for a thirty-centavo daily wage, half of which had to be spent on food.[16] Their flimsy spades, pickaxes, and drills shattered against the hard-rock surfaces, so that a blacksmith had to be available at all times to make repairs. Perhaps the biggest setback was the arrival of the bridge to span the Río Negro at Quetame. Built in New York City at a cost of three thousand pesos, pieces of the bridge were boxed into seventy-two cartons, shipped by sea to Barranquilla, and then sent up the Magdalena River to Honda. Mules carried the cartons to Bogotá and on to Quetame, but when workers assembled the bridge they discovered that it was too short to cross the chasm. Ever resourceful, González Várgas redesigned the wooden base for an additional cost of six thousand pesos and installed the jerry-rigged structure by the end of 1871.[17] Nicolás Pardo, a Bogotá lawyer who traveled to Villavicencio in November 1874, had high praise for the work of the "intelligent and patriotic engineer González Várgas," but he reported that at every step on the road between Bogotá and Quetame, "one finds a quagmire, a gorge, a precipice or a headlong slope," and that a section beyond Quetame between Servitá and Villavicencio was "nearly impassable."[18]

The outbreak of civil war in 1876 caused the government to default on its contract with González. The engineer continued construction at his own expense until December 1877, when after several months without reimbursement he gave up in disgust and went to Cúcuta to work on the San Buenaventura railroad. In 1880, the government reassessed the situation and determined that González had completed forty-five kilometers at a cost of nearly 70,000 pesos. It settled his claims for 2,499.55 pesos, a sum that included interest on the funds that had been withheld. Secretary of Development Gregorio Obregón reported that an additional 20,000 pesos was needed to repair war-related damage to the Quetame–Villavicencio section. He estimated that 148 kilometers remained to be built and that each new kilometer would cost 2,500 pesos. Thus, the total amount needed to build the road had swollen to 460,000 pesos or nearly two and one-half times the 1869 estimate.[19]

Work on the highway met with some progress and two setbacks during the next five years. In 1882, Emiliano Restrepo rebuilt the eighteen-kilometer segment between Susumuco and Villavicencio at a cost of ten thousand pesos, winning approval from Prefect Vicente Largarcha, who called it "one of the most important improvements in the last fifteen years for the Territory of San Martín."[20] Less fortunate was the effort to extend the road from Villavicencio to a port on the Guatiquía River, a Meta tributary. In 1881, Congress signed a contract and appropriated two thousand pesos for this project, but the road was never built for lack of agreement on the location of the river terminus.[21] In 1883, the iron bridge installed at so much expense in Quetame collapsed into the Río Negro after its wooden base had rotted away. Travelers were again reduced to crossing the river via a basket suspended from a cable or fording it with their cattle at great risk to life and limb.[22] After nearly fifteen years of sporadic construction, the condition of the Bogotá–Villavicencio highway fell far short of Radical expectations, but judging from the accounts of travelers, communication between the two cities had been improved. Ernst Röthlisberger, who made the trip in December 1883, found the road between Bogotá and Quetame quite hazardous, but pronounced the section between Quetame and Villavicencio "exceptionally" well laid out by the government engineers.[23]

Little improvement occurred on the mule trail connecting Gachetá, Ubalá, and Gachalá in Cundinamarca with Medina in San Martín and Cabuyaro on the Meta. In colonial times cattlemen had driven their herds from Apure and Arauca along this route, but by the nineteenth century the barrier posed by the cordillera between Medina and Gachetá discouraged all but the most foolhardy. In 1871, the vecinos of Medina raised 10,640 pesos in a campaign to improve the road, and Congress in 1874 voted 6,000 pesos for the project, although the money was never appropriated. Despite considerable local interest, nothing was accomplished, and the Gachetá–Cabuyaro route remained a highway of the future.[24]

The most successful road to the Territory of San Martín was built by private initiative between Colombia, Tolima, and Uribe. In the early 1860s, Nazario Lorenzana, Francisco A. Uribe, and Bernardo Herrera, founders of the Compañía de Colombia, acquired considerable land on the eastern slopes of the Eastern Cordillera for breeding mules and cattle and for exploiting cinchona forests. In 1865, President Murillo Toro authorized them to build a road from Tolima to the Llanos of San Martín, crossing the mountains at a place called Paso de las Cruces. Construction went quickly, and by 1870 the trail was open, offering easy passage for loaded mules, horsemen, and cattle. Since the trip from Colombia to Uribe took three or four days, the Compañía planted artificial pasture and food crops at intervals of twenty to twenty-five kilometers to serve as overnight rest stops. In May 1870, Secretary Camacho Roldán cited the partners for their achievement, reminding them that they must keep the road in good condition and could not charge tolls for its use.[25] The Colombia–Uribe route remained in service until the early twentieth century, but it continued to be a secondary route to the territory, perhaps due to its remoteness from Bogotá.

No road to the northern Llanos received preferential treatment from the national government. Law 11 of April 27, 1874, "on the promotion of colonization of the Territories of Casanare and San Martín," stated that the government would construct a camino de herradura from Tunja to a place in Casanare that could be reached by steamships traveling the tributaries of the lower Meta River and would award forty thousand hectares of baldíos to the company or individual who would build a road between Santander and Arauca; but no action was taken on either project. The secretaries of finance and development showed scant interest in highways to Casanare, and even though the prefects regularly complained about the isolation of the territory, their demands were not for a new road but for bridges, so that flooded rivers could be crossed during the rainy season.[26] Throughout the Federation Era, the most traveled road to Casanare left from Sogamoso, passing through Tópaga and Mangua, to cross over the San Ignacio peak of the Eastern Cordillera. From there, it descended to the Salina of Gámeza and followed the Labranzagrande River through fog and rain to the town of Labranzagrande. After it crossed the last Andean outcropping, the road divided, with a northern branch heading to Támara and Moreno and a southern branch to Zapatosa and Barroblanco. This road was regularly used by the ranchers of Casanare and Arauca, who in June and November rounded up their cattle to begin the long drive to the markets in Sogamoso. In June 1883, Alfred Hettner, a German geographer, completed the trip from Sogamoso to Labranzagrande in three days and predicted a brilliant future for the Llanos.[27] It is ironic to note that one hundred years later the condition of the road is much the same, and that in the 1990s it still requires twelve to thirteen hours of treacherous driving in a four-wheel drive vehicle to get from Sogamoso to Yopal, modern capital of Casanare.

Steam Navigation on the Meta River

A vision of steamboats sailing down the Meta and Orinoco rivers inspired Congress to support the Camino del Meta, for if Bogotá could be connected with the Meta it would no longer be dependent on the Magdalena River for communication with the outside world. Major deterrents to this goal were the unresolved boundary dispute with Venezuela and Caracas's refusal to allow Colombian ships to navigate the Orinoco. Little headway was made during the presidency of Antonio Guzmán Blanco (1870–1888), but while the diplomats wrangled on, one determined entrepreneur, José Bonnet, launched his steamboats on the Meta.

In 1868, the Colombian minister to Caracas, former president Manuel Murillo Toro and his Venezuelan counterpart, Fernando Arévalo, signed a treaty of navigation, transit, and customs that allowed mutual access to the rivers of both nations and subjected goods carried by Colombian ships on the Orinoco to customs only at the Arauca aduana. Unfortunately, this treaty along with five other agreements drawn up by the two ministers were rejected by their respective congresses. Two years later, Eustorgio Salgar refused to recognize Guzmán Blanco's government and permitted Venezuelan rebels to launch raids from Santander across the border into Táchira; but in 1874 tensions eased enough to permit talks to resume between Anibal Galindo and Julian Viso, representing Colombia and Venezuela respectively.[28] Galindo pressed hard but to no avail, for the acceptance of the principle that whichever state possessed sovereignty over the longest section of a river had the right to navigate it to the sea. In 1875, Gúzman Blanco terminated the negotiations, charging that Colombia was aiding Venezuelan revolutionaries along the border and was using its demand for free navigation as a ploy to extend its sovereignty over a larger portion of the Meta and Orinoco rivers.[29]

With border and navigation issues still to be resolved, Congress went ahead to pass Law 99 of July 10, 1870, authorizing the president to grant a twenty-year monopoly, with a subsidy of four thousand pesos the first year and two thousand pesos the second year, to an individual who would guarantee to sail a steamship from the confluence of the Meta and Orinoco to Cabuyaro every six months for four years. By 1881 there had been two bids for the contract, but neither was deemed acceptable. In 1882, Simon O'Leary offered a third proposal, also still-born, in which he promised to build a railroad between Bogotá and the Meta, in addition to putting steamships on the river.[30]

The morass of Venezuelan politics swamped two other commercial initiatives. In 1871, a Mr. Hancox, president of the Compañía de Vapores del Orinoco, wrote Camacho Roldán that he was planning to send a delegation of one hundred merchants from Trinidad and Ciudad Bolívar to Bogotá to discuss the issue of Meta–Orinoco trade with the secretary. This meeting never took place, for as Hancox was preparing a ship to go to Trinidad to pick up the merchants, Venezuelan rebels commandeered his vessel to transport their troops.[31] In the same year, Sergio Convers decided to explore the possibility of shipping coffee from Hacienda El Buque, near Villavicencio, directly down the Meta. Leaving from Caño Pachaquiaro in May, Convers sailed down the Río Negrito to the Humea, and then along the Meta and Orinoco to reach Ciudad Bolívar in forty-seven days. The governor of Guayana and the directors of the Compañía de Vapores del Orinoco proved receptive, but Guzmán Blanco put an end to the deal as soon as he learned about it. Still, the endeavor was not a total loss. Convers retraced his voyage back to the Territory of San Martín, bringing with him Venezuelan goods which he sold in Orocué, Cabuyaro, and Villavicencio.[32]

With the election of Rafael Núñez in 1880, relations between the two republics took a turn for the better. Renewed negotiations produced an agreement in 1881 to refer the boundary dispute to King Alfonso XII of Spain for arbitration. Both congresses ratified the treaty, and Alfonso XII agreed to accept the charge. His death in 1885 delayed the proceedings, but in 1891 Queen Regent María Cristina issued a decision that formed the basis for further negotiations until 1941.[33]

A beneficiary of the improved international climate was José Bonnet, a Frenchman born in 1847 who came to Colombia in 1865. Bonnet founded his commercial house in Bogotá in 1875. Soon afterward, he opened branch offices in Orocué and Villavicencio and acquired coffee plantations in the Llanos. In 1881, Guzmán Blanco agreed to let him introduce goods into Colombia, via the Orinoco and Meta, without paying duty at Ciudad Bolívar. Bonnet began shipping merchandise into

Orocué and Villavicencio, intending to reship the goods to Cundina-marca and Boyacá. Then, on September 13, 1882, Congress passed Law 61, which prohibited the importing of foreign merchandise from the territories into states that had no aduanas. Hacienda officials inter-preted the law retroactively against the French merchant, and by ex-ecutive order embargoed his goods stored in warehouses in Orocué and Villavicencio.

Bonnet protested vigorously. In a long memorial published in Bogotá in April 1884, he pointed out that for years Colombia had en-deavored to promote trade along the Meta. Bonnet, after considerable effort, had gained Venezuelan cooperation. He had purchased steam-ships, built warehouses, created ports on the Meta, and opened up roads to the interior, only to have his merchandise impounded. The longer the goods remained in the warehouses, the greater their vul-nerability to fire or theft by government officials; and he could not ship them back to Venezuela without incurring a substantial fine. Bonnet complained, "I have been arbitrarily persecuted [first] by the govern-ment, and afterwards by some ill-meaning people who do not want to see the immense advantages that will soon come to the country with the navigation of one of its most important rivers."[34] Salvador Cama-cho Roldán and other influential Radicals came to Bonnet's defense, and at length the government released his merchandise. In August 1884, the president gave him a new contract that guaranteed his right to bring goods into the states via the territories without paying duty.[35] From 1893 to 1896 Bonnet became the first to offer regular steamship service on the Meta, a feat that garnered him congratulations from the Colombian government, the Order del Busto del Libertador from Venezuela, and a nomination for the title of Chevalier de la Légion d'Honneur from France.[36]

Immigration

"In America to govern is to populate." Juan Bautista Alberdí's famus dictum revealed his awareness in 1852 of the impact of immi-grants in the western expansion of the United States and his anticipa-tion that a surge of Europeans would transform Argentina in the last half of the nineteenth century. Colombian Radicals accepted the va-lidity of Alberdí's formula. Their designation of wilderness areas as special territories had been done in the expectation that they would

The Actual Colombian-Venezuelan Border and the Demarcation Lines of 1834 and 1891

Caribbean Sea

Gulf of Venezuela

Maracaibo

Lake Maracaibo

R. Oro

R. Zulia

Venezuela

R. Tibú

Cúcuta

San Cristóbal

R. Apure

R. Uribante

R. Arauca

R. Otrá

R. Sarare

El Amparo

R. Capanaparo

Arauca

R. Sinaruco

R. Meta

Puerto Carreño

Colombia

R. Tomo

1834

R. Vichada

R. Orinoco

LEGEND

—— Present border

– – – 1891 demarcartion line

•••••• 1834 demarcartion line

R. Guaviare

San Fernando de Atabapo

R. Inírida

R. Atabapo

R. Orinoco

KMS. 0   50   100   150   200

R. Guainía

R. Negro

Adapted from: Daniel Valois Arce,
Reseña histórica sobre los límites de Colombia y Venezuela.
Medellín, 1970.

Brazil

be colonized by foreigners. Since many Bogotanos held an unrealistic conception of the Llanos as a healthy, incredibly fertile, and empty land, they believed that it was just a matter of time before Europeans would accept government inducements and settle there in large numbers.

This conviction went against the grain of past experience. Since Independence, the government had promoted European immigration. Braving the wrath of the church, Congress had promised prospective immigrants freedom of religion, naturalization after two years' residency, land on easy terms, and exemptions from taxes and military service. Despite these incentives, few arrived, for Europeans were leery of the fanatical Roman Catholicism of Colombia and alienated by its unstable political climate. In 1851, excluding Panama, there were less than 450 Europeans and North Americans in the republic, accounting for 0.02 percent of the population of 2,243,730.[37]

Radical optimism remained high. Seeking to capitalize on political unrest in Europe, Cuba, and the southern United States, Secretary Camacho Roldán launched in 1870 a many-faceted campaign to attract foreigners to Colombia and especially to the Llanos. On October 27, he wrote to Carlos O'Leary, British vice consul in Bogotá and agent for foreign creditors, that the government was willing to award baldíos to its creditors to pay off its debts. Particularly fine lands suitable for colonization were located in the Territory of San Martín, which was now organized in a fashion similar to the territories of the United States. Camacho Roldán continued:

In a word, this is a territory that promises much for the future and where the Executive Power believes that foreign creditors might ask with great advantage for the adjudication of their titles to public lands, or at least part of them, in order to send European immigration, to found colonies, to build roads and to sell within a few years titles that today are worth 20 or 30 centavos a hectare for two or three pesos.[38]

On December 1, he wrote to Jonathan H. Waters, a North American entrepreneur, that the president would grant, gratis, up to 2,680 hectares of baldíos (19,200 acres) in San Martín and up to 12,000 hectares (29,652 acres) in Casanare, on the condition that a colony of one thousand immigrants be established on the land. The government would pay the salaries of a schoolteacher, a missionary (either Catholic or Protestant), a doctor, and a judge or mayor elected by the colonists. It would pay for the expense of measuring and registering the land titles, and in Casanare it would pay for forty or fifty soldiers to restrain the Indians, a measure unnecessary in San Martín. Camacho Roldán assured Waters that the land, now worth very little, would appreciate with the arrival of immigrants and that Colombian migrants from the densely populated states of Boyacá and Cundinamarca would follow in the steps of the foreigners. He sent copies of this note to Colombian consuls in New York, Liverpool, London, Havre, Grimsby, Bremen, Hamburg, San Nazario, Florence, Amsterdam, Antwerp, Bordeaux, and Paris, and placed advertisements describing immigration opportunities in North American, English, German, Dutch, French, and Italian newspapers.[39]

In 1871, Congress appropriated twenty thousand pesos to promote immigration and passed, on June 9, Law 80 "on the protection of foreign immigrants." Law 80 instructed Colombian consuls to collect information about the best ways to attract potential immigrants from the countries where they were stationed. It charged all national and state employees to protect foreign immigrants and treat them on every occasion with courtesy and good will. Finally, it set up a "Junta de Inmigración" in each state. The juntas were to collect data from local businessmen about jobs and wages and assist newcomers by providing information about available employment, low interest loans, and health care.[40]

Despite these measures, with the exception of a number of Cubans (probably Spanish born) fleeing the Ten Years War (1868–1878), few Europeans came to Colombia. Already by 1874, Secretary of Finance and Development Aquileo Parra was rejecting the policy adopted by his predecessor. In his memoria, he wrote that Colombia had offered fertile lands, exemption from military service, ease of naturalization, and free institutions, but other countries provided much more. For Europeans accustomed to temperate climates, work in the hot lands along the coasts and rivers was nearly unsupportable. Colombia's cool highlands were already densely populated, and poor as the Europeans were, they were used to more comforts than the *campesinos* (peasants) enjoyed. They required better food, dress, and housing. As a result, they went to the United States or to Argentina, where they found agreeable climates and better-paid employment. Parra held out some hope for planned agricultural colonies, but he recommended that the government move slowly even on this option, since such colonies were difficult and costly to organize and only in Argentina had they met with some success.[41]

Still, dreams of attracting foreigners to the Llanos persisted. On September 14, 1881, in Chocontá, Cundinamarca, José Francisco Bayón, a well-known botanist, gave a speech addressed to President Rafael Núñez, urging him to people the plains with immigrants from the Canary Islands and Mozambique. Bayón argued that while the tropical climate made the plains unattractive to Europeans, they were certainly suited to immigrants from places of similar latitudes, especially since proper care could prevent fevers and excessive mortality. Among the equatorial countries, Australia and New Guinea had scant populations, but there was an abundance of people living in the Canary Islands and hard-working blacks in Mozambique, who could be transported up the Orinoco and Meta and resettled in San Martín and Casanare.[42] There is no record of Núñez's response to Bayón's novel suggestion, but by this time interest in the territories was fading, and the government was reluctant to finance any immigration scheme.

Foreigners did come to the Llanos—not the Europeans envisioned by Camacho Roldán, but Venezuelans who, as Codazzi predicted, were already acclimated to the heat and tropical diseases.[43] Contemporary accounts suggest that many people crossed over the border to escape the civil wars besetting Venezuela. In the 1830s, for example, Venezuelans from San Lorenzo, Apure, began a settlement at Arauquita. They worked hard and soon transformed the forests along the Arauca River into fields of plátano, corn, coffee, cacao, yuca, rice, and sugar cane. After the Federalist Wars ended in 1863, they were joined by David Mantilla, Tobias Valdivia, and General Policarpo Peraza—all from Barinas and on the losing side of the conflict.[44]

Orocué was founded sometime in the 1850s, also by Venezuelans. By 1860; the town consisted of the families of Juan Carvajal and Juan Sanabría, an elderly married couple who took care of the priest's house; the Díaz brothers from Sogamoso, who owned a warehouse; and an unspecified number of Sáliva Indians. As more Venezuelans arrived during the next decade, Orocué became Colombia's chief port on the lower Meta.[45]

In 1872, the prefect of Casanare, D. Acosta R., reported that a revolt against Gúzman Blanco had triggered a new wave of immigrants, to whom he granted asylum so long as they remained the prescribed distance away from the border. Six years later, Joaquín Díaz Escobar, who travelled extensively throughout the territory, observed that most of the inhabitants were Venezuelan or sons of Venezuelans coming from Apure or Guayana. The apureños, he added, were "verdaderamente Llaneros" (true Llaneros), while the *guayanos* were merchants, sailors, and educated people. The rest of the population were *casanareños* and *sanmartineros*, "also true Llaneros," or immigrants from Boyacá and Santander, "apócrifos Llaneros" (spurious Llaneros), who led a precarious existence.[46]

Venezuelans continued to pour into Arauca City and the surrounding plains. Ernesto Camejo, in *Breves apuntaciones sobre Arauca* (Bogotá, 1940), observes that in 1863 María Josefa Cisneros, the owner of the wealthiest hato near the town, began to sell off sections of her land to Venezuelan émigres, and her son, Pedro María Cisneros, married a woman from Barcelona who came to Arauca in 1868 with Patricio Harrigton [sic], a Danish national, and his Venezuelan wife. Camejo also cites an anonymous traveler who estimated Arauca City's population in 1890 at four thousand inhabitants "of which some ten are Europeans, one third are Colombians and the rest are Venezuelans."[47] This conclusion was confirmed by the Recoleto priest Daniel Delgado, who wrote that it was notorious that nearly all the hatos and *fundaciónes* between the Arauca and Pauto rivers were owned by Venezuelans who had taken refuge in Colombia during the time of civil wars in their country.[48]

If Venezuelans numerically and culturally dominated Arauca and, to a lesser extent, Casanare, they found a less than warm welcome in the Territory of San Martín. Prefect Rafael Vanegas wrote that in 1874 many Venezuelans had come up the Guaviare River to the port of Bolívar, a half-day's journey from San Martín City. They were artisans, merchants, and ranchers, who had planned to settle in the municipio which was the wealthiest in the territory in terms of cattle and hatos. By 1875, however, many were leaving, having encountered little food and outright hostility from the natives. Vanegas explained that the sanmartineros regarded the arrival of any foreigner to their town as a true calamity, since such a person "threatens their traditional semi-savage independence and lackadaisical ranching methods." Any challenge to their routine was a "tyranny" to which they could not conform.[49]

Racism was undoubtedly a factor in the Colombian behavior. Alfred Hettner, who visited Emiliano Restrepo's Hacienda Los Pavitos near Villavicencio in 1882, was deeply impressed by Restrepo's black Venezuelan mayordomo, whom he described as the "prototype of the Llanero" with his great stature, his physical energy, his scorn for book learning, his frivolous inclinations, and his love of pleasure. Decipher-

ing the mayordomo's "patois dialect," Hettner learned that he had
traveled all over the Llanos. The German observed:

Notable, in general, is the penetration of the Venezuelans in the Llanos, Negros
and Zambos for the most part, in contrast to the natives of the Colombian Llanos
who are essentially Indians and cholos, or mixtures of Indian and white. It appears
that this difference in the composition of the populations originated in the different types of cultural development, since there [Venezuela] large haciendas were
founded already in colonial times when slavery still existed, while here [Colom-
bia] settlement only seriously began in the present century.[50]

Colonization

Camacho Roldán hoped for European immigrants, but he was
realistic enough to realize that "colonization" of the territories meant
peopling them with Colombians. In 1869, he wrote that the nation
stood on the brink of a new age in its history, when landless peasants
from the densely populated Eastern Cordillera would stream down
into the empty eastern half of the country, lured by cheap and fertile
land.[51] To encourage such activity, the government pledged to improve the roads, build schools and churches, and provide good local
government in the territories; but above all, it sought to attract colonos
through grants of free land. How many actually came between 1863
and 1886 is difficult to ascertain, but it is likely that few highlanders,
fearing the fevers and the Indians, went to Casanare. The census of
the territory in 1870 showed a population of 26,066, a 40 percent increase over the 18,489 recorded in 1843; but Anibal Galindo, who analyzed these figures in 1876, found several glaring discrepancies and
concluded that the population might really be as low as 10,753, a
42 percent decline.[52] The accuracy of the lower figure was reinforced
by General Rafael Ortiz, who after surveying Casanare in 1888 by order of the secretary of war, estimated the Christian population at no
more than 13,000.[53] It was a different story in the Territory of San
Martín. The population there in 1870 was 4,056, up from 1,877 recorded in 1843; and officials reported campesinos migrating from Cáqueza, Cundinamarca, to Villavicencio; from the Valley of Gachalá in
Cundinamarca to Medina; and from Tolima to Uribe, via the road built
by the Compañía de Colombia. However many did arrive, they were
nearly all frustrated in their efforts to secure title to their land, in spite

of attempts by Congress to legislate a mechanism to help them legitimize their claims.

Before 1868 Llaneros had rarely bothered to obtain legal title to their land. Following the pattern predominant throughout New Granada, those who came to the plains in the aftermath of the War of Independence had been peasant farmers seeking economic opportunity. They built houses and planted small garden plots without attempting to register their claims. Likewise, the *ganaderos* (ranchers), surrounded as they were by seemingly endless plains, reckoned their wealth by the size of their herds. Making no improvements to the pasture, they moved their cattle to new lands at will and worried little about property rights. The government, for its part, used the public domain as a fiscal resource to support a bankrupt treasury. Congress issued territorial certificates redeemable in public bonds to finance the public debt and to pay military veterans and road contractors. "Freely bought and sold on the open market, these certificates were relatively inexpensive for men of means, though clearly beyond the reach of the peasants."[54] Even when the government tried to encourage family ownership—as was the case in 1843, when the president authorized the concession of one hundred fanegadas of baldíos to each family who would reside in one of the regions that the government planned to designate as a special territory—the wording of the law made it difficult for peasants to pay the costs of acquiring land, and most baldíos continued to go to landowning elites.[55]

These same contradictory tendencies characterized the land policies adopted for the territories after 1863. The Radicals wanted to create a nation of small farmers and to encourage at the same time the expansion of export agriculture, but the laws they passed posed problems for peasants and entrepreneurs. Article 24 of Law 39 of June 4, 1868, empowered the president to concede ten hectares of baldíos to each family who settled in the territory. Santos Gutiérrez's Decree of July 6, 1868, stated that the family head was to send a *memorial* to the prefect describing the land he/she wished to claim, supported by the sworn testimony of three witnesses that the land in question was baldío. If the petition was in order, the prefect granted provisional ownership and informed the president, who made the final resolution, after which the land was to be surveyed at the cost of the petitioner and duly notarized.[56]

While these requirements may seem simple, they posed insurmountable obstacles to the peasants who, being poor and illiterate, could not pay for the preparation of the memorial, let alone the costs of measuring the land. Those who managed to find the funds were so discouraged by the paperwork and bureaucratic delays that they withdrew from the proceedings.[57] To alleviate this difficulty, Congress passed Law 61 of June 24, 1874, stating that every individual who occupied uncultivated territory belonging to the nation and established on it a house and field acquired ownership to the land he/she cultivated, whatever its extension. A second article declared that if the colono placed cattle on baldíos or cultivated fields, he/she would receive for free, in addition to the property covered in the first article, a portion of the adjacent land.[58]

Law 61 cut the costs of landownership and put forward the principle that whoever put public lands to use by sowing crops or improving pastures was thereby qualified to receive that land for free, plus an adjacent undeveloped tract equal in size. In the Llanos, however, instead of protecting the rights of the farmers, this stipulation seems to have benefited the large cattle ranchers. Prefect Domingo Medina Martínez wrote, in 1880, that because of Law 61 ranchers encroaching on baldíos in Casanare believed that they were guaranteed all of the property they needed to pasture their cattle. Thus, an individual with two hundred head of cattle, would put up a rude house, seed enough plátano and sugar cane to feed three or four peons, build a corral, and consider himself the owner of as much land as might coincide with his fantastic imagination. This same individual would then impose certain obligations on the cultivators, who had the misfortune to remain within the perimeter of the land he had appropriated. If they refused to do what he asked, he forced them to move. As a result, whole towns that had started to form were destroyed by the ranchers, who looked with notable prejudice on those whom the law was supposed to favor. Medina Martínez urged the government to determine with precision who had the right to control the land, and to decide if it was "to be the cultivators, that is, the farmers (*labradores*), or the occupiers, that is, the ranchers (*creadores*)."[59]

In 1882, Congress passed Law 48 to reinforce the rights of the farmers. This law stated that "cultivators squatting on public land with shelter and crops will be considered possessors in good faith and shall not be deprived of possession except by sentences handed down in civil court." Colonos with annual crops were to receive the cultivated parcel and thirty additional hectares, while those who built fences could keep all the territory enclosed so long as it included no more than three times the area actually exploited. To qualify for a free grant, a cultivator had to have been working and living on the land for a minimum of five years.[60] Despite its good intentions, the law did not stop land usurpation in the Llanos, and in the view of Casanare's prefect, Trinidad Moreno, it was even counterproductive. He pointed out that in the open plains there was no water to use for irrigation or material for building fences. The grass was so hardy that only fire could destroy it. Moreno believed that many individuals who had resolved to come to Casanare and "challenge the elements, facing perhaps a premature death due to the climate and other hidden dangers," had given up because of lack of capital to overcome the obstacles set up by Law 48 for claiming land.[61]

The educated, wealthy entrepreneur had two additional ways to acquire land in the Llanos. The first was to use titles of concessions of baldíos given by the republic as military compensation. These titles were bought and sold on the open market and regularly quoted at thirty to forty centavos per hectare. The second method was to use "bonos territoriales" awarded to foreign creditors by Article 5 of the "Convenio" of November 22, 1860. In that year, bonos territoriales had been issued to equal 1,718,351 hectares. Part of these bonos were amortized in different regions of the country, but by 1868 there were still more than a million and a half hectares in circulation that were quoted between twelve and fourteen pennies per hectare in the London, Paris, and Amsterdam markets.

The procedure for claiming land was similar under both methods. Petitioners had to report the boundaries of the parcel desired, with the testimony of five witnesses who would swear before a national judge that the land was baldío. The petition with supporting evidence was submitted to the prefect, along with the bonos territoriales, or titles of concessions of baldíos to be used. The prefect appointed a surveyor to measure the land at the petitioner's cost. Then, he granted provisional approval and sent the file forward to the secretary of finance and development, who made the final decision on behalf of the president. Emiliano Restrepo, who explained these guidelines in 1870 in articles published in the Bogotá newspapers, *El Liberal* and *El Bien Público*, estimated that by observing these stipulations one could buy 2,500 hectares of land, sufficient for a large hacienda, for 1,125 pesos. Sold at public auction, the same parcel would cost less, but the title would not be clear.[62]

Although it was easier for the entrepreneur than for the colono to obtain land, there were still complications that tended to discourage large investors from moving out to the Llanos. Restrepo, for example, was critical of the decision embodied in the Código Fiscal of 1873, which stated that public land could not be sold for less than fifty centavos per hectare. The law's intent was to bring more money into the treasury, but its effect was to make it impossible to purchase baldíos through public auction. In addition, Law 61 of 1874 raised the price of land by requiring owners of cattle to fence in their herds in order to establish ownership, a costly procedure in the Llanos. Restrepo urged that both these measures be repealed because if settlers were to be attracted to the territory, land must be made available to them as cheaply as possible.[63]

In the fertile Sabana de Apiay, a legal battle of awesome proportions faced potential new investors. The Sabana de Apiay consisted of seventy-five thousand hectares of farmland and pasture, forming a large triangle bounded by the northern branch of the Río Negro, the Guatiquía, and the Eastern Cordillera. In the eighteenth century, the Jesuits had claimed much of this region for their Hacienda Apiay. After their expulsion, the vast estate was resold a number of times and was eventually purchased by Jacinta Rey. On Rey's death in 1792, her six children divided up the land. Soon, some sold their titles to others, so that by 1860 the number of people claiming to own shares in the so-called Community of Apiay had grown to three or four hundred, none of whom had clear title and all of whom were engaged in endless and protracted litigation. Apiay's fertility and its proximity to Villavicencio captured the interest of entrepreneurs who bought into the community or merely staked out their own claims. By 1868 there were seven substantial cattle ranches and two coffee haciendas—Ocoa and El Buque—on the savanna. In 1870, Restrepo warned that the claims of the *comuneros* were a stumbling block to the future development of Apiay, and he urged the national government to suppress the "community" and assign individual titles to the members with a clear delineation of each property. "These operations," he wrote, "already difficult today, will be much more difficult within a few years," for when large agricultural estates have been created, "the spirit of chicanery (*tinterillaje*), which is the ruin of incipient towns, will abound."[64]

A final problem for would-be investors was that much of the land officially designated as baldío in San Martín and Casanare was occupied by ganaderos who had no intention of applying for legal ownership. From time immemorial the ganaderos had calculated their wealth by the size of their herds rather than by hectares of land. Moving their cattle freely from one pasture to another, they saw no advantage in gaining title to the land or in improving it. In an age when forward-looking ranchers on the Caribbean coast and in the highlands were breeding selectively, putting up barbed wire, and sowing improved pasture, the Llaneros resisted such new-fangled notions. Restrepo wrote that if one explained to them the advantages of land improvement that would cost fifteen hundred or two thousand pesos, they replied that it would be a bad investment, since with the same amount of money they could purchase eighty to one hundred additional cattle, whose food cost them nothing. Restrepo believed that until such attitudes could be changed the Llaneros would "continue to have the character, type and conveniences of being a nomadic people differing in no respect from the Arabs, or the cattlemen of Manchuria, Mongolia or China."[65]

Table 3 lists all of the public-land grants officially awarded in Casanare between 1860 and 1889. The records published by the Ministerio de Industrias in 1931 show just ten grants, for a total of 42,272 hectares. Half the land awarded was in the municipio of Tame. With his two grants totaling 14,892.6 hectares, José Santos received the most land. The average award ranged between 2,300 and 5,000 hectares. Ignacio Vargas G. in 1860 got the smallest grant of 638.1 hectares. The scant number of awards over a thirty-year period is striking and bears out the assertions made by Rafael Ortiz, in 1888, that most of the "owners" in Casanare lacked title and that the territory was divided into large landholdings which were not well marked or legally constituted. He wrote, "Real estate is transmitted from father to son without deed or legal formulas, and if one wanted to rectify this point, it would occasion lawsuits and even armed struggles."[66]

The records for the Territory of San Martín are more extensive. Table 4 shows that between 1860 and 1885 fifty grants, totaling 324,405.9 hectares, were awarded to thirty-six individuals. The Compañía de Colombia received the most land, with 58,586.8 hectares, followed by Aparicio Escobar and associates, with 49,496.8, and Emiliano Restrepo, with 23,607.6. On the other end of the scale, there were six grants of less than 500 hectares, but two of these went to Restrepo and one to Indalecio Castilla, who had other much larger grants. Only three individuals could be said to be small landholders: Eduardo Monroy, with 307.8 hectares in Medina; Sebastián Lemos, with 46 hectares; and Félix Arciniegas, with 64 hectares in San Martín.

Table 3
Public Land Grants in Casanare, 1860–1889

Grantee	Municipio	Year	Hectares
Rufino Pineda	Tame	1860	2,301.3
Ignacio Vargas G.	Chire	1860	638.1
Antonio José Benítez	Chire	1864	2,304
Luis Guevara	Tame	1867	2,304
José Santos	Tame	1879	6,985.6
José Santos	Tame	1879	7,907
Juan B. Melgarejo	Orocué	1887	4,977
Juan B. Reyes	Orocué	1887	4,943
Alejandro B. Ruiz	Santa Elena	1889	4,981
Ricardo M. Ruiz	Santa Elena	1889	4,931
Total			42,272

Total Hectares by Municipios

Municipio	Total Grants	Total Hectares
Chire	2	2,942.1
Orocué	2	9,920
Santa Elena	2	9,912
Tame	4	19,497.9
	10	42,272

Grantees with Largest Holdings

Grantee	Total Grants	Total Hectares
José Santos	2	14,892.6
Alejandro B. Ruiz	1	4,981.8
Juan B. Melgarejo	1	23,607.6

Distribution of Grants by Size

Total Grants	Hectares
0	From 1 to 499
1	From 500 to 999
7	From 1,000 to 5,999
2	From 6,000 to 9,999
0	From 10,000 to 20,000
0	From 20,000 to 50,000

Source: "List of Public Land Grants, 1828–1931," *Memoria del Ministro de Industrias*, 1931, vol. 5, 321, 335.

Table 4
Public Land Grants in the Territory of San Martín, 1860–1885

Grantee	Municipio	Year	Hectares
Enrique Urdaneta	Medina	1866	737.3
Pedro Fortoul	Medina	1868	586.7
Nazario Lorenzana, et al.*	San Martín	1869	40,000
Nazario Lorenzana, et al.*	San Martín	1869	8,586.8
Eduardo Monroy	Medina	1870	307.7
Mariano Tanco	Bolívar	1870	5,181.2
José María Sarabia Ferro	Raicilla	1871	12,915.3
Emiliano Restrepo	?	1871	4,235.8
Antonio Pardo R.	?	1871	2,237.5
José María García	?	1871	10,000
José María Sarabia Ferro	?	1872	4,559.8
Celestino Castro y otro	Medina	1872	8,830
Francisco Piedrahita	Medina	1872	2,346
Pedro Restrepo U	?	1872	9,999.7
Mariano Tanco y otro	Medina	1873	4,755.4
Emiliano Restrepo	Villavicencio	1873	1,873.7
Eduardo Jaramillo R.	Villavicencio	1873	1,836.5
José Alonso	Medina and Cabuyaro	1873	11,102.5
Emiliano Restrepo	Villavicencio	1873	2,970.7
Francisco A. Uribe*	San Martín	1873	10,000
Aparicio Escobar, et al.	Medina and Villavo	1873	49,496.8
Carlos Bonito y otro	San Martín	1873	19,987
Bernardo Herrera	San Martín	1873	10,000
Lucio A. Restrepo	San Martín	1873	9,999.7
Emiliano Restrepo	Villavicencio	1873	6,091.8
Leonardo Cubillos	San Martín	1874	5,851.4
Leonardo Cubillos	San Martín	1874	2,032.8
Marcelino Gutiérrez	San Martín	1874	5,999.4
Emiliano Restrepo	Villavicencio	1874	998.7
Emiliano Restrepo	San Martín	1874	9,999.8
Marcelino Gutiérrez	San Martín	1874	8,227.8
José A. Mejía	San Martín	1874	9,999.4
Marcelino Gutiérez	Mesa de Fernando	1876	6,000
Luciano Perdomo	San Martín	1876	1,647.9
Indalecio Castilla	San Martín	1877	5,485.6
Emiliano Restrepo	Villavicencio	1878	362.5
Emiliano Restrepo	Villavicencio	1878	166.8
Primitivo Castro y otro	San Martín	1878	3,937
Emiliano Restrepo	Villavicencio	1878	1,143.6
Eugenio Martínez	San Martín	1878	2,330.8
Telmo Garzón	San Martín	1878	966.7

Table 4
Continued

Grantee	Municipio	Year	Hectares
Sebastián Lemos	San Martín	1878	46
Félix Arciniegas y otro	San Martín	1878	64
Juan de J. Bravo	San Martín	1878	2,613.2
Anastasio López	San Martín	1878	9,973.1
Casimiro Enciso	San Martín	1878	3,288.7
Felipe Rey	San Martín	1878	2,029.7
Indalecio Castilla	San Martín	1878	484.5
Leonardo Cubillos	San Martín	1878	1,549.1
Atanasio Rey	San Martín	1878	569.5
Total			324,405.9

Total Hectares by Municipios

Municipio	Total Grants	Total Hectares
Bolívar	1	5,181.2
Medina	6	17,563.1
San Juan de Arama	1	6,000
San Martín	26	175,669.9
Villavicencio	8	15,444.3
Unclassified		
Medina and Villavicencio	1	49,496
Medina and Cabuyaro	1	11,102.5
Raicilla	1	12,915.3
No municipio listed	5	31,032.8
Total	50	324,405.9

Grantees with Largest Holdings

Grantee	Total Grants	Total Hectares
Compañía de Colombia	3	58,586.8
Aparicio Escobar, et al.	1	49,496.8
Emiliano Restrepo	9	23,607.6
Marcelino Gutiérrez	3	20,227.2
José María Sarabia Ferro	2	17,475.1
Leonardo Cubillos	3	9,433.3
Indalecio Castilla	2	5,970.1

Table 4
Continued

Distribution of Grants by Size	
Total Grants	Hectares
6	From 1 to 499
5	From 500 to 999
17	From 1,000 to 5,999
15	From 6,000 to 9,999
5	From 10,000 to 20,000
2	From 20,000 to 50,000

*Compañía de Colombia associates.
Source: "List of Public Land Grants, 1828–1931," *Memoria del Ministro de Industrias*, 1931, vol. 5, 326–27.

Fifty-four percent of the land awarded was in the municipio of San Martín, reflecting the huge grants made to the Compañía de Colombia and Aparicio Escobar for the exploitation of forest products. It is clear that while hundreds of campesinos moved into the territory at this time, virtually none achieved their ultimate goal of becoming a property owner with a legally registered title.[67]

Civilization of the Indians

A top priority in devising the territorial system was to transform the Indians, estimated at twenty-one thousand in San Martín and fifty thousand in Casanare, into Colombian citizens. While some sedentary tribes, such as the Achaguas and Piapocos, were relatively open to assimilation into white society, the resistance of the nomadic Guahibos had grown steadily throughout the nineteenth century. Officials and citizens of Casanare pleaded with the government to send soldiers and missionaries to protect them from Guahibo attacks. To meet these needs, Congress passed four laws between 1868 and 1874, none of which became operative.

Law 40 of June 5, 1868, on "the civilization of the Indians," was adopted one day after the Territory of San Martín had been created. It stated that uncivilized Indians would be protected and treated as "Colombians worthy of the government's special care and attention."

It authorized the president to award to every Indian family who agreed to settle down twenty-five hectares of land, a house, clothes, animals, and tools paid for by the national treasury. The law empowered the president to send Christian missionaries to reduce the Indians. Tribes that resisted peaceful overtures and attacked towns were to be subdued and relocated at a designated site, where they could be instructed in Christianity, agriculture, and civilized life. Finally, Law 40 stated that garrisons (*guarniciones*) should be established at strategic points in the territories to safeguard commerce and mails.[68]

Since Congress neglected to appropriate funds, Law 40 remained a dead letter. On June 4, 1870, the legislators replaced it with Law 45, "on the reduction of savage Indians," which applied to natives throughout the country, but was aimed especially at the Guajiros on the Guajiro Peninsula. Law 45 ordered the president to sign contracts with whites who would agree to colonize a wilderness region and make it into a missionary center to reach out to the Indians. Each family in the colony was to receive ten hectares of baldíos, seeds, tools, and other necessities at the expense of the national government. As in Law 40, the president was to send missionaries to convert the Indians and maintain garrisons of soldiers to keep the peace. Law 45 provided a special annual subsidy of twenty-five thousand pesos to fund these activities, but again the money was never voted.[69]

The year 1874 brought two measures dealing with Indians. Law 11 of April 27, on the "development of colonization of the Territories of Casanare and San Martín," instructed the president to open contacts with unreduced Indians in the Llanos and learn as much as possible about their cultures. He was to set up commercial relations with them by promulgating treaties that would recognize their right to the territory they had traditionally occupied. In the case of the recalcitrant tribes who infested the northern bank of the Guaviare River, the president was to arrange for their submission, purchase their land, and relocate them farther south. Along with employing missionaries, he was to appoint two civil deputies (comisarios) in each territory, who would be responsible for improving Indian relations. Law 11 banned the sale of liquor to Indians not under white rule and augmented the garrisons with an armed flotilla that was to patrol the Casanare River.[70]

Law 66 of July 1, 1874, "on the reduction and civilization of the Indians," applied the concept of deputies and missionaries working in tandem to the entire country. This law divided national territory into six corregimientos for the purpose of subduing Indians: (1) Bogotá—

composed of Cundinamarca, Tolima, and the Territory of San Martín, with the capital at Bogotá; (2) Boyacá—composed of Boyacá and Casanare, with the capital at Tunja; (3) Magdalena, with the capital at Santa Marta; (4) Panama, with the capital at Panama; (5) Cauca, with the capital at Popayán, and (6) Santander, with the capital at Socorro. In each corregimiento capital, a six-member Junta General was to take charge of Indian relations. Each junta was to found a missionary college and sent out two missionaries to every major tribe within its jurisdiction. It was to distribute tools and domesticated animals to Indians who helped to construct roads and buildings, but the law specifically stated that Indians could not be obliged to work except for their own benefit. Once Indians had been forced into settlements, the president was to appoint a white deputy to govern them. Deputies and missionaries were to work together to protect the Indians and to keep the whites from seizing their land, selling them alcohol, or compelling them to work. Law 66 called for an annual subsidy of thirty-one thousand pesos from the national treasury—four thousand of which was assigned to Bogotá and six thousand to Boyacá.[71]

Like so many other pieces of Radical legislation, the Indian laws were imaginative and well meaning on paper but entirely unworkable in practice. Rafael Vanegas, who served as prefect of San Martín in 1874 and 1875, flatly stated that nothing fruitful had been accomplished with regard to the Indians since the creation of the territory because the laws passed by Congress "never correspond to the reality of the task." Rather than an elaborate system of deputies, Vanegas proposed that a priest should accompany the prefect on his regular visit to the territorial towns. Once the priest had met with the Indians and won their respect, they would volunteer to be baptized. Then, teachers could be sent to teach them to read and write. Vanegas warned that the Indians would resist any attempt to change their nomadic habits and that the best way to win them over was through such subtle measures as giving them the salt they so greatly coveted. He believed that in his capacity as prefect he could do much to gain their confidence if the government would only give him supplies to cover their small needs.[72]

In facing the formidable Guahibos, the prefects of Casanare were less sanguine about the government's ability to reduce the Indians. D. Acosta R. wrote in 1872 that Colombia should follow the example of the United States, for "the only way to protect the civilized population now from the Indians is to establish a permanent military force however small it may be." [73] In 1874, Gabriel Vargas reported that Guahibos had invaded the Corregimiento of Chita and were threatening Tame. He pleaded that action be taken "before the Indians acquire firearms and learn how to use them." The people in the interior do not understand the peril that we risk when we leave a town, he said. Here, he declared, the struggle is ongoing, and there is no time to find out who provoked it or who is to blame. The truly ferocious tribes, he pointed out, are the Guahibos, Chiricoas, Cuivas, and Yaruros, who completely dominate the Cravo Norte, Ele and Lipa rivers, and, at times, the Casanare River. "I doubt very much," Vargas concluded, "that a persevering policy of rectitude and generosity will make a mark on the heart of these beings of whom it can truly be said, 'they are large but terrible children.'" [74] By 1882 Prefect J. Trinidad Moreno was ready to take the issue a step further. Since Law 11 of 1874 has not worked, he wrote, the best way to deal with the Guahibos is "to conscript them into the Republican army which could be done without any violence or danger. They are inclined to get drunk. It would be easy to get them drunk and then disarm them and take them prisoner." He added, "The government simply does not understand the ferocious nature of these Indians which gets worse every year because they have totally forgotten whatever the Jesuits in the past might have taught them." [75]

The forlorn hope that missionaries would be able to pacify the Indians was doomed by the suppression of the religious communities in 1861 by T. C. Mosquera and the wave of repression that followed. Faced with the choice of renouncing their vows or leaving the country, several Dominicans, including Fray Antonio Acero, Dr. Simón López, Francisco Jiménez González, and José de Calasanz Vela, chose exile in the Llanos of San Martín, while Padre Santiago Pinilla, Fray Juan Nepomuceno Bustamente, and Padre Justo Pastor Rincón, all Recoletos, fled to Casanare. [76] They attempted to minister to the towns in the Llanos, but as they had no security or guarantees, they constantly feared that they would be apprehended and expelled.

Tensions eased after Mosquera's exile in 1867 and the election of Vicente Arbeláez as archbishop a year later. Arbeláez worked closely with Presidents Salgar, Murillo Toro, and Pérez to blunt Radical anticlericalism. A spokesman for moderation, he gave qualified support for the secular public education system embraced by Salgar, which was roundly denounced by the bishops of Popayán, Medellín, and Pasto; Conservatives; and right-wing Catholics. Arbeláez, however, could not revive the extinguished religious communities. When he received a request in 1871 from Alejandro Duarte to send missionaries to Casanare, there was little that he could do. Duarte wrote that only one of the three remaining priests in the territory regularly exercised his ministry, and he was aged and infirm. The settlers were waging a continual war against the Indians, provoked by their atrocities. If Arbeláez would assign priests to Arauca, Moreno, Támara, Tame, Trinidad, and Orocué and the government paid their salaries, Duarte assured him that the vecinos would supply them with food. Prefect Hilario Páez supported Duarte's plea, but Arbeláez replied that although he was working with President Salgar to start a mission in Casanare, there were not enough priests at the present time to fill the parishes that already existed.[77]

Church–state relations worsened as the decade went on. In July 1876, the Conservatives revolted to protest the election of Aquileo Parra to the presidency in the previous year. Although their grievances were primarily political, the Conservatives whipped up popular opposition to secular education to give their rebellion a religious hue. The two-year war cost 10 million pesos, left hundreds dead, and brought agriculture and industry to a standstill.[78] The Radicals emerged victorious and enacted reprisals against the Conservatives and the church, including sending the bishops of Popayán, Pasto, and Medellín into exile. It is evident that Arbeláez regarded a proposal in 1877 to detach Boyacá and Casanare from the Metropolitan See of Bogotá to form a separate diocese as a calculated measure to limit his political and economic power.[79] In spite of his opposition, Pope Leo XIII approved the plan on July 29, 1880, thus decreasing the financial revenue of the archdiocese by one-third.

The creation of Tunja diocese enhanced the possibilities of renewing the missions in Casanare because the new bishop would be physically closer to the Llanos. Arbeláez appointed his auxiliary bishop, Moisés Higuera, to serve as vicar governor of Tunja until the first titular bishop, Dr. Severo García, was installed in November 1882.[80] In 1881, Higuera named Miguel de Jesús Medina, formerly the párroco of Labranzagrande, to be Vicar of Casanare, and he founded a seminary in Nunchía to train young missionaries. After he took office, Bishop García allotted twelve hundred pesos for the school, and he urged the Colombian envoy at the Vatican to search in Europe for a religious order that would accept a missionary field in Casanare. In 1883, the Nunchía seminary ordained five new priests, destined for parishes in the Llanos. Higuera, now serving as Dean of the Cathedral of Bogotá, asked Congress for an subsidy of eight thousand pesos to support the seminary and to help start colegios for girls, but the civil war of 1884 halted these promising activities.[81]

While the religious revival in Casanare did not extend south of the Meta, the dedicated labors of an exiled Dominican, José de Calasanz Vela, kept the missionary spirit alive in the Territory of San Martín. Born in Gámbita, Santander, Vela entered the Dominican Order in 1859 and had just made his first profession when Mosquera dissolved the community. He joined the monks who chose exile in the Llanos over banishment from Colombia and remained in the territory until 1870. During the Salgar administration, he returned to Bogotá to complete his education and was ordained in 1872. After serving the parish of Cájica, Santander, for a year, he went back to Villavicencio, where he ministered to settlers and Indians until his death in 1895.[82]

For nearly three decades Padre Vela served the parishes of Villavicencio, San Juan de los Llanos, Jiramena, Uribe, San Martín, Cabuyaro, Sebástopol, and San Pedro de Arimena, traveling by horse, foot, and canoe to baptize children, perform marriages, and say mass. Visitors to the territory were vividly impressed by the Llanero priest. Röthlisberger, who met him in 1893, found a tall and robust man, with an expressive and kindly face, red cheeks, and a beautiful thick beard worn with the permission of his superiors. He wrote:

Padre Vela, in his white and black habit, was a splendid and masculine figure. But almost never, because of the fierce heat of that region, did he wear the habit of the order; in civilian clothes he looked more like a stout miller. He liked very much to ride horseback and to share the life of the Llaneros. He was a Llanero in the best sense of the word. He also had a small hato; he raised cattle and sold them. He had to do this because the government did not pay his salary punctually and because the inhabitants of the Llanos do not show any special largesse with their clergy.[83]

In 1887, Rufino Gutiérrez, a government inspector from Cundinamarca, wrote that Vela combined his zeal for the propagation of the faith and the moral and material progress of the territory with fertile and unceasing activity, a great knowledge of the Llanos, and exquisite tact to counsel his baptized parishioners and to catechize the Indians along the Meta and Ariari rivers. "He is generous, hospitable, charitable, of great practical sense and no little wisdom."[84]

Reminiscent of colonial Jesuits Juan Rivero and Joseph Gumilla,

Vela wrote detailed descriptions of the land and people. Archbishop Arbeláez ordered his lengthy report on the Meta missions of March 31, 1884, published in the *Anales Religiosos*, the official periodical of the diocese.[85] In 1889, under contract with the Ministry of Finance, Vela explored the Guaviare, Orinoco, and Vichada rivers to reach San Fernando de Atabapo, capital of the Venezuelan province of Amazonas. His account of his experiences and recommendations for the development of the Llanos south of the Meta, published in 1890, was influential in the creation of the Intendencia of Meta in 1897.[86] In 1895, Vela was thrown by a horse and died instantly. He was buried in Uribe and is still remembered today as a priest who brilliantly represented the church when its presence elsewhere in the Llanos was in deep eclipse.

Salt

Availability of salt was a perennial concern in the Llanos. Not only was it essential for human nutrition, but ranchers needed large quantities for their cattle, and traditionally, gifts of salt had been a practical way to entice Indians to settle down. Law 11 of April 27, 1874, "on the development of colonization of the Territories of Casanare and San Martín," recognized its importance by ordering the president to make low-priced salt available in the Llanos and stating that the price fixed on rock salt in the territories might not exceed for ten years the official price set for the nation in 1874.[87]

During the Federation Era, the central government retained the colonial monopoly on the production and sale of salt. There were eight national mines that produced three kinds of salt: *compactada* (consolidated), *caldero* (precipitated), and *vijua* (crude), but the huge works at Zipaquirá, Cundinamarca, accounted for over half the output. The government auctioned off the right to operate a mine to private investors, who agreed to produce a certain amount of salt each year to be sold at a fixed price in an official store, or *almacén*. Although inhabitants of the territories were exempt from other national taxes, they still had to pay the salt tax. Between 1865 and 1876 income from the salt monopoly ranged from 595,000 to 754,566 pesos in a given year, making up from 13 to 24 percent of federal revenues.[88]

In the Territory of San Martín, there were *salinas* (salt works) at Mámbita, Cumaral, and Upín. The government inexplicably prohibited operations at the Mámbita Salina, located high in the cordillera near the Río Guavio, which might have supplied the needs of the inhabitants of Medina, Ubalá, and Gachalá. The Cumaral Salina on the Río Guacavía, north of present-day Restrepo, had been abandoned in the midnineteenth century, so that by 1863 the clearing around it and the huts formerly used by the works had been reclaimed by forest. A few kilometers to the east, the Salina de Upín was still functioning. A solid bank of rock salt nine meters high, it was sandwiched between the forest and the Río Upín in a narrow gorge at the foot of the cordillera. Earth, trees, and debris driven down the mountain slopes by the rains covered the mine like a landslide during the rainy season. Water from the Río Upín transformed the gorge into a kind of sewer and the crystalline salt into a black, muddy precipitate.

Potentially a rich deposit, the Upín salina was operated in the most primitive fashion. The *contratista* (contractor) hired ten or twelve peons, who came to the mine when the rains ended in November and cleared off the layer of earth that had fallen on top of the salt. They used gunpowder charges to blow up chunks of salt and dirt from the bank, hacking the giant fragments into smaller pieces, or *vijua*, with pick axes. The peons carried the vijua over a rickety wooden bridge that spanned the river and stacked it in a miserable hut, grandly called the almacén. The mine closed when the rains returned in March. Any unsold salt was left to disintegrate in the humidity. Worked in this manner for four months, Upín produced an average of six thousand arrobas of vijua a year.[89]

In October 1868, the first prefect of San Martín Territory, Leonard Cubillos M. inspected the salina and condemned its ruinous state. The agent of the contratista could not produce his books. The buildings were small, badly constructed, and inadequate. Earth completely covered the mine. The road between Upín and Villavicencio was a hazardous footpath, and the official resguardo hired to prevent contraband consisted of two men, neither of whom lived at the mine and both completely ignorant about how to stop a theft. Cubillos recommended that the government close the mine, or, better yet, reorganize it so that it could produce compacted salt that was much preferred over vijua. He wrote:

If the Salina de Upín is put in order, with easy exploitation and superior quality salt, there would be much demand for this commodity in Medina, Villavicencio, San Martín and the other towns of the territory as well as the towns in the former department of Cáqueza, without excluding some in the State of Tolima whenever the road permitted it. Thus the national income would increase considerably and the towns mentioned would improve being able to obtain easily and of good quality one of the most necessary elements for life.[90]

Over the next twenty years the president signed contracts with a number of individuals. While some were more honest than others, the basic conditions of the mine described by Cubillos remained the same. The poor quality salt that it yielded was suitable only for cattle. Demand always exceeded supply, and the price was often as high as four pesos an arroba. The vecinos of Medina, Ubalá, and Gachalá regularly bought contraband salt collected illegally from the Mámbita Salina.[91] In 1886, Rufino Gutiérrez accused the government of artificially maintaining a high price on Upín salt so that it might not compete with salt from Zipaquirá.[92]

The situation was even more discouraging in Casanare. The official mines were the Salinas of Chita and Muneque on the slopes of the cordillera, but with no roads leading to them, it was difficult for Llaneros to buy salt there. In March 1870, Congress considered a bill for the development of the territories of Casanare and San Martín, which would have solved the problem by authorizing the president to establish almacenes in Moreno or Orocué, on the Meta River, and to arrange that salt be transported from Chita and Muneque to these sites and sold at reasonable prices. Unfortunately, this bill was never adopted, and the inhabitants of Casanare got most of their salt from Ciudad Bolívar, which, due to its high iodine content, was not suitable for cattle. In 1882, when the official price had risen to five pesos an arroba, Prefect Trinidad Moreno urged the government to lower the price and make salt more accessible.[93] His pleas fell on deaf ears. The call for better, cheaper salt was a monotonous litany that brought no reform.

Public Administration

Between 1868 and 1881, 91 percent of the 455,379.50 pesos that the federal government spent on the six territories went to pay the salaries of national employees—deputies, commissioners, prefects, judges, schoolteachers, hacienda officials, missionaries, and soldiers. The rest financed roads, jails, and schools.[94] The maintenance of a regular system of public administration was a novelty in several of the territories, and judging by the annual reports submitted by the prefects, they were more efficiently ruled than before. On the other hand, it was lapses in public administration that most annoyed the secretaries of government (as the interior portfolio was renamed in 1880), and prompted them to call for an end to the whole territorial system.

The election of commissioners and deputies to represent the territories in Congress was controversial for three reasons. First, since all other offices were appointive, these biennial elections were the only opportunity for the inhabitants to demonstrate their political allegiances. Party antagonisms in San Martín in 1871 were heated enough to force a second ballot for the commissioner, and after the election the residual bad feeling between the two sides kept the territory in turmoil for the next five years.[95] In 1874 and again in 1882, the election of a deputy brought Casanare to the verge of revolt, but despite alarms and conspiracies, in both instances the balloting took place without violence.

Second, the men who stood for election generally were not from the territories nor even especially public spirited. In 1884, Secretary of Government Ricardo Bercerra charged that many individuals accepted positions as prefects, secretaries, and judges in a remote territory with the sole intention of getting themselves elected commissioner so that they could come back to Bogotá with their salaries and travel expenses paid by the federal government.[96] Felipe Pérez, a supporter of the territorial system, nevertheless argued that the commissioners were unnecessary since the president could best decide on the specific needs of developing regions. He wrote, "The territories have no one now to send to Congress; it is Congress that should send to them the missionary, the school teacher, the engineer and the colonist."[97]

Third, from the standpoint of the casanareños, the reduction of their national influence to a single commissioner (upgraded to a deputy after the census of 1870 showed twenty-six thousand inhabitants in the territory) was the humiliating consummation of their political decline. As late as 1857 they had elected their own legislators, sent a senator and a representative to Congress, and voted in presidential elections. Señor D. Acosta R. was deeply impressed by the prevailing sense of bitterness when he arrived in Moreno in 1872 to take up his duties as prefect:

The people of Casanare have in truth suffered a long time in silence and with resignation. They have in their territory most of the savages that are in the nation.

The republic has done nothing to reduce these Indians; their borders are invaded from the neighboring republic (but more from passion than from government design). [They are] abandoned entirely by religion; commerce does not prosper as it should, and the cattle industry is in decadence. Public administration is not well-regulated at times because of bad political organization, and for some time they have been wanting to protest.[98]

The prefects, who were appointed by the president to two-year terms, exercised powers that were shared in the states between the governors and the legislators. While some of these men were of high ability—notably, Rafael Vanegas and Manuel A. Londoño in San Martín and J. Trinidad Moreno in Casanare—others were ill prepared for the responsibilities thrust upon them. Few qualified individuals would accept an appointment to a god-forsaken wilderness, and men who had been born there did not have the necessary influence to win the president's nomination. Many prefects performed their duties perfunctorily or not at all. During the eighteen years between 1869 and 1887, the secretaries of government received just eight of the required annual reports from the prefects of San Martín and five from their counterparts in Casanare.

In some cases, the prefect wasted a good deal of time overcoming the hostility of his constituents. D. Acosta R., quoted above, stated that he had gone to Casanare "with the purest intentions and the firmest plans to carry out my commission as well as I could," but he was met by a group of men who opposed him because he was not from Casanare. They threatened to revolt, supported by some Venezuela exiles "who have no respect for the territory," and by others "who want to depose the legitimate authority and declare themselves in open war with the general government."[99] Acosta managed to defuse their anger and restore peace, but other prefects were not so fortunate. In the judgment of Secretary Adolfo Vargas, the administration of Casanare and San Martín was destructive (*ruinosa*) and useless, and the political life was "a perennial evil produced and fed by the bad passions and animosities between the employees; those of the judiciary complain about those of the executive, and [controlling] the elections and the small sum that constitutes the budget is their only important mission."[100]

The prefect who went to Villavicencio was within three days' contact with Bogotá, could count on fairly reliable mail service, and ruled over a small population concentrated in a strip of territory close to the cordillera. By contrast, the capital of Casanare was moved twice: from Moreno to Tame in 1875, and from Tame to Nunchía in 1877, with each transfer creating confusion as the territorial offices were relocated.[101] Moreno, Tame, and Nunchía were equally remote from Bogotá, and there were continual complaints that mail was not received. Twenty-six thousand inhabitants were scattered throughout the immense territory, and lack of roads isolated the vecinos of El Viento and Arauca from the capital in the western piedmont. These conditions encouraged turmoil and made the prefect's job doubly challenging.

If the president experienced trouble in finding qualified prefects, the prefects had even more difficulty in finding men to serve as corregidores. According to Law 39 of June 4 and the Decree of July 6, 1868, the corregidores were key district officials. They were to work with the municipal councils, administer funds, and serve as judges of the first instance, but except in rare instances, they were to receive no salary, and in theory, those who accepted the appointment were required to separate themselves from their private businesses for a year. Prefect Manuel Antonio Londoño reported in 1879 that, in San Martín City, men from other places had held the post of corregidor for the last six years because "this job is hateful and anyone who accepts it does so for a short time and with repugnance."[102] From Casanare, Prefect A. Samudio wrote that there were few people whose occupations permitted them time to serve as corregidores without salary, and that he tried to appoint the most notable people of a district as corregidores, but they neglected their official duties to attend to their own affairs.[103] His successor, Trinidad Moreno, observed that if individuals nominated for the post were townspeople, they could not be very wealthy since "if they have even modest capital, they have herds in the Llanos and live there and are less aware of public matters." Moreno proposed unsuccessfully that the government assign a salary to the corregidores and order the municipalities to appoint separate judges of the first instance (*jueces parroquiales*) to reduce the demands placed on them.[104]

Public apathy in Villavicencio inhibited the municipal council and the corregidor. Prefect Rafael Vanegas wrote, in 1875, that the inertia of the principal citizens of the town defeated the best efforts of the officials. If he asked one of them to be the *personero* (tax collector) or treasurer, the person rudely replied, "I am a foreigner in this country," or "I will do nothing, absolutely nothing; you will waste time nominating me for such a post; I will resist all legal pressures, and I will not serve."[105] Four years later, Prefect Manuel Londoño could report little progress. He wrote that all the municipal councils were functioning except in Villavicencio, where it was impossible to get people to serve because they were lacking in public spirit. Only the schoolteacher had agreed to sit on the council, and that was because his job required him to do so.[106] The federal Supreme Court appointed a superior judge for each territory in the even-numbered years. These judges were supposed to visit all the corregimientos in their circuits every six months—a responsibility that was feasible in San Martín but physically impossible in Casanare. Prefect Acosta R. pointed out that when Boyacá had ruled Casanare, between 1857 and 1868, there had been two judicial circuits. Under the territorial system there was only one, and the vecinos in Arauca and El Viento could not exercise their civil rights because the judge who was based in Moreno could not get out to them.[107] When the judge did travel to Arauca, as was the case in 1882, he was forced to remain there for several weeks, creating considerable delay in the processing of cases in the piedmont towns.[108] All the judges were expected to make decisions based on a hodgepodge of legal codes. In some matters, the *Recopilación granadina*, compiled in 1845, was in effect; in others, laws adopted by Boyacá, and in still others, Law 39 and the Decree of July 6, 1868. None of the municipalities in Casanare had copies of these codes, an oversight that added to the general confusion.[109]

Inadequate jails complicated judicial proceedings. In San Martín, the districts maintained their own jails, but except for the jail in Pore, which was solidly built, the towns in Casanare either had none or used buildings of such flimsy construction that the prisoners readily escaped. The municipios allotted so little money to feed the prisoners that the corregidor hired them out to do obligatory personal labor for private citizens so they could earn their keep. By an agreement signed on August 27, 1869, convicted criminals from San Martín and Casanare were required to serve their sentences in the penitentiary in Cundinamarca.[110] Prefect Gabriel Vargas objected to this practice in 1874, explaining the that Llaneros were filled with horror at the prospect of having to live in the cold highlands, a situation "absolutely incompatible with their mode of being and semi-savage independence." He asked that a jail be built in Tame to house them instead, for "if to the loss of liberty is added the pain of obliging them to go to prison far from the land of their birth that they love so much, the punishment is increased so that for many, it is the equivalent of a true death sentence."[111]

By Law 39 Congress pledged to build a school in each corregimiento and to pay the salary of a teacher. The school reform initiated by the Organic Decree of Public Primary Instruction of November 1, 1870, had an impact even in the territories. In Casanare, primary schools increased from three in 1869 to twelve in 1872, enrolling 450 children. In that year, Prefect Acosta reported that all of the teachers were competent, and he singled out for special praise Eduardo Villega and Francisco Martínez, two Venezuelans who had fled their country after the Revolution of 1870 and were dedicating themselves to teaching children in Pore. In 1873, Prefect Fajardo announced that, aided by others, he had begun five schools for boys and three for girls, with a total enrollment of 430 students. Both Acosta and Fajardo contended that attendance would be higher if it were not for the fevers which decimated the population and the reluctance of some parents to send their children to school at all.[112]

A persistent problem was to find qualified teachers who would live in the Llanos. In 1873, Congress passed Law 25 of April 9, which provided funds to send three youths from each territory to normal schools in the interior for six years. Law 89 of 1876 expanded the program to offer scholarships to the newly founded National University for four students from Casanare and two from each of the other territories, but Prefect Vanegas pointed out that because of the poor quality of primary education in San Martín, no student was really qualified to attend normal school. Another complication arose when youths received these scholarships, for their parents were reluctant to let them go to the highlands. A third difficulty lay in getting the students, once they had graduated, to come back to the Llanos to teach.[113] In 1882, Prefect Moreno reported that Juan B. Abril, a graduate of the Normal School in Boyacá, refused to accept an assignment to teach in Cravo even though he was from Casanare and owed the territory for his *beca* (scholarship). "Cravo does not have a bad climate," he went on, "and the need for the teacher is real. As a result Sr. Abril has gone away without fulfilling his duties, and there has been no way to penalize him."[114] In that same year, Prefect Eliseo Forero pronounced public instruction in San Martín to be in a state of "prostration and decadence," even though six primary schools were still open. The teachers were not properly trained, and they were discouraged by their low salaries and the lack of school supplies. The teacher in Cabuyaro had worked without being paid for six months, and in San Martín City, final examinations could not be held because the teacher had committed suicide.[115]

Law 39 empowered the municipios to levy or maintain the direct, indirect, or personal taxes that had existed in the district prior to 1868 so long as the taxes were of purely local character and the revenues were used for the benefit of the locality. The chief sources of income were taxes on the slaughter of cattle and pigs (*degüello*), on the sale and export of *aguardiente*, and on gambling; the sales tax; and peaje, fines, and direct contributions. They were collected by the personero, who was appointed by the prefect. The money was used to improve roads, to subsidize salaries of teachers and priests, and to buy school furniture and office supplies. In 1875, Prefect Vanegas wrote that some levies imposed by the districts in San Martín, such as the tax on cattle exported to Cundinamarca, were technically illegal because they had not existed before 1868, but that all of his predecessors had tolerated this abuse because the vecinos did not object to the tax and the revenue it generated was needed to finance the local government. Such taxes, he argued, were justified because they were practical, did not fall on agricultural or forest products, and penalized only such pernicious vices as gambling and drinking.[116]

Joaquín Díaz Escobar's Plan to Develop Casanare

It can be seen from this summary of the federal government's efforts to construct roads, establish navigation on the Meta, encourage immigration and colonization, civilize Indians, make salt available, and improve public administration that the most discernible progress occurred in the Territory of San Martín. Casanare showed little gain, and except for the brief revival of missions between 1880 and 1885, its institutions and economy continued to disintegrate. This decline was denounced most energetically by Joaquín Díaz Escobar, who, in 1878, proposed an ambitious and comprehensive plan for developing the territory. Published in Bogotá in 1879 as *Bosquejo estadístico de la región oriental de Colombia: medios económicos para su conquista, sometimiento i desarrollo industrial i political*, it remains one of the most penetrating analyses of the problems and prospects of this section of the Llanos.

Joaquín Díaz Escobar was "an intelligent traveler, careful observer, and progressive merchant-missionary" who spent twenty years in Casanare.[117] In 1864, he unsuccessfully petitioned Congress for a contract to place steamships on the Meta River and reduce the Indians of Casanare. In 1875 he expanded his proposal, also offering to improve the climate of the Llanos and attract immigrants in exchange for a thirty-year lease on two salinas and the concession of thousands of hectares of baldíos. The war of 1876–77 terminated negotations, but undiscouraged, Díaz Escobar in 1878 put forward his third and most ambitious plan, meticulously outlined in *Bosquejo estadístico*, which he dedicated to Interior Secretary General Julian Trujillo and Dr. Aristedes D. Gutiérrez.

Díaz Escobar believed that all efforts to develop Casanare would fail because of the unhealthy climate, the great extension of land, bad soil, unpalatable grasses, fierce animals, extreme flooding, fevers, tropical disease, and the force of the hot wind. His solution was the "scientific" use of fire. Just as the Indians routinely burned grass in order to encourage new and more tender growth, Díaz Escobar argued that systematic burning of the plains during the six months of the dry season would destroy malicious insects, get rid of undesirable animals and vegetation, and allow the winds to neutralize the humidity, eliminating the pools of water that bred the germs of disease. Through its combustive power and radiation in the atmosphere, fire would destroy the organic elements that were poisoning the region and permit the introduction of improved pasture and cross-bred cattle. He wrote, "The weapon of fire—correctly applied and as part of an overall plan, can make the Llanos both habitable and productive." [118]

Systematic grass burning was the first step in Díaz Escobar's twenty-one-point plan to resuscitate Casanare. Other tactics included exploiting the salinas to obtain salt to civilize the Indians and improve cattle and commerce; promoting colonization by granting two hundred hectares of land to any family who would settle and work them for ten years; offering prizes to farmers who would plant coffee and sugar; facilitating river traffic by signing a treaty with Venezuela; moving the capitals of Casanare and San Martín to sites on the Meta River; prohibiting the slaughter of female cattle for ten years; and awarding a contract to an individual or company who would exploit an iron mine.

Díaz Escobar assured Congress that if his plan were implemented, Casanare "now abandoned to barbarism, beasts and death will become the most important region of all our territory." [119] Professors from the Schools of Natural Sciences and Medicine at the National University testified in his support, and in the end, Congress passed Law 55 of July 1, 1878, which authorized the president to appoint a scientific commission to examine his proposal. The law stated that if the commission reported favorably, and "it appears to it that Dr. Díaz has discovered something important," Díaz was to receive ten thousand pesos and up to fifty thousand hectares of baldíos in Casanare, and the government would proceed to implement the strategies he suggested. On the other hand, if the commission found Díaz's proposal unsatisfactory, the president was to award the ten thousand pesos to any other person who presented a complete study of the points enumerated that was judged satisfactory by the commission.[120]

By 1880 the commission had reached no decision, and a Senate committee drafted a bill modifying Law 55 so that Díaz Escobar could receive the ten thousand pesos immediately. Ricardo Vanegas E., chair of the committee, pointed out that Díaz Escobar had worked long and hard for progress in Casanare and that Law 55, which required the commission to prove his plan "infallible," was unrealistic "since only the Son of God might have been able with only the expression of his will, to show the sure and infallible way to combat . . . the fevers and the reasons behind the unhealthiness of those climates."[121] The bill passed first debate but died on second reading, so that nothing came of Díaz Escobar's scheme nor of another proposed in 1879 by General Reyes Patria, who promised within a short time to stimulate Casanare's commerce and industry, improve cattle, encourage colonization, and promote navigation on the Meta.[122]

The Failure of the Territorial Initiative

By the 1880s the territorial initiative had lost momentum, reflecting the waning influence of its sponsors. Between 1868 and 1874 the Radicals had launched many ambitious projects, but the disruptive election of 1875 broke up the uneasy consensus they had forged. The campaign was fiercely fought between Radical Aquileo Parra; Rafael Núñez, who was supported by moderate Liberals calling themselves Independents; and Bartolomé Calvo, a Conservative. After no candidate received the required five-state majority vote, Congress proclaimed Parra the victor, but the Conservatives and Independents cried fraud. The situation was especially precarious in Cauca, where the split between Radicals and Independents threatened the incumbent government. Meanwhile, the Conservative press began a bitter attack against federal and state institutions and whipped up popular resistance to the official secular schools.

The revolution began in Palmira, Cauca, in July 1876 and spread rapidly through the state. The presidents of Antioquia and Tolima openly supported the rebels, and Rafael Núñez, as president of Bolívar, gave his personal encouragement. Guerrilla warfare wracked Cundinamarca, Boyacá, and Santander, but decisive federal victories at Los Chancos (August 31, 1876), Garrapata (November 18, 1876), and El Cocuy (April 27, 1877) assured the preservation of the union.[123]

Despite their victory, the Radicals never regained their prewar ascendancy. A worldwide recession ended the commercial boom of the early 1870s. As exports fell, the 1878–79 budget showed a deficit of 5 million pesos. The civil war was costly, and it destroyed the delicate balance of power essential to the working of the federation. Government reprisals against the clergy for aiding the rebels alienated the Independents and aroused Conservative hatred. The military regime imposed on Antioquia increased Radical unpopularity. Beset by internal quarrels, the Radicals were unequal to the new challenges.[124]

In 1879, Rafael Núñez won the presidency by campaigning as an Independent with Conservative support. His 1880–1882 administration was really the first stage of *Regeneración,* a term often used by contemporary journalists and politicians to mean "fundamental action leading to political and economic progress," which Núñez officially adopted as a slogan upon being reelected in 1886. In 1880, his government revoked the oppressive measures passed against the clergy three years before. It opened negotiations with the Vatican for a new concordat. With congressional approval, Núñez established the right of the federal government to intervene in the domestic affairs of the states. He reorganized the executive branch into six ministries, awarding important cabinet posts to Conservatives. Although the Constitution of Rionegro remained in effect, the federal government was assuming a more dominant role.[125]

In contrast to Gil Colunje's rosy assessments of the progress made by the national territories in 1873 and 1874, the evaluations by the secretaries of government appointed after the 1876–77 war were uniformly pessimistic. Eustorgio Salgar, who as president had been one of the staunchest supporters of the territories, did not attempt to hide his disillusionment. In his *Memoria* of 1878, he wrote:

The situation in the territories is the same as it was before they were organized. The large sums that the national treasury has spent have not born true fruits in the work of colonization. On the contrary, the great distance of the capital from the territories greatly favors the abuses and irregularities that remain without correction. The instability in the personnel of their employees and the difficulties in postal communications are other hindrances to the effectiveness of the laws and executive action.[126]

José Araujo, in 1881, and Adolfo Vargas, in 1882, offered even more sobering indictments. Araujo wrote that the erection of the national territories was "a blind and ill-conceived imitation of the U.S.A. territories," which contradicts one of the fundamental principles of the federal system—local control. He went on to point out that national revenues had suffered. The federal deficit of $443,381.05 was approximately equal to the sum spent on the territories between 1868 and 1881 and would not have occurred if the territories had been administered by the states.[127] Adolfo Vargas added that it was wrong to take desperately needed funds away from the interior provinces and waste them on remote regions that would require the sacrifices of many generations in order to be developed.[128] Both secretaries agreed that their predecessors had greatly overestimated the wealth of the territories and that the glowing reports of explorers and journalists had created false expectations of rapid growth which could not happen without technical and scientific advancements.

Not everyone was convinced. Felipe Pérez, a former president of Boyacá who published his massive geography of Colombia in 1883, remained a faithful defender of the system. Pérez conceded that progress had not been uniform, but he insisted that for security reasons the government could not abandon these regions along international frontiers, nor could it return them to the states that had no resources to develop them. Instead, it should abolish the deputies and commissioners and use the money spent on their salaries to build schools, bridges, and roads; to buy tools and seed for the Indians; and to support missionaries. Quoting Gil Colunje's *Memoria* of 1873, Pérez reiterated, "These sections find themselves much more developed than when they were ruled by the States, and it is beyond doubt that they will achieve less if they go back to being administered in the previous fashion."[129]

By this time, Pérez was a voice crying in the dark. Secretary of Government Ricardo Becerra wrote in 1884: "No progress can be noted in the territories that has proceeded from an intelligent administration, and on the contrary, there have been many disturbances . . . there has not been nor is there now any administration of the National Territories and the secretaries of government have all recognized this fact in recent years." [130] Already, Law 77 of July 2, 1881, had returned the Territory of Bolívar to Santander. On November 2, 1883, the Boyacá Assembly sent a resolution to Congress, requesting the return of Casanare on the grounds that there was no government there except during elections and that a large group of casanareños were insisting that they be placed under Boyacá's rule. No further action was taken until the promulgation of the Constitution of 1886. Article 4 of this charter, the tenth in Colombia's history, reduced the states to departments and reincorporated all of the national territories into the departments to which they had formerly belonged. [131] By executive decrees issued in September 1886, Casanare and San Martín were reunited with Boyacá and Cundinamarca, and the territorial initiative was over.

The Balance Sheet

Law 39 of June 4, 1868, and the successive laws concerning the territories embodied the weaknesses and strengths of other Radical endeavors. On the one hand, with its naive anticipation of rapid transformation of the frontier regions into states, the system was, in certain ways, "a blind and ill-conceived imitation" of the Northwest Ordinance of 1785, which formed the basis for territorial incorporation in the United States. The Radicals overestimated the potential wealth of the wilderness regions and underestimated the time it would take to overcome the geographical obstacles to their development. Their reliance on the federal government to promote change was a blatant contradiction to their philosophical commitment to local control, states' rights, and laissez-faire economics. The country's dependence on international demand for its exports limited the amount of money that could be invested, especially when other major projects were under way, like the Great Northern Railway. [132] The anticlericalism of Radical leaders and the breach between church and state crippled attempts to revitalize the missions—always a critical element in the Colombian approach to frontier integration. Finally, the uncertain political climate and the premature fall of the Radicals from power doomed their experiment, just as it doomed the system of public primary education they had sponsored.

On the other hand, Law 39 offered a multifaceted approach to territorial development that was entirely consistent with national interests. With Venezuelan pressure on the east, Colombia could not continue to ignore Guajira and Arauca on its border. Conceived and supported by some of the most brilliant minds of the era, the law brought to public awareness regions that formerly had been ignored. The amounts spent by the federal government, admittedly insufficient, far exceeded the pittance that the states might have invested in areas so remote from their population centers. Moreover, in the Territory of San Martín growth did occur. The opening of the Colombia–Uribe road and improvements on the Bogotá–Villavicencio road facilitated the movement of entrepreneurs and colonos into the region. Exports of quinine, coffee, and rice were modest, but they pointed to an economy that in the future would transcend reliance on hides and meat. Even Secretary Araujo grudgingly admitted that of all the territories, San Martín was the one whose existence could best be justified, though he hastened to add that its administration had not been effective.[133]

Above all, despite their failure, the Radicals had established the principle that it was the national government's duty to take charge of wilderness regions. In 1892, the Conservatives, availing themselves of a clause in the Constitution of 1886 that gave Congress the right to separate the former territories from the departments to which they had been reincorporated, passed Law 13 of September 17 and restored San Martín and Casanare to Special Territory status. In a decade cut short by the War of the Thousand Days, the Conservatives would have their fling at developing the eastern frontier.

Illustrations by Edouard Riou from sketches drawn by Edouard André during his travels through the Territory of San Martín in 1875–76. André was a French botanist and editor of a scientific journal with a special interest in tropical nature. His account of his trip to the Llanos along with Riou's illustrations was first published in *Tour du Monde* [(Paris) 35: 1st sem. (1878), 129–224]. Riou's illustrations were later reproduced by Eduardo Acevedo Latorre in *Geografía pintoresca de Colombia* (Bogotá, 1968).

Villavicencio and the Llanos, 1875

André's arrival in Villavicencio

Hacienda in Cumaral

Salt mine at Upín

Coffee cultivation in the Llanos

5. Regeneration à la Llanera, 1886–99

*T*he victory in 1886 of Rafael Núñez, the Independents, and their Conservative allies signaled the rejection of the Radical Liberal doctrines that had dominated Colombia since 1849 and the triumph of a clear set of principles known as "Regeneration." Centralism, strengthened institutional authority, and close church–state cooperation—key elements of the program—were enshrined in the Constitution of 1886, which restored the authority of the central government by reducing the states to departments ruled by governors nominated by the president. The acts of alcaldes and municipal councils were subject to review by the governors—a measure that extended the centralization of authority to the local level. Under the new charter, the president and senators were elected indirectly for six-year terms and representatives for four years. Qualifications for voting included literacy or property ownership, and restrictions were placed on civil rights. The central government alone had the right to import, manufacture, and possess arms; the death penalty was restored for serious crimes, and censorship imposed on the press held it responsible for injury to personal honor and attacks on the public peace. Finally, Roman Catholicism was declared the religion of the nation, and a concordat signed with Pope Leo XIII granted further concessions and guarantees to the church. Although the constitution has been amended several times in the last one hundred years, it remains the fundamental charter of the republic.[1]

In his analysis of the events leading to the adoption of the Constitution of 1886, James Park concludes that Rafael Núñez, more than any other nineteenth-century Colombian, "transformed the country from a loosely-bound association of regions into a nation-state."[2] It is ironic that the document which integrated the Colombian heartland was a step backward in the administration of the national territories. Article 4 of Title I of the new charter stated that the national territories which had been directly administered by the central government under the Constitution of 1863 should be returned to the departments to which they had previously belonged—a process begun in 1881 with the reincorporation of the Territory of Bolívar to the state of Santander. By executive decrees in September 1886, Casanare and San Martín were returned to Boyacá and Cundinamarca. In the view of Humberto Plazas Olarte, the abolition of the territories under Núñez was "the culmination of the chaos" that had surrounded the irregular trajectory of their rule. "The Constitution of 1886 left vast regions without constitutional existence, in spite of their importance to national unity and the problems that affected them such as international frontiers, Indians, colonization, etc."[3]

Yet the Conservatives were not prepared to abandon the Llanos altogether. On September 17, 1892, Congress reestablished the territories of San Martín and Casanare by taking advantage of Article 6 of Title I of the constitution, which stated: "Congress may enact laws to separate the territories referred to in Article 4 from the departments in which they are now incorporated or to which they belonged and dispose of them as it may deem proper." Decree 392 of January 17, 1893, designated both regions as "National Intendancies" and set forth a series of dispositions regarding their organization and rule. This decree, in turn, was modified by Decree 392 of July 26, 1897, "on the administration of the National Intendancies." As this chapter will show, Regeneration à la Llanera meant administrative confusion, the renewal of missionary activity, improved transportation on the Meta River, and modest economic growth. Indifference toward the territories at the highest national level, coupled with systematic repression of the ousted Liberal party, encouraged a climate of political violence that eventually would erupt in the War of the Thousand Days.

Under Department Rule, 1886–1892

The return of Casanare and San Martín to Boyacá and Cundinamarca in September 1886 acknowledged the determination of departmental leaders to enhance their political influence on a national level and reflected the will of the central authorities to rid themselves of the financial drain of administering special regions—a policy roundly criticized during the first Núñez administration in 1880–82. In 1884, the Boyacá Assembly had requested control over Casanare, but it was soon evident that after receiving it, the department, like the nation, lacked the funds to create the "special, difficult and even costly administration" required by this extensive region with climate and customs distinct from highland Boyacá, a small dispersed population, and the need to develop natural resources, convert Indians, and defend the international border.[4] As the prefects who governed Casanare warned in their annual reports of 1889 and 1890, the economic situation of the province was so grave that if extensive support was not forthcoming, fifteen of its seventeen municipios would simply disappear.[5]

Cundinamarcan officials faced a similar dilemma. In 1886, the former Territory of San Martín had been divided. The districts of Villavicencio and San Martín City were attached to Oriente Province, with its capital at Fómeque, while Medina, Cabuyaro, San Pedro de Arimena, and Sebástopol became part of Guatavita Province, with its capital at Guatavita. In both arrangements, territory in the highlands was joined to portions of plains. Bad weather, horrendous roads, and difficult topography prevented highland authorities from visiting the Llanero towns, holding elections scheduled there, or providing them with adequate judicial services. By June 1892 the assemblies of Cundinamarca and Boyacá had each petitioned Congress for an annual subsidy of 100,000 pesos for the "protection, development and administration" of their Llanos regions, and on July 28 the Boyacense legislators passed a resolution asking that the national government take over the administration of Casanare completely.[6] Two weeks later, on August 9, the municipal council of Villavicencio, citing the region's decline under Cundinamarca's rule, requested new legislation that would enable the nation to sustain directly the municipios that composed the former Territory of San Martín.[7]

That the Núñez government was receptive to these requests is explained, at least in part, by its need to maintain an active Colombian presence along the disputed border with Venezuela. Negotiations over where to draw their common boundary had been going on since the breakup of Gran Colombia. Each nation based its claims on the principle of *uti possidetis juris*, as of 1810, with Venezuela demanding all of the territory controlled by the Captaincy General of Caracas' and Colombia all of the former Viceroyalty of New Granada. In 1881, they agreed to ask King Alfonso XII of Spain to arbitrate. At the king's death in 1885, Queen Regent María Cristina took over the assignment and, on September 17, 1891, handed down her decision, commonly referred to as the "Laudo."[8] In the meantime, Venezuela had awarded to the French Compañía General del Alto Orinoco a thirty-five year monopoly to exploit forest, vegetable, and mineral products in the Orinoco and Amazon valleys, to introduce steam navigation on the rivers, to build railroads, and to begin towns. The company based its headquarters at San Fernando de Atabapo on the Colombian border, and it quickly began extensive rubber and cacao plantations in Venezuelan Amazonas as well as in territory claimed by Colombia. The company's activities stimulated contraband that swept into Arauca virtually unchecked. In 1887, the secretary of war dispatched General Rafael Ortiz to Casanare, with orders to determine if war materials were being introduced illegally into Colombia via the Meta or Arauca rivers, to inspect the aduana in Orocué, and to report on general development possibilities in the region.

Ortiz submitted his report on March 18, 1888, after a four-month tour. He found that illegal weapons were not entering Colombia via the Meta because Venezuela, anxious to avert internal revolts, closely supervised the aduana at Ciudad Bolívar and threatened to revoke the monopoly of the Companîá General should it import war materials on the Orinoco. Regarding other types of contraband, Ortiz felt that the Colombian aduanas were ineffective but that the one in Arauca should be retained, despite its deficiencies, to collect taxes on exported cattle and as a symbol of Colombian sovereignty in a town "that believes itself Venezuelan because its inhabitants are Venezuelan."[9] He recommended that the aduana in Orocué be transferred to Cravo or San Rafael, at the intersection of the Pauto and Casanare rivers where trade could be monitored more efficiently.

Ortiz was pessimistic about the development potential of Casanare. Among the obstacles he cited were the unhealthy climate, poor soil, malnutrition of the inhabitants, the difficulties of navigating the Meta, and the fact that the small amount of savanna which had been improved for cattle grazing was controlled by a handful of ganaderos who transmitted their estates to their children without benefit of deed or legal formulas. Although there were perhaps 250,000 cattle in Casanare, the steady export of steers to Venezuela was draining the region of a major source of its wealth. Finally, Ortiz surveyed the Indian population which he estimated at 7,000—a figure considerably lower than the 24,000 listed in the official census. The general believed that missionaries were the appropriate agents to convert "this unhappy people" to Christian life, and he recommended that Tame be designated as the headquarters of the missionaries and the capital of the province (which in 1888 was still in Nunchía).[10]

At about the same time as Ortiz was reconnoitering Casanare, José de Calasanz Vela, the Dominican priest who had been in the

Llanos of San Martín since 1862, signed a contract with the secretary of finance in which he undertook to explore the wilderness south of the Meta by sailing down the Ariari and Guaviare rivers as far as San Fernando de Atabapo. Vela's principal goal was to catechize the Indians living along the riverbanks, but he also pledged to keep exact navigational records, report on the geography and climate, and catalogue the natural products that might be profitably exploited. Begun in March 1889, his odyssey lasted ten months and covered two thousand miles, mostly through unknown territory. Vela's report, submitted in June 1890, was later published under the title *Desde Villavicencio hasta San Fernando de Atabapo* (Cartagena, 1935–36), and with its penetrating observations on the Indians and the environment, it remains a valuable source for historians and anthropologists.[11]

Vela reached San Fernando de Atabapo in July 1889, after an exhausting journey by canoe down the Ariari and Guaviare rivers. He visited the Compañía General's extensive plantations, between the Inírida and Guaviare rivers, that produced large quantities of cacao and six hundred tons of rubber a year. What he saw convinced him that the Compañía had expanded into Colombian territory and was planning to build a road or even a railroad to the Orinoco. "Venezuela is not sleeping," he warned the secretary of finance, "and with untiring diligence it extends its radius of authority toward distant regions to the west. . . . It is necessary that patriotism be awakened and move our [Colombian] civilization and our laws to the far tributaries of the Orinoco."[12]

Unlike Ortiz, Vela was optimistic about the future of the areas he had explored. He asserted that the varied plant and animal resources were extraordinarily valuable, and the Indians, whose population he estimated at 21,531, could be civilized by missionaries. He urged the secretary to take immediate steps "to insure the rapid material, intellectual and moral colonization of our *llanuras orientales*," and among the measures he proposed were restoring the region to special territory status, ruled directly by the national government; lowering the price of salt; extending the telegraph line from Villavicencio to San Martín; building a road between Villavicencio and the port of La Cruz on the Meta; promoting steam navigation; founding a training college for missionaries in Villavicencio; and establishing settler colonies with military protection at San Pedro de Arimena and San Vicente on the Ariari River to extend Colombian control into these wilderness areas.[13]

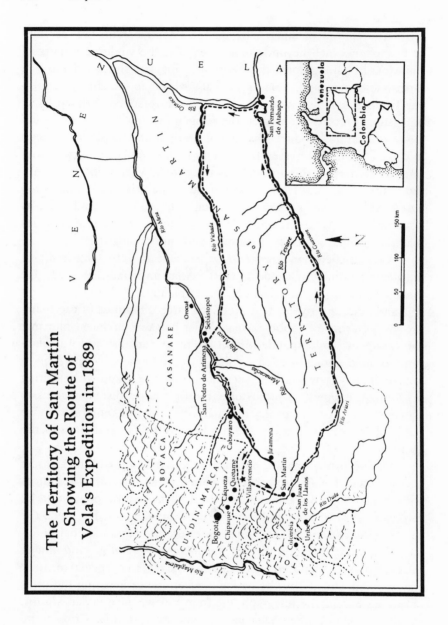

The Territory of San Martín Showing the Route of Vela's Expedition in 1889

National Intendancies, 1892–99

In 1892, Congress decided to revive the national territories, apparently swayed by the recommendations of Ortiz and Vela, the requests of Cundinamarca and Boyacá for assistance, and the Laudo of 1891, which awarded to Colombia the territory south and east of the Meta and Orinoco rivers (present-day Vichada and Vaupés) that Vela had just explored. In September, a Senate committee reported favorably on a bill to restore national control over the Llanos of Casanare and San Martín—regions the committee believed were "called by their topography, fertility of soil and abundance of natural wealth to be in the more or less remote future the center of a civilization more advanced than that of the Andean cordillera."[14] The bill passed second and third debate to become Law 13 of September 17, 1892. Taking effect on January 1, 1892, it separated the former territories of Casanare and San Martín from Boyacá and Cundinamarca and authorized the nation to administer said territories as it judged convenient, except for judicial matters which would continue to be ruled as in the rest of the republic.[15]

Decreto 392 of January 17, 1893, erected a national intendancy in each of the regions and outlined the organization of all branches of public administration. Written by Elisio Medina, a casanareño with considerable political experience, the decree reflected the needs of Casanare more than San Martín, which seems to have been added as an afterthought. Under Decreto 392, Casanare was divided into three provinces: Arauca, which included the municipios of Arauca and Arauquita; Orocué, including the municipios of Orocué, Maní, Cravo, Santa Elena, and Trinidad; and Támara, including the municipios of Támara, Chámeza, Chire, Lope, Marroquín, Moreno, Muneque, Nunchía, Pajarito, Pore, Sácama, Tame, and Ten. The capital of the intendancy was Támara, and aduanas were established in Arauca and Orocué. The intendant appointed prefects to rule Arauca and Orocué provinces, but ruled that of Támara directly. In addition, he was assigned control over the territory along the Venezuelan border that was granted to Colombia by the Laudo of 1891. The Intendancy of San Martín, with its capital at Villavicencio, was divided into the municipios of Cabuyaro, Medina, San Martín, Uribe, and Villavicencio.[16]

Until September 1894, the supervision of the intendancies was under the aegis of the secretary of justice, but with the suppression of that office, they were shifted to the secretary of government. By this time Elisio Medina, now serving as Casanare's first intendant, had discovered two major flaws in Decree 392. First, the creation of provinces in Casanare had produced an unwieldy bureaucracy, and second, the lack of independent judicial circuits deprived the Llaneros of their legal rights, since judges from Boyacá or Cundinamarca rarely went to Támara or Villavicencio to hear cases. A law passed on November 12, 1894, abolished the provinces and centralized the responsibilities of the prefect within the office of the intendant. A second organic decree, also numbered 392 but dated July 28, 1897, incorporated this feature and set up independent judicial circuits in both territories. Under this law, Casanare was composed of twenty municipios—Arauca, Arauquita, Cravo, Chámeza, Lope, Chire, Maní, Moreno, Nunchía, Marroquín, Pajarito, Pore, Sácama, Santa Elena, Támara, Tame, Ten, Trinidad, Zapatosa, and the capital, Orocué. San Martín had six municipios: Cabuyaro, Medina, San Martín, San Pedro de Arimena, Uribe, and the capital, Villavicencio.[17]

Administrative Chaos and Neglect

That five major reorganizations of territorial rule in eleven years created administrative chaos without addressing fundamental problems is well illustrated by the decisions to move the capital of Casanare from Nunchía to Tame in 1889; from Tame to Támara in 1891; and from Támara to Orocué in 1895. The designation of the provincial capital brought with it enhanced political status, a train of officials and their salaries, construction of public buildings, and expanded economic opportunities—advantages worth fighting over for the poverty-stricken towns in the Casanare piedmont. For example, after Nunchía became the capital in 1878, the municipio grew from 531 to 1,500 inhabitants in 1889, with 300 residing in the town itself. It received national dispatches and merchandise from abroad. Between 1882 and 1885, it was the seat of the auxiliary bishop of Casanare and had a seminary for missionaries.[18]

Key considerations in the selection of a capital were a healthy climate, accessibility to Sogamoso, Tunja, and Bogotá, and the question of whether the vecinos had enough influence with departmental and national authorities to win the designation. Judged by these criteria, the choice of Tame as capital in March 1889 appeared to be ideal. Connected by the Sarare road to Pamplona, the Cusirí road to Cocuy, and the Socha road to Tunja, all more or less functional, Tame had the additional advantage of being close to Arauca City, the largest and most prosperous town in the province. In that year, Prefect Benjamín Reyes Archila reported that the municipio had fifteen hundred inhabitants, with six hundred living in the urban center. The vecinos cultivated cacao, coffee, rice, and sugar cane, and the town was conveniently located for the missionaries to reach out to the Indians. Reyes Archila believed that the provincial capital in Tame would prosper if enough workers could be found and if the indolence and ignorance of the Indians could be overcome.[19] There was little time to test his assumption, for two years later the capital was transferred to Támara.

Organized as an Indian community as early as 1560, Támara had for a time been the capital of the Provincia de los Llanos in the eighteenth century. It was located on the Pauto River, with a temperate but humid climate due to the fog that strong winds pushed in from the Llanos during the rainy season. When Jorge Brisson visited there in February 1894, the town had been prospering since its designation as the capital of the intendancy. It had eight hundred inhabitants, with more arriving daily. New houses were being built, nearly a quarter of which had tile or zinc roofs. The town was exporting two thousand *cargas* (a measure equal to about six bushels) of coffee each year, and the stores were filled with goods from Bogotá and Ciudad Bolívar. There were carpenters, blacksmiths, tailors, and shoemakers. The Recoletos and the Hermanas de la Caridad had begun two schools, and from the only printing press in the Llanos came two periodicals, *La Gaceta Oficial de Casanare* and the religious newspaper *El Eco del Llano*. Despite these signs of progress, Brisson believed that Támara was not the best place for the capital, for the roads connecting it with Boyacá were often unpassable, its climate was too cold, and because it was perched on a ridge (*ensillada*), the town lacked room for expansion. He predicted that the capital would soon be moved to Orocué, which offered, along with a warmer climate, control of navigation on the Meta River.[20]

Llaneros were already lobbying Bogotá to transfer the headquarters of the intendancy to Orocué. On January 6, 1894, fifty-one vecinos of Nunchía petitioned President Núñez to approve a transfer. The capital, they argued, should have the best conditions for the health and comfort of people who visited it and should be able to confine prisoners securely. Támara, located in the piedmont, was too cold and unhealthy for inhabitants of the low-lying plains. Many times, these people preferred to renounce their rights rather than to risk the ill effect of a sudden change in climate that a trip to the capital entailed. Moreover, since Támara did not have a jail, prisoners were held in a small room that was almost in ruins. The town had scant space in which to expand, and it suffered from a water shortage that curtailed construction of new schools and public buildings. The vecinos tactfully concluded, "There are many other reasons we could cite, but we do not list them for fear of tiring you too much." [21]

Secretary of Government Luis María Holguín asked Intendant Elisio Medina for his opinion. On April 30, Medina responded that while in the future Orocué might be an appropriate capital, at the present time it lacked easy access to Boyacá and its hot climate was lethal for people who lived at higher elevations. Among the piedmont towns, Támara had the best location because it could get food and supplies from Boyacá without crossing dangerous rivers. It served the fertile section of the intendancy, which produced coffee and sugar cane and sent salt for the cattle in the Llanos. Contrary to what the Nunchía petitioners alleged, Támara had sufficient water and its climate did not pose any dangers. "Between the valley of Tolima or between the coast and Bogotá, for example, there is a difference of fifteen or eighteen degrees centigrade while between the Llanos and Támara there is only six degrees different. The inhabitants of the Llanos would benefit in health by coming occasionally to Támara." [22] In short, the prefect concluded, a change in capital would serve no good purpose and would even be prejudicial to public interests.

The capital stayed in Támara until 1895, when an executive decree transferred all government offices except the courts to Orocué. Writing a year later, Prefect Leonidas Norzagaray called the move a good one in view of Orocué's important military and commercial position on the Meta. He recommended that the judicial branch should likewise be relocated in Orocué for better administrative efficiency and the public interest. [23] The solution adopted near the end of 1896 was the creation of two judicial circuits for Casanare, one based in Támara and the other in Orocué, but due to the reluctance of qualified people to accept appointments in the Llanos, a judge did not arrive in Támara until March 1897 and not in Orocué until October. The fact that neither town had a jail can hardly have facilitated the dispensation of justice. [24]

The moving of the capital three times in six years inflamed local rivalries without solving the chronic administrative problems: lack of trained personnel and public buildings, inadequate sources of income, difficult communication with the interior, and the dearth of copies of law codes by which officials were supposed to rule. Moreover, in examining the policy of the Regeneration governments toward the Llanos, one cannot escape the conclusion that the attitude was one of indifference in comparison with the previous Liberal administrations. Neither Núñez; his *designado* Carlos Holguín, who exercised the presidency from 1888 to 1892; nor Miguel Antonio Caro, who served as the chief executive from 1892 to 1898, mentioned the national territories in their annual state of the union *mensajes*, and the organic decrees issued in 1893 and 1897 did not include coherent plans for colonization or economic development.[25] Caro's secretary of justice, Antonio María Rueda G., articulated well the prevailing lack of concern about the eastern frontier when he wrote in 1894 that Colombia should focus its limited resources on the development of the lower Magdalena, Panama, Guajira, and the Sierra Nevada. Rueda argued that the importance of the Llanos was strategic and international, rather than economic, and investment there was premature as long as Venezuela could strangle prosperity by its control of the Orinoco. He concluded, "The armed political convulsions, so frequent and terrible among our brothers on the other side of the Táchira River, are not a stimulus for the sacrifice that the colonization of the eastern region would demand from our strained treasury."[26]

Missions

If Regeneration governments were ambivalent about supporting national territories, they were steadfast in championing the evangelization of the Indians. Even before his election in 1880, Rafael Núñez called for religious toleration, reconciliation with the church, and mission revival. President José E. Otálora, in his message to Congress of February 3, 1884, condemned the abandonment of the 500,000 aborigines who lived in the remote jungles and plains. In his opinion, the only possible rationale for the territorial system, which had not justified the investment put into it, would have been the reestablishment of the missions.[27] Both the governors of Cundinamarca and Boyacá demanded missionaries after San Martín and Casanare had been reincorporated into their departments. By 1890, Secretary of Development Leonardo Canal could announce that the government was working closely with the clergy and the newly formed Society for the Propagation of the Faith and the Protection of Aborigines to promote missions and Indian agricultural colonies in the Llanos. On taking office in 1893 as the first intendant of Casanare, Elisio Medina urged the people "to help the missions and contribute to the civilization and development of this vast portion of Colombian soil, where now it is time for the rebirth of the hopes of the first missionaries and the shining sun of justice and restoration." [28]

Núñez began the reconciliation process during his first administration by negotiating with special papal envoy Monseñor Juan Bautista for the restoration of the religious orders. In 1882, the Dominicans, Recoletos, Franciscans, and other communities were reincorporated in Colombia. Congress repealed most of the anticlerical regulations enacted after the civil war of 1867–77, including the hated Law of Tuición. In addition to declaring Roman Catholicism as the national religion, the Constitution of 1886 stated that civil authorities could enforce respect for the church, public education was to be conducted in accord with Catholic teachings, and the church would be considered a juridical person in civil matters. In the Concordat of 1887, the government pledged to provide an annual subsidy to the church and compensation for losses suffered from the 1861 disamortization decree; it guaranteed its independence from civil interference and granted it substantial influence over education. This agreement, hailed by Catholics as a "model of mutual relations between church and state," initiated an era of expanding religious influence. [29]

In Article 25 of the concordat, the government assigned to the church in perpetuity an annual subsidy of 100,000 pesos for the support of dioceses, chapters, seminaries, missions, and other church activities. Law 150 of 1888 allotted 14,000 pesos from the budget for missions, of which 3,000 pesos was intended for Casanare, La Goajira, and Sierra Nevada. [30] By Law 72 of 1892, this annual subsidy was increased to 50,000 pesos, and the archdiocese of Bogotá and the newly created Tunja diocese contributed additional funds for this purpose. In 1893, Pope Leo XIII approved the creation of an apostolic vicariate (vicariato apostólico) for Casanare, based in Tame, and in 1897 an apostolic vicariate for San Martín, based in Villavicencio. [31] The actual labor of founding missions fell to three religious orders: the Recoletos and the Hermanas de la Caridad in Casanare, and the Salesians in San Martín.

Tomás C. Mosquera extinguished the Augustinian Recollects in 1861, fifteen years after their last missions in Casanare had disappeared. Their revival began in 1877, when the Superior General of the order in Spain reincorporated the Colombian chapter. In 1882, the handful of Recoletos still living in community at El Desierto de la Candelaria in Boyacá were recognized by Núñez, but real growth did not occur until the arrival of 1890 of Padre Fray Ezequiel Moreno and six other priests from Spain to start a novitiate at Candelaria. A year before, Juan Nepomuceno Rueda, bishop of Sebastópolis, had visited Casanare in the name of the bishop of Tunja, and had recommended that the newly reorganized Recoletos return to their former missions there. Secretary Canal supported this suggestion and made a formal request to Padre Moreno, who, as superior of the order, accepted the charge.[32]

In December 1890, Moreno, accompanied by Marcos Bartolomé, Manuel Fernández, and Isidoro Sáinz, left Tunja for their first reconnaissance of Casanare. They reached Orocué by the end of January. Bartolomé, Fernández, and Sáinz stayed there to begin working with the Indians, while Moreno continued his trip by passing through Trinidad, Moreno, San Salvador, Cravo Norte, Tame, Corozal, and San Lope before returning to Tunja in April 1891. Moreno was deeply impressed by the beauty of the Llanos. In a letter addressed to Padre Santiago Matute at Candelaria, dated January 25, 1891, he described his joy on seeing the plains for the first time as the missionaries crossed over the Cravo River. "What a beautiful panorama is presented by the view!" he wrote. "It is not possible to describe it; one must see it. In some directions one looks without seeing any object, and in others, trees and thickets that grow along the rivers and pools form the horizon. At times one feels as if he were on the high seas, seeing islands at a distance . . ." The Recoletos spent the night in a small hut near the river, and they had just begun their morning prayers when one of the *arrieros* (mule drivers) called to them that the sun was coming up. Moreno wrote:

I, who had heard from many people that sunrise in the Llanos is worthy of seeing, ended my prayer and left the hut to watch. In fact, as the *arriero* had said, the sun was enormous, lovely and beautiful. I have seen the sun rise over many oceans and I do not remember having seen it so large with the naked eye (*a la simple vista*). We prepared the altar immediately and celebrated a sung mass, the cantors being Brother Isidoro and Padres Manuel and Marcos. After elevating the host, they sang the Sacred Heart. The act was devout and moving. I at least confess that I felt myself moved when the thought came to me that in these immense plains no other sacrifice was being offered to God, and that the Lord would doubt-less receive it gladly.[33]

In seven other letters to Matute, Moreno wrote of his impressions of the Llanos and his enthusiasm for the mission. Subsequently published in Bogotá periodicals, his epistles stimulated much popular support for the efforts of the order.

In the meantime, Bartolomé, Fernández and Sáinz, from their base in Orocué, had started missions at Barrancopelado among the Guahibos, at Santa Elena among the Piapocos, and at San Juanito (also called Tagaste) among the Sálivas. In 1893, they were joined by Cayetano Fernández, Marcelino Ganuza, and Diácano Jiménez. The Recoletos made evangelization forays into Arauca and Tame. They compiled a dictionary and grammar of the Guahibo language. In 1894, Padre Moreno returned to Casanare as the first apostolic vicar, receiving a rousing reception in Támara. With customary energy, he organized his personnel as follows: two priests and a brother coadjutor in Arauca City; three priests and a brother in Orocué; one priest and a brother in Chámeza; and besides himself in Támara, three priests and a brother.

The Liberal revolt of 1895 disrupted the fledgling missions. In February, troops loyal to General Gabriel Vargas Santos seized Arauca City, and guerrilla chieftains soon took Orocué and Támara. The rebels harassed the Recoletos, extorted loans from them, and burned the church at Barrancopelado; but once the government had restored control in May, the work of the vicariate regained momentum. On April 12, 1896, Fray Nicolás Casas y Conde was named bishop of Casanare, replacing Ezequiel Moreno, who had been appointed bishop of Pasto. Casas y Conde came out to Támara in June, accompanied by several Hermanas de la Caridad who were to start schools for girls throughout the intendancy.[34] By 1898 there were sixteen Recoletos attending missions in Támara, Nunchía, Manare, Arauca, Chámeza, Orocué, and San Juanito; and the Hermanas de la Caridad had founded schools in Támara, Orocué, and San Juanito, and were preparing to open a new one in Manare. Citing these statistics, Marcelino Ganuza proudly concluded that "at no other time, not even during the period of the greatest prosperity and flourishing of the colonial missions, had Casanare been so well attended and fortunate in the spiritual realm as in those years preceding the revolution of 1899."[35]

In the Intendancy of San Martín, the Society of St. Francis de

Sales, popularly known as the Salesians, took charge of the missions in 1895. Founded by Dom Juan Bosco in Turin, Italy, in 1859, this religious congregation dedicated itself to the education of youth based upon reason, religion, and amibiability. Its method was to evaluate and employ all that was humanly useful in character formation—study, work, associative organization, and sports. The society grew so rapidly that after the death of its founder in 1888 there were 1,039 Salesians in fifty-seven foundations in Italy, Spain, France, England, Argentina, Uruguay, and Brazil. In 1889, Dom Bosco's successor, Miguel Rúa, signed a contract with the Colombian government, by which the society agreed to establish a school in Bogotá and begin a mission to the Indians.

The first group of nine Salesians reached Bogotá in February 1890. Led by Padre Evasio Rabagliati, they purchased the former convent of the nuns of Carmen and, by September, had opened the Colegio Salesiano de Leon XIII. Soon afterward, they began a home for vagrant boys and took over management of the Agua de Díos leper hospital in Tocaima, Cundinamarca. Shocked by the large number of lepers in Colombia and the lack of facilities to help them, Padre Rabagliati proposed to Vice President Caro in 1895 that the Salesians found a national leper hospital where all the afflicted could be brought together. Caro approved the project, and Rabagliati searched Santander and Boyacá for an appropriate site for the hospital. Then, in January 1895, while traveling with Dr. Gabriel Castañeda in the Llanos of San Martín, he discovered what appeared to be an ideal location between the Meta and Nare rivers. It was on this trip that Rabagliati became convinced that the Salesians should develop missions in the intendancy. He was still in Villavicencio when the outbreak of the revolution of 1895 postponed further action on either project.[36]

At that time, Fray José de Calasanz Vela, the Dominican who had explored the Ariari and Guaviare rivers in 1889, had been virtually the only missionary in the territory for thirty years. Carlos Cuervo Márquez, who met Vela in 1895, described him as "a worthy and valiant priest" who was the "center around which moves all the religious, political and social organization of the immense territory contained between the Meta and the Guaviare Rivers." He added, "Reverend Padre Vela is irreplaceable in the Llanos and what is to be regretted is that he does not have a young companion who he can educate in the employment of the sacred ministry of this special region."[37] Soon afterward, on December 6, 1895, Vela, on his way to Uribe, was thrown from his horse and killed instantly.[38] Receipt of this sad news further determined Archbishop Bernardo Herrera Restrepo to ask the Salesians to take over the missions in the intendancy.

Early in 1896, Rabagliati accepted responsibility for Villavicencio, San Martín, San Juan de Arama, Uribe, and Jiramena. On February 3, he left for Villavicencio accompanied by two priests, Leopoldo Ferraris and Ernesto Briata; an acolyte, Carlos Silva; and Antonio Pérez, brother coadjutor. Notwithstanding "the truly horrid state of the road," they arrived in Villavicencio in three days to find that the church was still in ruins, since a devastating fire of January 28, 1890, had leveled it and most of the town. The Salesians continued on to San Martín and decided to make their base there until the church could be rebuilt in Villavicencio. Rabagliati then returned to Bogotá for the start of Lent, while the others settled in to begin the mission.[39]

Toward the end of 1896, Padre Ernesto Briata sent a report on the missions to Dom Rúa, who now headed the order in Bogotá. Briata wrote of his recent pastoral visit to San Juan de Arama, Guejar, Uribe, and Villavicencio. He described the difficult travel conditions, the joyous welcome that the Llaneros gave the missionaries, and the somewhat bizarre churches he had encountered. For example, in San Juan de Arama, a town consisting of six *cabañas* (huts), the church built of wood and adobe with a thatched roof was like a "stable" :

The windows are rough and uneven holes; the altar looks like a shelf in an apothecary shop, with flasks and bottles for candle stick holders which at the same time they make known what their former contents was, they hold tallow candles. Three hideous statues occupy the upper part of the altar, so roughly carved that it is impossible to figure out the saints they represent. One lacks a nose, another hands and the other eyes; and they are so ridiculously dressed that they inspire everything except devotion. Nevertheless, these poor people venerate them and worship them with the same faith as if they might have been modelled with the chisel of Michaelangelo.[40]

In this humble church, Briata celebrated mass fifteen times, blessed two marriages, baptized fifteen children, heard confessions, and served holy communion to several people. He ended his report with a plea that he and Padre Leopoldo be given more help. If Dom Rúa could send four more Salesians to join them, then San Martín, Villavicencio, and Uribe each would have two priests.

In Bogotá, Dom Rúa pressed for authorization of the new leper hospital. Despite considerable support from authorities in Villavicencio to locate it in the Llanos, Congress instead chose a site on the

Pacific island of Coiba, four hundred kilometers southwest of Panama. Decree 145 of April 2, 1897, awarded the Salesians 60,000 pesos to start the hospital on Coiba and 140,000 pesos for developing existing facilities at Agua de Díos and two other places.[41] In the same year, Pope Leo XIII declared the Intendancy of San Martín an apostolic vicariate, and the Salesians expanded to three houses: Padre Briata, with coadjutor Jeremías Fernández and two acolytes, was based in Uribe; Padre Leopoldo Ferrari, coadjutor Antonio Pérez, and two acolytes remained in San Martín City, and Padre Tomás Tallone, brother Jesús Martínez, and acolyte Bernardo Romero lived in Villavicencio.

The letters from the Salesians written during this time, and reprinted by José Joaquín Ortega Torres in *La obra salesiana en Colombia: los primeros cincuenta años*, suggest that they were generally well received in the intendancy. One exception was Tomás Tallone, an Italian priest whose brusque, arrogant manner put him at odds with his Villavicencio congregation. The situation came to a head on Holy Saturday, April 10, 1898, when several vecinos asked and received permission from Tallone to take a saint from the still-uncompleted church and hold a procession in its honor. The priest did not participate in the ceremony, which ended normally enough with devotions held in a private home; but when the celebrants tried to return the saint to the church, they found the door locked on Tallone's orders. Not wishing to leave the image outside, they broke the door open "without force or scaling" (*sin fuerza ni escalamiento*) and placed it in its accustomed place. Tallone condemned this action as "desecration"; the vecinos maintained they had intended no disrespect and demanded that the priest be expelled. Archbishop Restrepo Herrera endorsed Tallone's decision and advised Intendant Elisio Silva to support him. By that time, however, Padre Rúa had ordered Tallone to return to Bogotá and the incident was closed.[42] In his annual *informe*, written just after the crisis, Silva wrote that the people sincerely wanted a new priest but only if he were Colombian. Father Tallone was virtuous and self-denying, but "he did not have well-developed the necessary traits to exercise his ministry in this region, where more than anything, it is indispensable to have good will and tact in dealing with the people."[43]

Navigation on the Meta River

Regeneration governments made little effort to improve communication and transportation to and within the Llanos, but they did score one major triumph—the inauguration of regular steamboat service on the Meta River between 1893 and 1899—an offshoot of the prolonged and rancorous negotiations with Venezuela over the international border. Far from ending the dispute, the announcement of the Spanish Laudo of 1891 merely took negotiations into a new stage. The Venezuelans were particularly unhappy with the queen regent's decision, believing that they should have won more territory in the Guajira Peninsula and the region drained by the Atabapo and Negro rivers (the present-day Colombian Guainía). General Joaquín Crespo, who seized power in 1892, resolved to pursue the issue vigorously, and thanks to the skill of his envoy, Dr. José Antonio Unda, Colombia, signed the Acta Declaración of 1894, in which both countries agreed to accept the Laudo of 1891 as a basis for future negotiations. In a second Treaty of Navigation and Commerce, signed on April 24, 1894, Colombia ceded to Venezuela the disputed territory in Guajira and Guainía, while Venezuela agreed to permit free navigation on the Orinoco, Atabapo, and Río Negro and to exempt all persons and cargo from imposts or duties. This treaty was never ratified, and in 1898 it was superseded by a new pact in which the two countries agreed to appoint mixed commissions to survey once again the entire border and to make recommendations for changes in the status quo established by the Laudo.[44] The upshot was that, until 1899, Venezuela allowed free trade along the Orinoco and Meta rivers, and the Colombians made the most of the opportunity.

In 1890, José Bonnet signed a contract with the Holguín government to begin steam navigation on the Meta and Orinoco. He pledged that his ship, *Libertador*, would make six round trips each year, traveling between Ciudad Bolívar and Orocué in the dry season and between Ciudad Bolívar and Cabuyaro in the rainy season. He agreed to build a warehouse in Orocué and to transport, at prices equivalent to those charged on the Magdalena, mail, missionaries, government officials, and soldiers. In exchange, the government promised Bonnet a three thousand-peso subsidy for each round trip and to press Venezuela to grant free trade along the river permanently. Finally, it awarded him thirty thousand hectares of baldíos along the Meta, on which he was to found three agricultural colonies, with each one consisting of at least ten families who would cultivate coffee, cacao, and other products suitable for export.[45]

Bonnet purchased the *Libertador* from the London firm of Yarrow and Company for 4,300 pounds sterling and had it outfitted in Trinidad by Charles Hardy, a Yarrow employee who also served as her captain. A miniature replica of the steamboats plying the Magdalena but without their cabins and other amenities, the *Libertador* was 24 feet wide and 124 feet long, including the rear paddle wheel. She had two decks eight and one-half feet apart, and on the passenger's deck a small restroom, a cabin shared by the captain and engineer, and another for the helmsman. The boiler on the bow and the eighty-four-horsepower engine on the stern near the wheel produced forty to one hundred fifty pounds of steam. The *Libertador's* average speed was nine miles an hour, but she could go as fast as twelve. With a crew of nineteen, she could carry one hundred and ten cattle and up to one hundred tons of cargo.[46]

Undoubtedly the most elegant ship to sail the Meta, the *Libertador* left Ciudad Bolívar on her maiden voyage on November 1, 1893. She carried cloth, hardware, wine, and foodstuffs on which no duty had been paid, a concession that provoked heated protests from local Venezuelan merchants. Her arrival on November 5 at 9:00 A.M. in Cabuyaro was greeted by "vivas" for the government and for José Bonnet. After she had anchored at the port of Barrigán on November 7, the intendant of San Martín, Habacuc Beltrán, telegraphed the minister of justice to ask him to inform Vice President Caro of the "general enthusiasm" that greeted her appearance, for "all see that this added to the measures taken by the government will redeem rich eastern region."[47] On the return voyage, the *Libertador* carried passengers, coffee, cacao, hides, and rubber, and took only five days to get to Ciudad Bolívar from Orocué.

Steam navigation quickened the economic pulse of the entire region. Travel time between Ciudad Bolívar and Orocué, which previously had taken sixty to eighty days depending on the season, now took from five to fifteen days.[48] Ramón Real, a Venezuelan merchant in Orocué, bought a smaller steamship, the *Boyacá*, and sailed it on the Pauto River, carrying coffee from Támara to Orocué and Ciudad Bolívar. In 1898, Casanare's intendant, Elisio Medina, asked the government to buy two steam launches from Yarrow and Company—one forty-five-feet long to patrol the Meta and Arauca rivers for the aduana. Congress supported his request in principal, but did not appropriate funds for the purchase.[49]

The chief beneficiary of the expanding commerce was Orocué, located on the left bank of the Meta, six hundred kilometers from Ciudad Bolívar. In 1894, Orocué had six hundred inhabitants and was showing signs of rapid growth. On his visit there, Jorge Brisson was impressed by the well-built houses on wide, clean streets illuminated by kerosene street lamps. José Bonnet, Ramón Real, and Franzius Aguilar had large commercial firms exporting coffee and cattle and importing foreign goods. Thanks to the aduana, trade was brisk, and in 1894 the exchange of commercial paper totalled 800,000 pesos, rivaling the volume of 1,050,000 pesos for that year in Arauca. The transfer of the intendancy capital to Orocué in 1896, and the opening of schools by the Recoletos and the Hermanas de la Caridad, further enhanced the town's status as "the sultan of the Llanura." As Brisson had predicted, Orocué's future seemed to be one of unlimited possibility.[50]

By 1898, however, dark clouds loomed on the horizon. Neither Venezuela nor Colombia had ratified the 1894 Treaty of Navigation and Commerce, and merchants in Ciudad Bolívar were demanding that Bonnet's shipments be stopped. Colombian rivals claimed that the government subsidy of three thousand pesos for each round trip of the *Libertador* gave the Frenchman an unfair advantage. The administrator of the aduana in Orocué charged that Bonnet varied his itinerary along the river and employed workers without government approval—both violations of his contract. In 1899, the secretary of finance cancelled the land grants awarded him in 1894 on the grounds that he had not fulfilled his obligations even though he had begun haciendas on two of the parcels and employed enough peons to raise coffee, sugar cane, and plátanos. In that same year, Cipriano Castro seized power in Caracas and banned free trade on the Meta and Orinoco. During the War of the Thousand Days, Colombian rebels commandeered the *Libertador* on the Apure River, and after the war was over, only its wreckage remained in Trinidad.[51] Bonnet was ruined, and it was not until the 1920s that there was another proposal to provide regular steamboat service on the Meta.[52]

The Railroad to the Meta

Bonnet's success in the mid-1890s encouraged other entrepreneurs to dream of connecting Bogotá to the Meta by locomotive, and ultimately to the Atlantic via steamships along the Orinoco. Tortuous mountain terrain, lack of capital and exports to pay the freight, and frequent political upheavals had failed to dampen the railroad fever that had engulfed Colombia since the 1870s. Work on eight different lines was under way by the time Núñez took office in 1886, with new projects proposed each year.[53] Given this climate of frenzied speculation, it is not surprising that many Llaneros believed that the railroad was the best way to break the geographic isolation of their region.

Juan de Díos Tavera put forward the first concrete plan in 1879, offering to build a railroad that would leave Bogotá for Duitama, with a western branch to Socorro and an eastern branch to the Unete River, a large tributary of the Meta. In a pamphlet entitled *Eco de Oriente*, Tavera explained that rail trade with the Meta River was the "first and most urgent necessity" for Boyacá and that Cundinamarca and Santander would also reap the benefits. He bolstered his argument with a letter written by a German engineer, J. Guillermo Bluhm, who expounded upon the development possibilities of the Llanos once railroads and steam navigation facilitated trade with the interior. The principal opponents to Tavera's scheme were individuals who believed that Santander and Cundinamarca would profit more from rail connections with the Magdalena, a position shared by the secretary of development who, within the space of fifty-five days in 1890, drew up contracts for three different lines to run from Bogotá to the Magdalena.[54]

The idea refused to die, however, and on August 30, 1892, *El Correo Nacional* of Bogotá reported that a high government official had received a letter from Caracas stating that a European firm was planning to build a railroad that would link the interior with the Meta. The newspaper backed the project, arguing that "opening the doors to our east by establishing steam navigation on the Meta, Arauca and Orinoco and a railroad to the great centers of consumption" would give easy, cheap communication with the exterior, broaden trade, and transform the national economy.[55] Eighty-two vecinos of Gachetá sent a petition to Congress supporting the proposed railroad and requesting that it be routed through their town so that it would open up trade with Bogotá as well as with the Meta.[56] In 1893, Secretary of Development J. M. Goenaga signed a contract with the London firm of Punchard, McTaggart, Louther, and Company to design plans for a railroad that would connect Bogotá to a port on the Meta navigable at all times to ships of three-foot draught. In due course, a team of English engineers arrived to examine three possible routes: the southern route, via Gachetá and the Guavio and Upía rivers; the Macanal route, via the Garagoa Valley to the municipio of Macanal in Boyacá; and the route through the Boquerón de Chipaque and along the Río Negro that would parallel the Bogotá–Villavicencio road. On completing their survey, the engineers recommended the third option through the Boquerón de Chipaque, estimating that it would require 190 kilometers of track to connect Bogotá with Puerto Banderas on the Humadea River (the present-day Metica River), a tributary of the Meta. The government appointed its own experts, Diódoro Sánchez and Manuel Ponce de León, to study this recommendation. When these engineers discovered several flaws—the most important being that the Humadea was not three-feet deep in the dry season—the plan was shelved and not revived again until 1916.[57]

Other Public Work Projects

The Regeneration governments made little progress on building highways. After Law 140 of 1888 called for improvements on the Bogotá–Villavicencio road and its extension to the Meta, vecinos of Gachetá and Chocontá sent separate petitions to Congress, each asking that the Camino del Meta be rerouted from its present course through Quetame and Cáqueza to pass through their town. Finding merit in their requests, Secretary Canal recommended in 1890 that the government build all three routes simultaneously so that they would converge on the same unidentified port on the Meta and "satisfy the interests of all the towns that would benefit from quick and easy communication with the eastern region."[58] This diplomatic solution was, of course, wholly impractical since the funds appropriated were insufficient to develop even one of the routes. In spite of the fact that many of its sections were unpassable in the rainy season, the Bogotá–Villavicencio road continued to be the principal highway to the Intendancy of San Martín.

In Decreto 392 of January 17, 1893, the government shifted responsibility for road construction to the intendants, so it was Elisio Medina who hired Jorge Brisson in February 1894 to survey Casanare and devise a coherent program of public works. Brisson, a civil engineer, traveled extensively throughout the intendancy before delivering his report to Medina on May 7. Navigation of the Meta topped his list of fundamental projects, and Brisson applauded the national subsidy to Bonnet's *Libertador* as a step in the right direction. Next, he advised completing the road between Lope and Cocuy and the Sarare Road, which, by linking Tame to towns in the department of Santander, would eliminate the necessity for ranchers in Casanare to use Venezuelan roads in order to reach the market in Cúcuta. Also on his list were constructing a road between Tame and Arauquita and a camino de herradura between Támara and the highlands; building a bridge over the Guanapalo River; and extending the telegraph line from Salina de Chita to Támara and Arauca. Brisson agreed with General Ortiz's suggestions that an aduana be located at a site called San Rafael, on the Meta, and that the capital of the intendancy be moved from Támara to Orocué. Brisson was optimistic about Casanare's future, but he warned that progress could only be achieved with help from Bogotá.

In summary, in our view, all light, all direction comes to us from the center, and we must look for our rudder for the boat that began to sail some months ago, and the rudder is in Bogotá. Therefore, telegraph and a good road to the interior; these are the first things that should preoccupy us in the area of public works.[59]

Within two years the capital was moved to Orocué and an aduana established at San Rafael, but as Brisson had feared, lack of money from Bogotá delayed improvements on roads and bridges. Congress did not appropriate funds, and local income was insufficient. Marco Antonio Torres, intendant in 1898, declared flatly that there was no money to repair the roads leading to Boyacá nor to construct new ones in Casanare. In San Martín, the situation was much the same. Intendant Antonio W. Robayo wrote in 1896 that the ten thousand pesos included in that year's budget were not nearly enough to pay for repairs on the Bogotá–Villavicencio road, let alone on the other five roads in the territory. He suggested that revenue from the liquor tax be used for road improvement, since opposition to the tax would be less if the public saw that the money was used for a good purpose; but Secretary of Government Antonio Roldán brusquely dismissed this proposal. Lack of money and public spirit on the part of the inhabitants of Casanare and San Martín was the reason little had been accomplished, he charged. Moreover, in the past much of the government's funds had been wasted on roads that were not useful, for it was obvious that during the summer no roads at all were needed on the Llanos, and when they were flooded in the winter travel could be accomplished by canoe. Given the reduced funds in the national treasury, Roldán was unwilling to increase financial support for roads in the intendancies.[60] From his attitude, it was clear that Brisson's "rudder" was not going to be found in Bogotá.

Economic Growth

In the Llanos as well as in the rest of Colombia, the expansion of agriculture, cattle ranching, and forest products during the 1890s conformed to the pattern set by the Liberals during the Federation Era. The cultivation of coffee, for example, which emerged during Regeneration as Colombia's leading export, expanded greatly in the 1860s in the Santanders, stimulated by improved transportation and a rise in world demand and prices. By the early 1870s, exports annually exceeded 100,000 sixty-kilo bags, and, along with sales of quinine, tobacco, and indigo, paid for the reforms undertaken during the first five years of the federation. After the Conservative revolt of 1876 disrupted the country, tobacco and indigo production never recovered. Quinine exports enjoyed a brief, final boom between 1877 and 1882, due to strong demand in the United States, Great Britain and France, but over the long haul, coffee proved to be the most durable commodity. Between 1887 and 1894, cultivation increased in Cundinamarca, Antioquia, and northern Tolima, as prices rose from 10.6 cents a pound to 18.8 cents a pound. Exports tripled, reaching 337,726 bags in 1894, to account for more than half the value of Colombian exports in that year. The collapse of this boom in 1896, sparked by a steep decline in world prices and demand, disrupted the ruling elite and contributed to the outbreak of the worst civil war in Colombian history, the War of the Thousand Days.[61]

Improved transportation via the Bogotá–Villavicencio road and the Meta River enabled the Llanos to participate in the coffee bonanza of the early 1870s. The entrepreneurs from Bogotá who settled in the Territory of San Martín had the capital and expertise to found estates devoted to export agriculture. Of the eight largest haciendas in 1875, El Buque, owned by Sergio Convers, and La Virginia, owned by Diego Suárez and Vicente LaFaurie, produced coffee, while Ocoa, owned by Narciso Reyes and Federico Silva, combined coffee with cacao, sugar cane, and cattle. With its 80,000 to 100,000 coffee trees, El Buque was said to be bigger than any coffee finca in Cundinamarca, and Ocoa, with 70,000 trees, was almost as large. All three estates had machines to hull, wash, and dry the beans, and El Buque had a hydraulic water wheel, windmill (*ventolina*), water tanks, and several workshops.[62] Thanks to the output of the three estates, in 1874 San Martín exported 90.4 metric tons of coffee valued at 20,642 pesos.

Production also rose in Casanare, where new technology was introduced by Venezuelans. Although there were some large fincas, most coffee was grown on small parcels, with production concentrated around Támara and Arauquita. Of the 251 metric tons exported by the territory in 1880, 140 metric tons came from Támara and 60 metric tons from Arauquita.[63]

In his perceptive study *Los Llanos: colonización y economía* (Bogotá, 1984), René de la Pedraja Tomán points out that coffee exports from the Llanos in the 1880s were noteworthy—not at the level exported by the Santanders and Cundinamarca, but considerably higher than the 86 metric tons produced annually in Antioquia. The boom ended in 1882–83, when after a sharp decline in prices, entrepreneurs in the Llanos failed to bounce back, while those in Antioquia were aided by the completion of a railroad to the Magdalena. By 1888 Antioquia was exporting 381 metric tons. By contrast, the haciendas in the Llanos remained isolated, too remote from the north coast to be competitive and dependent on Venezuelan goodwill for access to the Orinoco and the Atlantic. Locally, coffee remained important. It continued to be the chief export of Támara and Arauquita throughout the 1890s, and in Medina, a piedmont town in the Intendancy of San Martín, it touched off a violent struggle for land. On the large estates, however, Convers, Reyes, Silva, and Restrepo phased out coffee to rely on cacao, sugar cane, and cattle. In the end, De la Pedraja concludes, the coffee boom in the Llanos was "an isolated episode" that did not stimulate sustained development.[64]

Until the twentieth century agriculture played a secondary role to cattle raising in the Llanos. In Casanare, the number of cattle grew steadily from 61,166 in 1825 to 104,450 in 1856, and then slowed in the next twenty years, as the size of herds began to exceed the support limits of the natural grasses. To offset this difficulty, ranchers sent larger and larger numbers of cattle across the border to Apure for fattening before sending them on to Cúcuta via the San Camilo road through Venezuela. By 1874 a cattle census counted 109,240 head in the territory—35,000, or approximately one-third in the corregimiento of Arauca and another 20,000 around Orocué.[65]

The manner of operating a hato had changed little from the colonial era. The ganadero chose a site in the baldíos, where he built two or three small houses and corrals. He burned off the grass on some of the land so that tender new shoots could grow. Following a procedure known as "el pastoreo," he hired cowboys to drive the cattle to the new grass each day and to bring them back to the corral at night. After a month, the animals became accustomed to the unfenced pasture (*aquerenciar*) and could be allowed to graze unattended without fear of straying. The owner, who had to employ a large number of cowboys for the pastoreo phase, could get along once that was over, with his wife helping out as cook, and two or three workers besides himself to look after five hundred cattle, for if he hired a mayordomo, he would have to give him a share of the profits. About one-half of the animals would die during the first year, but in the second and third years this mortality would decline. After four years the cattle would begin to reproduce, and the owner could begin shipments of mature steers to markets in Venezuela or Cúcuta.[66]

Ranch size ranged from 200 to 25,000 cattle, with most herds averaging around 1,000. Daniel Delgado, the Recoleto missionary who traveled extensively through Casanare in 1908, listed by name 152 hatos in the territory, and he noticed a considerable difference in the life-styles of their owners. For example, at El Socorro, which was the largest hato in Arauca with more than 30,000 cattle, the Venezuelan proprietor, Victor Machado, had a beautiful house shaded by trees and adorned with rose bushes. "Every person employed by the hato, from the humble wranglers (*pica-cueros*) to the resplendent mayordomo, was efficiently used to complete the multiple tasks that a good operation of this sort demands." By contrast, at the neighboring hato of La Bendición, the house was "a sordid hut (*rancho*) of the most miserable type to be found here," even though the herd was almost as large as that at El Socorro. What draws one's attention in Casanare, wrote Delgado, is the number of people who live and die in misery and who, although they possess an annual income of eight to ten thousand pesos in gold, do not have any more comforts "than those a Guahibo can enjoy."[67]

At a time when ranchers in other parts of Colombia were experimenting with cross-breeding and artificial pastures, the only new technique adopted by ganaderos in Casanare was to try to provide salt for their animals in the belief that cattle would fatten more rapidly and be more docile. The difficulty was that the chief salinas—Cumaral, Upín, and Pajarito—did not produce sufficient quantities to satisfy the demand, and the government placed a high tax on their output while marine salt purchased from merchants in Ciudad Bolívar was subjected to Venezuelan duties and transportation costs.[68] With or without salt, the criollo cattle adapted to its hard life. Small, long-horned, slow-maturing and varicolored, the animals were hardy, resistant to heat and insects, fertile, and tolerant of mineral and nutrient deficiencies.[69] Because of the terrible roads and Casanare's distances from markets, they lost weight on long drives, but the practice of selling cattle by "el ojo" (by the head) minimized this disadvantage. As long as ranchers could use the Venezuelan road to get to Cúcuta or could send their cattle down the Orinoco, they could compete with ranchers in the highlands or on the coast. When the Venezuelans placed a heavy tax on Colombian exports, as they did in 1904 and again in 1909, casanareños preferred to sacrifice their cattle and salvage what they could from the sale of their hides.[70]

Ranchers in the Intendancy of San Martín were more innovative. Men like Emiliano Restrepo, Sergio Convers, Narciso Reyes, and Nicolás Castro experimented with cross-breeding and improved pasture. They regularly gave salt to their animals and urged their neighbors to do the same, though without much success. In 1874, when there were 40,305 cattle in the territory, the largest herds belonged to the Compañía de Colombia and Emiliano Restrepo. Ten years later, Alfred Hettner estimated that there might be as many as 120,000 cattle in the region. Records from 1892 show that, on the average, 45 cattle from Villavicencio were sacrificed each month in Cundinamarca, for a total of 549 during the year.[71] Although the precarious road to Bogotá remained a liability, cattle production in the intendancy was steady until the War of the Thousand Days.

Rubber, rather than coffee, was the export from the Llanos most closely associated with the Regeneration era, for after 1890 it replaced quinine as the principal product extracted from the forests of San Martín and Casanare. In the 1850s, world demand for quinine had triggered the exploitation of forests about Medina and soon spread from the Upía to the Guayabero rivers. By 1870 three companies dominated the extraction: the Compañía de San Martín in the north, from the Upía to the Humadea; the Compañía de Sumapaz in the center, from the Humadea to the Ariari; and the Compañía de Colombia in the south, from the Ariari to the Guayabero. There were also hundreds of colonos who invaded lands claimed by the companies to collect bark independently. In 1884, the collapse in world demand, due to competition from Ceylon and India, abruptly ended the quinine boom in the Llanos and forced companies and colonos alike to find a new product they could harvest from the forest with profit. As soon as they realized that rubber could play this role, they approached its extraction with the same mentality they had adopted with quinine—that the forest was an inexhaustible resource to be exploited according to the dictates of the market and in the most barbarous manner possible.[72]

During its heyday, between 1890 and 1913, the rubber boom was one of the most spectacular stages in the development of South American primary resources. The trees (*Hevea brasiliensis*) grew abundantly in the Amazon Basin, and from the early nineteenth century Brazil had exported small quantities of rubber. The discovery of the vulcanization process in 1845 and the invention of the pneumatic tire in 1890 sparked a new and seemingly insatiable demand for latex. For the next twenty years Brazil produced over 80 percent of the world's rubber, but the boom had an impact on all of the countries with Amazon territory. Speculators from Peru, Bolivia, and Colombia searched for rubber trees along the tributaries of the great river and staked out gargantuan tracts of land. They enticed laborers to come to these remote areas to collect the rubber or else they enslaved the Indians, forcing them to work in death-camplike conditions. A war was fought between Brazil and Bolivia over rubber-rich Acre (1899–1902), and elsewhere thousands of lives were lost as men sold their souls to harvest the "white gold." Yet the boom was destined to end almost as quickly as it had begun, due to competition from British rubber plantations in Malaysia that began production in 1900. Thanks to efficient management and abundant, cheap labor, Asian exports outstripped the South American supply in 1913, and the price of rubber fell from $4.42 per kilogram in 1910 to $1.40 in 1913 and $0.30 in 1921. Because of the unusual demand for rubber during World War I, production continued along some Amazon tributaries for a few more years, but well before 1930 exports from Peru, Bolivia, Colombia, and Brazil had fallen to a negligible quantity.[73]

In Colombia, the exploitation of rubber began around Cartagena in the 1860s and spread to Buenaventura and Tumaco on the Pacific Coast in the following decade. Speculators also invaded the forests of the middle Magdalena, but the trees there were not abundant and the rubber was soon exhausted. The frontier moved on to southern Tolima and reached the Llanos and Cáqueta in the late 1880s. By the beginning of the twentieth century it centered along the Putumayo River, with extensive operations in present-day Amazonas, Guainía, and Vaupés. Despite regional shifts, Colombian exports were fairly constant between 1870 and 1915, fluctuating between 300 and 600 tons annually. By contrast, Brazil exported during its peak years, between 1901 and 1912, an average of 34,500 tons a year.[74]

Exploration for rubber in the Llanos occurred first in the Territory of San Martín. As early as 1870 Hilario Ibarra extracted high-quality latex from rubber trees near Villavicencio, but his enterprise failed because the trees did not give enough sap to make the exercise profitable. Emiliano Restrepo, writing in 1875, postulated that the forests lying farther to the east and south of Villavicencio might prove more lucrative since they received more rain.[75] The Compañía de Colombia, owner of some sixty thousand hectares around Uribe, began producing rubber rather than cinchona in the 1880s. In December 1886, the original founders—Francisco Antonio Uribe, Bernardo Herrera, and Nazario Lorenzana y Montoya—dissolved the company, and after the death of his father on June 4, 1887, Carlos Uribe divided the assets between two new partnerships. The Compañía Herrera y Uribe took two-thirds of the original holdings and the Compañía Lorenzana y Montoya got the rest.[76] Both firms continued to produce rubber from their lands. In 1886, Carlos Uribe, along with two other men, received an additional fifteen thousand acres of national forest in the district of Uribe. The following year, the *Gaceta de Cundinamarca* announced that three grants each of ten thousand hectares had been awarded to three sets of partners in the municipio of Villavicencio. All grants were awarded for five years, for the purpose of extracting rubber and *copaiba* (balsam). The recipients could only work five thousand hectares at a time, and were required to take care of the trees in order to preserve their abundance and quality.[77]

Table 5 lists the public land grants awarded in the Intendancy of San Martín between 1887 and 1899, according to the official records in the Ministry of Industry. In those twelve years, there were fifty-eight grants to forty-five individuals, totalling 149,022.6 hectares. Over one-third of this land, or 58,649 hectares, was in Medina, followed by 29,024.5 in Villavicencio, 25,948.7 in San Martín, and 20,488.3 in Uribe. Cabuyaro lagged behind with 13,711.5 hectares, and there was a single grant in Cumaral for 1,200 hectares. In contrast to the period between 1860 and 1885, no grant larger than 5,000 hectares was awarded; however, José Bonnet received ten separate grants that totalled 43,867.6 hectares in Medina, Villavicencio, and Cabuyaro, and Sergio Convers added three new grants of 7,396 hectares to his already considerable holdings. There were six awards of 5,000 hectares; seventeen between 3,000 to 4,999 (of which eight went to Bonnet); and sixteen from 1,000 to 3,999 (including one to Bonnet). At the other end of the scale, there were eleven grants under 499 hectares and

Table 5
Public Land Grants in the Intendancy of San Martín, 1887–99

Grantee	Municipio	Year	Hectares
Leopoldo Reyes	Uribe	1887	346.2
Nicolás Munar	Uribe	1890	46
Daniel Cáceres	Uribe	1890	74
Pedro Tavera	Uribe	1890	66.8
Rafael González	Uribe	1890	88
Enrique Chacón	Uribe	1890	76.4
Felisa Calderón	Uribe	1890	36
Francisco Losada R.	Uribe	1890	2,000
Rufino Gutiérrez	Uribe	1891	5,000
Julio Fernández	Uribe	1891	4,999
Manuel J. Dueñas	Uribe	1891	5,000
Jesús Raldán	Medina	1891	98
Luis A. Von-Kokler	Medina	1892	5,000
Benito Rondón	San Martín	1892	2,980
Secundino Herrera	Uribe	1892	215.3
Isidro Ochoa	Uribe	1892	166.7
Segundo del Basto	Uribe	1892	138.5
Antonio Lobell, et al.	Uribe	1895	2,235.4
Luis Nariño	Medina	1895	4,207
Carlos Piedrahita	Medina	1896	4,022
Clímaco Manrique	Villavicencio	1896	1,596
Sergio Convers	Villavicencio	1896	4,400
Lorenzo Codazzi	Villavicencio	1896	4,692
Francisco Piedrahita	Medina	1896	971
José Bonnet	Medina	1896	4,970
Valentín Hernández	San Martín	1896	2,781.3
Pedro N. Hernández	San Martín	1896	5,000
Telésforo Barrera	San Martín	1896	5,000
Pedro Defrancisco	Villavicencio	1896	2,286
Pablo Cabo	San Martín	1896	2,000
José Bonnet	Villavicencio	1896	4,860.8
Mauricio Hernández	Villavicencio	1897	996.2
José Bonnet	Medina	1897	2,530
Sergio Convers	Villavicencio	1897	740
Sergio Convers	Villavicencio	1897	2,256
Emiliano Restrepo	San Martín	1897	2,000
Benigno Enciso	San Martín	1897	5,000
José Bonnet	Villavicencio	1897	2,938
Higinio Bunch	Medina	1897	1,196
José Bonnet	Cabuyaro	1897	4,134.5
Lorenzo Cuéllar y otro	Medina	1897	4,902.9

Table 5
Continued

Grantee	Municipio	Year	Hectares
Matilde Rojas de Castro	Cumaral	1897	1,200
José Bonnet	Cabuyaro	1897	4,788.5
Julio Montoya	Medina	1898	4,989.9
Mario E. Cubillos	San Martín	1898	513.4
Edmundo Cervantes	Medina	1898	3,118.1
Juan de Dios Ortiz	Medina	1898	987.9
Paulina Rosas	Villavicencio	1898	2,100
Francisco Acebedo L.	Medina	1898	4,788
Francisco Piñeros	Villavicencio	1898	621.7
Anacleto López	San Martín	1899	674
Hortensia Martín	Medina	1899	41.3
Juan de Dios Ortiz y otro	Medina	1899	1,970.3
José Bonnet	Medina	1899	4,976.2
José Bonnet	Medina	1899	4,945.2
José Bonnet	Medina	1899	4,935.8
José Bonnet	Cabuyaro	1899	4,788.5
Julio Vergara	Villavicencio	1899	1,537.8
Total			149,022.4

Total Hectares by Municipios

Municipio	Total Grants	Total Hectares
Cabuyaro	4	13,711.4
Cumaral	1	1,200
Medina	18	58,649.6
San Martín	9	25,949.7
Uribe	15	20,488.5
Villavicencio	12	29,024.5
Total	18	149,022.4

Grantees with Largest Holdings

Grantee	Total Grants	Total Hectares
José Bonnet	10	43,867.2
Sergio Convers	3	7,396

Table 5
Continued

Distribution of Grants by Size	
Total Grants	Hectares
11	From 1 to 499
8	From 500 to 999
16	From 1,000 to 3,999
17	From 3,000 to 4,999
6	5,000

Source: "List of Public Land Grants, 1828–1931," *Memoria del Ministro de Industrias*, 1931, vol. 5, 327–28.

eight between 500 to 999.[78] The records do not indicate the use that the land was to be put to. While some of the grants over 1,000 hectares might have been for cattle, it is a safe assumption that the majority of the recipients intended to collect rubber, with the action centered especially in Uribe, Medina, and Villavicencio. Similar statistics are not available for Casanare, but de la Pedraja Tomán states that by 1890 merchants in Orocué controlled the operations being conducted in Vaupés and Guainía, collecting the balls of latex in their warehouses and shipping them down the Meta and Orinoco to Ciudad Bolívar.[79] In both regions, scores of independent colonos searched for rubber in the baldíos without attempting to apply for ownership.

The Colombian government authorized rubber extraction on the condition that the trees not be destroyed, but companies and independent collectors routinely ignored this prohibition and felled the trees rather than tapping their sap in the Brazilian fashion. In 1887, Lisandro A. Moreno complained to the secretary of finance that the Compañía Herrera y Uribe was violating the terms of its grant by cutting down trees in the *aldea* of Uribe. The local authorities did nothing to stop the "numerous outrages," and the inhabitants of the isolated town acted "like savages even though they belong to social classes of some consideration."[80] Moreno was especially concerned that the loss of trees would leave many of the collectors without work, but the government was powerless to halt the practice. On July 18, 1898, Intendant Eliseo Silva assured the secretary of finance that he would "immediately give the order to the authorities of my jurisdiction so that they will stop the felling of the rubber tree forests," but his orders were ignored as easily as those of the local officials in Uribe.[81]

By that time, some attempt was being made to grow rubber on plantations. Enrique Cortés and Ismael José Romero published manuals explaining cultivation techniques and describing ways to counteract the more destructive forms of rubber collection.[82] The Compañía Herrera y Uribe began a plantation, La Mariana, with fifty thousand trees along the Guayabero River, but it was destroyed during the War of the Thousand Days. In 1910, Luis Convers Codazzi and Enrique Mistral started La Mistralia with twenty-five thousand trees near Villavicencio. They hired guards to keep the trees from being cut down by colonos, but they had to abandon the effort when low-cost Malaysian rubber drove prices down.[83]

Uribe

The growth of the town of Uribe was one of the most tangible consequences of the quinine and rubber booms. Founded by the Compañía de Colombia in the late 1860s, it served as the eastern terminus of its road to the Llanos from Colombia, Tolima. Company officials ran the town, which was populated by workers brought in from Tolima. Uribe's isolation enhanced their control. Although it was possible to get to Bogotá 350 kilometers away in eight days, by traveling first to Colombia and then north to the capital, direct communication with San Martín City, the municipio in which Uribe was located, was another matter, requiring a grueling trip through forests, plains, and over nearly one hundred rivers, including the treacherous Ariari. When Uribe was elevated to the status of corregimiento in 1880, the company paid the salary of the corregidor, notwithstanding the fact that his most important duty was to mediate disputes between it and the colonos. Under Decreto 392 of January 17, 1893, Uribe became a municipio. Two years later, the province of Uribe was created to be administered by a prefect and consisting of the municipio of Uribe and the corregimiento of San Juan de Arama, a small settlement halfway between Uribe and San Martín.

Uribe's remote location made it a favorite destination for criminals from the interior. In 1894, Alcalde Emilio Salazar told the secretary of justice that he was besieged with requests from Tolima authorities to return fugitives who were living in Uribe under assumed names, but without money and police to assist him there was little he could do.[84] In 1898, Intendant Eliseo Silva suggested that the alcalde's salary be raised from sixty to one hundred pesos a month in order to attract a reliable person who could keep order. "Most of the people [in Uribe] are simple and good and live off their work," Silva wrote, "but it is not unusual to find as well wayward people of bad character (*personas díscolas y de mal carácter*) who for the most trivial reasons get into fights with incalculable results. When to this situation is added the fact that Uribe is very far away from Villavicencio, the need for an adequately-paid alcalde is self-evident."[85]

In 1898, Uribe Province had three thousand inhabitants dedicated to cattle, agriculture, rubber collecting, and commerce. It contained 16,000 cattle, artificial pasture for 4,000 *novillos* (young bulls), 250,000 cacao trees, 300,000 coffee trees, and hundreds of hectares of sugar cane, plátano, yuca, and tobacco. Within the town, the Compañía Herrera y Uribe had built a church, priest's house, and jail, while the Compañía Lorenzana y Montoya paid for two schools. The Salesian missionaries, who first visited Uribe in 1897 and came to stay the following year, soon learned that the influence of the former company was pervasive. At the invitation of the Compañía Herrera y Uribe, Padre Ernesto Briata visited its three largest haciendas early in 1898. The first one, called Santander, was twenty-nine kilometers from Uribe and employed more than one hundred workers to grow cacao, sugar cane, and coffee. Four hours away was the rubber plantation La Mariana, which also had cacao, sugar cane, and corn fields. The third estate, described by Briata as a "villa rica" (rich country-house), had been built by the sons of Bernardo Herrera, "the young Herrera Umañas," and was named La Ilusión. It was primarily a cattle ranch, but there was also sugar cane, corn, tobacco, and eighty thousand cacao plants. Briata celebrated mass in "a place decently prepared" at La Ilusión, administered fifteen baptisms, and preached several sermons. He wrote Don Rúa that he was "exquisitely treated" by Don Juan Manuel Herrera, who was a nephew of Bernardo Herrera Restrepo, archbishop of Bogotá.[86] Padre Rodolfo Fierro, who directed the schools in Uribe, noted in his diary that Don Alberto Plot, the top company official in the town, was "an intelligent and powerful man who exercises a true *cacicazgo* (dictatorship) over all these regions." Plot was a French doctor and chemist who believed that bad nutrition was the cause of most diseases in the Llanos. For that reason, he supplied missionaries with coffee, milk, eggs, chickens, "passable" beef, port, and flour which Fierro used to make Italian specialties such as *tallarines al burro* and *all'uovo*.[87] Briata and Fierro agreed that without the continued support of the Compañía Herrera y Uribe, the town would cease to exist, a view shared by Intendant Silva. In his informe of 1898, Silva described the founders of the company as "tireless workers, true fighters for the progress of our country," taking their commercial enterprises to unexplored places, undaunted by dangers, defying sickness and privation of all kinds, subduing with courage worthy of imitation every kind of obstacle, and struggling hand to hand with nature in order to realize their goal of converting the wilderness into a rich and flourishing region, in the midst of which they had raised "a town as important for its commerce as it is congenial because of the culture of its inhabitants." If all we Colombians were men of such aspirations, he concluded, and if we followed their admirable example, "the fate of our beloved country would doubtlessly be very different."[88]

Conflicts over Land

Whether land was wanted to grow coffee, raise cattle, or extract rubber, bitter conflicts arose between colonos and entrepreneurs. Such conflicts were especially intense in Medina, a piedmont town north of Villavicencio on the Humea River. Alonso Ronquillo, a Dominican missionary, founded Medina in 1670, but its population disappeared by the beginning of the nineteenth century. Colonos from Cundinamarca rediscovered the site in the 1850s, attracted by the fertile lands and virgin forests. Taking advantage of a road from Gachetá, newly refurbished by Pastor Ospina in 1850, they moved into the area, staking out claims in the baldíos and cultivating cacao, coffee, sugar cane, rice, corn, plátanos, and yuca. Illiterate and isolated from Bogotá and Villavicencio, they were unaware of the procedures to gain legal possession of their land. Without the help of surveyors, they relied on natural landmarks for boundaries, such as trees, rocks in rivers, and caños. By 1871 Medina had a population of 1,796, and was organized as a corregimiento in the Territory of San Martín.[89]

Although Celestino Castro, Francisco Piedrahita, Mariano Tanco, José Alonso, and Aparicio Escobar acquired legally large grants of land in Medina in 1872 and 1873, entrepreneurial interest in the town intensified in the 1890s, stimulated by higher prices for coffee, the rubber boom, and prospects of improved transportation on the Meta, of which the Humea was a tributary. The applications for land made by entrepreneurs to the Ministry of Finance threatened the eviction of colonos who had been working on parts of the disputed territory for several decades. For example, in 1894, when Felipe Ruiz Quintero wanted 3,476 hectares, Intendant Jorge Novoa L. urged the secretary to deny his request. He pointed out that unlike Villavicencio, Medina was flourishing agriculturally because it had baldíos that were attractive to colonos. The lands Ruiz Quintero had his eye on were fertile, largely cultivated, and very close to the town. Not only would such an award harm those who had already settled there, but it would discourage others from coming to the territory. Rather than making a grant to a private individual, Novoa recommended that the government reserve land exclusively for colonization within a radius of three leagues around the town. Within five years the government, by charging rent on the parcels, could recover the sum it might have gained through adjudication.[90]

Ruiz Quintero did not get his land, but the records show that eleven of thirteen individuals who did acquire legal grants in Medina between 1891 and 1899 received 1,000 hectares or more, with the inevitable displacement of colonos. For example, in 1895 local authorities objected to the award of 2,500 hectares to Juan de Dios Ortiz because it usurped land cultivated by an "infinity of colonos and new settlers" on the river who were violently dispossessed. In another case, in 1896, the 971 hectares for which Francisco Piedrahita applied included the houses and fields of over sixty colonos who had been living there for twenty years. After Piedrahita was granted the land, he evicted many of these colonos and left others with reduced plots.[91] In spite of Law 61 of 1874 and Law 48 of 1882, which were intended to reinforce the rights of small farmers, only two land grants of less than 100 hectares were made in Medina in the 1890s—98 hectares to Jesús Raldán in 1891 and 41 hectares to Hortensia Martín in 1899.

It was perhaps poetic justice that the ruthlessness of the entrepreneurs did not always pay off in material gain. In 1898, Intendant Silva observed that although there had been an active movement to acquire baldíos in Medina since 1893 and fifteen fundaciónes had been started, the results did not correspond to "the sacrifices made by the honorable gentlemen who, scorning the comforts of life in the capital of the republic, have come to the virgin forests." Silva continued:

They invested money hoping to make a fortune. Just when they began to see the fruit of their work represented by coffee of good quality and other important products, the price of coffee began to fall, and all this money and work went up in smoke. If we add to this that some of these men are dedicated to *gatomaquía*—fabricating lawsuits against the authorities and peaceful citizens, so that the town is divided into two irreconcilable bands—all are Liberals—one easily understands that real estate is a casualty list of incredible proportions.[92]

Colonos invaded the forests near the salinas of Cumaral and Upín. In 1891, the mine's administrator, Juan Villegas, urged the secretary of finance to prohibit adjudication of nearby land and reserve it instead for the foundation of a colony. In such a colony, squatters could be permitted to have small plots without fear of destroying the forest "because firewood can be cut from the forest that remains on the Cordillera for some time." The colony would be a refuge for poor colonos tyrannized by entrepreneurs and would grow to become a town larger than Villavicencio because of the fertile land and good climate. There is no record of the secretary's reply, but a communication from Villegas's successor in 1898 indicated that colonos were continuing to fell trees near the Salina, a phenomenon observed as well by the administrator of the Salinas of Chita and Muneque in Casanare.[93]

The municipal council of Uribe also tried to keep land needed for the common good from falling into private hands. In 1889 it urged that Celestino González's petition for thirty hectares of baldíos be denied because the land in question contained the principal sources of the town's potable water and wood for fuel and construction. The council added that González was a front man for Julio Cáceres, who, "it was publicly known," had already acquired several parcels of land in violation of the law. As in the Medina and Cumaral cases, the council urged that land near the town be reserved for small plots as a way of attracting the poor people "who immigrate from all the Colombian departments to settle in Uribe."[94]

In Villavicencio, the entrepreneurs continued their unsuccessful struggle to liquidate the Community of Apiay. Ever since Emiliano Restrepo had first proposed that the community be suppressed and the area divided into clearly defined individual holdings, there had been intense speculation in buying and selling titles. In 1896, Sergio Convers began a partition suit to dissolve the community, but "there were many comuneros with many ambitions." The commotion was great, the laws inflexible, and the effort failed.[95] The comuneros became convinced that the division could not be completed. By 1899 their titles were depreciating, and they continued to lose value after the War of One Thousand Days, when more and more colonos invaded the land claimed by the community. The situation remained hopelessly deadlocked until 1918, when Convers went to court again to try to dissolve the community.

In Casanare, the paucity of official records concerning land adjudications support the assertion of General Rafael Ortiz that property ownership was not legally constituted. Most people claiming to be owners did not have titles and grazed their cattle on the baldíos. Their tendency was to claim "ownership" over large tracts so that a small number of "proprietors" controlled the area known as *sabana cautiva*, or grassland, which had been wrested from the Indians. Newcomers were forced to invade territory still held by Indians, provoking bloody reprisals. Conflicts between natives and ranchers increased in the 1880s around Orocué, where the Sálivas, occasionally backed by Venezuelans, stubbornly resisted efforts to dislodge them by attacking hatos and commerce on the Meta.[96] Other disputes arose when individuals who had received land under the provisions of Law 61 of 1874 evicted squatters by extending their claims over a much larger area. In 1893, Secretary Canal denounced this practice, citing a case in Casanare where a man granted 120 hectares had somehow gained title to 12,000 as well as another example in which an individual who had received 900 hectares in Boyacá also seized 5,000 hectares in Cundinamarca. Canal recommended that the procurator general should review all land grants in the Llanos to determine which were legitimate and which had been falsely obtained, but such a review was not carried out. In 1898, Intendant Marco Antonio Torres was still asking the secretary of finance to send him a list of the adjudications of baldíos in Casanare so he would know precisely who were legitimate landowners.[97]

Political Unrest

Conflicts over land, widespread and in many forms, exacerbated the climate of political unrest that prevailed in the intendancies in the 1890s. Decree 392 of January 17, 1893, stated that the nation should provide police to keep order in each territory, but due to lack of funding, the intendants found themselves without sufficient men and weapons to capture outlaws, settle local feuds, and put down rebellion. The need to station soldiers in Villavicencio and Támara was a recurrent theme in the correspondence between the intendants and Bogotá.

Uribe was not the only municipio in the Llanos infested with criminals. In June 1893, Comisario Antonio Rincón V. sent an urgent telegram to the secretary of justice, stating: "Criminals hiding in the town of San Martín are endangering the lives of peaceful families of the town. They flee to the *montaña* (forest) when force is shown and return when it is withdrawn."[98] In April 1894, Intendant Jorge Novoa telegraphed: "Insist absolutely on the necessity of sending at least ten or fifteen soldiers here, since there is no police. There are many wanted criminals and the authorities have no means to apprehend them."[99] This request was reiterated by Pioquinto Márquez C., who, as acting intendant, telegraphed in November 1894:

Last night Joaquín Rojas was murdered. They called me at one o'clock in the morning, and although I was completely alone, I went to help. Last night there was trouble between employees of the liquor monopoly and revolver shots. I am looking for the criminals . . . you understand that in our country and even in those more civilized, bayonettes are the basis of every stable system.[100]

In Casanare, San Pedro de Upía and Arauca City were especially turbulent. On July 8, 1893, Juan de Jesús González killed Erasmo Machado in San Pedro. The victim's brother demanded justice, and Intendant Elisio Medina sent out a *comisión* (posse) to catch the murderer, but the fugitive got away. On August 26, the alcalde of Cabuyaro reported that a gang of outlaws from San Pedro was attacking families and hatos in his district. Finally, in October, police sent from Orocué and Chámeza apprehended González and cleared the region between these two towns and the banks of the Meta, although some rustlers hidden on the right bank of the Upía remained at large.[101] In Arauca City, criminals and Venezuelan exiles found the customs revenue too good a temptation to pass up. Typical of many incidents was the prefect's report on November 21, 1893, that he had foiled a plot to attack the aduana and take its cash and weapons. Six conspirators, including an exiled Venezuelan general, had been captured, but most had escaped across the border.[102] In 1898, Intendant Torres again requested soldiers. He wrote that Arauca, because of its border location, was subject to the ebb and flow of political disturbances in Venezuela as well as in Colombia. "Short periods of bonanza and moral progress alternate there with rough attacks led by audacious men followed by outlaws and unemployed who at any moment were willing to risk all for all (*jugar el todo por el todo*)." A small police force in Arauca City had managed to keep order in spite of frequent rumors of local revolts prompted by events in Venezuela. So far, he concluded, these alarms had not posed an international threat, but it would be well advised to station soldiers in Orocué, where they could preserve order throughout the intendancy.[103]

While most Llanos towns did not have to contend with would-be Venezuelan revolutionaries, they were beset by political feuds born of traditional party hatreds. In Villavicencio, the murder of Antonio Rojas on December 6, 1898, brought a flurry of memorials written to the secretary of government by vecinos demanding retribution. Intendant Pantaleón Cortés S. explained that he had foreseen such an event coming because for some time the townspeople had been divided into two opposing groups—one of them Conservative, headed by the Reinas clan, and the other Liberal, led by several individuals including the recently slain Rojas. Cortés continued:

The Reinas are men of bad character and extremely aggressive as was Antonio Rojas and are wanted for several crimes. Two of them are already in jail, one is gravely wounded, and another, Oliverio Reina is a fugitive because less than two months ago, he killed a man in the streets of the town, and it has not been possible to arrest him even though he comes to town frequently. The citizens who ask you [the secretary of government] to organize a *comisión* to apprehend Reina are personal enemies of the fugitive and to accede to their request would be to condemn to death the criminal and perhaps some of those in the *comisión*. I have ordered the alcalde who is very competent and supportive of the government to arrest Oliverio Reina, but he explained that with the police the way they are today it would be very difficult to bring him to prison, and the reason is obvious; in small towns all the inhabitants are tied to each other by friendship or kinship (*parentezco*) and belong to one of the two militant bands, and no one wants to antagonize the other or in this case to become agents of the police in this place so that one cannot rely upon them. For these reasons I again ask you to send a squadron of national police. They would arrive free of previous commitments (*compromisos*), and for this reason they would provide an important service.[104]

The documents do not show whether police were sent or if Reina was ever captured, but the situation of two opposing camps splitting a town was not unusual. One of the longest running feuds developed in Medina, where personal hatreds kept the town in continuous turmoil in spite of the fact that all of the vecinos were Liberals. In November 1894, Intendant Tobías Hernández C. investigated complaints that the prefect, Heliodoro Ruiz, and his secretary, Guillermo Chaves, were harassing the priest, Higenio Bunch; the alcalde, Marco Aurelio Quimbay; and the personero, José Tomás Cola. Resolution of the matter was delayed by the outbreak in January of the Liberal revolt of 1895. Moisés Camacho, who became intendant at the close of the war, went to Medina in June 1895 to look into the matter because "there was no authority in that place." In his report written in October, he recalled, "Naturally my first concern was to find out if there were any friends of the Government there and put them in positions of authority. It is sad to say that I did not find there any person who had not taken part directly or indirectly in the *pronunciamiento* that took place in that town." Since Padre Higenio Bunch threatened to leave Medina unless Camacho could name an alcalde who would absolutely guarantee that he could carry out his ministry without interference, he decided to appoint Señor Cola, the former personero. Camacho reviewed a "centimeter of complaints" written to him by members of the opposing groups and concluded that the root of the problem lay in "personal rivalries." "If this office were to pay attention to the unceasing number of denouncements and complaints that arrive from this unfortunate town with every mail and with each one of the persons who come to complain, the only thing the intendant would be doing would be to write indictments (*sumarios*) and the office would have to be moved to Medina in order to carry them out." The long-term solution, Camacho concluded, was to create a circuit court in Villavicencio to process these suits and to provide adequate salaries to the alcaldes and other local employees, "since only in that way will honorable people who support the government come to this region."[105] By 1898 a circuit court had been established, and Intendant Silva reported that the new magistrate was kept busy studying the *sumarios* that arrived daily from Medina. Until the outbreak of the War of the Thousand Days, the town remained divided into two hostile bands, both out of favor with the authorities.[106]

The Liberal Revolt of 1895

Most of the intendants who served in the Llanos during the 1890s were capable individuals, and some, such as Eliseo Medina and Marco Antonio Torres, had a deep attachment to the region. Nevertheless, as Conservatives and representatives of the Holguín and Caro governments, which openly repressed their political opponents, they found themselves isolated in a population of firmly Liberal sympathies. Holguín and Caro's censorship of the press and control of elections—resulting in the fact that only two Liberals served in Congress between 1888 and 1904—left the Liberal party, in the words of Malcolm Deas, "not silenced but aggrieved and strengthened its bellicose factions. . . . A few men could start a civil war, and the electoral practices and the exclusiveness of the administrations up to 1899 were a standing pretext for them." [107]

Llanero antagonism to the national government was plainly evident to the intendants in Villavicencio. On July 12, 1894, Habacuc Beltrán wrote:

In many towns of the intendancy one observes movements against the authorities and a certain kind of social unrest that if it is not remedied, it is possible that this region will become the center of a revolutionary organization or undisciplined forces which are inclined to protest against what the government does even with the best intentions. [108]

Pioquinto Márquez C., in his letter of November 19, 1894, to the secretary of government, explained that he needed a squadron of soldiers not only because there were no police, but also because "most of the inhabitants of these regions have opinions contrary to that of the few employees that are with me. . . . Our opponents believe in absolute liberty and resent all monopolies, and the Bogotá–Villavicencio road is an easy way for them to get all kinds of weapons." [109] The permanent presence of soldiers, Márquez concluded, would inspire fear in those who are trying to ship arms.

In January 1895, the war faction of the Liberal party—a closely knit coalition of regional leaders—sent out a call for revolution. Devised by Eustacio de la Torre Narváez, a wealthy Cundinamarcan coffee grower, and Juan Félix de León, a law professor and newspaper editor from Santander, the plan was to seize the presidential palace and imprison Vice President Caro in a coup seconded by *pronunciamientos* in several departments. Warned in advance, Caro arrested de La Torre before he could act, but other conspirators, undeterred, "pronounced" on January 23 in Facatativá, Cundinamarca. Soon there were rebel armies in Santander, Boyacá, Tolima, and Casanare, but the revolution, opposed from the start by many important Liberals and dissident Conservatives, was doomed. Government troops, led by General Rafael Reyes, defeated the insurgents at La Tribuna, Cundinamarca, on January 29, and won other battles in Tolima, Boyacá, and Panamá. On March 15, Reyes delivered the decisive blow by defeating General Pedro María Pinzón at Enciso, Santander. Two days later, the rebels capitulated. Caro's preventive measures, his excellent choice of military commanders, and his ability to print money to pay for the war proved to be too much for the divided Liberal effort.[110]

General Gabriel Vargas Santos led the rebellion in Casanare. He was a distinguished military leader who had fought for the Liberal cause in the civil wars of 1860, 1877, and 1885. By the 1890s he had settled in Tame, where he owned several hatos and administered the salt mine at La Salina. As his Liberal sympathies were well known, it was no surprise when he organized an army in Venezuela and invaded Arauca in late January 1895, overwhelming the government garrison in Arauca City and confiscating the customs revenues. Vargas Santos exacted forced loans from the Recoletos before sending them into exile across the border. In the meantime, other rebels, shouting "¡Viva el gran Partido Radical!" took Orocué. They terrorized the Recoletos and burned their mission at Barrancopelado to prevent them from raising an Indian army. When the rebels finally withdrew at the end of February, Orocué looked as if it had been hit by a cholera epidemic, with many buildings in ruins. Another group of rebels seized Támara, but not until April. Led by a man identified as "Aguilar," they rode through the streets of the town, demanding money and shouting "vivas" and "mueras," seemingly oblivious to the fact that Pinzón had surrendered weeks before.[111]

In the Intendancy of San Martín, only Medina joined the revolution, although some Liberal guerrillas fled to Uribe after their defeat in Tolima. By February 2 Intendant Tobías Hernández had assembled fifty men, who pledged to defend the government but had no weapons. A few days later, General Rufino Gutiérrez appeared to take charge as *jefe civil y militar*. On learning that Orocué had fallen, Gutiérrez dispatched the "Ospina Camacho" regiment on March 15 to retake the town, unaware that the enemy had already abandoned it. By April Gutiérrez had restored peace in Medina and throughout the territory.[112]

In Casanare, Vargas Santos withdrew to Venezuela, but rebels continued to hold Támara until the arrival of an army from Boyacá, commanded by General Francisco Duarte Ruiz, convinced them that their cause was hopeless. General Duarte subdued the remaining pockets of resistance, and government authority was not challenged again, despite sporadic reports of uprisings in Orocué and Arauca. On October 8, Intendant Moíses Camacho acknowledged the lifting of the state of siege throughout the nation by Vice President Caro.[113]

The Liberal revolt of 1895 caused little material damage in the Llanos, but it did heighten political tensions. In Casanare, one of Duarte's officers, Juan Francisco Pérez, used his authority as jefe militar of the district between the Upía and Cravo to harass the inhabitants, "displacing legitimate authorities and appointing others arbitrarily, charging illegal taxes on *degüello* (slaughter) and aguardiente, and exacting forced loans."[114] In Villavicencio, Tobías Hernández, in following orders from Bogotá, removed officeholders sympathetic to the rebellion and replaced them with "friends of the government." On April 24, 1895, he confessed that, in Uribe, only the principal alcalde was a "friend of the government" and that he had removed the other officials and appointed "the most decided Conservatives that there are in this place." In San Martín, he made sure the schoolteachers were "friends of the government," but the notary was not and his appointment had been an accident. Medina was a special challenge since the whole town had been compromised by the revolution. Hernández was afraid to hold an election for the municipal council because the people who would win would not be supportive of the government. For that reason, the town remained without any local officials until June, when he appointed men he could trust.[115]

The Liberals smoldered under this overt repression. In Casanare, there were frequent rumors of unrest, of the return of Vargas Santos, and of weapons being shipped in clandestinely, via the Meta. The aduana in Arauca, reorganized in 1897, was still notoriously corrupt, and from Villavicencio Intendant Aristides Novoa wrote on May 11, 1896:

Radicals from here, turbulent and revolutionary, keep the town and territory in constant alarm. They form political groups, circulate false notices, denigrate the government, write articles and scandalous telegrams against the intendancy employees. . . . There is much speculation and unrest about when the next *pronunciamiento* will take place. We only have ten rifles and 250 shells. Even when we can count on our friends, we lack arms to organize a force.[116]

The results of the election of December 5, 1897, confirmed Novoa's contention that the government workers were a besieged group in the territory. In Villavicencio, there were 140 votes for the Liberal candidates for president and vice president, Miguel Samper and Foción Soto; 22 votes for Independent Rafael Reyes, who had withdrawn from the election; and only 18 votes for Manuel A. Sanclemente and José Manuel Morroquín, the government-supported "Nationalist" candidates who were declared the winners on February 1, 1898. Even more revealing is Intendant Francisco Duarte's account of election-day behavior. He informed Secretary of Government Antonio Roldán that Judge Nicasio Anzola voted for the Nationalists and did all he could to get other votes for them, but the fiscal of the court voted with the Liberals; the administrator of the Salina of Cumaral supported the *oposicionistas* and kept his employees from voting, and the administrator of the liquor monopoly "worked with much enthusiasm and activity with the Liberals" to defeat the government. Duarte suggested that the latter should forfeit his job with the liquor monopoly because of his disloyalty. "The *oposicionistas* are not only political enemies but also personal enemies, insulting the nationalist employees, forming threatening and suspicious circles, so that I have had to call together the few *nacionalistas* to reenforce the police in certain cases." In Duarte's view, the situation was untenable. "I beg you to send me an army contingent for otherwise it will be impossible for me to continue performing this job and I will irrevocably submit my resignation."[117] Secretary Roldán recommended that military forces be stationed in the intendancy, since the Llaneros "lacked sufficient discipline and character" to serve as policemen; but, as usual, no action was taken.[118] On the eve of the War of the Thousand Days, the Llanos were a whirlpool of political hatreds and popular resentment against the Conservative government in Bogotá.

A Summing Up

In summary, "Regeneration à la Llanera" was a mixed blessing. Administrative centralism, fundamental to Núñez's political agenda, brought down the system of territorial rule developed by the Liberals over a forty-year period. The return of San Andrés and Providencia, Bolívar, La Nevada y Motilones, Goajira, Casanare, and San Martín to their former departments, as mandated by the Constitution of 1886, was a step backward for the frontier regions since departmental governments had even less money to spend on them than Bogotá. It was not until after the resignation of Rafael Reyes, in 1909, that constitutional reform brought a new plan for the uniform rule of all of Colombia's peripheral territories.

The Llanos alone, among these regions, were singled out by

Congress in the 1890s to be ruled as intendancies. Although the Organic Decree 392 of January 17, 1893, was written by Elisio Medina, a longtime leader of Casanare, its flaws were immediately apparent; but the reforms embodied in Decree 392 of 1897 failed to remedy the ongoing problems of geographic isolation, disease, insufficient funds, land conflicts, and destruction of natural resources. Moreover, the policy of political exclusivism endorsed by Regeneration governments weakened Bogotá's ability to rule effectively over the fervently Liberal Llaneros. The Nationalist employees who went out to Villavicencio, Támara, or Orocué became a kind of occupation force with the Liberal Llaneros, ever attuned to party dictates from Bogotá and prepared to revolt at a minute's notice.

On a more positive note, reconciliation with the church brought a resurgence of missionary activity that was welcomed by officials and residents alike. The Recoletos, Hermanas de la Caridad, and Salesians who went out to the plains had the firm backing of civil and ecclesiastical authorities. They began schools in the towns and missions among the Indians. The Recoletos were especially energetic in their study of native cultures, compiling bilingual grammars and preaching the gospel in Guahibo. The Liberals who had suppressed the religious communities on ideological grounds had not hit upon an alternative way to integrate Indians into national life. With the restoration of the missions, the Regeneration governments reaffirmed the most basic institution of the Spanish American frontier, and priests and nuns mediated once again between whites and Indians.

Finally, despite the undercurrent of political unrest, the economy of the Llanos did fairly well throughout the 1890s. The Spanish Laudo of 1891 and the Treaty of Navigation and Commerce of 1894 temporarily eased the border dispute and opened the Meta and Orinoco to Colombian trade. Regular steamboat service facilitated the export of coffee, cacao, cattle, and hides. World demand for rubber encouraged the exploitation of forests and filled the gap left by the collapse of the quinine boom. The Liberal revolt of 1895 only dampened the general prosperity for a few months, so that it was not until 1899 that the vulnerability of the system was apparent. Cipriano Castro's seizure of power in Caracas and his repudiation of free trade on the Meta and Orinoco left the Llanos locked in isolation, and the outbreak of the War of the Thousand Days raised them to a level of violence that had not been experienced since the War of Independence.

6. War and Dictatorship, 1899–1909

$\mathcal{T}$he decade between 1899 and 1909 marked another turning point in Colombian history, for the War of the Thousand Days (1899–1902), the separation of Panama, in 1903, and the dictatorship of Rafael Reyes (1904–9) known as the *Quinquenio* laid the economic and political basis for the consolidation of the modern republic.[1] This era was no less pivotal for the Llanos. Violence disrupted the region for four years, as the people of San Martín, Casanare, and Arauca rallied against the government of Manuel Antonio Sanclemente and José Manuel Marroquín. The accession of Reyes to power in 1904 presaged the complete collapse of the territorial governance system that had been evolving since 1846. The following chapter will analyze the role played by the Llanos in the war's two phases, identified by Charles Bergquist in *Coffee and Conflict* as "The Gentlemen's War" (August 1899 to May 1900) and "The Guerrillas' War" (May 1900 to November 1902), and will then assess the legacy of the struggle within the region as it became apparent during the rule of Reyes.

The Gentlemen's War (August 1899 to May 1900)

As Helen Delpar has shown, "In the years after 1895 the Liberal party moved inexorably toward armed revolt against Regeneration."[2] Miguel Antonio Caro, who ended his administration in 1898 on bad terms with Congress, arranged a disastrous succession deliberately contrived to exclude the men of his own party who had demonstrated a willingness to compromise with his Liberal critics. His choice for president was the ailing octogenarian Manuel Antonio Sanclemente, and for vice-president José Manuel Marroquín—a seventy-year-old with no political experience. Both candidates were ratified in the election of 1897, defeating their Liberal challengers Miguel Samper and Foción Soto. Serving temporarily as chief executive before Sanclemente's arrival in the capital, Vice President Marroquín offered concessions in electoral, judicial, and press matters that might have satisfied the Liberal and Conservative dissidents, but Sanclemente withdrew these olive branches on taking possession of the presidency on November 3, 1898. Ill health soon forced him to desert Bogotá for Anapoima (Cundinamarca), where he continued to exercise his functions, but with the chief executive in a debilitating physical condition and the government weakened by fiscal problems, the militant wing of the Liberals began a revolution that lasted for three years and touched to a greater or lesser extent every section of the country.[3]

When General Juan Francisco Gómez Pinzón seized Socorro, Santander, on October 17, 1899, almost everyone believed that the conflict would be short and similar to earlier nineteenth-century revolts. On the rebel side, elite politicians and local caudillos volunteered to serve as officers, bringing with them their clients and dependent laborers as common soldiers. The government moved quickly to expand its army of just under nine thousand officers and men, while the traditional political leaders who were not engaged in fighting tried to work out a compromise between the opposing factions to end the crisis. Although the fighting was often desperate during the first ten months, the upper-class generals displayed a chivalrous concern for the dignity of their opponents, prompting the title, "The Gentlemen's War."

In the highlands during the Gentlemen's War, the Liberals recovered from early losses at Los Obispos, Nocaima, and Bucaramanga in Santander to win a major victory on December 15, 1899, at Peralonso, a valley west of Cúcuta, under the leadership of Rafael Uribe Uribe, Benjamín Herrera, and Justo L. Durán. Sobered by defeat, the Sanclemente government reorganized and strengthened its forces. Five months later, the two armies clashed again at Palonegro, near Bucaramanga. The encounter dragged on from May 11 to May 25. Pitting fourteen to twenty thousand government troops against half as many Liberals, it was the longest and most costly battle ever fought on Colombian soil. In the end, the determination of the Conservative commander, Próspero Pinzón, and the superior numbers of his forces turned the tide against rebel generals Uribe Uribe, Herrera, and Gabriel Vargas Santos. With one thousand dead and their army shattered, the Liberals had to retreat, but they were resolved to continue fighting elsewhere. The Battle of Palonegro ended the gentlemanly phase of the struggle and paved the way for a different kind of warfare.[4]

In the Llanos, the first news of the revolution in October 1899 unleashed enthusiastic support for the Liberal cause. Local guerrilla bands, armed with weapons brought in clandestinely from Venezuela, coalesced around three extraordinary leaders: Gabriel Vargas Santos, septuagenarian general and veteran of many earlier conflicts; Avelino Rosas, seasoned guerrilla fighter who had fought beside Antonio Maceo in the Spanish–Cuban–American War; and Tulio Varón, charismatic Liberal warrior from Tolima.

Gabriel Vargas Santos, often depicted as the stereotypical crude Llanero chieftain, actually was born into a distinguished family of Charalá, Santander, in 1827. As a youth, he received a classical education. He studied history and learned to read French and English, but he was drawn to a military career. He fought for the Radicals in the civil war of 1860 and earned a reputation for self-sacrificing patriotism. For example, when asked to comment on a plan to help Liberal soldiers proposed by the Convention of Rionegro, he reportedly replied, "We want nothing because we have only done our duty."[5]

Vargas Santos fought in the civil war of 1876–77, and by this time he had acquired several hatos near Tame, in Casanare. A slender man of nervous, plain gestures in battle, he evoked the aura of the mythic warrior whose very appearance animates the hearts of his followers. His contemporaries considered him a superb strategist who favored rapid and audacious confrontations with the enemy. Thus, when Daniel Hernández, Sergio Camargo, and Ricardo Gaitán Obeso began a new revolt in 1885, they were pleased when Vargas Santos agreed to take command. On this occasion, however, his actions were less than heroic. Rather than directly marching to attack the weak forces of the government in Bogotá, he opted instead to occupy Tunja, giving the government time to reorganize its army and eventually crush the rebellion. In the disillusioned view of his comrade-in-arms, Foción Soto, "The great moderation (*suma prudencia*) of General Vargas Santos avoided, I do not say the danger, but even the risk that we might fight."[6]

After his surrender, Vargas Santos returned to Tame where he continued to exercise considerable power as a ganadero and Liberal caudillo. Jorge Brisson, who visited him on March 5, 1894, described him as "a man of progress, and in spite of his age, active and very useful in these lands."[7] During the abortive revolt of 1895, the general seized Arauca for a few weeks in February, and once peace had been restored, authorities in Casanare closely monitored his activities. For example, on October 24, 1898, J. M. Arias sent a telegram from Tame to Secretary of Government Antonio Roldán to report that Vargas Santos had left town that morning to try to prevent the capture of some "criminals" wanted by the circuit judge of Támara, and who were his "favorites." The general was in an angry mood, cursing the officials and threatening to deal with them on his return to the territory. In reply, Roldán thanked Arias for his information and encouraged him to continue to guard public order zealously.[8]

In July 1899, as preparations for beginning the revolution were nearing completion, the Liberal directory in Bogotá looked for a supreme leader to replace Aquileo Parra, who had resigned on February 4. The "war" Liberals, led by Rafael Uribe Uribe and José María Ruiz, and the "peace" Liberals led by Parra, Miguel Samper, and Salvador Camacho Roldán, decided to nominate Vargas Santos, believing that his distinguished military record and his ties with both factions would make him an acceptable candidate. In October, Uribe Uribe and Ruiz met with "El Gran Viejo" in Tame and persuaded him to accept the position. The three planned to delay the revolt until the end of the year, but the momentum for action was too strong to be resisted. By the time Vargas Santos sent a telegram, dated October 19, to the Liberal directory, stressing the need for peace, Goméz Pinzón in Socorro; Ramón Neira in Ráquira, Boyacá; and Cenón Figueredo in Nocaima, Cundinamarca, had already declared war.[9]

Vargas Santos moved quickly to take control of Casanare. He dispatched General Primero with a group of armed men who reached Arauca on October 31, where they were joined by local rebels—Colombian and Venezuelan—who were encouraged by the news that Cipriano Castro had entered Caracas nine days before and seized power. Primero declared Arauca City in a state of war and under Liberal domination. He imprisoned three Recoleto missionaries—Antonio Caballero, Pablo Alegría, and Antonio Sibelo—and ordered them to give him three thousand pesos of gold. After some days in captivity, they managed to escape across the border where they remained in exile for the duration of the war. Primero also seized the steamboats *Boyacá* and *Colombia*, intending to use them to bring in weapons from Venezuela.[10]

By this time the rebellion had flared in the Intendancy of San Martín. On September 30, two hundred men attacked Villavicencio, easily overpowering Jefe Civil y Militar Juan Campela, the alcalde, Pedro Obando, and their force of eight policemen. Rebels also seized Uribe, Medina, and San Martín to control much of the territory. Learning on November 30 that General Mariano Ospina Chaparro was on his way from Bogotá with several hundred soldiers to restore order, they decided to evacuate Villavicencio, taking Campela and Obando with them. During the march to Cabuyaro, the prisoners managed to escape, returning to Villavicencio in time to see Ospina Camacho's triumphant entry into the city. Ospina Camacho reinstated Campela as jefe civil y militar and sent 350 soldiers to retake San Martín. Led by Colonel Eduardo Gómez, fifty of these men followed on foot the short, difficult path through the forest to San Martín City, while the rest on horseback and carrying supplies took the longer road that required fording several rivers. Eight leagues from Villavicencio, the large force caught up with a group of revolutionaries and overpowered them, seizing three hundred horses and two hundred cattle. Flushed with victory, they returned with their booty to Villavicencio, leaving Gómez and his fifty men to face alone more than six hundred rebels in San Martín City. The colonel waited for a week, but when the rest of the army did not come, he decided to return to Villavicencio without challenging the rebel stronghold, taking with him four Salesian missionaries who were no longer safe in San Martín. The rebels sniped away at the retreating soldiers, but by December 12 Gómez was back in Villavicencio with only one casualty.[11]

Ospina Camacho kept a firm hold on the capital of the intendancy, but the plains outside the city were in enemy hands. Around Christmas, the rebels were joined by Liberals fleeing Tolima, where they had been defeated on December 9 at the battle of El Playón, near the town of Colombia. Led by Tulio Varón, a fierce guerrilla fighter whose obsession was to kill Conservatives, they made their way to San Martín City and from there to Surimena, stopping at last in Santa Elena de Upía. There, they met General Gustavo Sánchez Núñez, who told them that the government had mounted strong outposts on the roads leading to Cundinamarca and Boyacá. Buoyed by "a very Colombian hope, that any day the situation would change," Varón resolved to stay in Upía.[12] Life in the camp was miserable, for the rebels were beset by disease and reduced to a diet of unsalted meat and plátanos. They concentrated on keeping their horses healthy, for without mounts they knew they would be helpless in the Llanos.

News of the arrival of General Avelino Rosas in Arauca galvanized revolutionaries throughout the Llanos. Born in Popayán in 1856, Rosas had dedicated his life to fighting for radical causes. At age sixteen, he took part in a military coup in Peru. He then went to Ecuador, where he joined an unsuccessful conspiracy against Gabriel García Moreno in 1875. In the Battle of La Granja in 1876, he defended the Liberal government of Cauca against a Conservative revolt, but in 1879 he supported Eliseo Payán's insurrection against the presidency of Modesto Garcés. In 1885, Rosas fought with the Radicals in the Battle of Paso de Moreno, earning his rank of general; but in 1887 he was exiled from Colombia, along with other "war" Liberals, by Rafael Núñez. Rosas went to Venezuela, where he participated in the so-called Legalista Revolution, which unseated General Raimundo Andueza Palacio and brought Joaquín Crespo to power in October 1892. Crespo, however, mistrusted his Colombian supporter and soon expelled him from the country.

Rosas was living in Curacao in 1895, when Antonio Maceo invited him to fight for Cuba's independence from Spain, and it was in this bloody conflict that he mastered the essentials of guerrilla warfare. Spurred on by the leadership of the Dominican warrior Máximo Gómez, Rosas performed the daring exploits that gained him the nickname "Lion of Cauca." By the time the war ended in July 1898, he had become a major general in the Cuban army and compiled the *Código de Maceo*—a manual for guerrilla fighters describing every aspect of irregular warfare from the proper attitude, training, and equipment of the individual soldier to internal organization, military tactics, and strategy of the group as a whole.[13]

In January 1899, Rosas sailed up the Meta from Arauca City to Orocué, with a handful of followers and copies of the *Código de Maceo*. Tulio Varón met him at the port and escorted him back to Santa Elena de Upía. The Tolimenses were disheartened initially by the small size of Rosas's retinue, for they had believed that he was bringing a complete army and enough weapons to enable the revolution to defeat the government, but their confidence was restored by his strong leadership. Rosas's presence in Upía infused new hope among the defeated guerrillas, who acclaimed him as their commander. Combining the men he had brought from Arauca with those he had found in Upía, Rosas organized two new cavalry squadrons. In one, he put the numerous generals, colonels, and other high officers, and in the other, the ordinary soldiers. Some members of the first group, becoming disenchanted, deserted and returned to Tolima where they spread lies about Rosas, but the rest followed him enthusiastically in a successful strike against the government garrison at Medina, where they seized a good supply of weapons.

From Medina, Rosas marched his men swiftly toward Villavicencio, sweeping over numerous government outposts set up to defend the road. Outside the capital, they exchanged shots with some government soldiers and tried to ascertain the size of the force inside the city. As soon as Rosas realized that he was facing more than two thousand soldiers, he started for San Martín City. Ospina Camacho followed, but in spite of the numerical superiority of his army, he could not break up the rebels' orderly retreat. On the contrary, Rosas inflicted losses on the government by ambushing the soldiers at every clump of trees or narrow gap in the road. At last, he reached a place called Las Peñas, between the Mestas de Guéjar and Uribe. He placed his men in an excellent defensive position and defeated Ospina Camacho in a battle that forced him to return to Villavicencio. Victorious Rosas continued his trek unmolested, arriving in Tolima in early March to join the army at General Aristóbulo Ibáñez.[14]

As guerrillas took over key points in the Llanos, and Rosas was organizing his followers in Upía, Gabriel Vargas Santos was leading an army of twelve hundred men over the cordillera to Santander. Learning of Uribe Uribe's momentous victory at Peralonso, west of Cúcuta, on December 15, El Gran Viejo had decided to join more actively in the fight. When he rode into Pamplona on December 25, Uribe Uribe proclaimed him supreme commander of the revolution and provisional president of the republic. In his reception speech, he addressed Vargas Santos with the following words:

They say that in one of your past wars, you went once through Casanare at twilight leading your army, and a Guahibo captain who knew you, cried out from the top of a great tree illuminated by the fantastic splendor of a sunset in the Llanos, "Goodbye, old Vargas, good heart!" (*Adiós, viejo Vargas, corazón bueno!*") That savage Indian knew how to define you better than anyone else. Good heart, magnanimous heart, heart capable of all acts of generosity and nobility—this is you, General, and for that reason you embody all the glories and pride of Liberalism. Welcome to the Supreme War Command. Your head, white as the plume of the French warrior, will show us the road of honor and of victory. Today is Christmas, General, the Christmas of Liberalism that with your first victory and with your arrival sees the rebirth of the trees of liberties . . . ¡Viva General Vargas Santos, Supreme Director of War and Provisional President of the Republic![15]

Uribe Uribe came to regret his warm endorsement, for he had expected Vargas Santos to be a figurehead, and when the general actually assumed direction of military operations, he was surprised and disappointed. Both he and General Herrera pressed Vargas Santos to take the offensive, capitalizing on the recent Peralonso victory to mount a strike against Bogotá and bring the government to its knees;

but El Gran Viejo rejected this strategy, preferring to march to Bucaramanga and wait for General Foción Soto and the weapons he was bringing from Maracaibo. This crucial decision lost for the Liberals all hope of ending the war quickly and infuriated Uribe Uribe, whom Vargas Santos had already alienated by appointing him his secretary while designating Herrera "Second Chief of the Revolution." [16]

Historians have joined with Uribe Uribe in faulting Vargas Santos's overcautious behavior in the months before the battle at Palonegro. As early as 1904, Carlos Adolfo Urueta wrote, "It is enough to say that General Vargas Santos showed himself completely incapable of preparing for the combat as well as directing the campaign." [17] In *La revolución de 1899*, originally published in Bogotá in 1938, Joaquín Tamayo concluded that the general devoted too much precious time in organizing public administration in the provinces of Pamplona and Cúcuta, in convincing Foción Soto to join the revolt, and later in forming two armies of the line commanded by Herrera and Uribe Uribe. "It had been a tremendous error to take General Vargas Santos from the bosom of his ranch in the Llanos in order to launch him into this whirlwind of discord, depriving the good patriarch of his favorite Llanos. It was not his epoch, and the men around him, too young for him, could not accept without protest his ideas and concepts of another era." [18] Moreover, as time went by, Vargas Santos showed no disposition to begin a campaign against the enemy. Max Grillo, who visited their camp, observed that while Uribe Uribe was seething inwardly, the supreme commander "was spending dead hours in an old wooden chair located in the middle of a vast room crammed with furniture and knickknacks. His appearance was that of a tired (*atediado*) man . . . hair whitened by the passing years, covered by a cap with an ironic tassel." [19]

Vargas Santos's vacillation was to have devastating consequences when fighting broke out on May 11 at Palonegro, not far from Bucaramanga. Although the well-equipped Conservative army, estimated at between fourteen and twenty thousand soldiers, outnumbered the Liberals two to one, savage Liberal attacks on their positions brought them to the verge of defeat at the end of three days. Sensing victory at hand, Uribe Uribe asked Vargas Santos to send him three thousand more men in order to launch a decisive strike. From his headquarters twenty-six kilometers away from the battle site, the Supreme Director responded by sending only a small detachment, enabling the Conservatives to mount a counterattack. Their superior numbers, better equipment, and excellent leadership by General Próspero Pinzón eventually turned the tide, and by May 15 the Conservatives beat back the Liberal offensive. The battle then took on a new, terrifying dimension for each army dug in, refusing to abandon the field. "As the days passed and the inconclusive fighting continued, the bodies of hundreds of dead men and animals lay bloated and decomposing between the lines, filling the air with their nauseating stench."[20] Finally, on May 23, the Conservatives, resupplied with ammunition, broke the stalemate and forced the Liberals to retreat, leaving two thousand dead and wounded, one thousand prisoners and eleven hundred sick or missing. Uribe Uribe blamed Vargas Santos for the defeat, and the old general later admitted that his error "consisted in not knowing the military position at Palonegro."[21] It was a costly mistake, for it widened the rift between him and Uribe Uribe and may have changed the destiny of Colombia for the next thirty years.[22]

The Guerrillas' War (June 1900 to September 1902)

The destruction of the Liberal army at Palonegro plunged the war into a new phase. Guerrilla bands led by Avelino Rosas, Tulio Varón, and others in southern and western Tolima, Bolívar, the Llanos, and both Pacific and Atlantic coasts kept the revolution alive. Although they were surrounded by well-equipped government troops, the guerrillas in their enclaves knew the terrain and had the support of the local people. "Resorting to surprise attacks, ambushes, and strategic retreats," they left trails of blood, burned buildings, and violence in the wake of their victories.[23] In the meantime, Uribe Uribe had some success in Magdalena, but by the end of 1900 he was defeated and joined Herrera and Vargas Santos in exile to search for international support to renew the war.

On the government side, the "Historical" Conservatives, who favored ending the war quickly, organized a coup on July 31, 1900, which unseated Sanclemente and installed Vice President José Manuel Marroquín. Marroquín's supporters believed that he would come to terms with the rebels. Instead, he adopted a hard line, appointing new military governors in the departments, and assigning the critical posts of governor of Cundinamarca and director of police to Arístides Fernández, a man determined to offer the Liberals no quarter. Marroquín followed this move by issuing decrees stating that recalcitrant revolutionaries would be treated as common criminals and subjected to increasingly harsh penalties imposed by military courts. Thus, on both sides, "a war that had begun as a conventional civil conflict between elites was transformed into a struggle of savage, irregular violence with distinct social and economic overtones." [24]

During the second phase of fighting, the government's presence in the Llanos was as tenuous as it was during the first. Following the pattern established in late 1899, the Conservatives held Villavicencio, Támara, and Orocué, while Liberal guerrillas roamed freely through the plains. When rebel leaders fled from Tolima and Cundinamarca to the Intendancy of San Martín or stole into Casanare from Venezuela, they found compatriots ready for action. Such a leader was Cesáreo Pulido, a seasoned, committed warrior from Cundinamarca who joined the rebels in San Martín in March 1901. Born in La Mesa in 1847, Pulido fought at age thirteen beside his father in the war of 1860 and later defended the Liberal government in the civil war of 1876–77. Working as a storekeeper, he became an implacable foe of Regeneration when some government soldiers allegedly mistreated his relatives in Viotá. In October 1899, he joined the revolution with twelve men and soon commanded many more. Pulido won an important victory at La Morada near Dolores, Tolima, on January 26, 1900. Later, he returned to Fusugasugá, Cundinamarca, where he built up his army and fought alongside Marco Aurelio Wilches and Juan MacAlister. When, by the end of 1900, a series of reverses had reduced their "Army of Oriente and the Llanos" to a handful of men directed by General Ruperto Aya, Pulido decided to go back to Dolores. Attacked there on all sides, he began a retreat to the Llanos, ordering his men to take separate routes and to reassemble in the comparative safety of the municipio of Uribe. [25]

Pulido spent the next five months in Uribe, rebuilding his treasury and his army. Aided by General Gabriel M. Calderón, he raised money to buy weapons by exacting "voluntary" contributions from all of the wealthy people in the district, "without distinction of political colors." [26] He bought large quantities of rubber harvested from the forests around Uribe and sold it at a good price in Orocué, a transaction managed with puritanical scruples by General Calderón. Pulido also expropriated cattle and rubber from the Compañía de Herrera y Uribe, eventually putting the owners out of business.

In early August, Alejandro Villoría led a thousand government soldiers over the cordillera from Colombia, Tolima, to attack Pulido.

The guerrilla leader with only 120 men evacuated Uribe, but the timely arrival of twenty cases of weapons, brought down the Meta River by General Emilio Santofimio, abruptly changed the balance of power. On August 24, Pulido soundly defeated Villoría at "Las Peñas," notwithstanding the disparity in numbers. After retaking Uribe, he went on to occupy Villavicencio and Quetame. Now firmly in control of much of the intendancy, he opened up contact with the rebel Ejército de Oriente, commanded by General Foción Soto, and accepted a position as Soto's subordinate.[27]

In January 1902, Pulido learned that Rafael Uribe Uribe was on his way to Casanare to organize a new offensive against the government. After his defeat on the Atlantic Coast in December 1900, the Liberal general had sought asylum in Caracas, where he talked with President Cipriano Castro about getting weapons for the struggle. Rebuffed by Castro, tired and discouraged, Uribe Uribe went to New York City, where on April 12, 1901, he proposed a peace agreement with the government that was rejected by the guerrillas still fighting throughout Colombia. Realizing his error, he renewed his support for the revolution in spite of the fact that the split between him and the official leadership—Vargas Santos, Soto, Herrera, and Durán—was irreconcilable.

In June 1901, Uribe Uribe returned to Caracas and managed to win Castro's approval for a joint Colombian and Venezuelan raid into Santander from Táchira. Before this offensive could begin, however, he found himself assisting the Venezuelan army in defending San Cristóbal from an invasion launched from Santander on July 26 by Castro's conservative opponents. The insurgency was put down, but Castro, hoping to avoid open war with Colombia, ordered that all Colombians who sought asylum in Venezuela should be disarmed, thus derailing Uribe Uribe's plans for a joint operation. Stranded in Táchira, he wasted the next four months by writing to Castro in fruitless attempts to change his mind.[28]

By December Uribe Uribe was tired of inaction. He resolved to bring down Morroquín's government in a bold maneuver reminiscent of Bolívar's Liberation Campaign. In an "Exposición" dated December 20, he explained to his officers that the way through the Llanos was "free, wide and clear of difficulties." The Liberal army waiting in Táchira could march across the plains to join General Eugenio Sarmiento's Army of Boyacá, and together they could penetrate the interior of Boyacá. The march through the Llanos, he argued "will save our existence as an Army and our dignity as men and as Colombians. . . . In the Llano we will be within our own country, with an abundance of resources and in complete control of our actions, that is to say, free to do what we think best." [29]

Uribe Uribe acted quickly on his plan. In Táchira, he assembled artillery, weapons, and 2,500 rebel soldiers. Crossing the Apure River, he led them through the Llanos of Apure and Arauca, reaching Tame on January 24 and Nunchía in early February, where Sarmiento and his army were waiting. Together, they marched on to Medina to meet Cesáreo Pulido, Emilio Santofimio, and their guerrilla troops. A few days later, they welcomed General Foción Soto, who made his way to their camp after escaping with four other Liberal generals from the Panóptico in Bogotá, where they had been imprisoned by Arístides Fernández. The officers agreed that although Vargas Santos, now living in Curaçao, was still the Supreme Director of the rebel army, Uribe Uribe should take over as Chief of Operations of the United Army and appoint Soto as his Subdirector. [30]

In Eastern Cundinamarca, the rebels had already begun to move. Victories at "Los Colorados," "La Aguadita," and "Alto de la Cruz" had forced the government to retreat toward Fusugasugá. General Juan MacAllister, leading another division, defeated regular troops at Usme, Cáqueza, Quetame, and Chipaque. As a result, the Liberals controlled an extensive region near the capital, while the government forces commanded by Minister of War Fernández were strongly entrenched in Soacha, where they could get help and supplies via the railroad. Uribe Uribe's plan was to lead the United Army in an attack on Gachalá, and from there to move on either to Guasca and Guatavita or to the Valley of Tenza. Accordingly, General Soto ordered MacAllister not to try to take Soacha until all of the troops had arrived from Medina.

Receipt of a telegram from Vargas Santos, dated January 21, 1902, disrupted this carefully laid strategy. The Supreme Director announced that General Herrera had triumphed on the Pacific Coast, and this news so excited MacAllister that he disobeyed Soto and attacked Soacha on February 23, without waiting for the others. In three hours of vicious combat, Fernández decisively defeated him. The rebels retreated first to Quetame and then to San Miguel, where they were met by Pulido and Santofimio leading the vanguard of the United Army. Alarmed by the unexpected setback, Pulido and Santofimio pushed on to Gachalá, and on March 9 they exchanged fire with the enemy at "Alto de la Cordillera." For two days they fought with restraint, rationing their scarce ammunition until the arrival of Uribe Uribe with the rest of the army and supplies changed the balance of power. Uribe Uribe took over the direction of the combat, and eventually the army fled, leaving behind much equipment that the rebels seized on their entry into Gachalá on March 13. On March 14, they seized Ubalá and Junín.

Victory now seemed assured as Uribe Uribe took part of the army to Chocontá, while Pulido and MacAllister led the rest to Guasca, but luck deserted them on March 17. At a place called El Moladero, General Ramón González Valencia, the most able among the Conservative officers, fell upon Uribe Uribe with a large, well-equipped army and completely routed his force. Four days later, an army led by General Nicolás Perdomo annihilated Pulido and MacAllister at El Guavio, ending Uribe Uribe's hope of replicating Bolívar's victory at the Battle of Boyacá.[31]

The Liberals were in full retreat, and once again the remnants of the shattered United Army gathered in Medina. On April 2, the officers signed the Act of Medina, in which they agreed to go their separate ways. Pulido would return to Tolima; the army of Santander and Boyacá would go to Boyacá; McAllister and the Cundinamarca Division would stay in the piedmont zone to threaten Villavicencio or to penetrate Oriente Province; and Uribe Uribe and Soto would travel to Curaçao to discuss with Vargas Santos the possibility of opening a campaign on the Atlantic Coast to gain control of the Magdalena River.[32]

Soto left immediately for Curaçao, but Uribe Uribe delayed his departure. On April 18, he issued a circular to the revolutionary leaders, suggesting that the time had come to consider seriously whether or not to sue for peace. "If my mission to Vargas Santos fails," he wrote, "I will tell you with the loyalty and honesty that is due companions in arms." In the meantime, he urged them to work together and to take advantage of the enemy's mistakes. "Cause disturbances in Tolima, recover if it is possible Villavicencio and Medina, and defend the entrances to the Llanos."[33] By the time Uribe Uribe got to Curaçao, Vargas Santos had already departed for New York City, but it was clear that the differences between them were too great for reconciliation. The general blamed El Gran Viejo for the revolution's reversals, and he seethed at the open criticism which Vargas Santos and his supporters directed at him. Rather than following Vargas Santos to New York and engaging him in a fruitless dialogue, he left Curaçao to join the rebel campaign in Magdalena.[34]

Both the government and the rebels were moving toward a final

truce, but their efforts at peacemaking were just as discombobulated
as their methods of carrying on the war. On June 12, Vice President
Morroquín declared a general pardon for all Liberals who laid down
their weapons, and many rebels hard pressed by government troops
accepted this offer. Others were captured and executed. By October
1902 there were only two Liberal armies of any size in the field—one
in the Department of Magdalena, led by Clodomiro Castillo and Uribe
Uribe, and the other in Panama, commanded by Benjamin Herrera.
On October 18, Castillo and Uribe Uribe accepted an armistice with
the government. Six days later they signed the Treaty of Neerlandia,
ending the war on the coast. On November 21, Herrera met with government leaders on a U.S. warship to sign the Treaty of Wisconsin,
and officially, at least, the War of the Thousand Days was over.[35]

In the Intendancy of San Martín, the government had already
regained control. After the Medina meeting on April 2, Cesáreo Pulido
started back to Tolima via San Martín and Uribe. Many of his men
deserted, disillusioned and torn by jealous rivalries. By the time he
had climbed the cordillera to the Páramo of Sumapaz, he had only a
handful of followers. Government troops captured Pulido on August 6.
A victim of the get-tough policies of Minister of War Fernández,
he was executed at El Espinal, Tolima, on September 13, despite
pleas for amnesty from distinguished Conservatives and priests. With
Pulido's death, rebels in the Llanos of San Martín knew that further
resistance was futile.[36]

The fragmentary information available suggests that the pacification of Casanare was more difficult. In his *Informe* of March 14,
1904, Intendant Teodoro J. Amézquita wrote that Generals García and
Arango, commanding the First and Second armies of Boyacá, reached
the territory in July 1902. They seized towns and ports as the rebels
retreated, but the violent methods they employed further alienated
inhabitants already hostile to the government. When murders, subver-
sion, and crime continued, General García ordered the jefe civil y militar (Amézquita does not give his name) and General Ramírez, who
headed the Próspero Pinzón Column, to restore order. The splitting
up of authority proved to be counterproductive, as rebel gangs hiding
along the banks of the Meta, Cravo, and Pauto rivers grew ever more
entrenched. Meanwhile, troops commanded by General R. Pulecio
clashed with rebels in Tame and might have won a decisive victory
except that Pulecio neglected to press his advantage, permitting his
adversaries to escape. Amézquita continued:

Finally the Government of Bogotá, through that of Boyacá, sent General Salamanca, who with true patriotic interest tirelessly fought against such multiple
problems as lack of money, food and housing for the troops; but surmounting all,
he rapidly organized *casanareño* troops, who supported the 1st Battalion of Boyacá
and the Neira Battalion, and began to fight with the enemy as soldiers on foot and
without pack animals through these vast and spacious pampas.[37]

Personally leading the Boyacá Battalion and the Llanero troops,
Salamanca defeated the rebels in a second battle at Tame, and the
Neira Battalion, led by two *ayudantes* from his staff, won another victory at Orocué in December 1902. Peace returned to Arauca after the
Venezuelan general, M. Chaves, killed the principal guerrilla leader
there, Julio Rueda, in February 1903. At about the same time, General Mariano Ospina Chaves, commander of the army in Eastern Cundinamarca, got the rebels in Mata de Palma to lay down their arms and
accept a truce. The intendancy was reestablished in April, and Ospina
Chaves served as interim intendant until the appointment of Amézquita in May. At last after three and one-half years, the fighting was
over in Casanare.[38]

The Impact of the War of the Thousand Days

The War of the Thousand Days ended the innumerable civil
wars sparked by deep-seated party hatreds in the nineteenth century,
but peace had been bought at a terrible price.[39] In 1903, Luis Eduardo
Villegas calculated that 100,000 men had died on the battlefield or
from disease, while thousands more were maimed for life.[40] Protracted
guerrilla fighting seriously compromised the discipline and morale of
the government army, and both sides pillaged the civilian population.
President Marroquín himself accused army officers of neglecting their
duties "to dedicate themselves to the buying and selling of mules,
livestock, provisions, and merchandise of every kind."[41] Economically, the long conflict worsened the effects of the coffee depression
by disrupting production and commerce and by prompting the government to sanction massive issues of paper money to finance the army.
Wartime damage to transportation and communication systems and
the general climate of insecurity restricted exports and imports and
discouraged productive investments. The struggle exacerbated Liberal and Conservative antipathies and left a legacy of hostility that
prevailed through the first half of the twentieth century. It also fanned

the flames of separatism. On November 3, 1903, Panama revolted and, with the aid of the United States, went on to secede from Colombia. Rumors of similar movements afoot in Cauca, Antioquia, and Casanare were widely circulated, and although none of these materialized, the authority of the central government was weakened.[42] The prosecution of the long, unpopular war and the loss of Panama discredited the rule by Regeneration proponents and paved the way for the dictatorship of Rafael Reyes between 1904 and 1909.

The war affected the Llanos in at least six ways. First, the continuous hostilities brought normal government functioning to a standstill. Military leaders wrested control of the intendancies from civilians. In December 1899, Juan Campela, jefe civil y militar in Villavicencio, complained to the secretary of government that General Ospina Camacho was usurping his prerogatives by issuing his own passports and refusing to recognize those authorized by Campela. The general ordered two of Campela's aides to march with his army to San Martín City, and when they refused, he threw one of them in jail. Already he had seized from the intendancy twenty-eight steers, fifteen cargas of *panela* (unrefined brown sugar), salt, iron, and nails, and declined to give any receipt. Campela assured the secretary that as "a Conservative by tradition and conviction and as an agent of the government," he would not put up with this kind of behavior, and he asked that a new commander be sent who would be faithful to his legal obligations, since Ospina Camacho was not fulfilling his mission with honor.[43]

As months passed, Bogotá, concerned with winning the war, could not appropriate money to pay for territorial administration. Both Intendant Amézquita in Casanare and his counterpart in San Martín, Tobías Hernández C., upon taking up their posts in 1903 discovered that most of the public employees had resigned because they were no longer being paid their salaries. There were no government buildings and no copies of the law codes. The judicial system had broken down, and the roads were in disrepair. On July 19, 1904, the Assembly of Boyacá described these conditions in a message to Congress which asked that Casanare be returned to departmental rule since the "expenses occasioned by the intendancy were excessive and without benefit to the inhabitants." The municipios of Sogamoso, Pajarito, Zapatosa, and Támara supported this request while Orocué, Arauca City, and Pore, preferring to remain under the national government, opposed it.[44] The secretary of government, Estéban Jaramillo, conceded that the intendancies were in a deplorable state, but he argued that the plan to civilize them "with the direct and exclusive action of the national government" should not be abandoned. The authorities, he wrote, should try all possible methods of administering the territories before agreeing to return them to the departments.[45]

A second consequence of the war was that both government and rebel troops plundered the inhabitants of the plains. Juan Campela, in the note previously cited protesting Ospina Camacho's actions, alleged that the general's soldiers had appropriated one hundred mules and horses from hatos without making any account to him and without giving receipts to their owners, many of whom were "foreigners, women or neutral persons." In another case, rebels had seized sixty-seven mules from Baptiste Broughter, a French citizen, some of which were subsequently recovered by government troops. When Campela ordered the officer who had found the mules to return them to Broughter because "the government cannot be responsible for reimbursing owners who do not sell them willingly," the man refused.[46] For their part, the rebels extorted money from the ganaderos and missionaries and took from the hatos whatever they needed. Cesáreo Pulido, when he was in Uribe, took so much cattle, rubber, and money from the Compañía de Herrera y Uribe that he effectively put it out of business.

To protect their interests, the ganaderos played the two sides off against each other. Such was the strategy adopted by Sergio and Luis Convers, owners of El Buque, the largest hacienda in the intendancy. With its rich sugar cane fields, coffee trees, and cattle, El Buque was a tempting prize. Sergio Convers, who was still a French citizen, charted a neutral course between the government and the rebels for several months. He supplied cattle to both on demand and aided all deserters who sought refuge in El Buque, regardless of their political affiliation, but eventually both sides accused him of treachery. Fearing for their lives, Sergio and his son Luis fled to Bogotá, as government soldiers took over the hacienda. When they returned in 1902, they found that all their workers had run away, and there was no one to harvest what remained of the coffee crop.[47]

Third, the fighting paralyzed commerce. The insecurity of the mountain trails to Cundinamarca and Boyacá disrupted the annual cattle drives to the interior. The government tightened its control of the salinas, making salt unavailable for domestic purposes.[48] Rebels seized the aduana in Arauca City, closing it for the duration of the war.

In 1900, they captured José Bonnet's ship *Libertador* in the Apure River. By 1904 its wreckage lay on the Island of Trinidad, and another merchant ship that had sailed the Meta had been sunk in the Orinoco, near Ciudad Bolívar. Only Ramón Real's steamship *Boyacá*, anchored in Orocué, survived the conflict, but by then Venezuela had revoked Colombia's right to use the rivers in its territory.[49]

Fourth, tense relations with Venezuela during the war encouraged border violations and stalled the work of the mixed commission appointed in 1899 to redraw the international boundary set by the Spanish Laudo. By May 27, 1900, the commissioners had agreed upon a division line from Guajira to the Atabapo, but they suspended their activities after the Colombian-assisted invasion of Táchira on July 26, 1901, leaving the region between the Atabapo and the Amazon still in dispute. Marroquín, determined not to lose any territory acquired in 1891, issued Decree 97 of September 20, 1900, which separated from the intendancies of Casanare and San Martín the area encompassing present-day Vichada, Vaupés, Caquetá, and Putumayo to form a new "Intendencia Oriental," with its capital in Maipure. He appointed Antonio Gutiérrez Rubio, a lawyer and member of the boundary commission, to serve as its first intendant. Rafael Reyes abolished the Intendencia Oriental in 1905, but its brief existence provided a precedent for organizing the Comisaría Especial del Vichada in 1913.[50]

Under rebel control for most of the war, Arauca City suffered especially because of its border location. Legal commerce was halted, and the fact that nearly all the residents were Venezuelans was an open challenge to Colombia's sovereignty. When Señor C. Mora arrived to reorganize the aduana in August 1904, he found that the town was "a den (*guarida*) in which are sheltered, because of the lack of authorities, an infinity of bandits who flaunt the laws." He wrote to the secretary of development: "Unfortunately there are very few Colombians who have not lost their respectability since, as a general rule, they have followed the example of the foreigners and lack political and social ideas with respect to our laws and love of country; they commit very grave crimes and go unpunished because of the ease by which they can move to our neighboring republic."[51] In this chaotic situation, the de facto rulers were a group of *gamonales* (local leaders), headed by Don Manuel Forero E. Mora, who believed that only a powerful authority sent from Bogotá could bring order to the city.

Fifth, the war disrupted the missions. The harassment of Recoletos in Casanare began in November 1899, when General Primero imprisoned the missionaries in Arauca City, but Avelino Rosas inflicted the greatest damage as he swept through Casanare between November and January 1900. In Chámeza, Manare, Orocué, and Moreno, Rosas's followers captured and insulted the priests, broke up missions, sacked their houses, and, in some cases, forced them into exile. The Apostolic Vicar, Bishop Nicolás Casas y Conde, denounced these actions, some of which he had seen with his own eyes and others that had been reported to him by letter, in a long diatribe dated April 15, 1900, and published in the same year under the title *Hechos de la revolución en las misions de Casanare* (Bogotá, 1900). Flatly rejecting Liberal allegations that the Recoletos were meddling in politics, Casas y Conde listed the attacks on each mission and summarized in fifteen points the charges against the rebels—a list that included insults to priestly dignity, illegal imprisonment, slander, robbery of church treasures, grave injury to a prelate by forcing him to abandon his territory, and depriving the faithful of the free exercise of their religion.[52] Liberals dismissed these accusations as exaggerations, but it is indisputable that missionary activity and public education, as it was administered by the Recoletos and the Hermanas de la Caridad, ended in Casanare by late 1900.[53]

Unrestrained by missionaries or Colombian officials, the Guahibos living along the lower Meta, Pauto, and Casanare rivers and between the Meta and Orinoco rivers stepped up their assaults against travelers and hatos and threatened to burn Orocué and Mata de Palma. According to Intendant Amézquita, criminals who escaped from the white towns were living with the Indians and inciting them to commit atrocities. Guahibos had forced the Sálivas, who had lived in the old mission of San Juanito, and several bands of Piapocos to abandon their *conucos* (garden plots) and flee to Venezuela or to other remote places.[54] Padre Daniel Delgado, during his travels through Casanare, repeatedly observed that Guahibos, provoked by white injustices, were attacking white settlements, and he described at length a situation bordering on open warfare between the two groups between 1906 and 1908.[55]

In the Intendancy of San Martín, the rebels forced the Salesians to leave San Martín City in December 1899 and to close their house there the following month. Soon afterward, they terminated their mission in Uribe but continued to work in Villavicencio, where government troops were in control. In August 1901, the Salesian superior, Dom Miguel Rúa, made the difficult journey to Villavicencio from

Bogotá and was agreeably surprised to find that reconstruction of the church after the 1890 fire was progressing satisfactorily, and that both morning and evening services were well attended. With few exceptions, the faithful received the holy sacraments, and in eleven days there were no less than thirteen hundred confessions and communions. The situation changed abruptly, however, after Rúa had returned to Bogotá and rebels led by Cesáreo Pulido occupied the city. Padre Ernesto Briata stayed on for a few months, but after the rebels sacked his house and took away whatever they wanted, he realized the mission was no longer viable.[56] In 1902, the Salesians closed their house in Villavicencio and regretfully relinquished their mission field in the Llanos, defeated by revolutionary violence and the insistence on the part of the papal apostolic delegate, Monseñor Vico, that Salesians must be at least thirty-five years old before they could work in the mission, a provision that the order could not meet.[57]

Sixth, and finally, the War of the Thousand Days contributed to the depopulation of the Llanos. Both sides impressed peasants and cowboys into their armies, and of the hundreds of casanareños and sanmartineros who were taken over the cordillera to fight in Tolima, Cundinamarca, Boyacá, or Santander, many were killed and many did not return. Others fled to Venezuela, or to the forests south of the Guaviare, to avoid the violence. Still others died in an epidemic of *viruela* (small pox) that swept across the plains.[58] Once peace had been proclaimed in 1904, the ganaderos complained that they could not get enough workers for their ranches and plantations. The partial census figures reported by the Ministry of Government in 1904 support this conclusion, especially in the case of Casanare. As can be seen in Table 6, the total population for towns in that intendancy was 12,555, or less than half of the official figure of 26,055 counted in the 1870 census and slightly under Rafael Ortiz's estimate of 13,000 in 1888. The 1904 total for the Intendancy of San Martín, however, was 4,957, a 14 percent increase over the 1870 census figure of 4,056.[59]

The Llanos during the Quinquenio, 1904–1909

The 1904 annual reports of the intendants of Casanare and San Martín were the first to be written since 1898 and the last to appear until 1911. Both Amézquita and Hernández described devastated, neglected regions plagued by violence and a stagnant economy. To help

Table 6
Population in the Intendancies of Casanare
and San Martín, 1904

Intendancy of Casanare	
Municipio	Inhabitants
Orocué*	3,000
Pore	906
Arauca	1,584
Arauquita	289
Todos los Santos*	3,000
Nunchía	531
Támara	1,880
Moreno	1,365
Total	12,555

Indendancy of San Martín	
Municipio	Inhabitants
San Martín	1,182
Uribe	460
Villavicencio	3,315
Total	4,957

*Probably no census was taken; the figure is an estimate.

Source: *Memoria del Ministerio del Gobierno*, 1904 (Bogotá, 1904), 210–227. The municipios of the intendancies were included in the population counts for the Departments of Boyacá and Cundinamarca.

them govern effectively, they asked for mounted police to maintain order; regular payments of the national subsidy; overhaul of the judicial system; restoration of the missions; improvement of roads and bridges; steamboats on the Meta; reorganization of the aduanas; and a colonization plan that would award free land to families willing to settle in the Llanos. As Hernández concluded:

These regions need a paternal government that will give them a way to live (*modo de vivir*), encourage immigration and colonization, and open land and river communication. If the government cannot do this, it should return the territories to the departments and see if they can provide enough money so that each of the municipios at least can have a primary school.[60]

These reports, submitted in March and April, received little attention from the politicians in Bogotá, who were in the midst of a hotly contested presidential campaign that pitted ultra-Conservative Joaquín Vélez against General Rafael Reyes—the man who had urged ratification in 1903 of the Hay-Herrán Treaty with the United States on the Panama Canal and who had tried to put down the Panama revolution, but without success. Initial balloting by electoral assembly showed Vélez with a slight edge, but the final tabulation gave Reyes the victory with 994 votes to 982 for his opponent. Vélez supporters immediately challenged 12 votes cast for Reyes by the Guajira Peninsula, where the election had taken place in a notoriously irregular fashion. In the end, the Gran Consejo Electoral decided the disputed votes in Reyes's favor just three days before the president was to be inaugurated.[61] On August 7, 1904, Reyes took office, calling for a program of national restoration.

At fifty-five, Reyes "resembled a general in the Kaiser's army with his tall figure, massive frame, and heavy mustache trained in the Teutonic fashion."[62] He was a frank admirer of Porfirio Díaz, whose achievements he had observed firsthand as head of the Colombian delegation to the 1901 Pan American Conference held in Mexico City. Impresario, adventurer, politician, and military leader, he planned to restore political harmony and modernize the nation by importing foreign technology, expanding the export sector, improving internal transportation and communication, and promoting industry and mechanized agriculture.[63] To implement these goals, he was prepared to adopt authoritarian measures. When Congress, in 1904, showed every intention of blocking action on his stated projects, Reyes took the unprecedented step of dissolving that body on December 13. In April 1905, he created his own bipartisan but extralegal National Assembly to stamp his presidential decrees with a seal of legitimacy. He extended his term of office from four to six years, and exiled or imprisoned critics who protested his policies too loudly. Surviving several assassination attempts, Reyes persevered in his dictatorship until June 13, 1909, when an unraveling financial system combined with public outrage over his campaign to win approval of tripartite treaties signed with the United States and Panamá to force his resignation. The general sailed for Europe and spent the next ten years traveling through

Africa, the Near East, the United States, and Latin America. In 1919
he returned to Bogotá, where he played the role of elder statesman
and published his fourth book, *Escritos varios* (Bogotá, 1920), a collection of short essays relating to all phases of his long and interesting
career. He died on February 18, 1921, the man who, in the words of
Darío Mesa, drew a line between the old and new Colombia.[64]

Historians find the Quinquenio a difficult period to evaluate.
Most agree that Reyes's insistence on representation for minority parties in the government, his curbing of guerrilla activity in the rural
areas, and the professionalization of the army and navy were valuable
accomplishments. Also earning high marks were the completion of
several railroads, improved steamships on the Magdalena, the promotion of textile manufacturing and the banana export industry. Bergquist calls Reyes's fiscal reorganization—which involved rationalizing
accounting and payment procedures, the setting up of a central bank,
and restoring Colombian credit abroad—an "unqualified success," yet
he notes that the political costs were high. Important local interests
suffered because of the centralization of departmental revenues, while
antagonism rose over the dictator's attempt to break down the departments into small political units and to transfer to the central executive
power control over immigration, foreign investments, and railroad construction. The system of fiscal monopolies gave rise to allegations of
graft, and the 1908 recession in Europe and the United States dried
up easy foreign credits to make borrowing abroad, essential to Reyes's
plan, more burdensome than ever.[65] Most of all, with the exception of
his closest collaborators such as Baldomiro Sanín Cano, José María
Quijano Wallis, and Jorge Holguín, the Colombian political elite found
Reyes's autocratic methods intolerable. In the view of Jesus María
Henao and Gerardo Arrubla, Reyes was one of Colombia's most efficient presidents, but "if he had thought more and acted less, if he had
urged his views more calmly, his administration would have been free
from the Caesarism which preoccupied him, would have gone along
with moral progress, with respect for the rights and personal guarantees of the citizens." Instead, he governed "without scruples, without
respect for the constitution that he helped to issue, without regard for
the law." Possessing the temperament of an autocrat, Reyes "had the
audacity and astuteness of General Mosquera but not his talents or
learning."[66]

Reyes's policies toward the Llanos are especially difficult to assess because there are few official reports, the subject is ignored in

secondary works, and the primary sources, if they exist, have yet to be fully investigated. On the basis of what can be ascertained, it appears that, besides supporting the missions, he proposed no new ideas for modernizing the plains and that his determination to divide the departments into small administrative units had the unfortunate effect of dismantling the national territorial system which had been evolving for several decades.

Reyes's neglect of the eastern frontier is all the more remarkable given his extensive experience in Putumayo as a young man and given the threat posed by Peru to Colombian Amazonia throughout his administration. Born in Boyacá in 1850, he joined his older brother Elías in commerce in Popayán in the late 1860s. After taking a business trip to Europe, he returned to Popayán with a scheme to explore Caquetá and open up trade with Brazil by putting steamships on the Putumayo River, a tributary of the Amazon. In 1874, accompanied by brothers Enrique and Nestor, Reyes crossed the cordillera southeast of Pasto and entered the unexplored *selvas* (jungles) of Caquetá. They found the Putumayo River after weeks of hardship, and aided by the Indians, the brothers sailed along it for twelve hundred miles to reach the Amazon, where they took passage on a steamer to Pará. Reyes then proceeded alone to Río de Janeiro, where he spoke with Dom Pedro II. Coming back to Pará he bought a small steamship, and the brothers retraced their journey to Colombia, having discovered a convenient water route to the Atlantic.

Except for brief intervals, Reyes remained in Caquetá for ten years. He explored the tributaries of the Upper Amazon, invested his family's fortune in the collection of cinchona, founding colonies and suppressing the Indian slave trade. Then, in 1884, a drop in the price of quinine caused his firm of Reyes Brothers and Company to crash, and tropical disease wiped out his settlements. Reyes gave up the enterprise and returned to Cali to become one of the foremost supporters of Rafael Núñez in the revolution of 1884 and, later, to hold positions in Congress, the cabinet, and the diplomatic corps.[67]

That Reyes had not forgotten these experiences was revealed in his inaugural address of August 7, 1904, when he stated:

Our eastern territory, whose incredible wealth has scarcely been guessed at by some sons of Colombia who have adventured into the inextricable labyrinths of those primordial forests or legalized with their own blood our sovereignty in such vast regions, awaits the efficacy of Colombian patriotism, so that through the decided assistance of the entire Nation, the treasures of that zone will be open to the country that some foreigners are exploiting right now in detriment to our rights. Covered with overgrowth (*maleza*), deserted and abandoned as well are the fertile pastures where in a not too distant past numerous herds used to graze. Our roads and transportation today are in worse condition perhaps than in the colonial era, and our isolation from the centers of civilization and progress is, for this reason, greater every day.[68]

The allusion to foreign encroachment on Colombian soil was an acknowledgement of Peruvian penetrations into the Putumayo River Basin and Alto Caquetá, a territory claimed by Colombia but over which Peru exercised informal jurisdiction from its Amazon city of Iquitos. Spurred by the rubber boom, Colombians had started to move into the region in the 1890s to exploit the rubber trees through the use of Indian collectors. At the same time, a Peruvian entrepreneur, Julio C. Arana, set up collection centers at El Encanto and La Chorrera, between the Caraparaná and Igara Paraná rivers, and began trading with the Colombians. In 1905, a conflict between the Peruvians and the Colombians was narrowly avoided by the signing of a treaty between the two countries recognizing the Putumayo River as a provisional international boundary. This agreement was later denounced, and agents for Arana pushed steadily north, enslaving Indians and massacring Colombian traders.

The Hacienda La Unión was the largest Colombian enterprise in the disputed area. Owned by Antonio Ordóñez and Antonio Martínez, it had assets of 100,000 pesos in 1907, as well as extensive cattle herds, and it employed five hundred Indians, who collected 60 tons of rubber annually. By contrast, the Casa Arana was producing 373 tons of rubber annually, and in 1907, Arana's men sacked the Hacienda La Union, driving out Ordóñez and Martínez. Now with a monopoly on the territory, Arana organized the Peruvian Amazon Company, chartered in England with a capital of 1 million pounds. It had one thousand white employees and seven thousand Indian collectors, some of whom were compelled to produce from fifty to sixty kilos of latex every ten days.[69] The company routinely conducted hunts to round up fleeing Indians. It pressed them into gangs and pushed them into the forests, in a daily routine of slave labor that killed them by the hundreds. In 1908, the newspapers of Iquitos were printing stories about hideous crimes occurring in the Putumayo, but the Peruvian government took no action.[70]

Neither did Colombia. Despite Peru's threat to Colombian Amazonia, Reyes did little to reinforce the Colombian presence there or to address the problems endemic to the Llanos. Perhaps it was because he was determined to rebuild the interior after the long war, but with the exception of the completion of a telegraph line to Támara, in 1908, his public-works programs ignored the plains. Diplomatic maneuvers to restore normal relations with Venezuela were stymied by Cipriano Castro's refusal to accept the credentials of plenipotentiaries dispatched to Caracas, and tensions remained high in Arauca.[71] Cattle ranching revived slowly in Casanare. Outside the center of the boom in Putumayo and Alto Caquetá, the exploitation of rubber trees in the Vichada forests south of Orocué continued sporadically. Only in the matter of missions did the government demonstrate any energy, and here the activity was sparked by a Convention on Missions signed with the Vatican by Reyes's predecessor, José Manuel Marroquín in 1902.

Under the 1902 agreement, Colombia gave the religious orders absolute authority to govern, police, educate, and control the Indians in wilderness areas, or in about 75 percent of the republic. They had jurisdiction over primary education for all people in these territories—white and Indian—as well as unlimited access to public lands to promote colonization. Even more important, church authorities had the right to reject nominees for positions in civil government if they regarded the individuals as unsuitable or as threatening to the Indians or the missionaries. The government pledged to provide 75,000 pesos annually to underwrite these activities, of which 11,500 were allotted to the Apostolic Vicariate of Casanare (including Arauca) and 2,500 to the Apostolic Prefecture of the Llanos of San Martín and Vichada. The Vatican assigned the Recoletos and the Hermanas de la Caridad to Casanare and Arauca. It awarded the Llanos of San Martín and Vichada to the Company of María (also known as the Montfort Fathers), and the Capuchins continued to be responsible for La Goajira, Caquetá, and Putumayo.[72] Throughout the Quinquenio, the government subsidized the missionaries financially and supported their work in education through the Ministry of Public Instruction.

At the end of 1903, Apostolic Vicar Nicolás Casas y Conde and several Recoletos returned to Casanare to rebuild their province out of the ashes left by the war. Despite a serious smallpox epidemic, by 1904 there were ten missionaries serving the seven *circumscripciones* of Támara, Manare, Nunchía, Chámeza, Orocué, San Juanito, and Arauca, and the Hermanas de la Caridad had opened schools in Támara, Manare, Nunchía, Ten, and Marroquín.[73]

In November 1904, Bishop Casas left Támara to lobby in Bogotá for more assistance. He conferred with Secretary of Public Instruction Carlos Cuervo Márquez and won from him nearly autonomous control over the direction and inspection of schools in the Vicariate without interference from the Ministry. He requested more educational supplies, including portraits of Jesus Christ, Pope Pius X, and Rafael Reyes, to be hung in every school. Casas also presented the government with a memorial entitled *Colonización de Casanare,* in which he called for the social and spiritual regeneration of the region by promoting its colonization by nationals, foreigners, civilians, soldiers, prisoners, or some combination of these groups. To revitalize agriculture and commerce, he proposed growing, spinning, and weaving cotton, fique, and other fibers on an expanded scale. Casas published the memorial, but it failed to win official endorsement.[74] Before he could return to Támara, the bishop died in Bogotá on April 5, 1906, at the age of fifty-two, worn out by his labors and by the ravages of the tropical climate that had reduced his once robust body to a "walking skeleton."[75]

Santos Ballesteros, who had previously served the missions of Arauca City, Orocué, Chámeza, and Támara, was chosen to succeed Casas. He took possession of the Vicariate in Támara on March 13, 1907. Ballesteros worked closely with the new secretary of public instruction, José María Rivas Groot, to expand education. By the end of the year there were five rural and twenty-four urban schools in Casanare, enrolling 954 boys and 633 girls, and a school for adults in Támara that was later reorganized as the Instituto Nacional de Artesanos.[76] These gains were made notwithstanding another smallpox epidemic, which forced the mission of Orocué to close temporarily and in spite of charges laid against the missionaries that the education they were offering in the schools of Arauca was "anti-Colombian" because the curriculum did not include Colombian history.

Daniel Delgado, who charts this growth between 1904 and 1907, suggests that the most difficult problem the Recoletos faced was preventing violent clashes between the Indians and the Llaneros. Events of the late nineteenth century had done little to ameliorate the deepseated antagonism between the two groups. For example, in 1870 Guahibos had destroyed the town of Manare, consisting of seven houses and several fundaciones, and began attacking travelers on their way to Cravo and Cuiloto. To punish the Indians, the prefect of the territory formed in Moreno a posse of two hundred armed men led by Venezuelan hacendado Pedro del Carmen Gutiérrez. Gutiérrez invited the Indians to meet in Caribabare to take part in a great feast. Two hundred and fifty Indians appeared. As they were eating, the whites fell upon them and massacred all but seven.[77] In another instance, a group of Guahibos came to Támara in 1899 to ask Bishop Casas for food. Casas gave them what he could, but after the Indians left the town they were ruthlessly killed on an hato near the Meta. The cause of the atrocity was never ascertained, but it was widely believed that the whites were retaliating because the Indians had killed some of their cattle.[78]

In 1906, the scattered violence in Arauca became a virtual war. On April 17, two hundred Indians surrounded the Fundación Santa Catalina on the banks of the Ariporo River. They killed four members of the family of Luis Gualdrón, who alone managed to escape, though he carried away arrows in most parts of his body. Six or eight whites vowed vengeance. When they came upon some Indians, they shot at them with rifles; but the Indians, instead of fleeing, turned furiously on their assailants, gravely wounding them. As tension mounted, owners of ranches between the Chire and the Ariporo rivers began abandoning their homes. In describing this situation, Delgado noted that the Indians were becoming bolder because they were being led by two or three whites who had escaped from prison. In spite of the increased violence, he urged the government to prevent private citizens from attacking Indians. If retaliation is necessary, he wrote, a respectable force should be organized with careful safeguards and according to a clearly Christian and civilized plan. "Expeditions of this kind are very delicate, because the death of a single Indian can be a virtue but when it is done without legitimate authority, it can degenerate into a vile assassination. According to our way of thinking there should be other ways to repress the outrages committed by the Indians.[79]

South of the Meta River, the Montfort Fathers and the Daughters of Wisdom (Hijas de la Sabiduría) entered the Llanos of San Martín after the Salesians had withdrawn. Both traced their origins to the Society of Mary, founded in France in 1705 by St. Louis Marie Grignion de Montfort, which expanded rapidly after the beatification of its founder in 1888. Dedicated to restoring the reign of Christ through the reign of Mary, the Montfort Fathers at the turn of the century were founding missions in Ireland, Denmark, Haiti, and Africa as well as South America. In August 1903, the first of their number, Eugenio Morón, arrived in Bogotá to assume his duties as Apostolic Prefect of the double prefecture of Vichada-Vaupés and the Llanos of San Martín. The following January, he left for Villavicencio accompanied by three Montfort Fathers, who had been transferred from Peru, and by the Salesian Ernesto Briata, who introduced them to the people of the prefecture and shared with them his past experiences. Five more missionaries came in 1905, two in 1906, and the Daughters of Wisdom began a school for girls in Villavicencio and Medina.[80]

Morón administered the dual prefecture until 1908, concentrating on organizing the parishes of Villavicencio, San Martín, and Medina. He founded the vice-parish of Surimena and visited Uribe on several occasions. In 1907, he undertook an expedition to Vichada, but illness forced him to stop at San Pedro de Arimena. He started out again the following year and, this time, reached Ucune where some Montfort Fathers had founded a mission. When he returned to Villavicencio, he learned that the pope had elevated the prefecture to an apostolic vicariate. Since Morón was not a bishop, he could no longer continue to head the province, so he resigned his post and retired to France.[81]

The most significant expansion of the Montfort Fathers took place under his successor, Don José María Guiot, who ruled from 1908 until sometime in the 1940s, but one important development during Morón's administration was the government's decision to establish a penal colony near the salinas of Cumaral and Upín, on some land donated by Emiliano Restrepo. The first prisoners arrived on June 22, 1907, most of whom had been convicted of political crimes. Under the direction of Lieutenant Benjamín Ferro, they built a camp and then began to work in the salt mine. Father Dionisio LeTendre, former cura of San Martín, served as chaplain at the settlement known as La Colonia, which at its height had eighty inmates and forty guards. In 1910, however, the government decided it was too expensive to maintain the prisoners in the Llanos and transferred them to the Panóptico in Bogotá. Despite their withdrawal, La Colonia did not die. Some exconvicts who remained at the settlement after completing their sentences were joined by colonos coming from Cáqueza and Guayatá, Boyacá. In 1912, La Colonia was incorporated as a municipio, and three years later its name was changed to Restrepo in honor of the original owner of the site. Moreover, the precedent of having a penal colony in the territory had been set, and in 1918 Congress returned to the idea, treating the Colonia Penal y Agrícola del Meta that was first located in Restrepo and later moved to Acacías.[82]

That Reyes regarded the Llanos as an appropriate place to punish criminals or troublesome enemies is demonstrated by his decision to exile a group of his critics to Orocué in 1905. In December 1904, a few days before the general dissolved Congress, some of his supporters circulated a pamphlet accusing anti-Reyista legislators of blocking his program. Those accused published a tract in their defense entitled "Explicación necesaria" (Necessary Explanation), which was widely circulated, inflaming the debate. Reyes, who would not tolerate dissension, settled the dispute by exiling all those who had signed the "Explicación necesaria" to Mocoa, in Putumayo, or Orocué, in Casanare. The legislators condemned to Mocoa ended up being confined in different towns in Cauca and Nariño for several months, but the thirteen banished to Orocué arrived at their destination after a difficult two-month journey.[83]

According to the memoirs of one of the prisoners, Ramón P. de Hoyos, boredom was the worst aspect of their ordeal. Well-housed by the principal merchant of the town, Ramón Real, the exiled *cachacos* (members of Bogotá's elite) played billiards, learned to dance the *joropo* and to play the *maracas*. They fished and bathed in the Meta River, read, and took long afternoon siestas, but tiring of this monotonous routine they began plotting ways to escape. By March they had hit on a plan to kidnap the commander of the local garrison and flee with him down the river to Ciudad Bolívar, but before they could act Reyes freed them unconditionally, and the legislators returned to Bogotá after five months of banishment.[84]

Reyes's biographer, Eduardo Lemaitre, in analyzing this incident, argues that the general's decision to exile his critics was a serious mistake since "Colombians will put up with all manner of atrocities between private citizens, but if the government takes the initiative, Liberals and Conservatives will unite to protest together," and if the government, trying to gain the good will of its enemies, lightens the punishment, then "the shouting is phenomenal and what was believed to be a remedy for the evil becomes an even worse evil." In this case, Reyes's actions gave cause to his opposition to brand him a tyrant. They continued their plotting against him, and one of the legislators exiled to Orocué, Miguel Abadía Méndez, emerged as a key player in his overthrow in 1909.[85]

If Reyes did little to promote progress in the Llanos, his determination to break down the regional elites who, in the past, had challenged the authority of the central government had a manifestly derogatory effect. Dismemberment of the nine traditional departments

(Antioquia, Bolívar, Boyacá, Cauca, Cundinamarca, Magdalena, Santander, Tolima, and Nariño) began with Law 17 of April 11, 1905,
which created three new departments (Galán, Caldas, and Atlántico)
and designated Bogotá as a capital district. Two weeks later, Law 46
of April 29 increased the number of departments to fifteen by adding
Tundama, Quesada, and Huila.[86] In June, Reyes convoked the National Assembly and ordered it to study a plan for a new territorial
division among other projects to reform the constitution. His secretary of government, Bonifacio Vélez, explained to the delegates that
reducing the size of departments would keep certain regions from
obstructing peace and good administration and would enhance the vitality of the municipio as the fundamental political unit of the republic. The assembly dutifully passed Law 63 of August 5, dividing Colombia into thirty-four departments, each subdivided into provinces
and municipios, and leaving Bogotá as a capital district. On August 31,
a second law suppressed the provinces, retaining municipios as the
only internal divisions of the departments.[87] By these acts, Reyes
hoped to cripple the power bases of his enemies and to encourage
economic growth in the subregions by giving them a distinctive administrative identity.[88]

Reorganization of the national intendancies was also under way.
The preamble to Legislative Decree 28 of January 31, 1905, explained
that it was "convenient that the Intendancies of Casanare and San
Martín be ruled by a single high authority close to the Executive
Power (*un solo Agente superior inmediato del Poder Ejecutivo*)" and of urgent necessity for Colombia to intensify its presence in its eastern territory in order to guard the borders, to found towns, and to civilize the
Indians. Accordingly, the decree joined Casanare and San Martín into
the single "Intendencia Nacional del Meta" and created two new intendancies of Alto Caquetá and Putumayo. It abolished the Intendencia Oriental erected in 1900, dividing its territory between the three
new intendancies. Finally, it instructed the president to work with the
ecclesiastical authorities to promote missions, enjoining him to develop commerce and reinforce national sovereignty in these regions by
granting concessions to exploit their forests.[89]

The territorial policy established by Decree 28 had been in force
for scarcely a year when a new law, Decree 290 of March 8, 1906, was
adopting suppressing the intendancies of Alto Caquetá and Putumayo
and incorporating their territory into the Departments of Nariño and
Cauca. Decree 290 reorganized the Intendencia Nacional del Meta. It

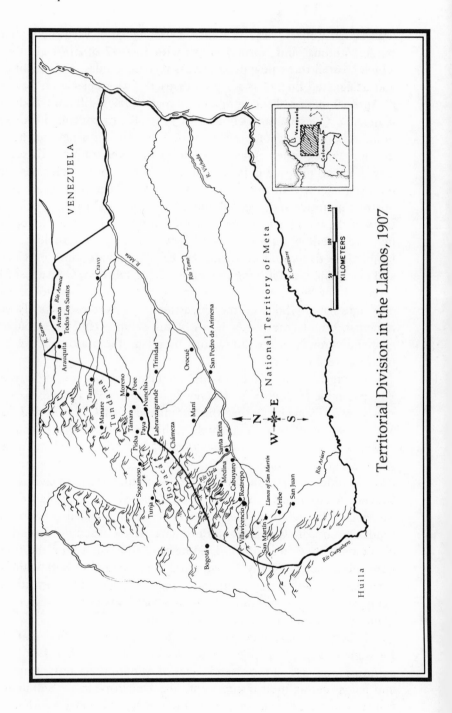

Territorial Division in the Llanos, 1907

split off several municipios that formerly were part of Casanare and attached them to the Departments of Boyacá, Huila, Quesada, and Tundama. Those that remained—Arauca, Arauquita, Cravo, Cabuyaro, Maní, Santa Elena, San Martín, Trinidad, and Villavicencio—continued to form the Territory of Meta, which was to be "administered by the government as it deems most convenient and according to special decrees that it will expedite."[90] Within fifteen months, Decree 778 of July 5, 1907, modified Decree 290 by readjusting the boundaries of the Territory of Meta. It added some of its land to the Departments of Boyacá and Quesada, and within the territory it erected the Provinces of Arauca and Casanare. The decree placed the territory under the jurisdiction of the Ministry of War, and Decree 1120 of September 7, 1907, completed this process by establishing the Jefatura Civil y Militar del Meta.[91]

In his *Memoria* of 1980, Secretary of Government Manuel P. Robles reported on developments in the national territories since 1904. The bulk of his remarks concerned Chocó and Goajira, but he did hail the creation of the intendancies of Putumayo and Alto Caquetá as an important step forward (apparently oblivious that these had already been abolished) and argued that the consolidation of San Martín and Casanare had placed the Llanos on the road to prosperity:

The Intendancies, so very necessary given the uses, habits and customs and general *ambiente* (environment) where they have been established and reorganized, have corresponded to the desire of the government to energize (*impulsar*) those privileged Colombian regions that need special laws for their administration. Through the Ministry of Government, the respective decrees have been dictated, whose excellent results we applaud.[92]

Measured against the neglected state of the Llanos, Robles's conclusions are an exercise in wishful thinking. As was the case with the reorganization of the departments, the ordinances passed during the Quinquenio regarding the intendancies were chaotic, ambiguous, and contradictory. The frequent changes confused all and satisfied none, inhibiting the elaboration of a genuine territorial policy. The result was the total breakdown of government. As Victor M. Salazar, secretary of government in 1922, commented, Reyes eliminated with a stroke the territories that had evolved between 1892 and 1905 and created others without giving them the administration they required in order to justify separating them from the departments.[93] The dictator's policies may have laid the foundation for the modern Colombian state, but they left the Llanos far behind. Their chronic difficulties, exacerbated by the War of the Thousand Days, remained unattended, and it fell to the Conservatives who came to power in 1909 to once again take up the challenge.

Eloy Palacios, a Venezuelan artist, painted a series of eighteen watercolors entitled "Una Crónica del Llano" (A Chronicle of the Llanos) in Caracas in 1912. While the scenes were of Venezuelan Llaneros, they were also representative of the people and landscapes of the Llanos of Arauca.

La Quesera. (The Dairy)

Llanero winter, the flood

Llanero musical group—harp, maracas, and four-string guitar

Roping wild cattle

Llanero cavalry

7. *The National Intendancy of Meta, 1909–30*

A few days before June 13, 1909, when Rafael Reyes startled Colombians by abruptly going into exile, the dictator presided over a congressional election that gave a majority to a newly organized party, the Republic Union. Led by Liberals and Historical Conservatives, this party was committed to a program of strict republicanism, bipartisan participation in government, and laissez-faire economics. Its members dominated the National Assembly that was installed on July 20, and after electing General Ramón González Valencia to complete Reyes's term of office, to August 7, 1910, they proceeded to dismantle most of the repressive measures of the Quinquenio. Within a few months they approved laws that reduced the presidential term to four years, prohibited immediate reelection, provided for annual meetings of Congress, restored direct presidential elections, and made provisions for minority representation. Yet, in other ways the Reyes legacy remained intact. Political stability replaced the fundamental ideological contentiousness, partisan exclusiveness, chronic civil war, and ephemeral constitutions that had characterized the decades before the dictator, and the new leaders continued his policy of promoting export growth and selective protectionism for domestic industry while repudiating measures that might threaten the interests of the large landowners.[1]

The National Assembly elected Carlos E. Restrepo, an Antioqueñan Conservative and leader of the Republic Union, as president for the period from 1910 to 1914. The next four presidents were also Conservatives, as the Liberals struggled to recover from their catastrophic defeat in the War of the Thousand Days. Despite the predominance of a single party, elections were held; public order was maintained, and upper-class civil liberties were generally respected. Many of the administrations were bipartisan in composition, and the principle of minority representation assured both traditional parties membership in the national legislative bodies.

The twenty-one years between 1909 and 1930, sometimes called the "Era of National Harmony" or the "Conservative Republic," saw the reorganization of territory rule. The Restrepo administration set up a system of national intendancies and special commissariats (*comi-*

sarías especiales) that remains in place today. Succeeding presidents spoke enthusiastically about the Llanos, but they failed to formulate practical programs to stimulate their development. As a result, much of the change that occurred was spontaneous—the unpredicted offshoot of the modernization of the Colombian interior that intensified the unique characteristics of each subregion. Civil officials were regularly installed in Meta, Arauca, and Casanare, but the dominant authorities often proved to be the missionaries who, by agreements hammered out during Regeneration and the Quinquenio, expanded their power over the civilization of the Indians to include many other aspects of life in the territories. After reviewing some key features of the Conservative Republic and the territorial system that was adopted, this chapter will focus on the history of the National Intendancy of Meta between 1909 and 1930, while chapter 8 will consider the Comisaría Especial of Arauca during this same period, and chapter 9 will take up the fate of Casanare as a province within the Department of Boyacá.

The Conservative Republic

One of the most important acts of the National Assembly in 1909 was to restore the territorial divisions that had existed in 1904 before Reyes came to power. Law 65 of December 14, 1909, divided the nation into ten departments—Antioquia, Bolívar, Boyacá, Cauca, Cundinamarca, Magdalena, Nariño, Panama, Santander, and Tolima; and two intendancies—Meta and Chocó. During the presidency of Carlos Restrepo, five new departments were added—Atlántico, Caldas, Huila, Norte de Santander, and Valle; and seven comisarías especiales—a new designation for undeveloped, peripheral regions. This configuration, unchanged until 1952, was dominated by two departments, Cundinamarca and Antioquia, whose hegemony was reinforced by the expansion of coffee as Colombia's chief export. Despite improvements in transportation and communication, the central government still had only a limited hold over provincial affairs. As Christopher Abel has pointed out, travel was costly, dangerous and slow, and politics was understood at the regional level in regional terms. Like the Austro-Hungarian Empire, Colombia continued to be a collection of heterogeneous regions throughout the first half of the twentieth century.[2]

The Cundinamarca–Antioquia ruling axis and the disorganization of the Liberal party enhanced Conservative control of the central government. Supporters of the Republic Union, including the peace factions of both parties, elected Restrepo as president in 1910. Although they failed to create a permanent national party, they did institutionalize the practice of accommodating the opposition and demonstrated that united allegiance to a presidential–congressional system by the upper class was an effective guarantee against individual and factional tyranny.[3] The official machinery, the church, the *caciques*, public opinion, and the direct vote all favored the Conservatives. In 1914, José Vicente Concha easily defeated his Republican Liberal opponent, winning 300,735 votes against 36,763. In 1918, Marco Fidel Suárez won 216,595 votes against 166,498 for Guillermo Valencia, a dissident Conservative who ran with Liberal support. In 1922, fraud, violence, and clerical participation enabled General Pedro Nel Ospina to triumph over General Benjamín Herrera, 413,619 votes to 256,213. When Liberals abstained in protest in 1926, Miguel Abadía Méndez won unopposed with 370,492 votes. Only in 1930, when the Conservatives divided their support between Guillermo Valencia and Alfredo Vásquez Cobo, did the Liberal nominee, Enrique Olaya Herrera, emerge victorious. Despite their continual shutout at the polls, the Liberals launched just two violent insurrections that were easily put down.[4] So long as the Conservatives abstained from meddling in their economic affairs or civil liberties, upper-class Liberals acquiesced to the system and were repaid, at times, with some cabinet or diplomatic post.

The Catholic church was the principal bulwark of Conservative rule. Briefly subdued by the War of the Thousand Days, it regained under Reyes its position of primacy authorized by the Constitution of 1886, the Concordat of 1887, and the Additional Convention of 1892. As John Lynch aptly observed, the church consolidated its power in four ways, offering a model to beleaguered clergy in other Latin American countries. First, it gave support and political legitimacy to the government in exchange for important privileges. Second, the superior education of the clergy made them indispensable to the functioning of local government. Third, the church controlled education and, therefore, the career prospects of many Colombians. Finally, the power of the church to open and close newspapers gave it the means of influencing the media and silencing its enemies—a definite advantage in the battle for public opinion.[5]

Christopher Abel underscores Lynch's assertions when he states that Bernardo Herrera Restrepo, archbishop from 1891 to 1928, probably exercised more civil authority than archbishops during the Spanish colony since, unlike the Hapsburg and Bourbon kings who ruled by divine right, Conservative presidents could not be elected without the prelate's *nihil obstat* and did not enjoy either his perpetual powers or his control over public consciousness. The bishops and párrocos were equally influential in the departments and municipios. Their superior education made them prominent leaders, and they exercised their influence as consultants to the alcaldes, supervisors of local education, and key figures in charity works, as well as by controlling popular diversions. Abel shows that on every level the church expected its clergy to intervene in politics against the Liberals. Throughout the period under discussion, priests were instructed to advise the faithful that there were two forms of sin: first, to be a Liberal and rebel against legitimate authority; and second, to support candidates that did not guarantee the church special concessions. Penitents who were not sincere could be denied absolution, for according to some priests the crime of being a Liberal was worse than committing murder, robbery, adultery, or incest.[6]

The growth of the export economy bolstered the Conservative hegemony. Between 1905 and 1929 total exports multiplied nine times. As coffee trees spread from Santander to Cundinamarca, Tolima, Antioquia, and Caldas, production increased by fifteen times. Exports of bananas from Santa Marta in the 1920s rose to 10 million stems. By the end of the decade petroleum was providing 20 percent of the export total, and Colombia had built a base in textiles, food processing, and other small consumer industries.[7] Although World War I temporarily halted expansion by closing many coffee markets and forcing the Concha administration to adopt a policy of retrenchment, prosperity returned in the 1920s, fueled by renewed coffee exports and the influx of foreign capital. The so-called Dance of the Millions began with the payment by the United States of 25 million dollars in indemnity to resolve the dispute over Panama in accordance with the Urrutia-Thompson Treaty of 1922. After President Ospina invited a U.S. financial mission, headed by Dr. Edwin Kemmerer, to modernize Colombia's banking and accounting system, the departments and the nation began to borrow extensively from abroad. Long-term debt rose from 27.5 million dollars in 1924 to 208 million dollars in 1928. Whereas the Suárez administration spent around 12 million pesos on public works, Ospina's spent 55 million and Abadía Méndez's 158 million. Much of this money was used to develop railroad and highway networks and to complete other public-works projects. Colombia moved into the modern age with the arrival of automobiles, the first aviation company, the first radio transmissions, motion pictures, and the formation of a national system of communication.[8]

The Territorial Policy of the Conservative Republic

With regard to territorial rule, the Conservatives wanted to mitigate the disruptive effects of Reyes's administrative shake-up and recapture continuity with the system begun under Regeneration. Led by Ramón González Valencia, the National Assembly endorsed the "intendancy" as an appropriate governance unit for peripheral regions, but there was considerable inconsistency in the laws that followed. Decree no. 238 of September 23, 1909, created the Intendancy of Meta, with its capital at Villavicencio and including the municipios of Villavicencio, Orocué and San Martín City. Article 1 of Law 65 of December 14, 1909, which redrew departmental boundaries, stated that the Territories of San Martín and Casanare, Caquetá, Goajira, and Chocó "will be administered directly by the national government as intendancies," but excepting the Intendancy of Meta, which had already been set up, and the Intendancy of Chocó, which would be created in April 1910, the former territories were subsequently reincorporated into their contiguous departments: Caquetá rejoined Cauca, Goajira returned to Magdalena, and Casanare, divided into the Provinces of Nunchía and Arauca, became part of Boyacá.[9]

During the Restrepo administration, Congress devised the comisaría especial, a new category reserved for regions of lesser importance and greater dependency on the central government than the intendancies. In 1911, Governor Rafael Castillo Mariño conceded that Boyacá could not govern the Province of Arauca effectively because of the immense distance between the region and Tunja, the lack of roads and telegraph, the large numbers of Venezuelans in Arauca City, and the department's inability to supply soldiers to secure the border.[10] Congress responded by passing Decree no. 306 of March 24, 1911, which created the Comisaría Especial of Arauca, with its capital at Arauca City, and the caseríos of Arauca City, Arauquita, Cravo, Todos los Santos, and El Viento. The decree called on the president to appoint a comisario to exercise the powers of governor, prefect, and alcalde; to promote the development of the caseríos into municipios; to

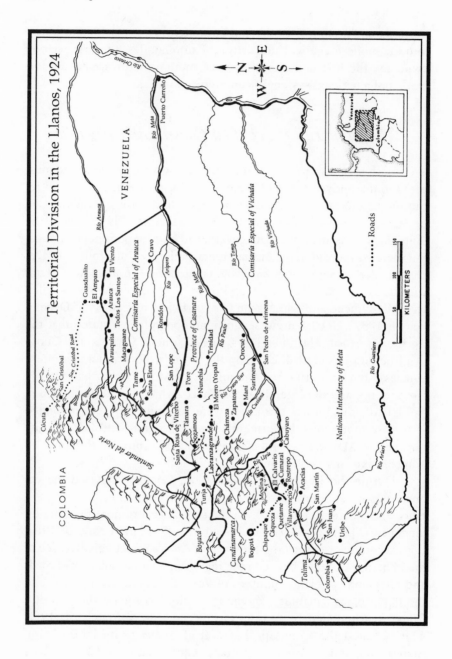

Territorial Division in the Llanos, 1924

defend national and sectional interest; to compile a census of property titles; to exercise notarial functions; and to supervise the customs house. To keep the peace, the comisario was assigned three agents from the national police force under the aegis of the Ministry of War.[11]

Two years later, Decree no. 523 of 1913 established the Comisaría Especial of Vichada by separating from the Intendancy of Meta the territory that lay east of the third meridian east of Bogotá (longitude 70°), bordered on the north by the Meta River, on the south by the Guaviare River, and on the east by Venezuela. Maipures was designated as the capital, and the comisario was given the same powers as his counterpart in Arauca except that he was subject to the fiscal and police laws of Cundinamarca. Before Restrepo left office, Congress created six other comisarías especiales: Caquetá, Putumayo, La Guajira, Vaupés, Juradó, and Urabá. All endured except for Juradó and Urabá, which were reintegrated into the Intendancy of Chocó and the Department of Antioquia, respectively.[12]

On August 12, 1913, Rafael Uribe Uribe, now a senator from Antioquia and the leader of the Liberal opposition in Congress, proposed a law to foster economic development in the Llanos. The plan called for the nation to establish a fifteen-year monopoly on salt production at Cumaral and Upín. Within a year of the law's enactment, the government would construct a road to link the mines with a navigable river, and six months later it would assemble a fleet of steamships to carry the salt to ranchers throughout the plains, to deliver mail, and to transport missionaries, civil officials, and military personnel. The salt would be sold to the ganaderos at a fixed price, and the government would tax cattle transported by water and land. Uribe Uribe argued that passage of this bill would stimulate ranching by ensuring a supply of cheap salt to the ganaderos. Easy availability of salt would encourage Indians to settle down. Improved river transport would lead to landownership, the introduction of fences and artificial pasture, and strengthen public security in the most isolated areas. The Llanos would be freed from dependence on Venezuela, and national defense would be strengthened. The bill was approved in committee on second debate, on September 15, 1913, but it faltered on the Senate floor. A year later, the assassination of Uribe Uribe on October 15, 1914, removed a forceful spokesman for the interests of the Llanos.[13]

Dissatisfaction with the progress of the intendancies and comisarías was not long in surfacing. In his annual message of 1915, President José Vicente Concha called for their complete reorganization because qualified people could not be found to fill the administrative posts and because they still lacked schools, roads, ports, and health and sanitary facilities.[14] In 1923, President Ospina again enumerated these problems and urged Congress

to infuse life, activity and development in those regions, impregnating them with the spirit of patriotism and attracting to them by securing life and property and the solicitude of scrupulous and respectable authorities, the desired population, labor, capital and initiative, and to give to these extremities for today and for tomorrow, the blood and soul of the Colombian nation one and indivisible.[15]

The legislators reacted to this noble charge by passing two measures in 1923. The first was Law 41 of July 19, which reorganized the intendancies and comisarías, creating the public offices that were necessary to govern them and assigning monthly subsidies from the national budget to sustain them. The second was Law 100, which promoted the colonization of the territories.[16]

More comprehensive, but no more effective, were two measures adopted during the Abadía Méndez administration. Inspired by a plan proposed by Miguel Triana in his book *Al Meta* (Bogotá, 1913), Law 52 of November 13, 1926, enjoined the national government to promote colonization, agriculture, ranching, and commerce by encouraging navigation of the rivers, opening roads to the interior, and facilitating salt production and the adjudication of land, or "in a word, to do all that is possible to organize the social life of the territories of San Martín, Casanare, Vichada, Vaupés, Arauca and the rest of the Llanos Orientales." It authorized the government to buy ships, to negotiate contracts for public works, to spend 100,000 pesos for a feasibility study for a railroad between Bogotá and the Meta River, and to assign 25,000 pesos annually for repairs on the Cravo national road connecting Sogamoso with the Meta River, via Labranzagrande.[17] Law 96 of 1928 established public-works committees (*juntas de obras públicas*) in each intendancy and comisaría to renew all proposed contracts for public works, formulate budgets, and make recommendations to the government on the contracts to be adopted. Plazas Olarte adds that the 1920s saw copious legislation dealing with the administration of baldíos but that the majority of these laws "did not pass beyond the realm of *expedientes* (file of papers bearing on a case) and official *infolios* (books in folio form)."[18]

Between 1909 and 1930 the Catholic church played a key role in governing the national territories. As mentioned in chapter 6, the 1902

Convenio on Missions signed between Colombia and the Vatican gave the religious orders control over the Indians in the territories and responsibility for the public education for all people in their jurisdiction, while the government pledged to provide seventy-five thousand pesos annually to support these activities. In 1908, the First Conference of Colombian Bishops created a National Junta on Missions to coordinate the drive to civilize the "savage tribes" and colonize frontier areas.[19] The work of various religious orders in the territories was well under way when international furor over atrocities in Putumayo focused world attention on the mistreatment of Indians in the remote jungles of Colombia and Peru.

In 1910, the British government, disturbed by persistent reports of alleged crimes committed by the Peruvian Amazon Company, directed its consul in Pará, Brazil, Roger Casement, to investigate the situation in Putumayo. Casement's report confirmed that the company had ruthlessly enslaved Indians, submitting them to refined tortures and corporal punishment and forcing women into concubinage and prostitution. He concluded that between 1900 and 1911 the Putumayo forests had yielded forty thousand tons of rubber at the appalling cost of thirty thousand lives. Casement's findings were confirmed by an American, W. E. Hardenberg, who visited the rubber camps and published a book exposing their horrors entitled *The Putumayo, The Devil's Paradise* (London, 1912). Reacting to public outrage, Colombia and Peru set up a mixed commission to conduct an on-the-spot inquiry, which revealed that the allegations were substantially correct. The scandal was particularly embarrassing for the Capuchins, who had jurisdiction over the Putumayo territory; and on June 7, 1912, Pope Pius X issued an encyclical, "Lacrimabili Statu," that condemned the "slavery to the devil and to criminals" into which the inhabitants of Putumayo had fallen and called on the South American bishops to take action to prevent further outrages.[20]

The Colombian bishops addressed the pope's directive at their Second Episcopal Conference in January 1913 by issuing the pastoral "Missions among the Unfaithful." In this document, they reaffirmed the need to convert the Indians in accordance with the Convenio of 1902. They emphasized that the missionaries must continue to wield complete control over the Indians in order to protect them from outside evils, and to promote their conversion they should undertake the foundation of towns; the construction of churches, schools, and roads; acquire boats for river transportation, and start homes for Indian children and farms, where adult natives could learn agricultural techniques. Asserting that their ardent desire was to win the Indians' souls for the faith and free them from their barbarous conditions, the bishops closed by urging all Colombians to support the missions with their money and prayers.[21]

Congress reacted to the Putumayo scandal by increasing its annual subsidy to the Junta de Misiones in 1912 to 100,000 pesos. In the years that followed, the missionaries continued to be important figures in the territories. It was they who ran the schools and hospitals, published newspapers, mobilized colonization, and not infrequently decided who would govern locally. On occasion, the powerful role of missionaries received intense national attention, with Liberals objecting to the political, judicial, and ecclesiastical monopoly exercised by members of the religious orders—many of whom were foreign citizens, over three-quarters of the republic—but for the most part, the question was "too distant to sustain public interest for long." In 1928, after "a gloomy debate of short duration because there were other more pressing problems," Congress renewed the Convenio of 1902 without amendment.[22]

The National Intendancy of Meta

The territorial policy elaborated by state and church, and summarized above, provides a backdrop for reviewing the history of the National Intendancy of Meta between 1909 and 1930. As the Montfort Fathers and the intendants extended their authority over Indian and white inhabitants of the Llanos, spontaneous immigration from eastern Cundinamarca, expanding cattle production for the highland markets, and the emergence of rice as a major cash crop fueled hope in Villavicencio and Bogotá that the territory was beginning to fulfill its destiny as "the future of Colombia." While rapid growth did not occur until after the Bogotá–Villavicencio highway was completely paved in 1936, the foundation for that growth was laid during the Conservative republic.

The consolidation of the municipios of Villavicencio, San Martín, and Orocué into the Intendancy of Meta, in 1909, proved to be just another temporary step in the search to settle the geographical dimensions of the territory. The region, which the Spanish called alternately and simultaneously the Llanos of San Juan and the Llanos of San Martín, had been in the nineteenth century a canton and a province in the Department of Cundinamarca, twice a national territory, and an intendancy; and, under Rafael Reyes, it was combined with Casanare to form a still larger intendancy. This tinkering with boundaries was not over, for in 1912 Congress reassigned Orocué to Casanare, and in 1913 it split off the eastern portion of Meta to form the Comisaría Especial of Vichada. The municipio of Medina, formerly a part of the territory, was awarded to Cundinamarca in 1910 and remained part of that department despite protests by Meta officials. As a steady stream of immigrants arrived, new districts were formed. Thus, by 1928 the National Intendancy of Meta consisted of four municipios: Villavicencio, Restrepo, San Martín City, and El Calvario; and six corregimientos: Uribe, Surimena, San Juanito, Cumaral, Acacías, and San Pedro de Arimena.[23]

The Intendants

According to the system elaborated in 1892 and 1897 and readopted by the National Assembly in 1909, the intendant appointed by the president controlled territorial government. He was responsible for maintaining order, overseeing the budget, inspecting local municipal councils, and working with the missionaries to promote public instruction, colonization, and economic development. Assisting him were two circuit judges from Cundinamarca—one for criminal and the other for civil cases—and a police force of twenty-five men. Each municipio had an alcalde and a five-member council. In Villavicencio there was also a *junta de caminos*, whose job was to repair national roads, using funds collected from tolls.[24]

Historian-archaeologist Miguel Triana, who spent several weeks traveling through the territory in 1912, described the intendant as a nominal official "without real initiative, without funds and nearly without subordinate employees to transmit his authority."[25] In truth, his powers, which appeared so broad on paper, were circumscribed by the fact that his appointment was normally for one year. Between 1909 and 1931, nineteen men held the post. Rubén Santacoloma, who served from February 7, 1925, until September 16, 1927, had the longest tenure, while Leopold L. León, one of four intendants appointed in 1929, had the shortest, ruling for eight weeks between August 8 and October 7, 1929.[26] The meagerness of national financial subsidy and the geographic isolation imposed other limitations. Intendant Timoteo Mora complained in 1916 that the nineteen thousand pesos assigned to his office were not enough to pay his employees and buy supplies. Moreover, he noted, government salaries were so low that qualified people would not accept the positions even if there had been money to pay them. His successor, Alfonso Rincón, asked that the budget be increased to help the municipios and corregimientos build offices, schools, and jails because their reduced local revenues could cover only the most pressing necessities. Santacoloma complained, in 1926, that most of the towns were lamentably backward because of the great distances between them, a lack of rapid communication, and public apathy. A telegraph line linked Villavicencio to Bogotá, but the extension of this line to San Martín had been destroyed during the War of the Thousand Days. The vast majority of the territory was completely isolated most of the year due to flooding that made the roads impassable.[27]

Judging by their informes, published annually with the memorias of the ministers of government, the intendants were men of varied ability, but they were all Conservative political appointees who had the disadvantage of ruling a region populated predominantly by men and women of Liberal sympathies. Triana observed:

Villavicencio is the headquarters for the political and ecclesiastical authorities who govern the national territory of Meta, or rather, who beam the social principal toward the Llanos (*irradian el principio social hacia la llanura*). . . . It is true that relative distance and isolation weaken, in proportion, the influence of the authorities of both orders, so that the people who live in those distant places are subjected to the Government and the Church by an obedience entirely voluntary and tenuous. . . . *Authority* which we citizens still think of as the sword and the cane (*el sable y el bastón*) does not appear in the center of the Llanos except as an intangible symbol without luster.[28]

Frequently, the intendants would request special laws to administer the Llanos, arguing that conditions there differed radically from the rest of the nation. They learned not to expect much from Bogotá. In 1915, Jacinto Rodríguez confessed that he was sure his report was of little interest to higher officials or the public, since it was evident that the national government knew nothing about the Llanos. Rodríguez urged Congress to pay more attention to the eastern territories and to provide them with an adequate, uniform administration, since under the present system "the laws of Boyacá are in force in some municipios; in others those of Cundinamarca, and most of these territories are like a Moor without a lord (*como moro sin señor*)."[29]

While Pablo V. León wrote in 1913 that the Llaneros were a "good sort, easy to govern, hardworking, and respectful of authority," other intendants reported that there were many crimes and registered their dissatisfaction with the size and organization of the police.[30] Court records for 1912 show that there were forty-seven blood crimes (homicides, injuries, quarrels, attempted assaults), thirty crimes against property (rustling, robbery, swindles, contraband), fifteen crimes against honesty (cohabitation, incest, rape, forced adultery), and twenty-seven miscellaneous crimes (perjury, slander, and vagrancy). Triana attributed most of the violence to abuse of aguardiente, and added that given the weakness of the authorities, the number of crimes was relatively insignificant.[31]

Cattle rustling was the most serious problem. Outlaws roamed the plains with impunity, preying on local ganaderos and receiving steers stolen from Cundinamarca, Boyacá, Santander, and Huila. Between 1923 and 1925 a gang led by Victor Espinal and Moisés Barón plundered the region, causing many to fear for their lives and property. Rubén Santacoloma finally broke their reign of terror. With an expanded police force, he captured some of the rustlers and recovered two hundred cattle. Barón and Espinal got away, but the latter was captured in Casanare and returned to jail in Villavicencio in 1925.[32]

Inflamed political hatreds, especially around election time, were another source of unrest. In the aftermath of the riot of April 22, 1923, Jorge Luna Ospina reported that the public had a tendency to defy his commands, but inflexible punishment was ending "such dangerous impulses as if by enchantment."[33] The calm he eventually imposed prevailed throughout the rest of the decade, so that when some socialist agitators arrived in 1927 to promote the ideas of Lenin and Trotsky, they returned to Bogotá without winning any converts.[34]

The Montfort Fathers

If there was continual turnover in civil government personnel, ecclesiastical rule, by contrast, was a model of stability. In 1908, the Vatican combined the Apostolic Prefecture of the Llanos of San Martín with the Apostolic Prefecture of the Intendencia Oriental to form the Apostolic Vicariate of the Llanos of San Martín, a jurisdiction that eventually included the Intendancy of Meta, the comisarías especiales of Vichada, Caquetá, and Putumayo, and the Prefecture of Vaupés. The spiritual leader of this enormous domain, which encompassed 350,000 square kilometers of plains and jungles, was the Illustrious Señor Doctor Don José María Guiot, a French citizen and Montfort Father who was consecrated bishop, *in partibus*, of Augustópolis and served as Apostolic Vicar from 1908 until 1936. The masculine and feminine orders of the Society of Mary, founded by St. Louis Marie Grignion de Montfort, had begun arriving in Villavicencio in 1905. By 1930 some thirty Montfort Fathers, most of them originally from France or Holland, had served in the Llanos as párrocos in the towns of the intendancy or as missionaries to the Indians in Vichada and Vaupés. The Daughters of Wisdom had houses in Villavicencio, San Martín, El Calvario, and Vichada. They taught boys and girls in schools and staffed the hospital founded in 1912. The Montfortian monopoly in the vicariate was not broken until 1921, when some Christian Brothers started a boys' school in Villavicencio. Later, nuns of the Order of Immaculate Mary and St. Catherine of Siena (María Inmaculada y Santa Catalina de Sena), founded in Antioquia in 1914, taught school in Vaupés.[35]

Since no more than ten or twelve religious were working in the vicariate at any one time, their presence in the outlying districts was as tenuous as that of the national officials. As Miguel Triana observed, "The immense extension of these parishes make their administration very difficult if not impossible with so few ecclesiastical personnel during the winter season which lasts for two-thirds of the year."[36] Nevertheless, in Villavicencio the Montfort Fathers were powerful figures. Assisting Bishop Guiot and residing in the capital were Juan Bautista Arnaud, who served as párroco of Villavicencio before leaving in 1912 to colonize the upper Guatequía River district; Gabriel Capdeville, who replaced Arnaud as párroco and served as Apostolic Provicar; and finally, Mauricio Dieres Monplaisir, first coadjutor, ecclesiastical notary, secretary of the vicariate, director of various social works, and school inspector in the absence of the bishop. Capable and energetic, these three men left their mark on life in the capital and in the settlements beyond.

When Bishop Guiot came to Villavicencio, there was no episcopal residence and the church was still only partially rebuilt after the devastation of the 1890 fire. Fortunately, Juan Bautista Arnaud was a competent architect and drew up plans for both buildings, and

Antonio Camargo, a local resident, supervised their construction. By 1917 the bishop had moved into his residence, and the church was nearing completion. Arnaud also collaborated with the alcalde, Colonel Heliodoro Moyano, to raise money for a hospital by holding Sunday bazaars. On July 20, 1910, they laid the cornerstone of the new facility. On November 1, 1911, the hospital opened its doors, managed by the Daughters of Wisdom with an annual government subsidy of eight hundred pesos that dropped to four hundred pesos in years of penury. Hamilton Rice, an American geographer delayed in Villavicencio in February 1912 by bad weather while on an expedition to the northwest Amazon Basin, wrote in his field report that the hospital had been built since his previous visit:

It was aviary as well as hospital such as would delight a Frank Buckland, for countless pigeons, fowls, ducks, and parrots roosted on the patients' beds or solemnly paraded on the mud floors. A brave and noble-hearted little Soeur de Sagesse did what she could to alleviate the sufferings of the wretched patients, but the absence of proper medical attendance and the pitiful stock of supplies made her task a discouraging and hopeless one.[37]

In 1912, Arnaud set off from Villavicencio to begin a colonization project along the upper Guatequía, and Gabriel Capdeville left his post as párroco in Medina to come to the capital. Although Capdeville had been born in France, his parents were Spaniards and he spoke Spanish without an accent, a talent that made him more acceptable to the Llaneros. Capdeville assisted the bishop and monitored the repairs on the church and episcopal residence. He organized the Santa Cecelia Boys Band, whose nineteen members, outfitted with handsome uniforms, played on patriotic occasions. He started the San José Bank which by 1917 had a capital of 4,006.41 pesos and 333 depositors. In that year, there were six primary schools in Villavicencio taught by the Daughters of Wisdom and inspected by Father Mauricio Dieres Monplaisir.[38]

As secretary of the vicariate, Monplaisir worked with Capdeville on social projects and edited the diocesan newspaper, *Eco de Oriente*, bringing out two mimeographed issues a month between May 15, 1913, and March 15, 1916. The installation of a printing press brought from France permitted the expansion of the operation, and beginning on April 12, 1916, *Eco de Oriente* (2d Epoca) made its weekly appearance as an elegantly printed periodical featuring national as well as local news. Monplaisir used the newspaper to propagate his political, moral, and social views and to promote progress in the intendancy.[39] He supported several bills introduced in Congress to build a railroad between Bogotá and the Meta River and encouraged the introduction of artificial pasture to improve the local cattle. An enthusiastic booster of Villavicencio, he wrote in an editorial of May 18, 1919, that the town had a small park, electric lights, and factories to process rice and sugar. Honorable and responsible merchants contributed to its active commerce:

Villavicencio is in effect an important city, worthy of paying attention to, not because it wants to make a point to those cities older in age, dignity and government, but because it sees with pain those people pretending to ignore its legitimate condition and the honor it has acquired . . . Villavicencio only wants to be understood for what it can and wants to be, a servant of the country and mother of its children.[40]

In 1915, a power plant built by Jorge Bejarano began generating electricity, and on November 24, 1916, Padre Mauricio showed the first motion pictures in Villavicencio, using a silent projector brought from France. Some ninety people assembled in the open-air Teatro Verdun, while Monplaisir, using a small pointer, interpreted the pictures that flashed across the screen. Six days later, *Eco de Oriente* printed the curious program, annotating the film titles with explanatory comments as follows:

1st Part: *Hippopotamus Hunt* (a very interesting film)
           Labor of Victorius
2nd Part: *Winter Sport in Switzerland* (travelogue)
           The Young Jules Verne (dream)
3rd Part: *The Spider* (scientific)
           The Perdition of the Apprentice (sensational)
           Encore. *The Departure of the Cyclist* (funny)[41]

On Friday, August 31, 1917, the work of the Montfort Fathers received a serious setback. At 6:30 A.M., a powerful earthquake shook Villavicencio and the surrounding area for fifteen seconds. The episcopal residence, the church, and the hospital roof each collapsed, killing a total of eight persons and injuring six others. Nearly all the houses made of adobe were destroyed. Damage was also severe in San Martín City, where tremors toppled the church and most of the houses.[42] Recovery was slow, and Bishop Guiot went to France to raise money for reconstruction, but by 1921 the church in Villavicencio had been rebuilt. The hospital was expanded and, in 1923, received a new zinc roof paid for by the government. In the meantime, Father Gabriel Capdeville, stricken with dysentery, retired to a monastery in Italy. As Bishop Guiot gradually withdrew from diocesan affairs, Father Mauricio, now párocco of Villavicencio, emerged as the most influential ecclesiastical figure in the vicariate.

Monplaisir did much to foster progress in the intendancy, but he was not uniformly revered. In the first place, he was a foreigner who spoke Spanish with a marked accent.[43] Secondly, in a region where most of the inhabitants identified themselves as Liberals, there was smoldering resentment against the priest's unabashed championing of the Conservatives. The tense political climate was revealed in an article published by the Bogotá Liberal daily *El Tiempo* on April 25, 1923, which described a bazaar held in Restrepo during the previous week and sponsored by Liberals to raise money to buy a printing press and to start a school. The local correspondent explained that a press and a school were the most urgent needs of Liberalism in the intendancy because the Marist Fathers monopolized the media with their political–religious newspaper "saturated with the most odious of policies," and because the government had unconditionally delivered public instruction "to a foreign community that does not permit official inspection or a review of its programs." He added that the bishop, in an effort to stop the event, had ordered a notice affixed to the church door stating:

We, José María Guiot, Apostolic Vicar of the Llanos of San Martín, warn our faithful that they all commit mortal sin if they take part in the Liberal bazaar, whether directly or indirectly, donating, buying or serving at tables.[44]

Despite this attempt at sabotage, the bazaar was a huge success. The Liberal party had raised five hundred pesos "to acquire the decisive elements that it needs for future struggles."[45]

Finally, while only Conservatives might be appointed intendants, not all of them found it easy to work with Padre Mauricio. As early as February 1919, a Liberal from Meta, writing under the pseudonym CELASP, published an article in *El Diario Nacional* accusing Bogotá of neglecting the intendancy and alleging that the efforts of the intendants were overpowered by the missionaries, who had all the moral and material advantages. "The Maristas," he charged, "made a crude war on the work of the intendants obstructing every project."[46] The most sweeping indictment came from Colonel Aristides Novoa, who served as intendant from May 22, 1922, to April 23, 1923. In his report to his successor, Jorge Luna Ospina, that he later published in *El Tiempo*, Novoa alleged that Padre Mauricio Dieres Monplaisir had forged an intolerable dictatorship over Meta and that, during the past twelve years Novoa had lived there,

All, absolutely all the gentlemen, who have served this intendancy with independence of character and civil dignity and most of the circuit judges, hacienda administrators, police chiefs and mayors have had friction and more or less serious disputes with the missionary that I am talking about, because they did not let him have his own way, because they did not give in to his demands and whims, because they did not servilely humble themselves before his dictatorial impositions and before his rough and uncivil treatment.[47]

A series of conflicts with Padre Mauricio marked Novoa's term of office, in spite of the fact that the colonel described himself as "a Conservative and a Catholic, by principle, by deep-seated conviction and by constant practice." The first confrontation came on October 12, 1922, when Novoa gave a speech during the celebration of the Fiesta de la Raza. Padre Mauricio objected to the tone of his remarks and complained to Bishop Guiot, who sent a telegram to the Minister of Public Instruction requesting that he censure Novoa. The feud escalated during the celebration of the Fiesta de la Paz on November 21. Novoa gave a patriotic speech to a large and respectable group of Liberals and asked them to join with the Conservatives and himself in singing the national hymn. Padre Mauricio left the plaza in disgust, returning later to pull down all the decorations and flags. On his instigation, Bishop Guiot sent another telegram to the minister of public instruction, accusing Novoa of not respecting the ecclesiastical authorities and of being the cause of "an extremely delicate situation that is getting worse by the moment."[48] On December 9, *El Tiempo* published both the telegram and Novoa's response, with the comment,

We are astounded: Villavicencio and the Meta region, in appearance a section of the republic is in reality an ecclesiastical colony, in which civil power is neither respected nor attended to, and which is ruled by the imperious orders of R. P. Maurice Dieres Monplaisir, párocco of Villavicencio, secretary of the episcopate, inspector of public instruction and French citizen who for some time has resided among us.[49]

The inevitable explosion came as preparations for congressional elections on May 12 were raising political temperatures, and Novoa was ending his term of office and arranging to turn over the government to Jorge Luna Ospina. On the evening of April 22, Oliverio Reina, part rancher and part bandit leader of a group of ultraconservative thugs, who enjoyed the patronage of Padre Mauricio, got into a bitter argument with a young Liberal, Efraín Chalarca, while they were drinking beer in a popular Villavicencio bar. Reina left the store in a rage and returned with some friends, with the obvious purpose of beating up Chalarca. As his assailants drew their pistols, Chalarca fired first, killing Reina instantly. Seeing their leader fall, Reina's companions shot Chalarca in both legs and proceeded to beat him to death, while men who had come to Chalarca's aid fought back, killing Antonio Ibagón. By this time an infuriated mob had gathered. Led by Rómulo Reina, nephew of Oliverio, they shouted, "Death to Liberalism," and went on a rampage, throwing stones at houses, breaking doors and windows. Informed of the uproar, Colonel Novoa rallied his force of six policemen, but they could not restore order. In the early hours of April 24, he telegraphed Minister of Government José Osorio for help, fearing that the enraged Conservatives would seize what arms were available in Villavicencio and make war on the Liberals.

While he waited for Osorio to reply, Novoa held a meeting of concerned citizens. He divided the men into two groups. To the first, made up of eight "honorable and clearsighted Conservatives," he gave weapons belonging to the government and instructed them to convince their copartisans to lay down their arms. The second group, consisting of unarmed Liberals and Conservatives, was to go through the streets to get those on both sides to stop fighting. As the two groups set out, Novoa sent a second telegraph to the minister of government, asking him to appoint a special investigator to conduct an impartial inquiry into the incident.[50]

The unrest continued until the arrival, on April 27, of the new intendant Jorge Luna Ospina, a nephew of President Ospina; the special investigator, Dr. José María Dávila Tello; and a squadron of cavalry. As Novoa left for Bogotá to tell his side of the story under military protection, Ospina offered ample guarantees to gain public confidence, and after a few days, the presence of the cavalry restored peace. By June Dr. Dávila Tello has charged six Liberals and two Conservatives with criminal actions and remanded them to Bogotá for trial. The cavalry remained for several months to prevent further unrest. When it was recalled to its regiment, many people threatened to leave the intendancy because they feared that the local police were insufficient to guarantee their security. In October 1923, the national government expanded the police force to twenty-five uniformed men. Luna Ospina stationed these officers in Villavicencio and the other municipios. In his annual report of 1924, he stated that they had carried out their duties well and were adequate for the normal needs of the intendancy.[51]

The violence in Villavicencio had national repercussions. The Liberal press of Bogotá gave full coverage to the events, and after his arrival in May, Colonel Novoa's account of the incident was printed, in full, in *El Tiempo*. Novoa accused Padre Monplaisir of deliberately obstructing his work as intendant. The priest used the *Eco de Oriente* "not only to criticize bitterly and unjustly the actions of the authorities but also to insult, jeer, and cowardly slander them." Moreover, he had a willing tool in Oliverio Reina. "Whenever he was hatching some political–religious problem or it was necessary to obtain some goal or to impede the fulfillment of some disposition," Monplaisir would summon Oliverio to his residence, and afterward the man would leave "in an angry mood to call together his gang, to drink, to shout threats and insults and spread panic in the town." The intendant's implication was clear. The events of April 22 may have gotten out of hand, but they were orchestrated by the French priest.[52] The editor of *El Tiempo* accepted the colonel's account, exclaiming that a travel–adventure novel could not include more interesting scenes of tropical life than those he had described. It was obvious that Padre Mauricio aspired to be lord and master of the intendancy, and the riot showed how a gang leader, "favored by friendships with important people, instills terror, ignores the authorities and finally falls by the violence he himself provoked." The Liberals lived under the threat of being attacked by bands incited by the missionaries, while the intendant must defend himself "as if he were in the desert, revolver in hand and risking life at every step." "The danger is latent," the editor warned. "At any moment, events could occur of the most serious consequence."[53]

Remarkably, the elections which had contributed to the crisis were held in complete calm on May 13. According to *El Tiempo*, in Villavicencio there were 192 votes for the Liberals and 475 for the Conservatives, with a large number of the former abstaining. *El Espectador* reported the totals for the intendancy as 906 votes for Liberals and 1,200 for Conservatives and Dissidents. Noting that the municipios of Cabuyaro and Uribe, "both completely Liberal, abstained from voting," it concluded that "with all, the Conservative triumph is truly Pyrrhic."[54]

The events of April 22 are important because they suggest that the influence exercised by the Montfort Fathers in Meta are consistent with the powerful role played by the Catholic church everywhere in Colombia in the 1920s. The extreme personal animosity between Novoa and Monplaisir, however, appears to be unique. The other intendants were able to accommodate themselves to the priest's domineering personality and, for the most part, civil and religious authorities cooperated to promote missions, public instruction, public health, and colonization.[55]

Missions, Schools, and Public Health

In accordance with the Convenio of 1902, the principal responsibilities of the Montfort Fathers were to civilize the Indians and establish schools throughout the vicariate. In 1913, Congress estimated that nearly 30,000 "savages" lived along the banks of the rivers in the eastern plains and appropriated 9,900 pesos to support missions in the Llanos of San Martín and 14,160 for those in Casanare.[56] The evidence suggests, however, that by the second decade of the twentieth century, few unconverted tribes still lived within the boundaries of the National Intendancy of Meta. Most of the parishes and vice-parishes, though poor and isolated, were populated by mestizos rather than Indians. In 1911, when Juan B. Arnaud left Villavicencio to colonize the upper Guatiquía, he anticipated that his push northward would bring him into contact with unreduced natives, but, as it turned out, his ministry was mostly among white and mestizo colonos. In 1916, Gabriel Capdeville described Uribe as a decaying town, nearly without inhabitants. The few people who lived there were not Indians but whites of "relaxed customs," and the priest, José M. Gourior gave them clothes and tools and helped them as best he could by teaching them hygiene, farming, and construction skills. San Pedro de Arimena, "a collection of fourteen straw houses" on the Meta River, was more of an Indian center. Natives came to the town to sell casabe, forest products, and handicrafts.[57] Some remained permanently while others stayed for a few weeks before moving on, but even here, according to Intendant Jerónimo Mutis, the Indians "were already nearly civilized."[58] In 1928, Intendant José Jesús Angel conceded that previous estimates of the native population had been inflated, for only a few thousand Indians remained in the territory, most of them located along the Guaviare River and the region drained by the Manacacías River.[59]

Given the lack of potential converts in Meta, the Montfort Fathers directed their missionary forays toward Vichada and Vaupés. In 1907, they started their first reductions in San José and San Amparo in Vichada, but these soon disappeared due to lack of resources and the nomadic nature of the Indians. In 1923, the order designated Cabuyaro as the official capital of the Vichada Mission, but six years later there was still little activity.[60] More impressive was the Montfort Papuri settlement, founded in 1913 by Huberto Damoiseaux and Pedro Barón in Vaupés near the Brazilian border on the Papuri River, a tributary of the Vaupés. By 1929 four missionaries under the direction of Padre Barón had formed six reductions of Cubeo Indians, two workshops, and numerous cultivated fields. Six sisters of the Order of Immaculate Mary taught in a school with more than one hundred native boys and girls, and plans were under way to inaugurate a dual radio–telephone station between Montfort Papuri and Villavicencio.[61]

Under the watchful eyes of Bishop Guiot and Padre Mauricio, opportunities for primary education expanded in the intendancy. In 1904 there were six schools: two in Villavicencio, two in San Martín, and two in Medina. By 1913 there were fifteen—three for boys, three for girls, and nine alternated with one sex attending in the mornings and the other in the afternoons. In 1926, the vicariate administered thirty-four schools—twenty-five in the Intendancy of Meta enrolling 1,103 children, two in Medina, three in Vaupés, and four in Vichada. There were still no secondary schools, although the order did found a seminary for its novices in the town of San Juanito, on the Guatiquía River. A night school planned for adult laborers and servants in Villavicencio did not materialize, but Bishop Guiot did begin a school for deaf-mutes in San Juanito that became the model for a similar school started later in Bogotá.[62]

The Daughters of Wisdom taught the children in the municipios, while local women, often barely able to read and write themselves, taught in the rural areas. Their salaries, when they were paid, ranged from twenty to fifty pesos a month. The curriculum included religious doctrine, sacred history, Colombian history, reading, writing, geography, Spanish, arithmetic, deportment, calisthenics, drawing, singing, natural history, and, for girls, sewing and embroidery. All the schools lacked textbooks and maps of Colombia. Attendance was sporadic, and in 1928 only 80 of 250 enrolled children in Villavicencio actually finished the four-year course. According to Intendant Angel, 50 percent of those who dropped out did so because of their parents' poverty and "the lack of a solid diet that makes it difficult for them to concentrate or because when they go home for lunch, the rain prevents them from returning."[63] To address these problems, the sisters in 1927 began serving breakfast and lunch in the schools. They also distributed clothes to the poorer children, so that needing decent apparel would not be an excuse to keep them at home.

Surely, many children missed classes because they were sick. The deplorable state of public health in the intendancy was a matter of concern for visitors and the authorities. According to Miguel Triana, morbidity was especially high in Villavicencio due to the excessive humidity and sharp temperature drops between day and night. Mosquitoes bred abundantly in stagnant pools and ponds, spreading malaria and yellow fever. Inadequate sanitary facilities, scarcity of potable water, and the lack of sewers intensified the dangers, particularly for immigrants from the temperate valleys of eastern Cundinamarca who were experiencing a tropical climate for the first time. While the mortality rate for the intendancy as a whole was 30 per 1,000 (or less than the rates for Mexico City, Lima, and Caracas), in Villavicencio it was a frightening 63.8 per 1,000.[64] Dr. Hamilton Rice, who visited the city about the same time as Triana, was impressed by the number of corpses that passed by his lodgings every day, carried by prisoners from the town jail in rough, uncovered coffins. "Villavicencio is no place for persons of nervous temperament," he observed, "nor are the people one begins to meet a day before the town is reached pleasant to look at, with their lemon-tinted, gaunt, emaciated faces and hands of horribly lethal thinness."[65]

Improvement of public health was the responsibility of the *médico oficial* (official doctor), a post created when the intendancy was organized in 1910. In 1913, the first man to hold this position, Dr. Isaac Flórez, informed the intendant that malaria and yellow fever were present in various forms, especially in rural areas infested by anopheles mosquitoes. Diseases of the liver and spleen were common. Syphilis, tuberculosis, and dysentery occurred in alarming proportions, but the most serious problem was uncinariasis (tropical anemia), or hookworm, which affected virtually every resident over a year old.[66]

While doctors had been aware for many decades of the dangers posed by malaria and yellow fever in tropical climates, the identification of tropical anemia as a parasitic disease was relatively recent. Unlike the other two, which are spread by mosquitoes, tropical anemia is caused by the larvae of the hookworm that live in the soil of hot, moist regions and enter the human body by penetrating the soles of bare feet. The larvae move into the bloodstream and pass by way of the lungs, throat, and stomach to the small intestine. There, they make their home, feasting and copulating, laying eggs that pass out with the stool and contaminate the soil so that other bare feet can pick up the new larvae, which hatch eggs. The host produces an anemia that saps vitality, cripples and kills, or leaves people emaciated with protruding shoulder blades, bloated stomachs, and swollen joints. By the beginning of the twentieth century, scientists had realized that hookworm was a disease that plagued millions of people in tropical and semitropical areas throughout the world. They had discovered that doses of thymol salts were effective in treating and eliminating the symptoms, and they recommended attacking the causes by disinfecting the soil, building sanitary privies, and educating people to wear shoes and practice good hygiene.[67]

The *médicos oficiales* of Meta repeatedly asked the national government to send them thymol capsules for individuals incapacitated by hookworm, and they did what they could to eliminate the unsanitary conditions that spawned it and other diseases. For example, in 1917, Dr. Teodosio F. Acero asserted that lack of sewers were causing inadequately drained water to seep into the houses of Villavicencio, forming breeding grounds for microorganisms that produced typhoid fever, dysentery, cholera, and tetanus. He recommended that the streets be cleared and the drains inspected; that the city ban the selling of meat in the streets, a practice which bred flies and mosquitoes; and that it widen the perimeter around the cemetery because decomposition and putrefaction of corpses lying in shallow graves was contributing to the epidemics.[68] In 1919, Dr. Flórez published in Villavicencio a book entitled *Enfermedades dominantes en los llanos de la región oriental de Colombia*. He formed a junta on hygiene to deal with ongoing health problems and, with the cooperation of Padre Mauricio, published information on disease prevention in *Eco de Oriente*.[69]

News that the Rockefeller Foundation was beginning a five-year campaign to eradicate hookworm in Colombia raised expectations that faster progress might be made in the future. In 1919, President Suárez signed an agreement with Dr. Louis Shapiro, a representative of the foundation. Shapiro promised to send medical personnel and laboratory equipment sufficient for treating up to fifty thousand cases of hookworm annually and to direct public-information indoctrination throughout the country. Suárez pledged to provide 100,000 pesos each year to subsidize these activities and to assign an office in the Ministry of Agriculture to coordinate the campaign. The Rockefeller Sanitary Commission began by conducting a hookworm survey throughout the country. Soon afterward, it started the first eradication centers in Tequendama Province of Cundinamarca and along the Magdalena River in Tolima.[70]

The campaign did not reach the Intendancy of Meta for another six years. In the meantime, local authorities with scant resources struggled to control the disease. In May 1925, Intendant Rubén Santacoloma informed Minister of Government Ramón Rodríguez Diago that he was planning with the aid of his son, Dr. Nestor Santacoloma, and two other doctors to finance a sanitarium where the sick could receive care and attention. He asked for Rodríguez Diago's approval, "since negligence will bring a fatal degeneration of the race," and also urged him to send the Sanitary Commission which, with its knowledge and experience, could help "to broaden this campaign against that disease which decimates the towns of the Llanos."[71] When members of the Sanitary Commission finally did arrive in Villavicencio later that year, they dosed hundreds of people with thymol salts, but their plans to build sewers and privies were delayed for want of materials. In 1928, the médico oficial, Dr. José Antonio Concha, reported that malaria, yellow fever, tuberculosis, venereal disease, and syphilis were still taking a heavy toll, and he called for a renewed effort against hookworm in the countryside. His successor in 1931, Dr. Gustavo Ruiz Mora, could only observe, "There is still a terrifyingly high rate of infant mortality and an alarming advance of malaria and hookworm."[72]

Colonization

Despite the menace of disease and high mortality, the population of Villavicencio and the intendancy grew by leaps and bounds. The census figures in table 7 show that between 1904 and 1918 the population of Villavicencio grew from 3,315 to 4,774, an increase of 44 percent. At the same time, the regional population more than

Table 7
Population of the Meta Region and
Villavicencio, 1832–1938

Year	Meta Region	Villavicencio
1832	1,530[a]	
1843	1,877[b]	
1870	4,056[b]	800[c]
1904	4,957[d]	3,315[d]
1912[e]	9,039	4,774
1918[f]	11,671	4,736
1938[g]	51,674	24,315

Sources: a. Montenegro Colon, *Geografía general*, III, 550.

b. Galindo, *Anuario estadístico*, 1876, 20.

c. Restrepo, *Una excursión al territorio de San Martín*, 39.

d. MMG, 1904, 210–227.

e. Baquero, "Departamento del Meta," 93.

f. *Censo de población de la República de Colombia, 1918* (Bogotá, 1923).

g. DANE, *Estadísticas históricas*, 1975.

doubled, going from 4,957 to 11,671. By 1938 the city had reached 24,315 and the region 51,674, registering the fastest population growth for that period in the nation.[73] Some of the migrants were seasonal, coming from eastern Cundinamarca to earn high wages during planting and harvesting and then returning home, but most streamed into the intendancy with every intention of remaining permanently. There were two organized colonization projects—the settlement of the upper Guatiquía River, led by Padre Juan B. Arnaud, and the founding of a penal colony in Acacías by the national government. In addition, Congress reformed the laws regulating baldíos to make it easier for small farmers to claim their land.

The Guatiquía River Basin stretches north of Villavicencio to the Cordillera de Peñas Blancas and contains more than thirty thousand hectares of land. It was densely settled by Indians and Spaniards in the seventeenth century, but after Independence these people disappeared, and dense forest reclaimed the cultivated fields. In the 1870s, colonos from Fómeque began exploring the area for cinchona trees. Founding a caserío, or small village, at El Baldío, they managed to thrive despite their isolation from other towns in Cundinamarca and Meta. In 1910, when they asked the authorities to help them build a road between El Baldío and Villavicencio, Bishop Guiot decided to send Padre Juan B. Arnaud to reconnoiter the area. Arnaud returned brimming with enthusiasm about its development potential, and Guiot authorized him to begin a mission in the upper Guatiquía.

Arnaud set out for the second time in December 1911, with a subsidy of four hundred pesos. He worked with the people of El Baldío to build a new town, El Calvario, clearing the forests with machetes and axes. Progress came swiftly. By 1917 there were 533 inhabitants, twenty-six houses, a chapel, priest's house, inn and store, *alcaldía* (mayor's office), prison, market, and a school taught by the Daughters of Wisdom. In the meantime, Arnaud pushed up the Guatiquía, and at a site that could serve as a stopping place on a future road leading from Medina to Villavicencio and ultimately to Cabuyaro, he founded San Juanito. Colonos came with their cattle, building houses and planting fields of plátano. When El Calvario was elevated to municipio status, San Juanito was designated as a corregimiento. Here, the Montfort Fathers began their seminary and a school for deaf-mutes. Arnaud planned a third settlement, San Francisco, three and one-half hours from El Calvario in the direction of Fómeque, but its existence proved to be ephemeral.[74]

Since the prosperity of El Calvario and San Juanito depended on easy access to Villavicencio, Arnaud used 4,500 pesos and colono labor to build a camino de herradura. By 1923 it was possible to travel between the towns without much difficulty. All along the road the settlers planted crops, and at least thirty parcels were devoted to pasture for hundreds of cattle, horses, mules, and burros. By 1929 the municipio had grown to three thousand inhabitants, and Arnaud was at work on a new road that would unite Bogotá with the Llanos by passing through El Chingaza, San Juanito, Villavicencio, Restrepo, and Medina.[75]

The national government was also interested in encouraging the rapid settlement of frontier areas by peasant families to provide an agricultural base for the industrialization that engulfed the country after World War I. After 1917, Congress, in association with the Ministry of Industries, began a program to sponsor government-financed colonies that would become poles of attraction for other settlers. The legislators agreed to aid people accepted into the new colonies with transportation, loans for food and tools, and free surveys of the land.

They authorized several penal colonies and, in 1928, disclosed plans for purely agricultural communities in Tolima, western Valle, Huila, Chocó, and Caquetá.[76]

One of the new penal colonies was located in Restrepo, in the Intendancy of Meta. Although President Carlos E. Restrepo, in 1910, closed the first prison established there in 1905 on the grounds that it was not cost effective, the notion that the Llanos might be settled by excriminals who had learned the value of honest work continued to have its proponents. In November 1918, Congress passed Law 60 creating the Penal and Agricultural Colony of Meta and established it once again in Restrepo. The law stipulated that men convicted of stealing or cattle rustling in Tolima, Cundinamarca, Boyacá, Arauca, Vichada, and Vaupés would be sent to the colony, where they would be put to work on public projects and farming the land. Six months after they had completed their sentences, they would receive title to seven hectares of land. In addition, Law 60 offered seven hectares of land to volunteer colonists, who would receive their titles within a year so long as they were actually cultivating at least one-half of their claim.[77]

The second penal colony was no more successful than the first. Fifty prisoners had arrived by 1920 and were put to work building a bridge over the Guatiquía, but Intendant Jerónimo Mutis was not satisfied with the arrangements. He pointed out that the prisoners were indifferent workers unless they saw how they could benefit, and the need to deploy fifty national policemen to guard them on the job was not very practical. Mutis felt that the intendancy rather than the national police should administer the prison, and he pointed out that the two thousand residents of Restrepo resented having criminals in their midst. A year later, calling the colony a failure, he suggested that it be relocated in the corregimiento of Acacías, on the Ariari River—a site blessed with a healthy climate and fertile land that was already farmed by five hundred settlers who had moved there from Gutiérrez, Cundinamarca.[78]

In 1922, Congress suppressed the Restrepo facility and passed Law 105 authorizing a new penal colony in Acacías. President Pedro Nel Ospina, who visited the intendancy in February 1923, was a strong supporter of the project, asserting that it would be a "powerful factor of moralization, a center of population of exceptional importance . . . and a model establishment of its kind, of permanent rather than transitory character and destined to exercise great influence over our Lla-nuras Orientales."[79] On June 2, 1924, he issued Decrees 1130 and 1131, which inaugurated the Acacías Penal and Agricultural Colony and designated it as a place of incarceration for vagrants and convicted criminals of Cundinamarca, Boyacá, and Atlántico.[80]

Between 1924 and 1932 the prison population at Acacías fluctu-ated between 130 and 220 men supervised by 50 to 60 guards. Work-ing in gangs, they planted sugar cane, tobacco, and cotton. They im-proved one road leading from Acacías to San Miguel and another that went toward Bogotá through Caño Acacitas. They repaired the bridge over the Guayuriba and began work on a hydroelectric plant and a telegraph line between Acacías and Villavicencio. A town grew up around the prison, and by 1928 there were 800 inhabitants primarily engaged in cultivating rice. In 1932, the Dirección General de Pri-siones of the Ministry of Government took over the Penal and Agri-cultural Colony, which remained the only penitentiary in the inten-dency until the 1960s.[81]

In her study of land policy, Catherine LeGrand has shown that the Colombian government in the 1920s adopted a position that was vigorously pro-colono, as opposed to encouraging large entrepreneurs. Policymakers stressed the need to reform the structure of landholding to stimulate economic growth. "Specifically they advocated the spread of family farms in the well-founded belief that small producers work the soil more intensively than large landowners," and because of a "resurgence of the Liberal concern to foster the formation of a rural middle class that had marked the reforms of the mid-nineteenth cen-tury."[82] The call for penal and agricultural colonies was one dimension of this strategy. Far more important was their attempt to reform land-tenure laws, to make it easier for small settlers to gain title to their claims.

Contributing to this change in focus were two new laws and a historic Supreme Court decision. In 1917, Congress passed Law 71, which exempted settlers with holdings of twenty hectares or less from having to hire a surveyor, buy official paper, or pay postage in applying to Bogotá for their titles—all requirements that had made grants costly. In 1926, Law 47 simplified grant procedures for colonos even more and promised that the government would give them credit, tools, and seed. Then, in that same year, the Colombian Supreme Court handed down a landmark decision "intended to facilitate official colonization by strengthening the government's position in its relations with private individuals. The justices ruled that henceforth all land in Colombia would be presumed public land unless proven differently. Only by showing the original title by which the state had alienated a given tract of land from the national domain could a landowner sustain his or her legal right to that property."[83] The ruling's effect was to withdraw legal sanction from many of the large estates consolidated in frontier regions in early years, since most landlords did not have the first titles that the court required. It also enabled the government to recover public land illegally appropriated from the national domain. Finally, until 1926 anyone could contest a settler's grant application by saying that the land was private property, but after 1926 this ploy was no longer possible. These changes meant that "so long as a small cultivator filed the correct paperwork, he or she was assured of legal title to the land."[84]

The impact of these reforms in the Intendancy of Meta is not completely clear. Table 8 lists the public-land grants awarded between 1908 and 1931. Only six grants were registered between 1908 and 1917—three in Villavicencio and three in San Martín, all ranging from 800 to 1,000 hectares. Between 1918 and 1931, thirty-seven grants were awarded. While six of these ranged from 1,500 to 2,500 hectares, twenty-seven others, or 73 percent, were for 20 hectares or less—nineteen in San Martín, eight in El Calvario, and one in Uribe. These figures suggest that it was easier for small settlers to gain title after 1918 than before, yet when one considers the hundreds of colonos who were relocating to the intendency, very few of them actually did become legal owners.

The comments made by the intendants suggest that many were frustrated despite the reforms. In 1924, Luna Ospina reported that he was enforcing Law 71 of 1917, but there was great confusion over the rights of people who had been occupying land without formal title.[85] In 1926, Santacoloma stated that fourteen of forty-four applications for land submitted that year had been abandoned, while the rest were pending. He added that only a few people possessed titles, and many of those who did pretended to own much larger tracts, "not permitting that anyone occupy them, which disturbs the development of agriculture and cattle." Another problem giving rise to constant law suits was that "former possessors have sold their small improvements with rights to thousands of hectares that have not been cultivated nor occupied with cattle as the government requires."[86]

Table 8
Public Land Grants in the Intendancy of Meta, 1908–1931

Grantee	Municipio	Year	Hectares
Mario E. Cubillos	Villavicencio	1908	808.6
Baronio Arciniegas	Villavicencio	1908	1,000
Eduardo Gómez	Villavicencio	1908	1,000
Santana Hernández	San Martín	1908	800
Manuel Rincón	San Martín	1911	?
Gregorio Parrado	San Martín	1911	1,000
Félix N. Jaramillo	San Martín	1919	20
Apolinar López	San Martín	1920	20
Araceli Hernández de T.	San Martín	1920	20
Heliodoro Torres	San Martín	1920	20
Ignacio Santamaría	San Martín	1920	20
Jesús Urrego	San Martín	1920	20
Matilde Ruiz de Rozo	San Martín	1920	20
Juan Rozo	San Martín	1920	20
Agapito Sanabría	San Martín	1921	20
Teresa S. de Mora	San Martín	1921	20
Alfredo Sánchez C.	San Martín	1921	20
Antonio Solano	San Martín	1921	20
Victor A. Franco	El Calvario	1921	2,500
Rafael Arias	Uribe	1922	20
Manuel del Castillo	El Calvario	1923	1,664
Agapito Sanabria	San Martín	1923	.4
Lorenzo Hernández	San Martín	1923	20
Antonio R. Lara	San Martín	1923	20
Miguel Abadía Méndez	Restrepo	1924	2,500
Gregorio Aroca	San Martín	1924	20
Abraham Peña	El Calvario	1924	20
Antonio Pérez	El Calvario	1924	4
José Sarmiento	El Calvario	1924	10
Santiago A. Velásquez	San Martín	1924	20
Jacobo Ramos	San Martín	1924	8
Pablo E. Hernández	San Martín	1925	20
Francisco Sarmiento	El Calvario	1925	10
Teodolinda Carrillo	El Calvario	1925	20
Luis Raabe	Uribe	1926	1,578.8
Valentin Ossa	Uribe	1926	785.8
Ernesto Muss	Uribe	1926	2,221
Adán Guatavita	El Calvario	1926	8
Neftalí Daza	Sucre	1928	20
Manuel Pacheco	Villavicencio	1929	942.3
Manuel Pacheco	Villavicencio	1930	942.3

Table 8
Continued

Grantee	Municipio	Year	Hectares
Santos M. Santos	Villavicencio	1930	646.7
Urbain Marie Francois Fondut	Villavicencio	1931	2,449.3
Total			21,299.2

Total Hectares by Municipios

Municipio	Total Grants	Total Hectares
El Calvario	8	4,236
Restrepo	1	2,500
San Martín	22	2,148.4
Sucre	1	20
Uribe	4	4,605.6
Villavicencio	7	7,789.2
	43	21,299.2

Grantees with Largest Holdings

Grantee	Total Grants	Total Hectares
Victor A. Franco	1	2,500
Miguel Abadía Méndez	1	2,500
Urbain Marie Francois Fondut	1	2,449.3
Ernesto Muss	1	2,221

Distribution of Grants by Size

Total Grants	Hectares
27	From 1 to 20
0	From 20 to 499
6	From 500 to 999
9	From 1,000 to 2,500
1	?

Source: *Memoria del Ministro de Industrias,* 1931 (Bogotá, 1931), V, 328; 353–54; 405–6.
LeGrand, *Frontier Expansion,* 198.

Still pending was the dissolution of the Community of Apiay. In 1918, Sergio Convers signed a contract with more than two hundred comuneros, by which they agreed to cede him their titles in exchange for a certain number of hectares to be awarded based on years and extent of occupancy once the land had been measured. Convers planned to deliver the land by September 1919, but the division apparently did not take place. In 1928, Intendant José Jesús Angel wrote that the existence of the Community of Apiay continued to block the development of "the most beautiful portion and best cultivated area of land in the intendency."[87]

Angel went on to state that, in spite of the land-tenure reforms, many people were unwilling to sink their capital into baldíos, having seen so many unjust procedures used against poor colonos. Of the 8,400,000 hectares of baldíos in the intendancy, about 8 percent was being utilized. Ranchers grazed cattle on some 500,000 hectares. An additional 30,000 hectares contained improved pasture, and another 10,000 was cultivated with different food crops, especially rice. Much of this land that was occupied was still officially "baldío." Between 1872 and 1928, 214,581 hectares had been adjudicated, but many of those who had received title never developed their claims, while others fled the region to avoid being recruited into armies during the wars so that the land had returned to its natural wild state. Legislation regarding tenure was a "confusion of dispositions." Angel recommended that all of the land laws be compiled and organized into a code. "What we need are just, clear, precise laws which favor the proprietors and especially the poor."[88]

In 1929, geographer and engineer Peregrino Ossa V. published an article in the *Revista Nacional de Agricultura,* suggesting that the problem was even more severe than Angel had indicated. "Ownership of property is not known in the Llanos," he wrote, "because all of the plains are baldíos, and even if some of them have been legally awarded, the documentation does not exist or is incomplete so that all is reduced to the right of possession [or who is actually living on the land]."[89] Because of the extraordinary floods and droughts, cattle in Meta need a great extension of land, and ranchers occupy the plains without stability, moving from place to place. Alongside the fundaciones that show genuine growth are an "infinity of individuals who, like parasites, squat on the baldíos and steal the cattle, keeping the industry from advancing." Ossa called for special legislation that would take into account the unique conditions of the Llanos and allow greater flexibility and more liberality in adjudication. As it stands, he concluded, "Acquisition of land here by our present laws is virtually impossible."[90]

Economic Growth

Undeterred by legalities, colonos moved into the intendancy and began cultivating plots of land. The road between Bogotá and Villavicencio was little better than a hazardous mule trail, yet trade between the two cities doubled between 1913 and 1925. Exports of coffee declined, since the Llanos could no longer compete with harvests from other regions, but shipments of corn, yuca, and plátano grew steadily, and the widespread cultivation of rice sparked an agricultural revolution. The intendancy was beginning to assume its contemporary role of providing foodstuffs for the large highland market.

The newcomers who cleared the land around Villavicencio, Restrepo, and El Calvario soon discovered that rice grown without irrigation and with the most rudimentary care would give yields of five hundred to one in four months. Individual farmers could harvest and sack the crop by hand and transport it by pack mule to be milled. By 1920 there were three hydraulically powered mills to choose from: one in Villavicencio, which also produced electricity, owned by Jorge Bejarano; another on the Convers hacienda, El Buque; and a third in Restrepo owned by Francisco Arango U. At the mills the rice was dried, threshed, hulled, and sacked. Its high quality was appreciated in Bogotá, where it brought a good price. In 1923, the intendancy produced 103,500 arrobas of rice grown on 2,250 hectares, and valued at 207,000 pesos. Total exports from the territory doubled from 51,255 arrobas (including rice, corn, and plátanos) in 1913 to 118,295 arrobas in 1925, including 91,840 arrobas of rice, 21,530 arrobas of plátanos, and 4,925 arrobas of corn.[91]

Dramatic changes were also taking place in cattle production— still Meta's principal resource, notwithstanding the poor quality of Llanos grass and the difficulty of driving the steers up the cordillera to market. As early as 1869 Emiliano Restrepo had urged fellow ranchers to plant improved pasture called *pasto gorda*, or *yaragua*, so that they could fatten steers on their own land. Few ganaderos had followed his lead, preferring to sell their skinny animals at a low price to other ranchers who would take them to Magdalena or Tolima and fatten them for a year before selling them for beef at a substantial profit. Then, in 1919, Plácido Castro L., a ganadero from San Martín, presented a report to the Sociedad de Agricultores de Colombia in Bogotá describing his three-year effort to cultivate pasto gorda on his land using seeds provided by José María Uribe. Castro found that, with irrigation, the pasto gorda had readily substituted itself for the native grass. He predicted that if it were introduced on a large scale, the Intendency of Meta might become a new Argentina.[92] Castro's success encouraged others to experiment, and the number of hectares of improved pasture increased from 500 in 1921 to 2,104 in 1922. In that year, the intendant jubilantly reported that ranchers in Casanare and Arauca who used to take their cattle to Sogamoso were sending the animals for fattening in pastures outside Villavicencio. Between 1922 and 1925 annual cattle fairs were held in Villavicencio, and the number of animals in the intendency increased from 49,196 to 77,045. Exports grew as well. In 1913, 3,630 cattle left Villavicencio for Bogotá. By 1925 the number had quadrupled to 16,235, of which 74 percent, or 12,000, had been fattened on improved pasture.[93]

The boom in agriculture and cattle did not extend to rubber collection, which peaked in 1913 when the intendency shipped 1,011 cargas (9,099 arrobas) to Bogotá, valued at 113,737 pesos or more than all of the cattle exported the same year. By 1925, however, the price of rubber had plummeted from 2 pesos to 40 centavos a pound. Only 130 arrobas left Villavicencio, most of it collected in Vaupés by colonos who cut down trees in the national forests, oblivious to laws prohibiting the destruction of the trees. The situation of these colonos worsened throughout the 1920s. In 1919 and 1920, the government passed laws forbidding the collection of rubber in the national forests without a legal contract. In 1921, Intendant Mutis asked the minister of agriculture to waive these laws and allow colonos who had illegally extracted rubber and brought it to Villavicencio to send it on to Bogotá. "There are many unhappy people in Vaupés," he wrote, "who are occupied in this work without incentive or hope of progress since the cost of transportation will price the articles out of competition." Mutis urged the minister to help those "who remain in the forest as human wrecks without the means of returning to civilized society."[94] The request was not granted, but even if it had been, it would not have aided the colonos nor halted the precipitous collapse of Amazonian rubber output in the face of east Asian competition.

Quickening trade transformed Villavicencio from a sleepy village to a bustling entrepôt. The intendency sent rice, corn, plátanos, cattle, and hides to the highlands in exchange for flour, soap, food, beer, oil, wire, machines, and domestic and foreign manufactured goods. Bogotá traders came with their merchandise to Villavicencio, and from there they supplied the surrounding towns as far away as Orocué. They sold hats, textiles, hammocks, *bayetones* (large woolen ponchos), *alpargatas* (sandals), and other *chucherías* (gewgaws) which appealed to the Llaneros. Venezuelan merchants came, bringing goods and money. By 1928 there were two commercial houses of the first order (*casas de primer orden*) in Villavicencio, with capital of forty thousand pesos—Echeverría Brothers and Rueda Sierra and Company. Factories included Jorge Bejarano's electric plant, which had been milling rice and making ice since 1915; Uribe and Arango's soft drink plant; and others that produced soap and tobacco. Still lacking was a bank, but Intendant Angel wrote in 1928 that the city was perfectly capable of supporting one and suggested that a branch of the Banco Agrícola Hipotecario be opened there soon.[95]

Railroads and Highways

The heavy traffic between Bogotá and Villavicencio confirmed the growing symbiotic relationship between the highlands and the Llanos, and renewed hopes that either the national government or that of Cundinamarca would build a railroad to circumvent the slow, dangerous Bogotá–Villavicencio highway. It will be recalled that in 1890 Núñez signed a contract with the Belgian–English firm Punchard, McTaggart, Louther, and Company to build the Ferrocarril del Meta. In 1894, Punchard's engineers surveyed three possible paths that the train might take and recommended the so-called southern route. Juan N. González Vásquez, an engineer who had helped lay out the national road to Meta in 1872, began cutting the trace which, after leaving Bogotá, passed through Usme, the Alto de Santa Rosa, and Nazareth before following the Río Blanco to the Río Negro and on to Acacías and Villavicencio. In the meantime, the Society of Colombian Engineers rejected the Punchard plan, the war of 1895 forced all work to be suspended, and the government cancelled the contract in 1897.[96]

In September 1916, Representative Francisco Barbosa from Bogotá revived the idea by introducing a bill authorizing a railroad between Bogotá and the Meta River, following the Punchard cut. A reviewing committee supported it, arguing that the proposed railroad would bring many benefits: "National life will receive an incalculable propulsion, public wealth will multiply, there will be greater communication between departments, and in the general atmosphere of well-being we can put into exercise all of our latent national energy." [97] In Villavicencio, the *Eco de Oriente* greeted Barbosa's plan with enthusiasm. On September 14, 1916, Juan Bautista Arnaud wrote, "The railroad that is to come from Bogotá to the Llanos is of vital importance for the entire nation." All the towns along the route would benefit, and Villavicencio would become the center of a vast commercial network—"the place where the Bogotá eagle could come down to get supplies and if necessary defend the entrance to its royal nest." [98]

On September 28, the newspaper published another article signed by "La Cooperativa," stating that there were no insurmountable obstacles facing the project, and the railroad, once completed, would fill a tremendous need. It would run through a region that some day would have more than 200,000 inhabitants. Valuable products grown in the Llanos could easily reach the capital, and rubber production would be stimulated since the latex would no longer have to be shipped down the Orinoco. The railroad would create jobs for young people, prevent North American rice from flooding Colombian markets, encourage transport along the Meta and Orinoco rivers, and contribute to the defense of the international border. [99] Two weeks later, Padre Mauricio Monplaisir sent a telegram to Congress urging approval. In the end, the deputies did pass the bill, but it stalled in the upper house, when senators raised questions about where the money to build the railroad would come from and whether the proposed route was the best way to get to the Meta. [100]

As the Senate was deciding to table the Ferrocarril del Meta, the Cundinamarca Assembly, at the behest of Governor José Ramón Lago, began debating another project—the Ferrocarril de Oriente. The route of this proposed railroad would have passed through Tunjuelo, Yomasa, Chipaque, Cáqueza, Quetame, Monteredondo, Río Guatiquía, Villavicencio, and the Río Ocoa to reach an undesignated port on the Meta—a distance of 190 kilometers. The pros and cons of the scheme were widely discussed in Bogotá's daily newspapers. On March 4 and March 6, 1917, Alfredo Ramos Urdaneta published two articles in *El Diario Nacional*, arguing that the railroad "was the necessary key and the undebatable axis of the development and progress of the republic and of the eastern towns." Its length was not excessive, and if the Punchard cut was used rather than the new route that had been suggested, the cost would be only thirty thousand pesos a kilometer. Ramos Urdaneta recognized that such a sum was beyond the resources of the department, but he believed that a loan floated by popular subscription would be taken up with alacrity by capitalists in Cundinamarca and elsewhere.[101] Enrique Uribe Ramírez, writing in *El Nuevo Tiempo* on March 21, pointed out that Colombian engineers had rejected the Punchard cut for several valid reasons, not the least of which being the fact that it would have terminated on the Humadea River, an unnavigable tributary of the Meta. He suggested that Governor Lago appoint a commission of engineers to study possible routes and also to explore the possibility of building a train powered by electricity.[102] The idea of an electric train was supported by Edmundo Ramos, on April 10 in *El Diario Nacional*, on the grounds that such trains were superior in their construction to steam engines and had been used successfully in the subways of Paris, London, and New York City.[103]

Others were more skeptical. "On Railroads," an April 26 article in *El Diario Nacional* signed by "J.," questioned whether the Ferrocarril de Oriente was really necessary when the country could benefit far more from railroads linking Bogotá north to the Atlantic and south to the Pacific. "J." reminded his readers that with the ongoing war in Europe, the United States was the only source for construction materials, and prices were very high. Given this situation, it would be far better to complete projects already begun than to start a new one.[104]

Back in Villavicencio, Padre Mauricio energetically campaigned for the railroad. Between August 21 and December 1917 he published *Ferrocarril del Meta*—a bimonthly periodical featuring articles and manifestos by local citizens in support of the project. In one typical article, Padre Mauricio wrote that the railroad would foster "intimate, close, cordial, and rapid ties between Cundinamarca and the Llanos," for while it was true that the Llanos needed supplies from Bogotá, it was equally true that the capital could not overlook the Llanos as its "*granero* or *dispensa natural*" (fruitful, grain-producing country or natural pantry). When one considered the importance of the Meta River, it was evident that Bogotá was the head and Villavicencio the heart of an organic system that encompassed all of the Llanos Orientales. The Ferrocarril de Oriente was indispensable from a national as well as regional viewpoint.[105]

After much discussion, the only project to gain the approval of the Cundinamarca Assembly was an electric trolley line that was to leave the Parque de los Mártires in Bogotá by Carrera 13 and head south to Yomasa and Tunjuelito in the municipio of Usme, and might in the future serve as the first leg of a rail connection to the Llanos. Directed by Dr. Francisco Olarte Camacho, construction on the Tranvía de Oriente began August 15, 1917. Ten years later, he had completed fourteen kilometers of the route to Yomasa. Cundinamarca renewed its contract with Olarte Camacho so that he might continue the line to Chipaque. Ordenanza 42 of 1926 reorganized the company, raising its capital assets to 1,500,000 pesos divided into 30,000 shares at 50 pesos a share. The department took 15,001 shares and private parties took 7,182, with the rest opened to public subscription. In February 1928, Olarte Camacho began laying track toward Usme, and by 1930 26 kilometers were in service, carrying 106,569 passengers and 5,161 tons of freight in that year. The onset of the Great Depression postponed any hopes of extending the line to the Llanos. After decades of dreams and hopes, the Ferrocarril del Meta was abandoned forever.[106]

Fortunately, endeavors to modernize the Bogotá–Villavicencio highway had a happier outcome. In 1922, the Ministry of Public Works began upgrading the 125-kilometer road. By 1926 five hundred prisoners had rebuilt the 30-kilometer section between Bogotá and Chipaque at an expense of 142,488 pesos. By 1929, 17 additional kilometers to Cáqueza had been improved, costing 994,548 pesos. The remaining 78 kilometers were completed between 1930 and 1936, at a cost of 749,893 pesos. The final cost of the highway was 15,895 pesos per kilometer, for a total of 1,886,929 pesos, including maintenance during construction, feasibility studies, and bridges over the Cáqueza, Sáname and Negro rivers and the quebradas of Susumuco and Pipiral.[107] Although the improvements had only reached Cáqueza by 1930, leaders in Meta were optimistic. As Intendant Santacoloma wrote, "Today we are still limited by lack of labor and the high cost of transport, but when we can count on a road to this region from the populated centers of Cundinamarca, the rice industry and others will develop on an unimagined scale."[108]

Internal transportation within the intendency was still quite difficult. In 1923, the national government did launch a steamboat on the Meta, but it provided no money to maintain local roads that were annually disrupted by flooding rivers. The bridge over the Guatiquía that connected Villavicencio with Restrepo, the Salina of Upín, and Casanare required constant attention. In 1918, excessive humidity rotted its floor and the cables sustaining it, and a year later the bridge collapsed, not to be rebuilt until 1929.[109] The other principal bridge over the Guayariba that linked Villavicencio with San Martín City was located, for some obscure reason, in an overgrown area away from the road so that it was not convenient to travelers. The lack of a telegraph line between the two cities further isolated San Martín City, for the wires that had been strung in the 1890s had been cut during the War of the Thousand Days and were not repaired until the 1930s.[110]

The most dramatic event in transportation occurred on March 26, 1928, when Lieutenant Camilo Daza and Lieutenant Colonel Fidel Abadía Méndez landed an airplane in Villavicencio twenty minutes after taking off from Bogotá. The enormous possibilities presented by easy communication by air between points long isolated by flooding rivers were not lost on local officials. Using a motion picture camera that Lieutenant Daza had brought with him, Padre Mauricio began to make films of the Llanos that could be shown in Bogotá to encourage highlanders to live and invest in Meta. A *Sociedad Anónima de Aviación Llanero* was founded with a capital of 100,000 pesos divided into 100 shares at 8,000 pesos each to promote aviation, and Intendant Angel urged the Minister of Government to support the company which could take over the duty of carrying mail between Bogotá, Arauca, Vaupés and Vichada.[111] With the arrival of the airplane, a new age had begun—an age that would see its fulfillment under Alfonso López and his Revolution on March of the 1930s.

8. The Comisaría Especial of Arauca, 1909–30

*ℐ*f conflict between civil and religious authorities and economic growth were the leitmotivs of the history of Meta between 1909 and 1930, in Arauca they were the clash between civil and military authorities and the attempt of the national government to secure a border region overwhelmingly populated by Venezuelans, where events were more often precipitated by decisions made in Caracas or San Fernando de Apure than in Bogotá. Fear of Venezuelan annexation prompted Carlos E. Restrepo to separate the province from Casanare and to reorganize it as a comisaría especial in 1911. Tense border relations and diplomatic haggling over the Laudo of 1891 kept Arauca in the national spotlight for the next fifteen years. After the Swiss government arbitrated the bitter boundary dispute in 1922, relations between the two countries improved, but Colombia's demand for free navigation along the Orinoco remained an unresolved issue. In contrast to Meta, Arauca's economy declined in the 1920s, and by the end of the decade little progress had been made in breaking down its geographic, economic, and cultural isolation from the rest of the republic.

Arauca in 1909

Although Law 65 of December 14, 1909, which reorganized the departments, stated that the national government should rule Casanare as an intendancy, in the months that followed the region was turned over to Boyacá to administer as two provinces, Nunchía and Arauca. The Province of Arauca included the municipios of Arauquita, Arauca City, and Cravo Norte, and had an area of about fifteen thousand square kilometers—two-thirds of which was open plains subject to heavy flooding nine months of the year, while the rest was forested. Shaped like a trapezoid, it was bordered on the east by the municipios of Tame and San Lope, in the Province of Nunchía, and on the south by the Casanare and Meta rivers. The Arauca River, on the north, marked the international border with Apure State in Venezuela. An imaginary line established by the Laudo of 1891 formed the eastern boundary, but since neither Colombia nor Venezuela had accepted the Spanish queen's decision, this line, as well as some areas along the Arauca River, were vigorously contested.[1]

In 1909, the only agricultural zone within the province was situated in the western municipio of Arauquita. Located on the Arauca River, across from Santa Rosa in Venezuela, the town of Arauquita had twenty-five to forty houses and an estimated population of 289. The vecinos grew cacao, plátanos, corn, sugar cane, and other crops that they shipped in *bongos* east to downstream settlements. Given the fertility of their fields, they could have sent food to the Colombian highlands as well, but the road that led to Tame, Labranzagrande, and Chita was treacherous for lack of bridges over the rivers intersecting it, and the long-promised Sarare Road to link Arauquita with Pamplona in Norte de Santander remained a highway of the future.[2]

The rest of the province was devoted to cattle. Daniel Delgado counted forty-nine hatos and fundaciones in the area bounded by the Arauca, San Ignacio, and Casanare rivers, and Miguel Triana estimated that 150,000 cattle grazed on the vast sabanas.[3] Before the War of the Thousand Days, ganaderos had exported 10,000 steers annually to Apure. They also shipped cattle to Cúcuta, paying tolls to Caracas to use the Venezuela road that went from El Amparo to Guasualito and San Cristóbal. High tariffs imposed on imported Colombian cattle by Cipriano Castro, and continued by Juan Vicente Gómez after he seized power in 1908, closed off the lucrative Venezuelan market. To compensate for this loss of income, many ganaderos slaughtered their animals for their hides or resorted to collecting the fragile, snowy white feathers of the *garzas* (herons) that inhabited the swamps, lagoons, and rivers of their grasslands, and which fetched in Europe, where they were used to decorate women's clothes, the extraordinary price of five hundred dollars a pound.[4]

Ever since its founding in 1782, Arauca City had served as the entrepôt for this section of the Llanos, capitalizing on its border location and on its access to the river traffic along the Arauca, Meta, and Orinoco. As capital of the province, it had 3,472 inhabitants and the offices of the aduana, national treasury, circuit court, and *prefecturía*. It had an alcaldía and municipal council, a police garrison, three schools, and a church with a handsome cedar altar carved by Hermano Isidoro of the Recoletos. Trade was brisk with El Amparo across the river, where steamboats ended their long journey from Ciudad Bolívar. Delgado saw more than sixty stores on the main street of the town.

Their proprietors were Venezuelans, French, Italians, and Turks who exported hides and feathers and imported liquors, textiles, food, shoes, and other merchandise.[5]

Arauca City administered two settlements along the river as corregimientos. Todos los Santos, located halfway between Arauquita and Arauca City, had been an important port in the late nineteenth century, but extensive flooding of the river had reduced its population to 247 people and left half of its forty houses unoccupied. To the east of Arauca City was El Viento, with a population of 430, separated by the border from the Venezuelan town of Elorza. The 1891 Laudo had awarded El Viento to Venezuela, but Colombia refused to accept this decision and continued to insist that it was part of Arauca.[6]

Cravo Norte, lying to the southeast, was the third municipio in the province. Located at the juncture of the Casanare and Cravo rivers, it had been founded by the Venezuelan Socorro Figueroa in 1856, and in 1909 had five hundred inhabitants. It had a casa municipal, a chapel, and a schoolhouse, though as yet no classes were being offered. Raising cattle was the principal economic activity, and of the fundaciones around the town, two—Caño Rico and La Margarita— were large enough to be called hatos.[7]

While, in many ways, Arauca's geography and the life-style of its people were similar to those of Meta and Casanare, the all-pervasive Venezuelan influence made the territory unique. In the first place, the population was 90 percent Venezuelan. Ever since colonial times, Venezuelans had moved freely across the border, and their numbers swelled during the Federalist Wars of the 1860s, when constant turmoil in their homeland made life dangerous and difficult. Venezuelans founded the towns in Arauca, and Venezuelan culture was all pervasive. Delgado wrote that while Arauca City had a certain cosmopolitan sophistication, the people who lived on the hatos, fundaciones, and small towns were strongly *llanera* in their outlook:

Llanera are their customs; *llanera*, their religion and morality; *llanera* their diversions. It is clear; the *araucanos* are nearly all originally from the Llanos of Venezuela, and as such, are lovers of aguardiente and of cock fights, tireless dancers and *tiple* players.[8]

Triana agreed, noting that nearly all the owners of large hatos, transport enterprises, and stores were Venezuelans. He added, "The Venezuelan Llanero, better accustomed to the climate by his long sojourn in the plains of his own country and with a mixture of African blood

that gives him tropical atavisms, is the one who truly characterizes the
regional type and who imposes his customs, tastes, style and supersti-
tions, [and] who provides a model for the Colombian Llanero who
comes from the highlands and has mixed Indian blood."⁹

Secondly, Venezuela manipulated Arauca's economy by its control of the road to the west and the river to the east. Rather than face
the delays that driving their cattle through Colombian territory created, the Araucanos paid the tolls to use the San Cristóbal road to
Cúcuta, relying on the goodwill of the governors of Apure, Barinas,
and Táchira. With the exception of the 1890s, when José Bonnet's
steamship sailed from Ciudad Bolívar to Arauca, the Venezuelans steadfastly refused to recognize Colombia's right to free navigation on rivers
running through their republic to the Atlantic. Castro restored the prohibition during the War of the Thousand Days, so that the merchants
of Arauca City looked on glumly as steamboats owned and captained
by Venezuelans put in at El Amparo across the river. Compelled to
import their goods through Venezuelan middlemen, they paid duty at
Ciudad Bolívar and again at Arauca, raising their prices to unaccept-
ably high levels. Not surprisingly, two-thirds of the provincial trade
was contraband, for the Colombian aduana had only seven badly paid
men to guard a border of 150 leagues. At times, only Venezuelan cur-
rency circulated. In 1912, Comisario Pedro León Acosta reported that
Venezuelan merchants had collected all Colombian coinage in Arauca
City, restamped it as Venezuelan, and reintroduced it at 100 percent
profit! ¹⁰

Finally, Arauca inevitably was caught up in Venezuelan regional
and national political turmoils. Would-be revolutionaries found the
Colombian plains a convenient place to organize invasions into Apure,
and their activities, which included extorting cattle and horses from
local ranchers, made them indistinguishable from the run-of-the-mill
outlaws who plagued the region. In 1909, 1911, and 1912, opponents
of Apure's president, Dr. José Rafael Gabaldón, launched ill-fated
raids from Arauca, and after Gómez overthrew Castro in 1908, the
defeated president's supporters plotted their vengeance in Arauca. To
crush them, Gómez did not hesitate to order their assassinations or
to send troops across the Arauca River, with or without Colombian
permission. His high-handed actions reinforced fears of an impending Venezuelan invasion, or even of the annexation of the entire
province.¹¹

The insecurity of the border and the overwhelming problems

facing law-abiding citizens of Arauca were aptly summarized by Max Carriazo, in a series of articles published in *El Nuevo Tiempo* in 1910 and later gathered together in a pamphlet, *Llanos Orientales*, dedicated to Rafael Uribe Uribe. Carriazo, a Liberal who had fought with Uribe Uribe in the War of the Thousand Days, discussed such topics as the need for salt, civilization of the Indians, the hunting of garza feathers, baldíos and colonization, customs, commerce, and free trade. Charging that Bogotá had systematically neglected Arauca to the point of carelessly omitting the province from the official map of the republic published in 1908, he listed thirty-six complaints that Araucanos could legitimately lodge against the government, including excessive taxation, rule by corrupt officials, lack of means of communication, and the threat of Venezuelan attacks. With far less provocation, he warned, Panama had separated from the republic. Unless Bogotá took immediate action on at least some of these grievances, Arauca might well follow Panama's lead.[12]

President Restrepo needed little convincing. The governor of Boyacá, Rafael Castillo Mariño, had already informed him that the department could not effectively rule the far-flung Province of Arauca and that "the creation of a comisaría especial is indispensable given the situation, in which as I have said, is found that region."[13] On March 24, 1911, Restrepo issued Decree no. 306 placing Arauca under the direct rule of the national government as a comisaría especial with of five municipios: Arauca City (capital), Arauquita, Cravo Norte, Todos los Santos, and El Viento.

A National Territory

The definitive boundaries of the new comisaría did not take shape until 1924. From the start, there was considerable sentiment within Arauca that the municipios of Tame and San Lope, still ruled by Boyacá, belonged geographically to the Llanos rather than the highlands and could be more effectively administered from Arauca City than from Tunja. For example, Comisario Aristides Vaca requested in 1920 that Tame and San Lope be annexed to the comisaría because they were too isolated from Tunja to be patrolled by departmental police. When bandits from Arauca hid there, Vaca could not pursue them himself without getting permission from the prefect of Támara, an inconvenient and time-consuming process.[14] Governor

Luis A. Mariño Ariza opposed the loss of more territory from his department, but by Decree no. 1000 of July 6, 1923, President Pedro Nel Ospina added Tame and San Lope to the comisaría.[15] A year later, in accordance with the boundary decision laid down by Swiss arbitrators on July 30, 1924, Colombia surrendered El Viento to Venezuela, and Colombians who had been living there moved south of the newly drawn border to settle in Villanueva. With the addition of Tame and San Lope and the loss of El Viento, Arauca had attained its present-day configuration ov 23,500 square kilometers.[16]

The internal divisions of the comisaría also saw some alteration between 1911 and 1931 as one new town was founded and two older ones decayed. In 1920, Luis Felipe Hernández, a Llanero from Guárico, started a fundación on the left bank of the Casanare River, midway between Tame and Cravo Norte. The following year, three more Venezuelans arrived. Planting fields and raising pigs and cattle, they prospered by supplying food to travelers along the river. Hernández called the settlement El Padre because a priest had once said mass there, but no one could remember his name. As the community continued to grow, El Padre became a corregimiento in 1923, and in 1931 the vecinos adopted a new name, Rondón.[17] Of the older towns, Arauca City, Arauquita, and Tame continued to attract settlers, but the 392 people who lived in Todos Los Santos in 1919 were so scattered throughout the municipio that it was difficult to find candidates for local offices, and in Cravo Norte elections could not be held for lack of Colombian residents. Eventually, the comisario was forced to suppress these municipios, along with that of San Lope. In 1931, the territory consisted of three municipios: Arauca City—the capital—with the corregimientos of Cravo Norte, Rondón, Villanueva, and Todos los Santos; Tame, with the corregimientos of San Lope, San Salvador, Macaguane, and El Bando; and Arauquita.[18]

Although Decree no. 306 of 1911 gave the comisario broadly based power, his influence, as in the case of the intendant of Meta, was more theoretical than real. The comisario exercised all the faculties that were divided between governors, prefects, and alcaldes in the departments. He was responsible for supervising government, fostering the growth of settlements into municipios, drawing up a tax roll of property owners, inspecting the aduana, and promoting the general interests of the territory. Inhibiting his effectiveness was the small annual subsidy of fourteen hundred pesos with which he was supposed to administer the territory and the fact that his tenure was limited to one year. Between 1911 and 1930 seventeen men served as comisario, and only one, Paulo Miller Puyo, was appointed twice (in 1926 and 1929). More important, however, was the fact that Decree no. 306 specifically assigned responsibility for public order and defense to a squadron of national police directed by the Ministry of War in Bogotá, and which, by Law 100 of 1913, was expanded to include two hundred men assigned to Arauca.[19] With constant turmoil by would-be revolutionaries, threats of invasion, and the activities of outlaws and bandits, the police in the territory had their work cut out for them, yet conflicts between the comisario and the local police chief—be he a general or a colonel—severely inhibited their ability to keep the peace. Lack of cooperation between the civil and military authorities was a telling factor in the two most serious challenges to Colombian rule in Arauca—Pérez Soto's invasion in April 1916 and the Gómez rebellion in December of that same year.

Pérez Soto's Invasion

In December 1915, Pedro Pérez Delgado tried to topple the government of General Vincencio Pérez Soto, caudillo president of Apure. Pérez Soto defeated Pérez Delgado, who retreated with his followers to Arauca, where he occupied himself with stealing cattle. By March rumors that he was planning to attack Arauca City prompted the comisario, Marco Torres Elicechea, to urge the police chief, Sergeant Major Villalobos, to apprehend him before he could carry out his scheme. Villalobos refused, explaining that he would respond only to orders from the minister of war in Bogotá. When rumors of the impending attack persisted, General Pérez Soto himself offered to come to Elicechea's aid and defend the city.

Learning of the crisis, President José Vicente Concha declined Pérez Soto's aid, and ordered the commander-in-chief of the frontier police in Cúcuta, General Daniel Ortiz, to march with his men to Arauca using the San Cristóbal road. President Juan Vicente Gómez gave Ortiz permission to travel through Venezuelan territory, but before he could get to Arauca, Pérez Delgado attacked the Venezuelan border town of Elorza on April 3, killing twenty-two people. Thoroughly provoked by this new outrage, General Pérez Soto pursued the outlaws, invading Arauca with the consent of Comisario Torres Elicechea, who was immediately jailed by Sergeant Major Villalobos for treason. Happily, General Ortiz arrived soon and took command. He released Torres Elicechea and persuaded Pérez Soto to withdraw. After capturing Pérez Delgado and some of his gang at La Cañada near Arauca City, Ortiz remanded them to Boyacá for trial. He continued to patrol the Llanos until July, when, with the arrival of the new comisario, Estéban Escallón, he returned with his troops to Cúcuta.[20]

President Concha placed high priority on improving relations with Venezuela, and 1916 was a critical year. Juan Vicente Gómez's overthrow of Cipriano Castro had paved the way for the resumption of diplomatic ties in 1910, broken nine years before by Colombia. While Pérez Delgado was attacking Elorza, the Colombian foreign minister, Marco Fidel Suárez, was negotiating with Venezuelan plenipotentiary Demetrio Lozada Díaz for a new agreement to submit the disputed border for arbitration. As a consequence, in his annual report to Congress in July 1916, Suárez downplayed the violation of Colombian sovereignty by Pérez Soto, pointing out that it was regrettable but understandable if, at times, Venezuelan forces crossed over the border in pursuit of bandits.[21] Minister of Government Miguel Abadía Méndez, in his report, attributed the crisis to Villalobos's refusal to take orders from Torres Elicechea. To avoid this bottleneck, he suggested that the police chief should be placed under the authority of the comisario by an executive decree—a recommendation which Concha adopted but which, as events were to prove, failed to clear up the difficulty.[22]

Beyond this step, Bogotá did nothing to reduce tension in the comisaría, which was heightened by the unchecked activities of outlaws. A correspondent from Arauca, writing in *El Diario Nacional*, reported on July 18, 1916, that bandits in groups of six, ten, twenty, and even fifty, armed with Mausers, Winchesters, and other precision weapons, were roaming through the territory at will and terrorizing the peaceful inhabitants. "The quantity of cattle lost is terrifying; the robberies are daily," he wrote, "and the principal cause of this situation is the anarchy that has nearly always existed between the civil and military authorities." He added that if Sergeant Major Villalobos had supported Comisario Torres Elicechea, he could have prevented the attack on Elorza, and the arrival of Comisario Escallón to Arauca City only made matters worse.[23] A Bogotano without experience in the Llanos, Escallón lacked diplomacy and tolerance. Within weeks he alienated many Araucanos. He failed to foster cooperation with either the new police commander, Captain Alberto Santos, or General Pérez

Soto, and he relentlessly harassed his personal enemies.[24] One of the latter, Humberto Gómez, fled to Apure and began plotting revenge.

La Humbertera

Humberto Gómez, blond, blue-eyed, and deeply tanned, was twenty-nine years old in 1916. Born in Santander, he lived as a child in Sogamoso and Cúcuta, where he learned rudimentary pharmacy and carpentry from his foster father. An intelligent, audacious young man, he moved to Guárico, Venezuela, where he won the patronage of the local caudillos, the Gabaldón brothers. Sometime after 1911 he settled in Arauca, married, and worked as mayordomo on the hato Las Delicias.[25] Some of his neighbors regarded Gómez as nothing more than an honest cattleman. Others alleged that he and the Gabaldón brothers were trafficking illegally in garza feathers. In the opinion of a former comisario, Eduardo Carvajal, who knew him personally, Gómez was "one of many vicious products of the Colombian and Venezuelan interior who flee to the frontier to avoid jail and who take advantage of the freedom there to commit new crimes."[26] Evidently, Comisario Escallón shared this view, for all accounts agree that it was Escallón's tireless persecution of Gómez that drove him into Venezuela in September 1916.

While in exile, Humberto plotted his move against Escallón. His plan to capture Arauca City and sack the government treasury won the allegiance of former followers of Pérez Delgado who were still at liberty. Later, other malcontents, including some soldiers discharged by Captain Santos for insubordination, joined the conspiracy. Humberto armed his men from a cache of Mausers and Winchesters hidden by Pérez Delgado, and by mid-December he was ready.

General Escallón refused to take seriously warnings he received of Humberto's impending attack, and his obstinance supplied the outlaw with an opportunity on December 29. By sending one police squadron to the Llanos to search for an overdue mail delivery and another commanded by Captain Santos to Cravo Norte, he foolishly left the garrison in Arauca City with only twenty defenders.[27] Before dawn on December 30, Humberto and thirty-seven companions crossed the Arauca River, where they were joined by Eloy Sánchez and twelve others. Proceeding stealthily to the plaza, they killed the

sentinel. Then shouting "Viva la República de Arauca!" they attacked
the barracks. The shots awoke General Escallón, who rushed out of
the comisaría with a carbine. Advancing bravely, he was mortally
wounded in the stomach by a bullet fired by a man later identified as
Pedro Antonio Alvarez. After the fighting, Gómez ordered Escallón
carried to the house of his brother-in-law, Atilio D'Anello, where he
died at 1:00 P.M.[28]

By noon Humberto controlled the city. Thirteen police were
dead. Commandeering the town arsenal, he seized 5,000 pesos from
the treasury and 150 pesos from the aduana. Gómez burned the archives of the comisaría and the circuit court. He imprisoned all those
who opposed him and demanded ransom for Marco Torres Elicechea,
General Luis Nieto, Colonel Alejandro Díaz, Colonel Manuel Molano
Briceño, and Alfonso and Zoilo Escallón, sons of the slain comisario.[29]
Later, he sent a posse to trap Captain Santos. Finding him in the
Llanos south of Arauca City on January 1, the rebels forced Santos to
retreat to Pore. With no other Colombian force to challenge him, the
former contrabandista was "Master of Arauca."

While vengeance and booty were his primary motives, Gómez
endeavored to give his actions an ideological cast. He told the terrified
Araucanos that his insurrection was part of a general Liberal revolt
throughout Colombia and that President Concha, Minister Suárez, and
other high officials were already in jail. In the *Proclamación* dated January 4, allegedly composed by his secretary, Luis Romero, and circulated widely in the Llanos, Gómez announced that the practice of
sending corrupt officials to Arauca had ended, and he called to arms
all Liberals, Republicans, and Araucanos. He declared Arauca a Republic and named himself as jefe civil y militar.[30] His ample supplies
of horses, aguardiente, and guns attracted new recruits, who swelled
his army to three hundred men. Throughout January they roamed the
Llanos, attacking hatos and carrying off cattle and horses. As accounts
of unprovoked atrocities circulated, peaceful settlers fled to the forests
or to safety in El Amparo. Especially notorious was the cruelty of one
of Humberto's lieutenants, Monte de Oca, who beheaded children
with his machete. It was said that Humberto himself was afraid of this
bloodthirsty Venezuelan and one evening ordered his men to tie him
up. The next day, he delivered Monte de Oca to the Venezuelan army,
who obligingly executed him.[31]

Gómez planned to hold Arauca City until he had collected enough
booty to make a profitable retreat into Venezuela or Brazil, before

the Colombian army might arrive. Despite reports that he was marching with a thousand men on Tame, Orocué, and even Tunja, the only town he occupied besides Arauca City was Cravo Norte. By the end of January his army was already beginning to dwindle. Gómez released his prisoners through the mediation of the president of Apure, Pérez Soto. His last attack fell on El Viento, where he burned and sacked the business district. Then, on February 3, along with most of his officers, a large quantity of hides, merchandise, and horses, he crossed the border and was captured by the Venezuelan army.[32] The "Republic of Arauca" dissolved five days before the first Colombian soldier appeared on the scene.

The "Humbertera," as it came to be called, differed from dozens of previous violent border incidents in the killing of the comisario, the audacity of its leader, and the political overtones of his essentially criminal motivations. In contrast to their lack of interest in the invasion of Pérez Soto, the Bogotá newspapers vied with one another to report the latest developments in the Gómez revolt. Their coverage of the fumbling attempts of President Concha to restore order and of the alleged excesses of the two expeditionary armies soon transformed the revolt into a national scandal, the "Arauca Affair," and exposed the fragile hegemony exercised by Colombia over the distant territory.

To begin with, Concha did not know that a Colombian province had fallen until four days after the fact because there was no telegraph in Arauca City, and a telegram dispatched by the Colombian consul in El Amparo had to be relayed through San Cristóbal and Cúcuta to reach San Carlos Palace by January 3. Other telegrams followed from Nunchía, Cúcuta, and Orocué, telling of the murder of Escallón and the alarm sweeping the Llanos. From Pore, Captain Santos wired that he had eighty men ready to resist Humberto but only eighteen horses, and General Ignacio Suárez in Nunchía reported that he was assembling volunteers and supplies to defend Tame.[33]

Concha hesitated. On December 16, he had warmly congratulated Juan Vicente Gómez on the eighth anniversary of his coming to power, and, above all, he did not want to disrupt relations while the Venezuelan legislature was debating the new arbitration treaty signed on November 3.[34] Although the news from Arauca suggested that the insurrection was not politically inspired, the report on January 8 that Humberto was marching on Tame required action. On January 9, Concha declared a state of siege in the Comisaría Especial of Arauca, the prefecture of Nunchía, and the district of Orocué in Boyacá. He ordered General Salomón Correal, director of the national police, to march with two hundred men from Bogotá to Arauca, going first to Villavicencio, continuing on to Orocué, and from there to the besieged city. He wired General Daniel Ortiz in Cúcuta to mobilize the frontier police and to request permission from Venezuela to use the San Cristóbal road. Finally, on January 11, he appointed General Jesús García as civil and military jefe of Arauca, with orders to raise a volunteer army in Boyacá and Casanare and to proceed to Arauca via the Chita road to restore Colombian sovereignty.[35]

The decision to send two armies to put down the revolt indicated the depth of Concha's concern. The policemen set off first, leaving Bogotá on January 10. *El Diario Nacional* stated: "Yesterday we saw them for the last time, each with his suit of light denim and his hammock under his arm. They could be heard to speak of Arauca as something far away and terrible, and they go out to fight Humberto Gómez just as the settlers centuries ago went out to fight the savage hordes of Don Lope de Aguirre."[36] General Correal and his men reached Villavicencio on January 15, continuing by boat down the Meta River to Orocué. In the meantime, General García went to Tunja, where he organized two volunteer infantry battalions, "El Albán" and "El Chita." Accompanied by the Soublette Battalion from the regular army, they left for Arauca, taking the Chita road. García stopped in Tame, where he incorporated some Llanero cavalrymen into his force. On February 9, he reached Arauca City to learn that Humberto had fled five days before, leaving many buildings in ruins and the plaza littered with dead animals, burned papers, and bloodied clothing.[37] On García's orders, General Correal waited in Orocué for a few days to deter any attempt by Gómez to flee to Brazil. Then he and his policemen continued on to Arauca City, arriving on February 25 to aid in the cleanup operations.

García went first to El Amparo to assure Venezuelan authorities of his desire for cordial relations and to urge dozens of Araucanos to return home. To round up outlaws still at large, he selected one of Humberto's former prisoners, General Manuel Molano Briceño, who, with thirty-four Llaneros, combed the territory along the Arauca River for fugitives. When Molano Briceño returned with his prisoners, stories were already circulating that his men had committed atrocities against innocent people. The general quickly dispersed his group, but unfortunately for him, one of the alleged victims was a Venezuelan whose relatives complained to the Venezuelan consul, who, in turn,

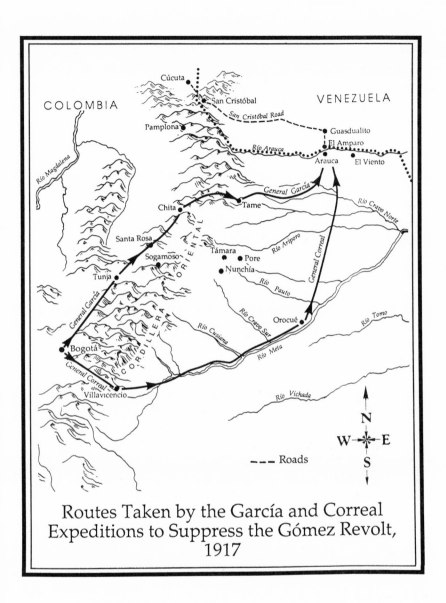

Routes Taken by the García and Correal
Expeditions to Suppress the Gómez Revolt,
1917

demanded an investigation. At Venezuelan insistence, the Colombian minister of war, Salvador Franco, sent a special commission to look into the allegations. The commission stayed in Arauca for nineteen days, conducting an inquiry which exonerated Molano Briceño of any wrongdoing.[38]

García assumed the powers of investigating judge (*funcionario de instrucción*) and drew up indictments against Humberto's suspected collaborators. He heard three hundred sworn testimonies over a fifty-eight-day period. Then he charged forty Araucanos with complicity, including Atilio D'Anello, Humberto's brother-in-law.[39] On April 24, these prisoners, with an armed escort, began the arduous trip to Santa Rosa de Viterbo, Boyacá, where they were to be tried. García appointed Luis Camejo as jefe civil of Arauca and met with members of the reconstituted municipal council to discuss the needs of the comisaría. The council composed a statement describing Arauca's problems, which the general included in his final report to the ministers of government and war. He also authorized some immediate reforms, such as reorganizing the local revenue to yield more money for salaries and public works.[40]

On March 17, President Concha lifted the stated of siege in Boyacá and ordered Correal and his policemen to return to Bogotá. García's troops departed a month later, after the general had handed over command to the new comisario especial, Aristides Novoa. General Gabriel Rojas Robayo remained with 250 border police to keep peace. While Minister of Foreign Relations Suárez haggled with President Gómez for the extradition of Humberto and fifty-six of his companions, Concha ended the state of siege in Arauca on April 30.[41]

The Arauca Affair

As far as the government was concerned, the incident was over, but the arrival in Santa Rosa, on May 19, of García's prisoners, loudly proclaiming their innocence, quickly dispelled this illusion. Accusing García's soldiers of having committed atrocities far worse than those of Humberto, the prisoners found an eager listener in G. Pérez Sarmiento, reporter for Bogotá's leading Liberal newspaper, *El Diario Nacional*. Pérez Sarmiento's telegraphed dispatches from Santa Rosa transformed the "Humbertera" into the "Arauca Affair," a national scandal that brought into question not only the conduct of Generals

García, Correal, and Molano Briceño, but also the policies of President Concha, his minister of government, and his minister of war. Goaded by the press, Concha was forced to open a new inquiry, and the Araucanos found a champion in Enrique Olaya Herrera, founder of *El Diario Nacional* and Liberal congressman who was destined to become president of Colombia in 1930. Olaya saw the scandal as an opportunity to unite his fragmented party against the Conservative government, and he lobbied energetically to convince Congress to open its own investigation.

Even before May 19, the press had assiduously followed the unfolding of the insurrection. The death of Comisario Escallón and the boldness of Humberto captured public attention. Articles about Humberto's victims, interviews with former comisaría officials, telegrams, official statements, and photographs filled the front pages while editorials expressed diverse political viewpoints.[42] *El Nuevo Tiempo*, a staunch supporter of Concha, declared that the vicious criminals in Arauca deserved firm punishment, welcomed the state of siege declaration, and applauded General García's appointment as commander-in-chief. In Tunja, the militant *La Unión Conservador* gleefully published the political sections of Gómez's January proclamation and accused the Liberal Party chief in Boyacá, Enrique Santos, of inciting Humberto to revolt through irresponsible editorials in his periodical, *La Linterna*.[43] The Liberal press—*El Diario Nacional, El Espectador, El Tiempo*, and *Gil Blas*—criticized the government's response to the crisis. While conceding that Humberto was an outlaw, they argued that his actions were partially justified by years of official corruption and neglect in the Llanos. Olaya Herrera's editorials in *El Diario Nacional* pressed Concha on several decisions: Was the state of siege necessary? Why were two expeditions sent? Why was the regular army not mobilized? How was it that Venezuela could get troops to the border within a week, when Colombia needed forty-five days?[44]

Pérez Sarmiento's dispatches at the end of May raised new questions about the handling of the insurrection. Atilio D'Anello, Francisco Vitta, Saturnino Buena, and the other prisoners steadfastly maintained their innocence, contending that General García had rounded up anyone he could find, regardless of lack of evidence. They charged that the expeditionary officers had extorted money, horses, and equipment from them, and they described in detail atrocities committed by General Molano Briceño's men in their arrest of former followers of Humberto.[45] Eyewitnesses swore that at Guaratarito, Las Delicias,

Cabuyares, Villanueva, and El Yopal these irregular troops had bru-
tally executed seventeen innocent men. The most terrible killings
occurred at Villanueva, where, according to one account, Molano Briceño's men tied two Venezuelans, Luis Cobos and Francisco Ramírez,
to a tree and slowly dismembered them with a machete:

> He (Cobos) did not cry out once when the machete cut off his arm. Afterwards
> they cut off his other arm and then his legs. Maddened like jackals by the blood
> his butchers repeated their blows prolonging his agony until finally one of them,
> perhaps the least cruel, with a single stroke severed his head from his body. Ra-
> mírez watched the death with immense heroism. . . . They repeated on him the
> execution of Cobos. The bodies were then thrown into the Arauca River . . .⁴⁶

As these details appeared under the apt headline "Hair-raising
Crimes," Pérez Sarmiento raised another sensitive issue by charging
that the national police had also committed crimes. By General Correal's
admission, twenty-four agents had been jailed in Tunja on their return
from Arauca for gambling, drunkenness, and insubordination. While
these charges were not as grave as those lodged against Molano Briceño's
men, Pérez Sarmiento argued that they were serious enough to reopen
the matter of the government's decision to send police and the volunteer force raised by General García rather than relying on the regular
army. General García had required a staff of ten generals to direct one
thousand men, and his punitive expedition had been guilty of immo-
rality and lack of discipline. It had been costly as well. Pérez Sarmiento charged that it was entirely possible that the government had
spent over 150,000 pesos on the operation.⁴⁷

Liberal newspapers throughout Colombia took up the cry. Expressing sympathy for the Santa Rosa prisoners and horror at the
atrocities, they demanded an official inquiry. *El Fiscal* from Socorro
wrote, "Those guilty in connection with Gómez should be punished,
but the character of reprisals that sacrifice innocent victims is unpar-
donable."⁴⁸ *El Universal* of Barranquilla warned that if the government
did not investigate and punish the guilty, "it would become identified
with those savage crimes committed not by outlaws but by an organized body of military agents in a country that calls itself Christian
and civilized."⁴⁹ The intensity of public opinion forced President
Concha to announce on June 1 that he had ordered the attorney general
of the nation to investigate the accusations. On August 1, spurred by
the Santa Rosa court's unconditional release of the Arauca prisoners,
the Chamber of Representatives opened its own investigation.

In response to these charges, General García submitted two reports in June and July to the ministers of war and government and published letters in *El Nuevo Tiempo*. Concha issued the *Exposición*, in which he explained his decisions and reproduced copies of relevant documents as well as García's reports. Ministers Franco, Suárez, and Abadía Méndez dealt at length with Arauca in their annual reports of July 1917, and Franco and Abadía Méndez spoke before the Chamber of Representatives on September 8. *El Nuevo Tiempo* and other Conservative newspapers published letters from expeditionary officers justifying their conduct. Their arguments can be briefly summarized as follows: García flatly rejected the claim made by the Santa Rosa prisoners that they had been unfairly accused and maintained that any expropriations he had ordered were legal under the state of siege. He admitted that some executions had been committed by Molano Briceño's men, but asserted that the victims had been incontrovertibly implicated in the insurrection. Moreover, Molano Briceño had not ordered the killings and knew nothing about them until afterward. Minister Franco supported García's position, stating that General Molano Briceño was a respected Liberal and a trusted companion of General Uribe Uribe. If atrocities had occurred, the appropriate court would punish the guilty. In the meantime, his office had received many letters from Araucanos who applauded the efforts of the expeditionary forces to rid the Llanos of outlaws.[50] Minister of Government Abadía Méndez defended the actions of the national police. The government had sent them to Arauca because the police were the appropriate security branch to deal with violence of a criminal nature. While it was true that some agents were in jail, no officers had been denounced. Abadía Méndez insisted that the imprisonment of policemen, rather than reflecting a lack of discipline, only showed that even their small offenses would not go unpunished.[51]

Concha and Franco both justified the crucial decision to send a volunteer force instead of the standing army. The president noted that the tropical environment, the transportation difficulties, and the lack of horses and other equipment would have greatly hindered the regular army. Jesús García was a general-in-chief on the official army roster, and a brave officer familiar with the Llanos. He had not promoted the officers who had joined his staff, and he had tried to select Liberals as well as Conservatives for these positions. Concha set the cost of operation at 107,061.90 pesos, or 46,999.67 pesos for García's expedition and 60,173.23 for Correal's.[52] He declared that only the most indispensable military measures had been taken and that they had proved adequate to restore order. Minister Franco seconded the report of the president. In his view, the expeditionary forces had overcome many difficulties, and they deserved recognition rather than reproach.[53]

García's reports and the statements by Concha, Franco, and Abadía Méndez carried the day, for the attorney general ended his investigation by exonerating the government. After Franco and Abadía Méndez had testified before the Chamber of Representatives, Olaya Herrera made a final attempt to keep the issue alive. On September 9, he summed up the case for the opposition in a long speech and offered a new resolution that the Chamber should continue the investigation of the war ministry and required that the minister of government report on measures he had taken in Arauca to prevent the recurrence of atrocities.[54] Representative Montoya Arbeláez, a member of the Conservative majority, spoke against Olaya's motion, insisting that the ministers had performed their duties in accordance with the constitution and that General García's conduct had been entirely correct. "I am tired of hearing so many unfounded incriminations against the government," he concluded.[55] His colleagues shared his weariness, and when the vote was called, they resoundedly rejected Olaya's resolution.

The "Aaruca Affair" had ended. On September 21, *El Diario Nacional* printed, without comment, under the caption "Epilogue and Summary," Law 3 of September 15, 1917, which assigned to the Ministry of War an additional 270,000 pesos to cover the cost of the García expedition.[56] Having failed to unite the Liberals around army reform or frontier security, Olaya Herrera abandoned Arauca for other concerns. For the national government, too, the comisaría was no longer a critical issue. On July 20, 1917, a ceremony in Caracas marked the ratification of the treaty to submit the disputed boundary to the Swiss government for arbitration, and President Gómez conferred on Concha the Order of the Liberator—First Class.[57] In March 1918, Venezuela agreed to extradite Humberto and fifty of his companions, but whether they ever returned to Colombia remains a mystery. After this date, there is no further mention of Gómez, either in official documents or the newspapers, and a thorough search of the archives of the Tribunal Superior at Santa Rosa de Viterbo uncovered no evidence that a trial was held.[58] The silence of the press on matters relating to Arauca after September 1917 bears out the prophecy made by the editor of *Correo Liberal* in Medellín, on learning of the release of the Santa Rosa prisoners:

It is certain that no further mention of the matter will be made. Things in Colombia manage to go along with the same monotony. It is like what happens when an object falls into a quiet pool of water. The agitated waves make concentric circles to the banks where all movement dies. The glacial-like surface of the dead pond continues, monotonously sad, reflecting our inertia and our lack of civic spirit.[59]

Securing the Border after 1917

Besides overcoming domestic criticism of his handling of the Humbertera, President Concha also had achieved his principal goal of maintaining cordial relations with Venezuela. Foreign Minister Suárez had nothing but praise for Venezuela's cooperation during the crisis. In his memoria of July 1917, he pointed out that General Pérez Soto had seized the revolutionaries as soon as they crossed the border and was holding them until extradition could be arranged. As soon as Humberto had deposed the comisaría authorities, the general had pledged his support to the Colombian consul in El Amparo. Venezuela permitted the transport of Colombian troops through its territory, and private Venezuelan citizens paid the ransom of at least one of Humberto's victims, Marco Antonio Torres. With regard to the events in Arauca, Suárez asserted, "The Venezuelan government has worked in a just and friendly way according to international law and the agreements adopted at the Bolivarian Convention of Caracas in 1911."[60]

Venezuela continued to reject Colombia's demand for free navigation on the Orinoco, but it did accept the ruling of the Swiss government on the boundary arbitration, handed down on March 24, 1922—a ruling widely regarded as favoring Colombia. The Swiss determined that the two countries could go ahead and occupy the territories that had been adjudicated under the Spanish Laudo of 1891 and other regions divided by uncontested natural boundaries such as rivers and mountains, while at the same time continuing to negotiate the specific portions of the border still under dispute.[61] In accordance with this decision, Colombia turned over the municipio of El Viento to Venezuela on April 30, 1924, and in 1928 the two governments set up mixed commissions of engineers to review the six segments of the border that remained in doubt. A definitive boundary treaty was not signed until 1941, but after decades of frustrated negotiations, genuine headway had been made.

This cooperation was all the more remarkable when one considers that the Comisaría Especial of Arauca continued to be a breeding ground for Venezuelan revolutionaries throughout the 1920s and a haven for outlaws of all descriptions. In 1919, Comisario Julio Acosta complained that the Bogotá press maligned Arauca by constantly insinuating that only criminals lived in the territory, yet his own report showed that, in the previous year, public order had been disturbed by rumors of an armed attack against the police garrison, by a revolution in the Páez District of Apure, and by the depredations of a Venezuelan cattle rustler, Baudilio Escalona. Evidently, Escalona proved to be the most serious problem, for when he threatened to attack Arauca City, Acosta and the jefe of the frontier police could not agree on a course of action. Once more, General Vincencio Pérez Soto arrived at the border to offer weapons and men to capture the outlaw. After some discussion, Acosta accepted the loan of fifty rifles and some ammunition. The police pursued Escalona, killing three of his gang and capturing ten others, along with their horses and guns. Escalona remained free and found time to attack Elorza in 1920, before the Venezuelans finally apprehended him.[62]

In spite of the publicity surrounding the Humbertera and Concha's efforts to improve defense of the border, the comisaría was as vulnerable as before. The government reorganized the frontier police in 1918, and throughout the 1920s between 150 and 200 agents were stationed in Arauca. The formation of a cavalry unit to complement the infantry was approved in 1918, but it did not become operational until 1922. Friction continued between the comisarios and the police jefes. In 1923, the latter refused to act without direct orders from the Dirección General de Policía in Bogotá. Comisario Heliadoro Polanía complained that this attitude was inconvenient, especially since telegraph service between Bogotá and Arauca was not reliable and orders sent by the Dirección General might never arrive. "The dual authority is very serious since the Jefe de Policía does not consider his authority less than that of the Comisario, and when they don't get along, a struggle develops that hinders action."[63]

There were also charges of police improprieties. On July 26, 1919, P. M. Reyes of Hato Corozal dispatched a telegram to Congress claiming that police, at the behest of Venezuelan authorities, were killing Venezuelan exiles living in Arauca. On November 16, 1922, *El Tiempo* published a telegram sent by three Araucanos to the minister of government, charging that police had illegally taken over the supervision of the slaughter of cattle and the weighing of meat in flagrant disregard of the objections of the butchers and of previous orders from the government to desist. In 1929, Comisario Paulo Miller Puyo reported that the police were causing disturbances at night and that when they were sent out to the Llanos on some assignment they became "dictators" and forgot about following orders. At that very moment, a detail of police sent to Villanueva to prevent some revolutionaries led by General Arévalo Cedeño from crossing into Colombian territory were terrorizing the corregimiento, introducing contraband brandy, and holding dances every night. Miller Puyo recommended that policemen assigned to Arauca be rotated each year because the agents who stayed longer acquired bad habits and quickly corrupted the new recruits.[64] His remarks suggest that the frontier police, undermanned, underpaid, and inclined to look after their own interests, were ill equipped to control revolutionaries or outlaws.

The Indians

Guahibo Indians posed another threat to peace in the comisaría. Unlike the natives in the Intendancy of Meta, who had either accommodated themselves to Colombian rule or withdrawn to remote sections of the territory, the estimated three thousand to thirty-five hundred Guahibos in Arauca nourished a passionate hatred of the whites that was fully reciprocated. Superbly adapted to the Llanos environment, these nomads were organized in capitanías. Although they cultivated crops, they readily deserted their fields when it was necessary. They raided isolated hatos and towns, and during the rainy season, traveled easily by canoe over the flooded sabanas to kill cattle stranded on islands of land. Efforts to reduce them and force them to work achieved scant success. In 1913, Indalecio Yáñez convinced Marcelino, a Guahibo captain with two hundred followers, to build a road between Arauca City to Salibón. A year later, Ezequiel Tocaría hired some Macaguanes to work on the road between Arauca City and Tame, but these cases were exceptions.[65] Those whites who approached the Indians soon discovered that their nomadic instincts made them reluctant to settle permanently in one place, while their memory of past betrayals instilled them with a deep distrust of the whites.

White frustration, fear, and anger toward the Indians were well expressed by Comisario Eduardo Carvajal, when he reported in 1914 that it was impossible to deal with the Guahibos since they "remained silent and anonymous in strict solidarity." They despised work and "lived by the most cynical and shameful pillage, attacking in gangs and killing with a maximum of cruelty and treachery." Carvajal wrote that everyday he received complaints from peaceful proprietors who had seen their ranches razed and their animals devoured by these Indians. Moreover, in defending themselves the whites were at a disadvantage because they had to obey the laws, while the Indians could do whatever they liked without fear of penalty. Carvajal believed that since the government would not permit whites to imprison an entire tribe or to hunt them down like animals, the best solution would be to force the Guahibos to relocate in a region with a cold climate where they would have to build houses, wear clothes, and plant crops in order to survive.[66] Between 1914 and 1930 several other comisarios voiced support for this draconian approach, although the government does not seem to have ever seriously considered adopting it.

The Missionaries

Missionaries, the traditional instrument of Indian control, conversion, and integration wielded far less power in Arauca than in Meta during the first decades of the twentieth century. Until 1916 the comisaría was part of the Apostolic Vicariate of Casanare, administered by the Recoletos under the leadership of Apostolic Vicar Santos Ballesteros. The capital of the vicariate was Támara, and the Recoletos concentrated their scarce resources within the Province of Nunchía. Just two priests were assigned to the comisaría, Antonio Caballero and Francisco Corra, both of whom taught schools in Arauca City and only ventured outside the town to minister to the white ganaderos. In 1916, the ecclesiastical authorities detached Chita, La Salina, and Arauca from the vicariate to form a separate Apostolic Prefecture. They assigned the new province to the Congregation of the Mission, also known as the Lazarists and/or Vincentians, an order founded by St. Vincent de Paul in France in 1617 and established in Colombia in 1870. Directed by Emilio Larquére, who served as Apostolic Prefect from 1916 to 1928, the Lazarists established their capital in Chita. Although Larquére did make one recognizance trip among the Indians in Arauca, in general he was content to focus the work of the order on the spiritual, educational, and health needs of the whites.[67]

The Lazarists got off to a shaky start, for they had just settled in Arauca City when Pérez Delgado began his rampage. Then, Humberto Gómez sacked their house in Arauca City and burned down their house in El Viento. With the arrival of General García, however, calm was restored, and the priests could set to work in earnest. By 1920 Larquére had nine Lazarists scattered throughout the prefecture: Padres Bermúdez and Puyo in Chita; Padre Catalano in La Salina; Padres Calas and Motoa in Tame, with responsibility for Macaguane, San Lope, San Salvador, and El Banco; and Padres José Villanea, Victor Cabal, and Victor Fernández in Arauca City, who also had charge of El Viento, Cravo Norte, Camoruco, Arauquita, and the hatos along the Banadía River to the banks of the Meta. In 1917, the first Daughters of Charity of St. Vincent de Paul arrived to take charge of the schools. Three years later they had houses in Chita, Tame, and Arauca City.[68]

The Lazarists were not deterred by the notorious irreligiosity of the Araucanos. In his annual report of 1917, Padre Larquére observed with satisfaction that many communicants in Arauca City had celebrated Holy Week with solemnity and order. "The Llanero is not refractory to religion," he wrote. "It is only through lack of instruction that they are superstitious . . . one feels that Christian life penetrates little by little in this way, and with the schools we will watch over the youth giving their education a solidly religious base."[69]

Nevertheless, the comisaría presented enormous difficulties. In Tame, the missionaries did not have a house and had to haul water from a source more than half a league from the town. In Macaguane, a fire on July 21, 1919, burned down two houses, the school, and the chapel, destroying a magnificently carved wooden *retablo* (altar-piece) that had belonged to the Jesuits in the eighteenth century. Spiritual progress in Arauquita was minimal that year, "due to the indifference not to say hostility of its inhabitants." Larquére attributed this recalcitrance to the presence in the town of many "adventurers" who posed a constant threat to social tranquility and to the influence of Doctor Forero, who scandalized the region with his moral and intellectual perversion and his freewheeling life-style.[70] Finally, proximity to Venezuela posed special problems. In 1918, for example, at the invitation of the jefe of Guasdualito, the Lazarists crossed over the border to offer sacraments to Venezuelans in the border towns, but when they returned the following year, having received permission to do so from the Bishops of Calabozo and Mérida, a new jefe threatened to throw them in jail for fomenting insurrection. Larquére interceded for the priests and managed to get them back to Arauca, but he protested the high-handed action of the jefe and also the Venezuelan practice of sending agents across the border to assassinate exiles living peacefully in Colombia. [71]

Organization of primary schools was the principal activity of the missionaries in the prefecture. By 1926 there were three schools in Arauca City, two in Tame and one each in Arauquita, Cravo, Camoruco, Macaguane, El Banco, and San Lope, with a total enrollment of 386 students. Some of these schools were barely functional. When the teachers were not members of the religious orders, they lacked all pedagogical preparation and earned thirty pesos a month less than the salary of an illiterate *jornalero* (day worker). Textbooks and supplies dispatched from Bogotá arrived after long delays, and the hot climate, chronic illness of the children, and indifference of the parents worked against effective instruction. Probably, the Daughters of Charity offered the best education in their school for girls in Arauca City. Consisting of three classrooms and a dormitory for boarders, this school had the support of the municipal council and enrolled the daughters of the leading citizens of the capital. [72]

The missionaries collaborated with civil officials to improve health conditions in the comisaría. As in the Intendancy of Meta, hookworm, malaria, and syphilis afflicted much of the population, and cases of rheumatism and beriberi were also reported. Excessive heat and humidity, bad diet, and lack of popular awareness intensified the dangers posed by these diseases. Dr. Julio Pérez Hoyos, who organized the first Junta de Sanidad in 1913, estimated that the mortality rate in children was 65 percent. In 1917, there was a dysentery epidemic, and in November and December of 1919, two hundred people died of influenza, many of them children or elderly. These deaths prompted a decision on the part of Padre Larquére and Comisario Julio Acosta to start a hospital in Arauca City. A junta consisting of Acosta, Dr. Pérez Hoyos, and párroco José Villanea persuaded the Daughters of Charity to donate their residence to house the new facility. The hospital opened on March 28, 1920, with beds for ten patients who were cared for by the sisters and local doctors. The numbers of sick who came daily revealed the need for a larger building. In 1922, the comisaría began a planned expansion to create three twenty-bed wards—one for soldiers, one for men, and one for women—and five individual rooms for pensioners. By July half of the new addition had been completed, and Padre Larquére noted that it was especially important that the police knew that there was some place they could get attention when they were sick since they were often terrified at the thought of having to live in the Llanos.[73] Besides the hospital, little progress was made in fighting the causes of disease. The Rockefeller Sanitation Commission did not visit Arauca, although Comisario Miller Puyo requested it to come in 1926.

Communication

In erecting the Comisaría Especial of Arauca, Congress hoped to break down the isolation of a portion of the Llanos that occupied a strategic section of the border with Venezuela. President Restrepo endorsed two projects to improve communication—a direct telegraph line, made by extending the wire from Pore to Arauca City, and the completion of Sarare Road to connect Arauca City with Pamplona. Eventually, the telegraph line was installed, but the Sarare Road project remained an unfulfilled aspiration.

Recognizing in 1913 that the Colombian telegraph offices nearest Arauca City were hundreds of kilometers away in Cúcuta, La Salina, and Pore, Congress authorized twenty thousand pesos to extend the line from Pore to the capital of the comisaría, passing through Tame and Arauquita. Work on the project was sporadic until the Humbertera exposed the vulnerability of the border and the critical urgency for swift communication. In March 1917, construction began in earnest, supervised by Agustín Landínez Vargas. Twenty of the sixty leagues of line to be strung passed through dense jungle, and the rest through open but heavily flooded plains, where, in some places, the peons worked in water up to their waists. Six hundred men lost their lives before the line was completed at a cost of fifty thousand pesos, with stations in Arauquita, Todos los Santos, and Arauca City.[74] On July 20, 1917, Comisario Aristides Novoa sent the first telegram from Arauca City to President Concha and Minister Abadía Méndez, stating:

The people of the comisaría and the municipio are exhilarated and profoundly grateful to the government. They have commissioned me to extend to you their thanks. With such a saving instrument that the supreme powers have given us, I hope to consolidate order, always insecure here, and face any situation that arises. The organization of the service of the line is well-established. Inspector Manuel Antonio Manrique assures me that communication will continue in spite of the heavy rains (*crudo invierno*).[75]

Inspector Manrique's confidence was misplaced. By 1919 Comisario Julio Acosta was reporting frequent disruptions in communication, lasting up to fifteen days. Besides the minor inconvenience caused by the inexplicable decision to call the station located in Arauquita "Guadual" instead of "Arauquita," there were two fundamental difficulties. First, Landínez Vargas has installed substandard poles in the plains section of the route. They snapped quickly and subsequently had to be replaced. Second, the trace cut through the forest was so narrow that strong winds blew trees down on the line. Although the government hired two inspectors and twelve guards to patrol, they were insufficient to keep the wires open. Throughout the 1920s service was frequently suspended without warning, but when the line was clear, messages could be received and sent to the interior within two hours—a definite improvement over the pre-Humbertera years.[76]

The Sarare Road was another matter. For decades residents of Norte de Santander and the Llanos had urged the building of a highway through Colombian territory, which would link Arauca City with Pamplona and Cúcuta and eliminate the need to pay tolls to Venezuela to use the San Cristóbal Road. In 1912, Araucanos spent 70,000 pesos in gold for the privilege of driving their cattle through Venezuela, and as Comisario Jerónimo Mutis pointed out, if ever Venezuela decided to close the road for any reason, not a single steer from Arauca would be able to reach the Cúcuta market. On August 23, 1912, thirty-two Araucanos signed a memorial addressed to the presidents of the Senate and Chamber, urging them to support a subsidy to build a Colombia road, for "to connect us with the interior is to free industry, facilitate commerce, obeying the progressive march whose development is wealth." A year later Congress appropriated 9,672.56 pesos to build a road between Arauca City and Salivón–Banadía, which would eventually connect with the section between Banadía and Pamplona being constructed by the Department of Norte de Santander.[77]

Progress on the road was sporadic, in spite of the fact that the Humbertera dramatically demonstrated the need for an all-Colombian route to Arauca. In 1920, Congress approved a bond issue of 100,000 pesos and a subsidy of 24,000 pesos, but it is unlikely that these funds ever materialized. The route itself was difficult because of exuberant vegetation. Workers would spent months clearing a trace of several kilometers, only to see the forest return and obliterate it. In 1926, Comisario Miller Puyo reported that several herds of cattle were traveling over the road, even though it was not finished, with a maximum delay of twenty days, but during the rainy season the route was unreliable. By 1930 the most viable land route to the interior continued to be the San Cristóbal Road through Venezuela, and officials were still calling for the completion of the Sarare Road as the principal way to break down the isolation of the comisaría.[78]

Travelers in a hurry relied on the rivers. Motor launches plied the Meta and Arauca in the 1920s, but the most common boats were bongos. The bongos carried the mail, which was supposed to come from Bogotá three times a month via Villavicencio, Orocué, and Cravo Norte or from Tunja via Chita, Tame, Arauquita, and Arauca City. In 1929, Comisario Miller Puyo complained that the conductors who brought the mail from Villavicencio were careless and unreliable. During the rainy season, newspapers, official correspondence, and private letters would arrive in a completely illegible state because the carriers had not protected the mail sacks from the rain or flood water. Mail from Chita was even more unpredictable, since after the conductors delivered it to Arauquita it awaited the arrival of some traveler who was going on to Arauca City, who would agree to take it with him, and such people were not very concerned about making sure that the letters reached the offices to which they had been destined.[79]

Garza Feathers and Cattle

In 1918, the comisaría collected 1,789 pesos in monthly revenue from the liquor monopoly, degüello, and stamped paper, while incurring expenditures of 9,000 pesos.[80] Bogotá provided a subsidy to make up the difference, but beyond this minimal aid, the erection of Arauca into a national territory did nothing to revive its economy, which declined steadily as a consequence of the collapse in the market for heron feathers and the decay of cattle ranching.

The European demand for feathers, which reached boom proportions during La Belle Époque (1890–1914), was to have tragic consequences for the Llaneros and for thousands of egrets inhabiting the swamps, lagoons, and rivers of Arauca and Casanare. The birds—known locally as the *garza real* (*Casmerodius albus*) and *chumbita* (*C. egretta thula thula*)—formed an important part of the ecology of the plains, eating the insects that infested the cattle as well as ticks, toads, and worms.[81] Between June and October they congregated in their ancestral nesting places called *garceros*. The spectacle of their annual return to the Llanos was vividly described by Rómulo Gallegos in his 1929 novel *Doña Bárbara:*

> The numberless flocks were still arriving. Wearied by their long flight, they rested, swaying on the flexible branches of the forest trees, or, being thirsty, flew to the rim of the marsh, so that the woods and waters were covered with white. They seemed to recognize each other, and to exchange impressions of their journey . . . herons of one flock greeted those of another returned from some distant land. . . . At times there would be a scuffle for a branch of the roosting-tree, or the remains of a nest built the year before.
>
> The wild ducks, the scarlet flamingos, the blue herons, the cotuas, the gavanes and the wild blue chickens, none of whom had migrated flew up to greet the travelers. . . . The marsh was filled to overflowing, for the winter had set in with a will.[82]

In the nineteenth century, the Llaneros esteemed the nesting grounds not for their beauty, but as a source of income. While raising their young, the birds shed quantities of feathers, turning the marsh into a snowy forest:

> In the trees, in the nests built in them, and around the pools was the whiteness of thousands and thousands of herons; while on every side in the branches, in the shoals floating over the muddy water of the swamp, lay the white frost of feathers shed during the night.[83]

Feathers shed in nesting grounds on baldíos belonged to anyone who took the trouble to harvest them; and since European dress makers paid up to twenty U.S. dollars for a pound of wing feathers, called aigrettes, which they used to decorate women's hats, ranchers carefully protected the garceros on lands that they claimed in order to make the most of this lucrative resource. The collecting began at dawn, and Gallegos wrote that the peons would start out in canoes, but in their eagerness to reach the feathers, they would jump into the water, defying death in a dozen hidden forms, "shouting and singing, for the Plainsman never works in silence."[84] After the plumes were gathered, they selected the wing feathers and sorted them into fine and ordinary categories, according to their shape and general condition. Ten feathers weighed a gram and five thousand—the output of seventy egrets—made a pound. When only the moulted feathers were harvested, the nesting grounds of Arauca and Casanare produced altogether something under a hundred pounds of aigrettes a year.[85]

The situation changed, however, when a lavish use of feathers to ornament women's fashions in Europe after 1890 drove the price paid for a pound of aigrettes to five hundred U.S. dollars and even a thousand U.S. dollars for a pound of *grifa*, or the smaller feathers of the *chumbita*. Lured by the prospect of fast profits, armed men invaded the garceros and shot the birds, rather than waiting to collect feathers that they moulted naturally. The massacre of the adult herons doomed the fledglings to starvation. It was estimated that in each garcero ten to twenty thousand birds died each year. By 1909 Arauca was exporting annually 126 to 132 pounds of aigrettes and 5 to 12 pounds of grifa, while Orocué was averaging 150 pounds.[86]

Corruption and violence increased with the scale of hunting. In 1906, for example, the prefect of Nunchía, citing a national law passed in 1906 regulating baldíos, claimed for his district the income from the nesting grounds on public lands. He proceeded to grant licenses to individuals to hunt in specific garceros, on the condition that they surrender to him half their earnings. Since only the prefect's friends had a chance to obtain licenses, others who collected feathers did so illegally. Moreover, the prefect was claiming control over nesting grounds regarded up to that time as private property. When owners attempted to defend their rights with guns, clashes between opposing bands occurred, turning the garceros into places of bloody strife. In 1910, Max Carriazo recounted this incident and other abuses, and warned that due to the complete lack of regulation, "the Araucanos are now killing the goose that lays the golden eggs."[87]

Once Arauca was designated a comisaría especial, feathers became a national concern. In 1913, President Restrepo issued a series of decrees, declaring that garceros on baldíos belonged to the nation; that money from the tax on feathers would go to the municipios; that killing birds on public or private land was prohibited; and that violators must pay a two-peso fine for every heron shot. Laudatory in intent, these laws were unenforceable. A two-peso fine was not stiff enough to prevent the killing of a bird whose feathers were worth many times that amount, and authorities in the comisaría did not have sufficient men to police the garceros. Rustlers added garza poaching to their exploits. Masked men invaded the marshes, shot the birds, sold the feathers to merchants clandestinely, and swaggered through the streets of Arauca City, spending their ill-gotten gain before the eyes of the helpless officials.[88]

Fortunately for the herons, changes in fashion prompted by the outbreak of World War I foreshadowed the end of this contemptible trade. In August 1914, women's dresses were still following the elaborate lines of the past, but hats became more sober and materials plainer. By 1915 designers shortened skirts and replaced the formerly lavish use of feathers with an occasional decorative plume. The impact on demand for feathers was immediate, for in that year the price per pound of aigrettes and grifa fell by 80 percent. Meanwhile, vigorous lobbying by animal-protection societies produced laws in Europe and the United States forbidding the importation of bird feathers. In Arauca and Casanare herons were still hunted, but diminished demand, lower profits, restrictive legislation, and the near extermination of the garzas and chumbitas reduced exports once as high as 250 pounds a year to 50 pounds in 1926 and still less in the years that followed.[89]

Like the coterminous rubber boom, the feather boom failed to provide a solid economic base for the comisaría and contributed to the general climate of unrest and social alienation that produced the Humbertera and other border violence. The decimation of the birds brought a corresponding rise in insect pests, which descended in hordes on the already beleaguered cattle.[90] Perhaps the best that can be said is that enough herons were left when the boom was over to permit recovery of the species, and today garzas and chumbitas are again abundant in the Llanos of Arauca and Casanare.

More serious than the collapse of the feather trade was a decline in cattle herds and exports that became especially severe in the 1920s. In 1921, Comisario Pantaleón Cortés estimated that there were 160,000 cattle in Arauca and exports of 30,000 novillos a year. Five years later, Comisario Miller Puyo reported that exports had dwindled to 6,000 novillos a year, and asserted, "I can guarantee that in all the Comisaría there are grazing no more than 60,000 cattle."[91] High Venezuelan tariffs on Colombian cattle lay at the root of the problem. Finding that it was no longer profitable to export their animals, ranchers slaughtered them for hides, and the practice of killing females before they reached reproductive age was widespread. To control this destructive habit, Comisario Luis Castillo R. in 1925 placed a tax on the slaughter of female cows, but his decree exempted animals declared unfit to reproduce. Taking advantage of this loophole, the ranchers intentionally mutilated the females—cutting their teats or udders and blaming the carib fish—in order to kill them without penalty. Miller Puyo deplored this behavior and urged Congress to pass a more comprehensive law that would prevent it from occurring.[92]

Unchecked raids by rustlers took an equally heavy toll on the cattle. In an insightful essay, "La ganadería en los Llanos Orientales," published in the *Revista Nacional de Agricultura* in September 1929, geographer, Peregrino Ossa V. pointed out that many men went to the Llanos lured by the high daily wages paid to vaqueros by the hato owners. When they got to Casanare or Arauca, they found that they could earn a living more easily by gambling in the towns or by stealing other people's cattle. Such individuals would build a rude house (*en zancos*) that was little more than an unfurnished lean-to in the plains. They kept no cattle, planted no crops. Equipped with a saddle, a lasso, and a gun, they stole and killed steers, taking a portion of the meat and the hides, which they sold to pay for their needs and vices. The system, Ossa wrote, was disastrous because the disappearance of the cattle keeps it from multiplying, and when the ganaderos tried to stop the rustlers, the latter "hide behind the fact that the land is baldío, and they have as much right to stay on it as anybody else." The solution, he believed, was to promote true colonization that would permit immigrants to gain legal title to land and to create a mounted police force capable of containing the outlaws.[93]

Unlike their counterparts in Meta, the ganaderos of Arauca did nothing to improve their cattle. Comisario Pantaleón Cortés, in a letter to the editor of the *Revista Nacional de Agricultura*, dated December 31, 1921, lamented the unwillingness of the ranchers to plant improved pasture, to crossbreed their animals, or to provide them with salt. He explained that while cattle on the open plains did not require as much care as those nearer the mountains, salt made them gentler and more resistant to disease. Salt did not occur naturally in Arauca, and the ranchers had to import sea salt from Venezuela or rock salt from the mines in Cumaral and Upín—an expense they were reluctant to make. As a result, Cortés asserted, cattle in Arauca were vulnerable to many fatal diseases. Even worse off were the horses and mules that demanded daily attention because they suffered from *hormiguilla* (a hoof disease), ulcers, goiters, and *renguera*, which could kill as many as four thousand animals during an epidemic. Cortés recommended salt and selective breeding to save the cattle industry in Arauca, but while it was easy to suggest a solution, putting it into practice was far more difficult.[94] In 1929, Congress tried to combat disease by requiring ganaderos to dip their animals in chemical baths. The law was unworkable in Arauca, where cement for building tanks had to be imported from Europe or the U.S., and at a cost far higher than the value of the cattle. Rather than adopt the practice, the ganaderos preferred to slaughter their cattle or sell their ranches. Resistance to change, rustling, lack of markets, and substandard cattle combined to transform an industry that had flourished thirty years before into a pitiful vestige of its former condition. An article published in *El Araucano* on September 22, 1935, entitled "Cattle Ranching: A Retrospective Look," lamented that in the combined municipios of Arauca and Cravo Norte there were fewer cattle grazing than had existed in 1898 on just two or three hatos. The author concluded, "Today the Llanos are poor of cattle but filled with families who live in misery."[95]

In summary, the erection of Arauca into a comisaría especial in 1911 intensified Colombia's official presence in a volatile border province, but it exacerbated the conflict between civil and military authorities and failed to correct the underlying conditions that sent Arauca into an economic tailspin. The Humbertera and the Arauca Affair brought to national attention the plight of this region so geographically isolated from the Colombian interior, but prompted no far-reaching reforms. Throughout 1917, Bogotá and Tunja periodicals published letters from Araucanos expressing hope that the Humbertera would shake the government out of its lethargy. "Humberto Gómez had an ideal which was more than vengeance," wrote J. M. Salazar Alvarez in May 1917. "We need roads, capital, immigrants and missionaries. . . . We need free navigation on the Orinoco, honest rulers to administer justice and a strong garrison."[96] Araucanos such as Salazar Alvarez attempted without success to initiate reforms on their own. In October 1917, Comisario Aristides Novoa announced the meeting of a "Congress of Llaneros" to draw up a special law code adapted to the needs of the plains. His telegram describing the project brought encouraging replies from national officials. In February 1918, delegates met in Arauca City and composed a law code based on the Venezuelan "Ley de los Llanos." Novoa sent the draft to Congress, but it was not approved.[97]

In the presidential election of 1918, voters in Casanare and Arauca backed Guillermo Valencia, who ran as an unendorsed Conservative against Marco Fidel Suárez, the official candidate. In a letter addressed to Carlos J. Durán and published in *La Linterna* on January 18, 1918, Valencia promised that if he were elected he would see that the Llanos would get a special law code, increased security, road construction, and medical aid.[98] This program won him 179 votes from Arauca and 601 from Casanare, while his opponent received only 17 from Arauca and 155 from Casanare. Nationally, Valencia ran a poor second to Suárez, garnering 166,598 votes to 216,545 for his opponent.[99] Alfonso López in 1934 was the first president to give the Llanos preferential treatment, and even his program had far less impact on Arauca than it did on Meta. In the comisaría especial, rapid change awaited the discovery of extensive reservoirs of petroleum, which did not occur until 1979.[100]

Emiliano Restrepo
Echavarría.
[Luis de Greiff, *Semblanzas
y comentarios* (Bogotá:
Editorial ABC, 1942.
p. 107.)]

Restrepo was a Liberal lawyer,
journalist and entrepreneur who
became one of the largest
landowners in the Territory of
San Martín in the 1870s. His
book, *Una excursión a los Llanos
de San Martín* (Bogotá, 1870),
which promoted the
development of the territory,
encouraged the Radicals in
Bogotá to regard the plains
south of the Meta River as the
"future of Colombia."

José de Calasanz Vela
(1859–1895)
[*Trocha* (Villavicencio)
No. 174 (July 1990). p. 28.]

Vela was a Dominican
missionary who served whites
and Indians in the Territory of
San Martín for three decades, In
1889, under contract with the
Ministry of Finance, Vela
explored the Guaviare, Orinoco,
and Vichada rivers to reach San
Fernando de Atabapo on the
Venezuelan border. His report
published in 1890 helped to
convince the government of the
need to reconstitute the
National Intendency of San
Martín in 1893. This
photograph was taken in 1892
three years before Vela's death.

Rafael Uribe Uribe
(1859–1914)
[Rafael Serrano Camargo,
El General Uribe (Bogotá:
Tercer Mundo, 1976.
Cover.)]
Uribe Uribe was a Liberal
general, legislator, statesman
and diplomat. During the War of
the Thousand Days he led a
rebel army through the Llanos
of Casanare in January 1902 in a
bold but unsuccessful attempt to
vanquish the Conservative
forces entrenched in the Eastern
Cordillera. Uribe Uribe's defeat
at the battle of El Moladero on
March 17, 1902 contributed to
the ultimate collapse and
surrender of Liberal forces the
following November.

Mauricio Dieres Monplaisir
[*Bodas de plata misionales de
la Compañia de María en
Colombia, 1904–1929*
(Villavicencio, 1929. p. 117.)]
The French priest and
missionary Monplaisir was a
member of the Company of
Mary who came to Villavicencio
in the early twentieth century.
As secretary of the Vicariate
Apostolic of the Llanos of San
Martín, he wielded enormous
authority in the national
territory in the 1920s and 1930s.
His personal feud with
Intendant Colonel Aristides
Novoa provoked a riot in
Villavicencio on April 22, 1923
and the arrival of soldiers from
Bogotá to restore order.

Humberto Gómez
[*El Gráfico* (Bogotá) 7:338
(March 24, 1917).
Reprinted in the *Boletín
Cultural y Bibliográfico*
(Bogotá) 24:20 (1989),
p. 38.]
Gómez was a rancher and
alleged outlaw who seized
control of Arauca City on
December 30, 1916 and
murdered the comisario,
Estéban Escallón. His revolt
known as "La Humbertera" was
the most serious challenge to
Colombian rule on the
Venezuelan border. Although
the government restored order
within a few months, criticisms
of the behavior of the
pacification forces set off a major
scandal in the administration of
José Vicente Concha.

José Eustasio Rivera
[*José Eustasio Rivera 1888–
1988*. (Bogotá: Colcultura-
Biblioteca Nacional-Banco
de la República-Biblioteca
Luis Angel Arango,
February, 1988.)
Frontispiece.]
Rivera was a poet, author,
lawyer, diplomat, and explorer
of Colombian Amazonia. His
novel, *La Vorágine*, published in
1924, has been celebrated for its
dramatic exposé of the
enslavement of rubber collectors
in Vichada, but it was also a
brilliant portrayal of life in
Casanare that revitalized the
myth of the Llanos as a
"devourer of men."

296

9. Casanare: Province of Boyacá, 1909–30

*T*he Restrepo administration's decision to restore Casanare to Boyacá, while designating Meta, Vichada, and Arauca as national territories, was a pragmatic move designed to appease regional leaders. Settled primarily by immigrants from highland Boyacá, Casanare had been integrated into the department already on three occasions— 1821–31, 1857–68, and 1889–92. In 1911, alarmed by the unrest on the Venezuelan border, the Tunja elite agreed to the dismemberment of Arauca, but they resisted proposals to place Casanare under a special government.[1] While the Apostolic Vicariate directed civilization of the Indians and public instruction with subsidies from the national government, the political and economic fate of Casanare was shaped by its status as a province of Boyacá. As this chapter will show, between 1909 and 1930 the problems plaguing the Llanos since the War of Independence lingered on, for if Bogotá had few resources to allot to the national territories, Tunja had still less to invest in a region geographically isolated from its heartland and possessing a strikingly different way of life. The colonos who went to Támara, Nunchía, or Orocué to seek their fortunes soon learned that survival depended on their own meager resources, and with the publication of José Eustasio Rivera's startling novel *La Vorágine*, the romantic myths inspired by the exotic tropical plains and their picturesque inhabitants took on a more menacing character.

Casanare in 1918

As in the case of Meta and Arauca, the territorial organization of Casanare was frequently readjusted in the first quarter of the twentieth century. Law 65 of December 14, 1909, suppressed the Department of Santa Rosa created by Reyes, and reestablished the Department of Boyacá as it had existed in 1905. A few months later, leaders in Tunja began to rule the former Intendancy of Casanare, dividing its municipios into two provinces: Nunchía, containing Moreno, Manare, Pore, Maní, Ten, Sácama, Támara, Nunchía (the capital), Marroquín,

Tame, San Lope, and Trinidad; and Arauca, containing Arauca City (the capital), Arauquita, and Cravo Norte. On March 24, 1911, Carlos E. Restrepo detached the Province of Arauca by Executive Decree no. 306 to create a comisaría especial. Law 100 of 1912 took the municipio of Orocué away from the Intendancy of Meta and added it to Nunchía Province. In 1919, the Boyacá Assembly passed Ordenanza 8 of May 1, changing its name to Casanare and moving the capital to Támara. Ordenanza 33 of April 9, 1921, returned the capital to Nunchía. In 1920, Ordenanza 8 of April 12 segregated La Trinidad, Maní, and Orocué into the Province of Olmedilla, with Orocué as the capital, but another ordenanza suppressed it on April 19, 1922. Finally, on July 3, 1923, Boyacá ceded San Lope and Tame to the Comisaría Especial of Arauca, and the Province of Casanare assumed its definitive form, encompassing 24,000 square kilometers of territory between the Meta and Casanare rivers.[2] To minimize confusion, this chapter will consider this final delineation as the limits of Casanare for the period under study.

Measured in square kilometers, Casanare was approximately the same size as Arauca and one-third that of Meta, but its population of 17,125, as determined by the reasonably reliable census of 1918, was two and one-half times the population of Arauca and nearly 50 percent larger than that of Meta. About one-half of the people, or 8,889, lived in Marroquín, Nunchía, Sácama, Támara, and Ten—all municipios in the *cerro*, or highlands. Many of them owned hatos or fundaciónes in the open plains south and east, but they visited these properties only during the dry season and left them in the care of mayordomos for the rest of the year. Another 4,382 people lived in Manare, Maní, Moreno, and Pore in the *pie de cerro*, the base of the cordillera. In the previous century, Pore and Moreno had been capitals of Casanare, but beset by hot, unhealthy climates, they, like Manare and Maní, had fallen into a state of decay. Finally, 3,854 people lived in Trinidad and Orocué, towns in the open Llanos imbued with a true "llanero culture," open to Venezuelan influence, and in close proximity with unreduced Indians.[3] The gulf between the towns in the highlands and those in the plains was marked. As Prefect Servio Tulio Acosta observed:

The inhabitants of the cerro are completely different from the pure Llaneros—(who are) nomads, models of work, independence, honor, virility and frankness. In the cerro, the people live close to the life in the interior, to the life dominated by politics and hatreds. In the Llano one breathes better and the life of the Llanero is far from petty avarices (*mezquinidades*). In the vast region of the pampa, the only god is work and the only faith is permanent struggle. Every day the sun kindles fires of weariness, and the afternoon heat goes on burning in its crimson forge.[4]

Where one town came naturally to dominate in Meta and Arauca, three municipios competed for supremacy in Casanare—Támara and Nunchía in the cerro, and Orocué on the Meta River. Támara, situated amid a dense Indian population on the Pauta River and surrounded by land suitable for agriculture, was the largest urban center in the territory, beginning in the sixteenth century. By 1918, many of its 3,463 people still lived from their fields, cultivating coffee, corn, sugar cane, vanilla, and beautiful orchids that were prized in the interior. Támara's climate was temperate but humid, due to fog pushed in during the rainy season by violent winds from the Llanos. It had a church and a casa municipal, but most of the buildings were adobe and thatched with straw. Since 1892 it had been the seat of the bishop of the Apostolic Vicariate and headquarters for the Recoletos. It was also the home of the most powerful man in Casanare, General Benjamín Perdomo, a provincial jefe of the Conservative party who ran the city with a tight *rosca* (small band of influential persons) made up of family members. With all these advantages, it is somewhat surprising that Támara served as the capital of the province in the twentieth century only briefly, between 1918 and 1921, losing out to its neighbor and rival, Nunchía.[5]

Founded in 1748, Nunchía had become the second largest city in the province by 1918, with a population of 3,058. Stopping there in 1909, on his expedition to retrace the route of Bolívar's Liberation Campaign, Hiram Bingham regarded it as a place of importance:

It has two priests, a blacksmith, a carpenter, a tailor, a shoemaker, a saddle-maker, two telegraph operators, and a courthouse which is more than can be said of any place we have seen for two months. There are almost no ruins here, and the town appears to be fairly prosperous. The shops contain little besides cotton cloth, alcoholic liquors, provisions such as cassava, plantains, buns, canned salmon, and a few specifics, such as copaiba oil for snake bites and other troubles. We are told that during the rainy season, *bongos* are able to come up the Tocaría River to a place four miles away from which goods are easily brought to Nunchía. As the river has not been navigable for some months, there is almost no business at present.[6]

Nunchía's isolation was a liability, for the road to the interior was blocked by enormous mud holes (*enterrazales*) that, during the rainy season, took a toll on the muleteers and their beasts, who transported foodstuffs of prime necessity to the city. Nevertheless, its designation as capital enhanced its stature and prompted the construction of a new alcaldía in 1923 and the installation of electricity. In addition to schools run by the Hermanas de la Caridad, it had a small library named in honor of Salvador Camacho Roldán, who was born in Nunchía in 1827.[7]

More than one hundred kilometers southeast was Orocué, a key port on the Meta River. It had 2,474 inhabitants, according to the 1918 census, although Miguel Triana, who passed through in 1912, put the population at 556, of which "160 know how to read and write."[8] The town had wide streets and thatched-roof houses built of bamboo plastered over with clay. It had an aduana and was the center of a flourishing grazing district with numerous hatos and fundaciones. Near the river were three large commercial houses owned by José Bonnet, Ramón Real, and the Franzius brothers. Cattle, hides, rubber, feathers, coffee, and Indian crafts were the chief articles of export. Triana noted that the merchants had three steam launches, one of which, the *Isabel*, was twenty tons and gave public service. The bulk of the river traffic consisted of *lanchas de vela* (sail boats), bongos, and canoes, often captained by Sáliva Indians, who offered travelers passage to Ciudad Bolívar. The town had a pulsing vitality that was not lost on H. L. Mozans, who stayed there overnight as a guest of Ramón Real. The North American described his host as one of the richest men in the Llanos:

Besides owning the largest business house in Orocué—which is a distributing point for the great Casanare territory—he is the proprietor of several of the largest hatos in the country and counts his cattle by tens of thousands. In addition to all this, he has various other interests that yield him a handsome income. He enjoys the reputation of being a millionaire, and the reputation is apparently justified.[9]

Triana urged the national government to invest millions of pesos in Orocué because of its economic and military importance as a port on the Meta. Indeed, the town had been the capital of the Intendancy of Casanare between 1897 and 1905, but its hot climate and distance from Tunja put it out of favor with the people of the interior. It was the capital of Olmedilla from April 1920 until April 1922, when the assembly abolished the province for lack of funds and qualified people to hold government posts. After 1922 Orucué fell on hard times. Venezuela's refusal to allow free navigation on the Orinoco strangled commerce, as did the collapse of the feather and rubber booms. On

February 25 and April 13, 1926, two fires destroyed more than fifty houses and reduced much of the city to ashes. The national government had already closed the aduana and removed the piquet of police. Two years later, Prefect Horacio Perdomo commented, "This town which serves as a sentry on the east of the country has been forgotten by our Congress."[10]

Provincial Rule

The Constitution of 1886, which outlined the political organization of the departments, determined the administrative structure of Casanare as a province of Boyacá. Under this system, the president of the republic appointed the governor of Boyacá for a three-year term. The governor named three secretaries to assist him with public administration, government, and treasury–public instruction. A popularly elected assembly, composed of twenty-seven deputies serving two-year terms, made up the legislative branch. The deputies debated fiscal and economic policies and passed *ordenanzas* that had the character of departmental laws. They also determined internal territorial divisions.[11] Between 1910 and 1930 there were twelve provinces ruled by prefects appointed by the governor. Each province was subdivided into municipios governed by the alcaldes, who were appointed by the prefect, and popularly elected municipal councils. The municipios were responsible for administering corregimientos, or settlements within their districts that were not large enough to be full-fledged towns. The bishop of Tunja had ecclesiastical jurisdiction over all of Boyacá, except the Apostolic Vicariate of Casanare.

The department was divided into other configurations for fiscal purposes, military control, and judicial matters. To elect four deputies to the assembly, the provinces of Casanare and Sugamuxi were joined in a single "*círculo electoral.*" Since Sugamuxi, with its capital at Sogamoso, had four times the population of Casanare, its candidates always won, leaving the Llanos without any representation. In 1929, Prefect Horacio Perdomo protested that this arrangement was manifestly unfair. He added, "I have heard it said that Casanare does not vote. That is not true. In this province elections are clean and without fraud because the casanareño, although he is not in direct contact with civilization, lives spiritually within political morality and is a good patriot."[12]

In *Los territorios nacionales*, published in 1944, Humberto Plazas

Olarte charged that the prefecture was a "bureaucratic device suffocated by indolence and mountains of paperwork," and under the rule of Boyacá, Casanare saw all its former greatness disappear.[13] While these allegations are valid to some extent, it is important to note that Casanare was the poorest province in one of the poorest departments of the republic, and its fundamental problems were well established before it became part of Boyacá. Nor is it true, as Plazas Olarte states, that no governor ever visited Casanare. During the furor surrounding the Humbertera, there was much discussion in the assembly and the press over how to rescue Casanare from the conditions that had generated the revolt, and the former commander-in-chief of the expedition to capture Humberto, General Jesús García, made an official inspection of the province after his appointment as governor of Boyacá on September 16, 1918.

In his annual message of March 1, 1920, García identified as critical areas the difficulty of travel within Casanare, the lack of municipal authority, the small salaries paid to officials, the impossibility of maintaining public safety, the poverty of the inhabitants, and their inclination to migrate to the interior to protect their economic interests and escape the danger of personal insecurity. Pointing out that most of what was written about Casanare was "literary conceit," García urged the assembly to send a delegation to the province to observe life there firsthand. His other recommendations included fiscal reform, the creation of a separate prefecture in Orocué, improving the Chipaviejo road between Socotá and Támara, appointing an official doctor, expanding the powers of the corregidores, and helping the municipios in the cerro repair their roads.[14] Although the assembly did reform the tax system, set up the Province of Olmedilla, and vote a two-hundred-peso subsidy for the Chipaviejo Road, the ordenanzas it passed were later discarded. As with Law 52 of November 1926, approved by Congress to promote colonization in the Llanos, departmental measures were generally inoperative and made little headway in improving conditions in the region.

The prefect, as the chief administrator of Casanare, had powers commensurate with those exercised by the intendant of Meta and the comisario of Arauca. He supervised government, maintained public security, worked with the missionaries, encouraged municipal growth, and made recommendations to the governor for reform. Each year, he was required to submit a report on the state of the province, which was published with the annual message of the governor. A search of the departmental archives in Tunja turned up reports for eleven of the twenty-one years between 1911 and 1932, written by eight different prefects. Ignacio Suárez served for three years (1914, 1915, 1917) as did Abelardo Fernández (1919, 1920, 1921), and Horacio Perdomo served for two (1928 and 1930). Five other men held office for a year. The prefects were Conservatives, but unlike the officials in the national territories, they were natives of Casanare with strong ties to the region. Their reports varied from perfunctory statements to insightful analyses of regional realities, yet one suspects that Plazas Olarte's criticism of the prefecture as "a scarcely functioning bureaucracy based on favoritism" is not without substance. In 1938, when Rafael LaRotta went to Nunchía to take up his duties as the new prefect, he discovered that his predecessor had left the office in a chaotic condition:

The place is a dirty, dilapidated little room. The archive is a *maremagnum* of papers, shapeless mounds of the remains of *informes* devoured by termites; the furniture consists of three tables in a bad state, three broken stools and two bookcases. Nothing has been done since last year: (there are) scattered memorials that have not been processed; incomplete *expedientes* mixing up penal with civil matters; the official periodicals in sealed packages unopened: there is no stamp. The budget for office supplies was cashed but nothing was purchased, etc. The person in charge of the prefectura slept in the office where he held parties many nights so that the citizens had to see the following day the spectacle of the intimate belongings of the official without a screen to hide them discreetly from view.[15]

Except in Támara, Nunchía, and Orocué, municipal government was equally haphazard. Since elections for municipal councils were rarely held, the badly paid alcaldes were the only officials in some towns. As Prefect Acosta wrote in 1932, they had to attend to Don Fulano or Don Sutano without the aid of secretaries or judges, and "not always well-intentioned persons took advantage of their incapacity and ignorance."[16] Competent individuals were reluctant to accept appointments to jobs that were so little rewarding. When Prefect Ernesto Flórez asked Salomon Castro to be the alcalde of Maní, Castro refused for five reasons: (1) Maní could not legally sustain itself, (2) its inhabitants did not lend themselves to be governed, (3) its inhabitants systematically opposed authority, (4) the municipal government could not be formed without qualified people, and (5) Maní did not have any income, and the liquor tax could not be collected because there was no treasurer. Flórez added that there was no school in Maní, and no one there knew how to read and write. Observing that Manare and Sácama were in a similar state, he recommended that all three municipios be reduced to corregimientos.[17]

A Stagnating Economy

Absolute poverty lay at the root of the dysfunctional bureaucracy. Table 9 shows the revenues and expenses of the provinces of Boyacá, as reported in 1916. Casanare, the most destitute, generated 6,159.57 pesos in taxes that year, or less than one-sixth of the revenue of the two richest provinces, Centro and Occidente. Only Valderrama, with an income of 9,599.80 pesos, came close to it in penury; all the other provinces produced more than 16,000 pesos annually. The breakdown of taxes collected in Casanare's municipios in 1916, shown in Table 10, supports the prefects' repeated assertions that the towns could not pay for their most urgent needs. Manare, Maní, Sácama, and Ten collected less than 265 pesos during the entire year, and only Nunchía and Orocué produced more than 1,000. Inflated salaries and a high

Table 9
Revenues and Expenses of the Provinces
of Boyacá, 1916[1]
(Colombian Pesos)

Province	Revenues	Expenditures
Centro	35,265.37	35,265.37
Gutiérrez	28,754.12	28,754.12
Márquez	20,529.07	20,529.07
Neira	20,020.61	20,020.61
Norte	19,425,58	19,425.58
Nunchía	6,159.57	6,159.57
Occidente	34,794.50	34,794.50
Oriente	16,495.35	16,495.35
Ricaurte	16,954.73	16,954.73
Sugamuxi	32,665.21	32,665.21
Tundama	31,724.91	31,621.67
Valderrama	9,559.80	9,559.80
Total	272,388.82	272,285.58

[1]Informe del Gobernador de Boyacá, 1917, xix.

Table 10
Revenues and Expenses of the Municipios of Casanare, 1916[1]
(Colombian pesos)

| | Revenues | | | | Total |
	Common	Pub. Instru.	Roads	Total	Expenses
Manare	195	—	30	225	225
Maní	60	164	—	224	224
Marroquín	30	436.60	90	556.60	556.60
Moreno	651.03	102	100	853.03	853.03
Nunchía	773.20	—	450	1,223.20	1,223.20
Orocué	1,314.95	184.32	375.50	1,874.77	1,874.77
Pore	—	—	—	—	—
Sácama	194.52	42	24.75	261.27	261.77
Támara	—	—	—	—	—
Ten	92	24	25	140	140
Trinidad	280.20	321.50	200	801.70	801.70
Total	4,590.90	1,274.42	1,294.25	6,159.57	6,159.57

Cost of Living in Tunja and Orocué as Seen in Prices of Food, 1935[2]
(price by carga)

	Sugar	Panela	Salt	Corn	Beans
Tunja	17.24	13.25	10.00	14.10	21.06
Orocué	32.50	30.00	18.00	20.00	31.87

Average Day Wage for Manual Workers
in Different Municipios of Boyacá, 1935[3]

	Day Wage with Food	Day Wage without Food
Nunchía	.25	.80
Orocué	.50	1.00
Pore	.30	.60
Tunja	.15	.50
Sogamoso	.20	.40

[1] *Informe del Gobernador de Boyacá*, 1917, XVI–XVII.
[2] Medina, *Geografía económica de Colombia* 475.
[3] Ibid., 477.

cost of living presented Orocué with additional problems. As Table 10 reveals, prices for basic foodstuffs in Orocué were double that of the interior, while manual laborers received wages two or three times as high. Even though more revenue was collected, it was not sufficient to cover the expenses incurred by the city.[18]

The principal sources of income were the liquor and degüello taxes that were used to pay the salaries of provincial employees. Prefect Suárez noted in 1915 that the taxes on tobacco and land transfers produced little revenue—the first because tobacco introduced into the province had already been taxed, and the second because all land in Casanare was baldío and no one bothered to register his/her land title.[19] Prefect Jiménez Herredia pointed out that of eighteen taxes that the assembly authorized municipios to collect in 1910, eleven were inapplicable in Casanare due to the lack of agriculture, while several of the remaining seven could not be collected. For example, a tax imposed on the sale of cattle failed because there were not enough police to ensure that it was paid in all the towns and because many ganaderos did not sell their cattle in the municipios of the Llanos, but in the markets of the interior and paid the taxes there.[20] In 1911, at the height of the boom in heron feathers, the assembly declared that those wishing to exploit a garcero would have to apply to the secretary of finance for a license. Twenty-five percent of the money collected was to support public instruction in the municipios, where the garceros were located, and the rest was to be used for the construction of the Cravo and Pajarito roads. By 1914 the assembly had ceded the entire income from this tax to the municipios, but by this time the feather market had collapsed, and the receipts were "illusory."[21]

After 1915 ranching remained the sole industry. In 1936, Juan Medina estimated that there were 152,184 cattle on 94 hatos and fundaciónes between the Casanare and Pauto rivers, 142,277 cattle on 51 hatos and fundaciones between the Pauto and Cusiana rivers, and 240,681 cattle on 100 hatos and fundaciones between the Cusiana and Upía rivers, for a total of 535,142 cattle on 245 hatos and fundaciones.[22] While these figures seem substantial, the herds were not reproducing themselves, due to the practice of killing females.

As in Arauca, disease struck down many, and the unwillingness of ganaderos to experiment with cross-breeding or improved pasture meant that their animals could not compete with those produced in other sections of the republic. Most would have provided salt for their herds, but without roads to the Salinas of Chita and Upín, it was expensive and difficult to obtain. Prefect Horacio Perdomo, pondering these problems in 1929, urged lawmakers to learn from the example of Venezuela. Twenty years later, when the cattle industry there had slumped, Caracas gave it a powerful impulse so that from twenty thousand to thirty thousand head of Venezuelan cattle now passed through the Colombian Llanos each year to Villavicencio or Labranzagrande to be sold in the markets of Cundinamarca and Boyacá. The legislative bodies and the executives should think seriously about the eastern regions, Perdomo wrote. "They have to Colombianize the commerce of these Llanuras, and the only way is to help the Casanareño expand his industry with roads, salt and money." [23]

Roads

By 1921 all the municipios of Casanare except Sácama, Ten, and Manare had telegraph offices, but lacking roads, they were more isolated than Arauca City, where ganaderos could go through Venezuela to get their cattle to Cúcuta. The principal route into the province was the Cravo Road, which left Sogamoso and passed through Labranzagrande and El Morro on its way to the Meta River. Congress consistently supported construction of this so-called national road, voting a subsidy of 3,750 pesos in 1912, which was increased in 1926 to 25,000 pesos. By 1931 the road had reached to the Río Tocaría and was the preferred route for twenty-five thousand cattle that left Casanare each year for Santander, Cundinamarca, and Tolima. [24] Due to its prime location on the road, the corregimiento of El Morro thrived while Marroquín, thirty miles away, remained cut off from commerce. In 1923, Prefect Ernesto Flórez recommended moving the municipality to El Morro, where there was already a telegraph office, a greater number of houses, and a good climate. The transfer was carried out in 1936, and six years later El Morro was renamed Yopal. [25]

Departmental support for other roads, even those leading directly to the interior, was not forthcoming. In 1914, Prefect Suárez declared that roads were the most neglected aspect of the province and that "except for the Cravo Road which is regularly composed, it can be said that no one can enter Casanare without exposing himself to great dangers." [26] Governor García, after his official visit in 1919, pledged money for the Chipaviejo Road connecting Socotá with Támara, and despite lack of steady funding, this route became the second most important one. In 1935, farmers in Támara sent 2,500 cargas of coffee to Bogotá along it, but the path was so treacherous that even the short distance between Támara and Socha required two days of travel by mule.[27] The municipios lacked money to repair roads in the interior of the Llanos. In 1921, Prefect Abelardo Fernández chastised the Assembly for passing an ordenanza excluding the municipios of Casanare from road taxes. He wrote, "Perhaps the deputies were thinking that all the towns in Casanare were in the Llanos and therefore did not need roads forgetting that some of them are in the Cordillera and desperately need to maintain their roads. Even the towns in the Llanos have to maintain their roads in the winter."[28]

Given the difficulties of overland travel, casanareños were not immune from the railroad fever that swept Colombia in the postwar era. In 1920, the municipal council of Nunchía wrote to Congress urging completion of the Ferrocarriles del Norte and Casanare, and in 1929 congressmen debated a proposal to authorize the construction of a railroad to connect Casanare with Tunja via the provinces of Márquez, Neira, and Oriente. Senator Pompilio Gutiérrez, speaking in support of the bill, pointed out that Casanare, so neglected by previous governments, had enormous wealth and thousands of kilometers of navigable rivers. The railroad would develop economic ties between the interior and Casanare, provide a bridge between the Magdalena and Meta rivers, and make available to Colombia in the future "a source of incalculable prosperity." President Abadía Mendez signed it into law on October 10, 1929, but steps were never taken to implement it.[29]

Public Safety

Between 1909 and 1930 the most serious challenge to Colombian sovereignty in Casanare was Humberto Gómez's revolt on December 30, 1916, described in chapter 8. The governor of Boyacá, Domingo A. Cambariza, reacted quickly to the crisis. On January 10, he appointed General Benjamín Perdomo as prefect of Nunchía, with orders to mobilize defense throughout the region. Then he asked President Concha to declare a state of siege and to provide money to pay the volunteer fighters "because the department does not have any treasury funds of importance and has absolutely no way to supply money to help the prefect and the alcaldes organize troops."[30] Since the fighting took place in Tame and Arauca, there was no bloodshed in Casanare, but the crisis spawned a vitriolic debate in the Tunja press about Perdomo's conduct and contributed to the general climate of insecurity that reigned throughout the Llanos.

Within a week of his appointment as prefect, General Perdomo gathered together one hundred men and horses. He ordered fellow Conservative, General Ignacio Suárez A., and General Manuel José Nieto, a Liberal from Moreno, to raise troops and to meet him in Tame. He also alerted the alcaldes to take measures to defend their municipios and to prevent "unknown individuals free transit who instill suspicion."[31] At the same time, General Jesús García, named by Concha as commander-in-chief of the expeditionary forces, left Bogotá for Sogamoso, where, on January 15, he formed the Albán Battalion from volunteers from the surrounding towns. With these men he marched on to Chita, and on January 24 he organized there a second battalion of men from Sugamuxi, Valderrama, and Tundama. Three days later, the supply Soublette Battalion from the regular army arrived, and García set off with the three divisions, taking the Chita road. When he appeared in Tame on February 2, he found Generals Suárez and Nieto waiting, and General Perdomo arrived on February 5. García incorporated the Casanare troops into his force and continued on to Arauca City, where he discovered that Gómez had already escaped across the border. Since the cleanup operation was confined to the comisaría especial, President Concha lifted the state of siege in Casanare and dispersed the volunteer armies on March 17.[32]

In Tunja, Enrique Santos, head of the Liberal Directory of Boyacá and editor of the militant *La Linterna*, quickly disassociated his party from Humberto's claims of carrying out a Liberal revolution. In a letter published in *El Espectador* on January 13, he called Gómez a common criminal. "There is not a trace of political motive for this deplorable movement," he wrote. "Even the most extreme Conservatives do not blame the Liberals for those events. All the great hacendados of the Llano, Liberals without exception, have offered their persons and their property to pursue the bandits."[33]

Santos supported García's expeditionary army, but when Liberals from Támara complained that General Perdomo was extorting loans, cattle, and horses for his volunteer force, he gave full attention to their allegations in the February 6 issue of his newspaper. The prefect of Nunchía replied with a blistering telegram, which appeared in *La Unión Conservador*, denouncing "the lying, slanderous information published yesterday by *La Linterna* that I took forced loans in Támara."[34] The Conservative periodical included a second telegram signed by fifteen Liberals from Támara who refuted all the accusations against Perdomo, but Santos kept up his editorial attack.

Perdomo's rebuttal, dated Nunchía, March 5, and published by *La Unión Conservador* on April 13, reveals the intensity of party antagonisms in Casanare. Demanding that Santos either stop defaming him or provide specific details and names of the Liberals allegedly mistreated, the general accused the editor of inventing persecutions in order to persuade Governor Combariza to appoint a new prefect who would not be from Casanare. He swore that he had not offended any Liberal in word or deed, and he accused Santos of launching a vendetta against him because he was a Conservative and because Támara was a town "with a conservative majority that goes in the vanguard of the towns of Casanare morally and materially due to the efforts of the Conservatives for if it were Liberal, it would be in worse decadence, especially in moral matters." Perdomo dared Santos to compare his actions with those of Liberal generals, and he would see that he had fulfilled his duties with honor. He concluded:

It is incredible that the editor of *La Linterna* can continue imagining that I persecute Liberals and that I permit my agents to commit abuses in this land of Casanare where I was born. . . . If the Liberals of Casanare were men of judgment and political honor, they would recognize my good intentions for Casanare and support me in order to work together for the benefit of the region without expecting to be directed by foreign elements that bring them only vices and bad customs.[35]

Despite his protestations, it is not unlikely that Perdomo did extort money and horses to organize his army, since the lack of police made this strategy a pragmatic method of controlling outlaws. The prefects continually pleaded for expanded police protection. In 1914, when Ignacio Suárez reported that there had been three murders in Trinidad and an armed assault against the alcalde, he stated that disorders were constant in that town due to the activities of Venezuelan exiles, and he urged that police be stationed there and in Tame to keep the peace. His successor, Alejandro Motto, observed that in the entire comisaría there were just two departmental policemen and they were assigned to Orocué. To apprehend bandits in the other municipios, the alcaldes appointed "comisarios" who, since they were unpaid, did only what they wanted to do.[36] After the Humbertera, the

Assembly ordered a detachment of the Guardia de Boyacá to Casanare, but these men proved ill equipped to control violence in the Llanos. By 1919 there was a sergeant, corporal, and eight guards stationed in Támara, and a corporal and five more guards in Tame. Prefect Abelardo Fernández praised their conduct, but lamented that their rations were too small to cover their basic necessities. Moreover, they had no horses. In order to track down bandits, they had to ask the ranchers to loan them mounts, and if the ranchers refused to cooperate, as was often the case, the bandits remained at large. For example, when Faustino Jara and his band began raiding hatos around Trinidad in 1921, the prefect of Olmedilla, Manuel Forrero Mariño, telegraphed the landowners requesting horses for the police. When none responded, they set off on foot. The police eventually reached Trinidad, but after crossing the flooded plains in heavy winter, they were in no condition to fight Jara. Forrero Mariño urged the Assembly to help the guardía by creating a body of mounted *baquianos* (men who knew the Llanos well), who could accompany them on weekly trips through the Llanos and reassure the ganaderos by their presence. The assembly did pass Ordenanza 27 of 1921, authorizing a cavalry. For lack of money, the order was never carried out.[37]

In 1927, Governor Nicolás García Samudio, citing the large number of outlaws in Casanare, asked the national government for two thousand pesos to buy horses and saddles for the Guardía de Boyacá stationed there. When the subsidy was not forthcoming, the assembly placed a fifty-centavo tax on each slaughtered steer to raise money, but the court suspended the ordenanza. In 1928 a new gang appeared in Trinidad led by José Palacios, a Venezuelan. The guardía could not stop him from raiding the fundaciones, and after several months of terror, the ganaderos joined in his pursuit. Finally, the police killed Palacios when he injudiciously came into the town, and aided by "expert Llaneros" they managed to capture the rest of his men.[38] Two years later public security was still a critical issue. Prefect Domingo E. Medina wrote that eight departmental guards were not sufficient to chase down all the outlaws in the province, including one Cruz María Figueredo, who had already committed two murders. "The lack of a body of well-mounted police composed of men skilled in the Llanos for this kind of activity has impeded the capture of the criminal. It is necessary to augment the guard with Llaneros and to give them good horses."[39]

Indians and Missionaries

Indians were another threat to public safety. In 1914, Ignacio Suárez estimated that there were three thousand natives in the province, including "nomadic and completely savage" Guahibos and Chiricoas, "nearly civilized" Sálivas and Piapocos, and the remnants of formerly large tribes of Achaguas and Tunebos, who lived near Barronegro, Mundonuevo, and Covario. As in Arauca, the Guahibos hated the whites for taking their land and killing their chiefs. They systematically raided ranches and homes around Orocué, and the ganaderos retaliated with equal ferocity. Noting that the attacks were spreading to hatos along the Casanare River, Suárez pledged, "This office will try through an agreement with the missionaries to handle this delicate situation."[40]

The Recoletos had been in Casanare since 1892, when it was designated an Apostolic Vicariate. At the death of Padre Nicolás Casas in 1905, Santos Ballesteros, titular bishop of Carfarnaún, became the third apostolic vicar, holding that office until 1933. In 1916, the erection of the Apostolic Prefecture of Arauca left the Vicariate with some 45,000 square kilometers of territory. The bishop lived in Támara, and for most of this period there were ten missionaries working in Támara, Nunchía, Moreno, Orocué, and Chámeza. The Hermanas de la Caridad, who left Casanare during the War of the Thousand Days, returned in 1918 to teach school and assist the sick.[41]

Hoping to maximize his limited resources, Ballesteros resolved to concentrate on converting the Sálivas near Orocué. These Indians had helped to found the town in the 1860s and still resided there in large numbers, selling food and handicrafts to the whites and working as boatmen on the Meta River. Ballesteros rejected the traditional method of sending priests out to live with the natives, considering it too difficult, too expensive, and not very productive. Instead, he decided to found a school in Orocué, where the Sálivas could bring their children to live and study with the Hermanas de la Caridad. At first, town officials opposed the plan, but by 1917 the bishop won them over. Using two thousand pesos from the Junta de Misiones, he began to build the school, completing it in 1919. The Hermanas de la Caridad returned to Orocué in July 1919 and started to teach the Indian children. By the middle of 1919 the school enrolled 102 pupils.[42]

Once the school was functioning, Ballesteros began negotiations to buy a cattle hato to support the missions and aid in the reduction of Indians along the Ariporo, Casanare, and Meta rivers. In February 1920, he paid seven thousand pesos to Dr. José María Oropesa for El Algarrobo, a hato with good land in an area frequented by Guahibos. The Recoletos purchased 150 tame cattle and took possession of the monthsestate in January 1921. The next years were fraught with difficulties, forcing temporary suspension of classes in the Indian school, but the worst setback was a devastating fire that swept through Orocué on February 25, 1926, destroying more than fifty buildings, including the school and the nuns' residence. Once again, the Hermanas de la Caridad left the town and did not come back until March 2, 1928.[43]

The Recoleto efforts to convert Indians during the rule of Bishop Ballesteros seem halfhearted when compared to their labors during the 1890s, but this perception may be influenced by a lack of documentation to equal the books published by Daniel Delgado, Marcelino Ganuza, Pedro Fabo, and Santiago Matute, which described the earlier achievements. In 1931, Ballesteros asserted that all of the Sálivas and Tunebos had been Christianized, but that the Guahibos continued their barbaric ways.[44] Prefect Servio Tulio Acosta agreed, stating that there were some five thousand Sálivas who spoke Spanish and knew some of the truths of the Catholic religion. The Guahibos, on the other hand, were still "ferocious and perfectly savage," taking pleasure in attacking the whites. The ganaderos of Orocué lived in constant fear that their homes would be burned, their cattle seized, and their employees murdered. Moreover, the number of Indians was actually increasing, since the Venezuelans had begun to use airplanes to frighten Guahibos in their territory into immigrating to Casanare. Acosta called for the creation of a special guard to help the ganaderos defend their land against the savages.[45]

Education and Health

Besides proselytizing Indians, the Recoletos attended to the spiritual needs of the whites and were in charge of public education. The national government provided six hundred pesos a month for teachers' salaries, books, and supplies, and Bishop Ballesteros was the official School Inspector. In 1913, there were boys' schools in Moreno, Orocué, Nunchía, Támara, Tame, and Ten; girls' schools in Moreno, Orocué, Nunchía, Támara, Tame, and Ten; alternated

schools in Chámeza, Chire, La Trinidad, Manare, Marroquín, Pajarito, Pore, Nunchía, San Lope, Támara, and Tauramena; and rural
schools in Ten and Támara—for a total of twenty-four. This number
fluctuated during the next two decades. In 1919, there were fifteen
primary schools enrolling 713 students, and in 1928, thirty-two schools
enrolling 878 students. The Colegio San Agustín, a secondary school
for boys founded in Támara in 1912 by Padres Agustín Cuervas and
Nicasio Balisa, had sixteen boarders and fourteen day students, while
the Hermanas de la Caridad prepared young women to be elementary
schoolteachers in colegios in Támara and Nunchía.[46]

Bishop Ballesteros was proud of the schools. He liked to empha-
size that they were taught by women who had graduated from the
colegios in Támara and Nunchía "because we cannot hope that young
ladies who graduate from the Normal School of Chapinero will come
to teach in Casanare."[47] Nevertheless, the quality of education was
spotty. As in Meta and Casanare, the children were ill nourished,
chronically sick, and frequently absent from class. The teachers, when
they were not religious, were barely literate. Their salaries were insufficient to support themselves, let alone their families. A reporter for
La Linterna, who was very critical of the colegio in Támara which he
visited in March 1916, remarked that he had not seen a decent school
anywhere in Casanare.[48] In 1935, Prefect Leonidas Cuellar T. wrote
that the instruction given in the primary schools by the Hermanas de
la Caridad was rudimentary. Even when pressured by their alcaldes,
the people of Sácama, Ten, and Moreno refused to send their children, citing the incompetence of the teachers. Cuellar believed that
the department should take complete charge of the schools, using the
educational subsidy from the national government to develop better
public instruction.[49]

In October 1931, the *Revista de Misiones* published a revealing
interview with Santos Ballesteros, who, at the age of sixty-one, had
spent thirty-eight years in Casanare. The bishop discussed the work
of his order, and at the prodding of the reporter, he spoke at length
about the region and its inhabitants. In response to a question as to
whether Casanare was as fierce as some people said, he conceded that
the Llanos were not as "delightful as Bogotá." There were no roads in
the summer, and in the winter the plains became a lake. "There are
fevers, malaria, snakes and similar things, but one can live there with
precautions and saying goodbye to vices." Ballesteros attributed the
ongoing economic crisis to a lack of industry, the decline of the market

for garza feathers, and the low price for cattle. Given this misery, it was appropriate, he argued, that the patron saint of the region was Nuestra Señora de los Dolores (Our Lady of Sorrows), titular of the Manare Mission and queen of Casanare:

> In Casanare one suffers much, and it is necessary to have a patron saint who knows how to share in the sufferings of the Llaneros, and no one could be better for that than Madre Dolorosa, the Virgen de los Dolores. Her festival is celebrated on January 6. The Casanareños venerate her deeply, and all attend this festival who are not materially impeded.[50]

In no area did the people of Casanare suffer more than in matters of health, for in a region where 70 percent of the inhabitants had some form of hookworm, malnutrition, malaria, dysentery, tuberculosis, or syphilis, there was not a single hospital or qualified doctor to attend them before the 1930s. Representatives of the Rockefeller Sanitation Commission did not come to the province, and the missionaries limited their involvement to publishing an occasional informative article on tropical anemia in *El Propagador* and to the nursing performed by the Hermanas. When casanareños fell ill, they doused themselves with folk remedies, consulted ignorant quacks, or purchased patent medicines hawked by "roving exploiters." If they could no longer work, their only resource was to beg for charity in the streets or throw themselves on the mercy of the local alcalde, who would try to find some way to sustain them "until fate might decide their situation."[51]

Without any medical help, the prefects resigned themselves to reporting epidemics each year and pleading with the department to send a doctor. In 1916, dysentery killed thirty people in Trinidad, with other cases appearing in Nunchía, Orocué, Moreno, and Chire. The next year, a "pernicious fever," probably malaria activated by heavy rains, infected an alarming number of people in Orocué and the surrounding hatos. In 1918, a strange disease causing high fevers, violent gastric pain, and black vomit broke out in Ten. At first believed to be yellow fever, it was later identified as typhoid. In 1923, the dominant scourges were malaria, tropical anemia, and "epidemics of a rebel character which frequently decimate the towns because this province does not have any doctors."[52] Fatal epidemics of smallpox, influenza, and whooping cough occurred in 1928. In 1932, Prefect Luis Reyes wrote that although mortality was extraordinarily high, especially in the winter, the government had still not sent a doctor to visit the towns.[53]

At least two other threats to public health went unresolved. In 1916, a reporter for *La Linterna* wrote that warehouses containing hides and tanks of poison were contaminating Orocué. He asked the prefect to inspect the buildings since the "merchants of this town always have their own way," and it is clear to anyone "with scientific knowledge that the situation is dangerous." [54] More pervasive throughout the Llanos was the dangerous practice of fishing in the rivers with dynamite. In 1917, the prefect issued a decree forbidding the use of dynamite, but it was patently ignored. In 1928 and again in 1929, Horacio Perdomo asked the Assembly to prohibit the practice with severe penalties, since many people were being killed or grievously injured through the incautious use of explosives. [55]

Colonization

Defying the dismal economy, lack of roads, violence, and high mortality, colonos came to Casanare between 1909 and 1930, leaving their towns in the Boyacá highlands to seek a better life in the Llanos. Table 11 lists the census figures for the municipios of the province for 1905, 1912, 1918, and 1928. Although such figures are notoriously unreliable, they do suggest demographic trends. Since most authorities rarely estimated the population of Casanare at under 12,000, it is likely that the census of 1905 was undercounted, but a comparison between the 1912 and 1918 figures suggests that the population grew by 48.7 percent, from 12,895 to 25,481, or at a slightly higher rate than the department as a whole, which increased from 583,078 to 950,264, or 45.1 percent. During this period, the population of the entire republic increased from 5,472,604 to 7,851,000, or 43.5 percent. Growth within Casanare was not universal; the population of Sácama declined, and Pore, Moreno, and Manare grew but little. On the other hand, Támara more than doubled, and Nunchía, Orocué, and Marroquín (Yopal) registered large increases.

The Ministerio de Industrias has not published a list of land titles awarded in Casanare in the first half of the twentieth century, and it is clear that most colonists staked out their parcels without bothering to try for legal ownership. Nevertheless, there were conflicts between ganaderos who claimed to own land and the colonos who settled on it. Three cases uncovered by Professor Catherine LeGrand in the Min-

Table 11
Population of Casanare, Boyacá, and Colombia, as Reported in the Censuses of 1905, 1912, 1918, and 1928 [1]

Municipio	1905	1912	1918	1928
Manare	—	1,092	1,322	1,800
Maní	—	735	881	1,182
Marroquín (Yopal)	946	1,092	1,382	2,363
Moreno	1,365	1,238	1,197	1,505
Nunchía	531	2,888	3,058	4,301
Orocué	1,488	—	2,474	3,031
Pore	906	891	982	933
Sácama	524	356	214	324
Támara	1,880	2,775	3,463	6,112
Ten	452	734	772	1,689
Trinidad	111	1,119	1,380	2,241
Total	8,203	12,895	17,125	25,481

Department of Boyacá				
Total	515,209	583,078	645,562	950,264

Republic of Colombia				
Total	4,303,687	5,472,604	5,855,077	7,851,000

[1] Medina R., *Geografía económica de Colombia*, 147–78.

isterio de Industrias archive, "Correspondencia de Baldios," offer tantalizing glimpses into the complexities of the disputes.

In the first case, the alcalde of Trinidad wrote to the attorney general on May 4, 1917, on behalf of twenty-three colonos who were being threatened with dispossession. The colonos had settled thirty years before at "Santa Rita," a parcel adjudicated in 1846 but abandoned by the owner in 1884. Until recently, they had raised their cattle without problem. Then Manuel Abella had appeared. Declaring that he was the rightful owner of "Santa Rita," he sought their expulsion.[56]

The second case arose in Marroquín and dragged on for several years. It began in 1922, when Heliodoro Reina claimed most of the land in the corregimiento of El Morro and demanded that colonos pay him rent for cutting wood in the forests and grazing their cattle on "his" plains. Contending that he had purchased the land from Indians whose titles dated back to the colonial era, he threatened to throw the colonos out if they refused to pay what he asked. The colonos wrote to the attorney general to protest that Reina's titles were illegal and to ask him to declare the land officially baldío. The municipal council of Marroquín supported their petition and added that because Reina had the backing of department officials, it could not protect them. Two years later the situation was unresolved. The president of the council wrote again to the attorney general, asking him to issue a ruling since the colonos were anxious to be redeemed from their status of "slaves disguised by the name of *arrendatarios* (renters)."[57]

The third case concerned "El Amparo," a large section of land in the Pauto River Valley, in the municipio of Nunchía. Many colonos had moved there believing it to be baldío and because it was along the route of the projected Chipaviejo Road. They built their houses and planted crops, but in 1926 a new "owner" claimed to have gained title over all the land and threatened to dispossess them. The prefect, in reporting the case to the Ministerio de Industrias, urged justice for the colonos, explaining:

With relatively small exceptions, the territory of Casanare is baldío, and there are an infinity of colonos settled here with crops and cattle. A few ambitious ones have deeds of possession drawn up which they use to disturb others within their boundaries until they oblige them to sell out.[58]

The documents found by LeGrand do not reveal how or if any of these cases were settled, but they do demonstrate that colonos coming to Casanare, without legal protection of any kind, were harassed by the ganaderos. A common abuse condemned by the prefects in 1926 and 1929 was prompted by a resolution passed by the Ministerio de Industrias in 1924, declaring that ranchers might travel freely with their cattle throughout Casanare. The ganaderos interpreted this law as the right to drive their cattle to market through pastures laboriously developed by colonos. They permitted their hungry herds to devour the grass and water intended for the colonos' animals, and in one or two days destroyed the work of ten or twenty years. To make matters worse, they often made off with some of the colono's cattle when they started on their way again. Prefect Perdomo urged the Ministerio de Industrias to impose severe sanctions on those who engaged in such practices. "The roads for common use are known," he asserted, "and the *comerciantes* must be made to stay on them."[59]

José Eustasio Rivera

Casanaré's most celebrated lawsuit began in Orocué in 1918, and it was not a struggle between colonos and ganaderos, but a bitter fight between would-be heirs to a large hato called Mata de Palma. In April of that year, José Nieto, an energetic boyacense who had lived in Orocué since 1910, visited the offices of a young Bogotá lawyer and poet, José Eustasio Rivera. Nieto explained that he had bought some cattle from a rich ganadero, Don Ramón Oropeza, whose extensive lands, including Mata de Palma, had passed at his death into the hands of his son-in-law Jacinto Estévez. Other relatives had challenged the legacy, and then Jacinto himself died, complicating the matter further. Nieto was soliciting Rivera's legal services on behalf of himself and another contender, Alfredo Santos. The lawyer, who had an irresistible urge to visit Casanare, agreed to take the case.[60] His experiences in Orocué during the next two years provided material for a novel he would publish in 1924. Entitled *La Vorágine* (*The Vortex*), the book gained instant fame as an exposé of the enslavement of rubber collectors in Vichada, but it was also a brilliant portrayal of life in the Llanos that revived and transformed the legends that had surrounded Casanare since the War of Independence.

Rivera's fascination with the Llanos had flared two years earlier, when he went on a hunting trip near Villavicencio before beginning his final year of law school. Born in Neiva in 1888, he held a minor government post there in 1906, receiving a scholarship to study at the Escuela Normal Superior in Bogotá. As he completed the three-year course, he began writing poetry in the Parnassian style then in vogue in the capital. A member of the Conservative party, in 1909 he took part in the student protests against the Cortés–Root–Arosemena Treaty, which would have legalized the separation of Panama. In 1912, Rivera entered the Faculty of Law and Political Science at the Universidad Nacional, accepted a position with the Ministry of Government, and dedicated himself to his literary pursuits.[61] By January 1916, needing a break from these activities, he decided to vacation in the National Intendancy of Meta, lured by the prospect of losing himself in exuberant nature. He rode down the Bogotá–Villavicencio road, first on horseback and then by mule, and, like all travelers before him, was deeply impressed by the beauty of the changing landscape. Rivera spent two happy weeks with friends at Hacienda *Barrancas,*several kilometers beyond Villavicencio. As he hunted and fished, he fell in love with the region and its people, so that when it was time to return to Bogotá, he felt like "a criminal having to go back to jail." [62] In the words of his biographer Eduardo Neale-Silva, Rivera "remembered the Llanos with nostalgia [as] limitless plains open to all hope that seemed to cleanse man of obscure passions, inviting him to live within the fresh air, free as the birds." [63]

With such positive memories, Rivera jumped at the chance to represent Nieto and Santos in Orocué, especially since his legal specialization was the liquidation of inheritances. He left Bogotá on April 11, 1918, traveling again to Villavicencio, and from there on to Puerto Barrigón, where he hired a bongo to take him down the Meta to Orocué. Compared with Bogotá, Orocué had few amenities, but Rivera, installed in Nieto's house, was delighted to be in the Llanos again. He presented his letters of introduction to the circuit judge, but as he began to study the documents of the case, he realized that his clients were trying to cheat the rightful heiress, Doña Josefa Oropeza, out of Mata de Palma. Rivera remonstrated with Nieto, and when the latter angrily denounced him, he made up his mind to switch sides and represent Doña Josefa in order to see justice done.

The case moved slowly, and Rivera passed the time hunting, learning the peculiarities of different rivers, Indian customs, frontier incidents, and all the minutiae of life in the Llanos. He engaged in various deals to buy and sell cattle. Little by little, he penetrated the local culture, getting to know the people and sharing with them their pleasures and adversities.[64] By the middle of 1919, when the case had been reviewed by three different judges and was in danger of stagnating, Rivera succeeded in having it transferred to the court in Santa Rosa de Viterbo. He moved to Sogamoso to be near the seat of the tribunal, but on September 24, 1919, the judge decided for Nieto and Santos and against Doña Josefa. Disillusioned, Rivera returned to Orocué, concluded his business affairs, and went back to Bogotá in February 1920.

After publishing his first major poem, *Tierra de Promisión (Land of Promise)*, in 1921 and visiting Peru, Mexico, and the United States as part of a Colombian delegation to the national celebrations of those countries, Rivera went to Sogamoso where he began to write a novel about Casanare. With the first part finished in September, he accepted a post as a secretary-lawyer to the Colombian–Venezuelan Commission, appointed to determine the border between Vichada and Venezuelan Amazonas. The commissioners sailed down the Orinoco by canoe to San Fernando de Atabapo, and then proceeded to explore more than two hundred leagues of water along the Guaviare, Atabapo, and Inirida rivers. During this voyage Rivera discovered both the incredible beauty of the jungle and the brutal exploitation of the rubber workers, which he regarded as a national crime. Eventually, however, he was forced to leave the commission, his health broken by bouts of malarial fever. He returned to Bogotá from Manaus, Brazil, in September 1923, determined to devote the last two sections of his unfinished novel to telling the story of the rubber workers.[65]

La Vorágine, published in August 1924, was an immediate success, for Rivera's passionate defense of the rubber collectors and of Colombian sovereignty in the jungle struck an intensely nationalistic chord. As the last of a generation of Romantic novels authored by Colombians between 1886 and 1930, *La Vorágine* can be analyzed in three ways: "as a romantic allegory, as an urban intellectual's frightened vision of the barbarism of his country, and as a novel of protest."[66] It has been the subject of countless articles and reviews, in which critics usually focus on the nightmarish world of the protagonist, Arturo Cova, and Rivera's powerful descriptions of an omnipotent jungle.[67] From the standpoint of the history of the Llanos, however, it is the first section of the book that has particular interest, for Rivera, in describing the customs and people of Casanare, revitalized the romantic myths about the region and elevated them to a new plane.

Romantic Views of Casanare and La Vorágine

José María Samper was the first to cast the popular conceptions of Casanare and casanareños in the romantic, *costumbrista* mold that dominated Colombian literature in the second half of the nineteenth century. In *Ensayo sobre las revoluciones políticas y la condición social de las repúblicas colombianas* (Paris, 1861), he identified the types of people who inhabited the diverse regions of New Granada. After describing the bogotano, *antioqueño*, and the *indio pastuso*, Samper takes up the Llanero—the Colombian gaucho, "but a gaucho infinitely more poetic, more accessible, less barbarous" than those on the Argentine pampa:

> He is a type from a comic opera *par excellence,* in which are allied the heroic and the pastoral, the dramatic and the very humorous, in a most unusual mixture. Shepherd of the immense, free herds; rider, bullfighter, celebrated swimmer; fabulous cavalry soldier; poet of the pampas and of savage passions; a gallant artist in his way, the Llanero is a union between civilization and barbarism . . . between society with all its more or less artificial conventions and the imposing solitude of the deserts, where only nature rules with her immortal grandeur and solemn majesty.[68]

The land over which this "gaucho" rides is very different from Colombia's mountainous interior, for its "orchards" are forests of palm trees, its "roads" are "interminable plains of unlimited horizon covered with giant grass," and the Llanero's companions are "fat steers" and "indomitable horses." Samper's cowboy wears a felt hat, poncho, short pants, a colorful neckerchief, goatskin chaps, and hemp sandals. He carries a saber and a huge knife. Close at hand are his *tiple* or *bandola*–types of guitars used to accompany his songs called *galerones.* Fiercely independent, the Llanero, according to Samper, has never served the cause of oppression nor of dictatorship. "When liberty is in danger, he responds enthusiastically to the first call," and after the war is over, he does not ask for a reward because in combat, "he is an artist of death who loves art for art's sake as any other."[69]

These stereotypes reappear in many books and traveler accounts published years after Samper's time. For example, Francisco Javier Vergara y Velasco, in *Nueva geografía de Colombia* (Bogotá, 1901), refers to the inhabitant of Casanare as "a classic type in our national history":

> He is the Llanero accustomed from infancy to tame the wild horse . . . to struggle with the wild bull . . . to swim across flooded rivers infested with crocodiles, to conquer beasts in singular combat. The Llaneros, robust, with uncommon poetic sense, requiring few necessities, knowledgeable about the terrain, and capable of moving with extraordinary speed, were centaurs and hardened soldiers before having seen a battlefield, which explains their importance in the great war, and although this has changed with modern weapons, they are the only ones capable of dominating these regions.[70]

Vergara y Velasco gives a detailed, technical description of the landforms and subregions of the Llanos and suggests that because of the

Indians, wild animals, diseases, and floods, many years will pass before they will be fully cultivated. Yet even the rational geographer is captured by the spell cast by the plains, which is "imposing even when sad for their apparent immobility." It is a region, he writes, rich in spectacles of exceptional beauty, such as the grass fires, hurricanes that destroy the palm trees, and the rising and setting sun–a region where the sight of the full moon "is a poem as melancholy as it is indescribable":

The Llano is not for the man of other horizons; but he who passes some time in it, can not abandon it and remains conquered by it in such a way, so that later, when he comes to see the mountains, he retreats with fright back to his *conucos* fearful of losing those mysterious and interminable lonely places (*soledades*).[71]

Similarly, José María Vergara y Vergara, in *Historia de la literatura en Nueva Granada* (Bogotá, 1902), writes, "The Llanero is a distinct type among New Granadans . . . his eternal struggle against a ferocious and grandiose nature; his life in the desert and in the struggle, his nomadic home and his only occupation as cowboy have given him a unique character." A son of the desert, the Llanero "is an enthusiastic lover of poetry and of music, and he can pass an entire night, and the nights that follow as well, playing his *tiple* or *bandolín* and singing his *coplas* or his verses (*jácaras*)."[72]

Two other examples can be found in the books by Jorge Brisson, the engineer who proposed a development plan for Casanare in 1896, and by H. J. Mozans, the indefatigable Yankee minister who traveled through the Venezuelan and Colombian Llanos in 1907. In the introduction to *Casanare* (Bogotá, 1896), Brisson affirms:

The great and melancholy Llanura, cut by rivers that are bordered by forests varying from ten to five thousand meters in width, is one of the most surprising and majestic manifestations of nature. The most valiant and daring man is made timid by respectful admiration, when he takes in with his eyes and his mind those unknown and virgin solitudes, only crossed by wild animals and by human beings who by their primitive nature recall the mysterious origins of our race."[73]

When H. J. Mozans left the forests around the Meta River and saw the plains of Casanare for the first time, he was euphoric:

The landscape before us was indeed beautiful, entrancing as a vision, fair as the Happy Valley of Rasselas. Exulting in a new sense of freedom and stirred by many overmastering emotions, we could but exclaim with Byron,

"Beautiful!
How beautiful is all this beautiful world!
How glorious in its action and in itself!" [74]

Mozans found the Llanos lovelier than their North American counter-parts, and populated by fat, sleek cattle–as "large as any we had ever seen on the plains of Texas or Nebraska." [75] He agreed with Samper, Vergara y Velasco, and Vergara y Vergara that the Llanero "was abso-lutely unique among his countrymen." Give a Llanero a horse–he wrote–a lance, gun, poncho, and hammock, and he is completely in-dependent, at home wherever the setting sun may happen to find him. "Having these things, he is happy, and although he may be poor in all other worldly goods, he is ever ready merrily to sing:

Con mi lanza mi caballo	With my lance and my horse
No me importa la fortuna	I care not for fortune
Alumbre o no alumbre el sol	Or whether or not the sun shines
Brille o no brille la luna	or the moon gives light. [76]

This image of the merry, picturesque cowboy seems strangely out of kilter with the grim problems that faced the inhabitants of Casa-nare in the first quarter of the twentieth century—violence, disease, poverty, and lack of political power—a fact that more perceptive con-temporary observers were quick to point out. In his survey of Colom-bia written in 1913, businessman Phanor J. Eder concluded that the vaunted richness of the Llanos was a myth, and that only a few sec-tions of Casanare were capable of being developed with massive finan-cial investments. As for the Llanero, he wrote:

The old type Llanero, half Spanish, half Indian, the wild, brave, restless, devil-may-care cowboy, a "Cossack of the Colombian Steppes" and a boastful Tartarin full of poetic fire, rolled into one, is rapidly disappearing. Vanished is the poetry and romance of his life, if it ever really existed outside his remarkable *cantos*. . . . He seems to have tamed down completely, in spite of the solitary, open-air life, and in spite of the continuance of a certain element of danger, battling with the elements–encounters with jaguars, reptiles, and savage Indians are, however, in fact, the rarest episodes in the life of even the most daring and exposed Llanero. [77]

Eder's view was antedated by Hiram Bingham who, on his trip through the Llanos in 1906, was deeply impressed by the misery of the cowboys, whom he described as being "rather wild, restless and shiftless–not caring to work except on horseback." Even more pathetic were the horseless peons who worked on the hatos. They were "dirty and unkempt." Their scantily clad children suffered from malaria and enlarged spleens. Their food was wretched and infrequent, and they were tormented by clouds of insects. Altogether, Bingham concluded, "they seem to be content with less than any civilized people that I have ever seen."[78] Finally, J. M. Vargas Vergara, cited by Eder as a "Colombian authority," whose articles on the eastern plains were published in 1909 in the *Boletín de Obras Públicas*, challenged the prevailing notion that the Llanos "were a privileged region that have no equal for exuberance and fertility of soil." He wrote:

In my opinion there are no poorer lands nor any less suitable for agriculture in the whole Republic. . . . Where is the fertility of the Llanos? I have seen the pasture insufficient even to breed cattle and have seen them die for lack of nourishment. . . . The Llanos are fertile only for him who knows them not.[79]

José Eustasio Rivera did know the Llanos, and his book was the first widely read Colombian novel to describe Llanero life in detail.[80] Critic Roberto Simón Crespi notes that the moral indifference and spirit of independence of the cowboys in *La Vorágine* are reminiscent of the attitudes of the gauchos in Domingo Sarmiento's *Facundo o civilización y barbarie* (1845). Rivera's epic of Casanare is rich in *costumbrismo*. Man, in his struggle against nature, is triumphant and celebrates his victory with "aguardiente, boasting, duels, and elegies to the masculine spirit of the descendants of the conquistadors," but according to Crespi, *La Vorágine* presents the inhabitants of Casanare "outside their historical and objective context." They are proud and defiant people, "but, also, and Rivera does *not* tell us this, [they are] an exploited and forgotten people, the pariahs of civilization."[81]

In his treatment of the landscape, Rivera brilliantly juxtaposes against the romantic vision of tropical paradise an even stronger image of green hell. This transfer is achieved by recording the changing perceptions of Arturo Cova and his companion Alicia of their environment. When the two first arrive in the Llanos, Cova is confident that he can dominate "Casanare, that strange land of plain and jungle, of drought and flood, of cattle men and hostile Indians." As he and Alicia sip their coffee in the freshness of early dawn on the plains, they are overwhelmed by the fragrance of the lush grasses, plowed earth, and newly cut timbers.

An unexpected joy swelled our veins; while our spirits, flowing amply like the pampas, felt grateful for life and existence. "Casanare is fascinating!" Alicia repeated. "I don't know what its charm is, but I felt somehow released, just as soon as I stepped on the plains."[82]

Later, Cova confesses, "I even felt like imprisoning myself forever in those fascinating plains, living with Alicia in a smiling home, which I myself would build on the banks of a river of opaque waters, or on one of those verdant knolls where a sea-green pool sleeps in the shadow of a palm."[83] Later, however, as the lovers cross from plain to plain, and river to river, they learn of the terrors of the region. No longer a happy kingdom, the Llanos become for them a grotesque nightmare, just as the rains had changed fertile savannas into desolate swamps. Cova writes:

With water to our waists we followed the trail of the guides, foreheads bathed in sweat, the pack we carried damp and moist, hungry, emaciated, spending the night on elevations covered by inhospitable thickets, without fire, without bed, without protection or shelter. Those regions are merciless in drought or rainy season . . .

Summer scorched the torrid plains, and the cattle, in the blazing heat, moved here and there in restless search for water. Heifers scraped the parched bed of a winding creek, where in other days they had drunk. A dying horse lay near them, nostrils plunged in the dry mud . . . and then after some rain, the territory reversed its hostility. Foxes, cavies, and rabbits clambered up tree trunks, fleeing the floods; and the cattle now chewing on the tall grass with water to the haunches, lost their udders under the savage teeth of the carib fish. . . . Over those hostile regions we marched barefooted like the legendary heros of the Conquest.[84]

Rivera set out to destroy the European concept of a tamed nature, and in *La Vorágine* the hellish view of nature prevails. The influence that his celebrated novel had on shaping Colombian impressions of the Llanos should not be underestimated. Eduardo Zuleta Angel, a contemporary of Rivera who served in the cabinet of President Alfonso Pumarejo López in the 1930s, asserted that *La Vorágine* convinced many young Bogotanos, who had thought of Casanare as a place to make their fortunes, that to go there would be a dreadful mistake. It was commonly believed "that he who became enchanted by the Llanos would gain nothing more after a few months of being there than to have his clothes eaten up by moths. . . . No one was tempted to follow the example of Arturo Cova. No one was interested in gambling his life, when after a thousand absurd adventures, violence would win."[85] An anonymous article published in *Revista Pan* in 1937 underscored Zuleta Angel's comments by stating that in the early 1930s, Colombians had come to regard the Llanos as a "devourer of men." Those people who did travel there were animated solely by the desire to appear heroic and to be able to return to the altiplano with "frightening stories of cannibals, wild beasts, and poisonous snakes." Such stories were accepted by the public and by government officials at face value, so that it was not until the completion of the Bogotá– Villavicencio highway and the proliferation of air travel throughout the region, that the Llanos recovered their appeal as a place where Colombians might begin a new life.[86]

In summary, between 1909 and 1930 Casanare showed scant signs of progress. Lacking Meta's advantage of proximity to Bogotá and Arauca's importance as a strategic region on the Venezuelan border, the province languished under Boyacá's departmental rule. In spite of the arrival of many colonos, its economy stagnated, the material well-being of the people declined, and the missionaries, traditionally a powerful force in the Llanos, were surprisingly inept in civilizing the Indians or in improving public education. Popular concern for the exploited rubber workers of Vichada, which had been awakened by *La Vorágine*, did not extend to the Llaneros, and the myth of Casanare as a "devourer of men" only increased the cultural isolation of the region. These conditions combined to make Casanare an ideal refuge for criminals from other parts of the country, and during the Violencia, the undeclared civil war that swept through Colombia between 1948 and 1960, they would convert the province into a major theatre for guerrilla activity.

Conclusions

As Enrique Olaya Herrera put on the presidential sash on August 7, 1930, and Colombia was beginning its one hundredth year of independent existence, its eastern frontier appeared to be much the same as in the time of Spanish rule. Most of the people were clustered in small towns near the cordillera, isolated from one another and from the interior by wide expanses of plains, forests, rivers, and mountain peaks. Numbering less than 50,000 they accounted not even for 1 percent of Columbia's population of 7,851,000. Cattle ranching remained the principal activity, and the hatos and fundaciones were organized along traditional lines. In some regions, the Indians had been assimilated into Colombian society, but in others they were engaged in bitter warfare with the whites. Missionaries continued to bear primary responsibility for their subjugation. The Llanos remained a place of refuge for fugitives from the highlands and would-be Venezuelan revolutionaries. Violence was endemic. The cowboys had developed a distinctive culture, but like the peons and colonos, they lived in poverty, beset by disease, without legal guarantees, and vulnerable to exploitation by gamonales.

Yet a closer look at the frontier reveals that important changes had taken place between 1830 and 1930. Perhaps the most dramatic development was the shift of the focal point of settlement from Casanare to Meta. During Spanish rule, the fortunes of the Provincia de los Llanos were linked to the rich and populous Provincia of Tunja, and nearly all the towns, hatos, and missions were located north of the Meta River. The decay of these towns in the first half of the nineteenth century mirrored the political and economic decline of the Department of Boyacá within New Granada. Meanwhile, in the 1840s, colonos from Cundinamarca began to move into the Llanos of San Martín, followed by entrepreneurs from Bogotá. With its highway link to the altiplano, the steady inflow of new settlers, and preferential treatment from Radical and Conservative administrations, the Intendancy of Meta manifested by the twentieth century a dynamism unmatched by Casanare, now ruled by Boyacá, or Arauca, isolated on the Venezuelan border.

Settlers came to the Llanos either from the interior or from Venezuela. They staked out claims in the baldíos, cultivating food crops or raising cattle. The government passed laws in 1874, 1882, and 1926 to make it easier for them to gain legal title to their land, but in the Llanos, as in other parts of the country, the laws were ineffective. In Meta, less than one hundred land titles were registered between 1860 and 1930; in Casanare and Arauca, officials insisted that all the land was baldío despite its occupation by small and large ranchers. The colonos simply squatted on the land, and even after they had been there for decades, disputes arose between them and entrepreneurs who claimed prior ownership to their property.

The influx of new people contributed to the coalescence of regional identities within the Llanos. Until 1913 Arauca was part of Casanare, but even in 1830 its relative prosperity set it apart from the other municipios in the province. The isolation of Tame, Trinidad, and Arauca City from Tunja, Nunchía, and Támara, and the predominance of Venezuelans fostered a unique subculture and an independent spirit. Similarly, the movement of people from Cundinamarca and Tolima into the Llanos of San Martín gave Meta a distinctive unity, while Casanare remained the home of the traditional Colombian "Llaneros"—a mixture of immigrants from Boyacá and Santander and Indians, divided between the settlers in the piedmont with ties to Tunja and Sogamoso and those on the open plains with more affinity with Venezuela.

In all three regions, old and new towns led a precarious existence. In Casanare, colonial towns such as Pore, Manare, Ten, and Zapatosa stagnated. The Archivo Nacional contains numerous solicitudes from vecinos requesting permission to move their municipality because of unhealthy climate, isolation, economic necessity, or Indian attacks. The capital of Casanare was changed twelve times between 1830 and 1930 and was located variously at Pore, Támara, Moreno, Tame, Nunchía, and Orocué. Of the towns founded in the nineteenth century, only Villavicencio and Orocué achieved an enduring vitality, and they were both destroyed twice by fire.

The Llanos was really two frontiers, for if to the west was the Colombian highlands, to the east was Venezuela, and the Venezuelan factor was increasingly influential. Almost constant civil wars in that country during the nineteenth century produced a stream of refugees who fled to the relative peace of the Colombian plains. The border between Arauca and Apure was a zone of tension, as caudillos on both sides crossed the line with impunity to conscript cattle and men. In many towns, Venezuelans greatly outnumbered the Colombians. In 1830, a local group in Casanare voted to secede from Colombia to join Venezuela, and in 1904, after the loss of Panama, rumors of secessionist plots circulated once again. Nearly every Colombian administration negotiated with Venezuela over the location of the international boundary and for the right of free navigation on the Orinoco. Venezuelan cattle traveled through Arauca and Casanare on their way to Colombian markets, and Colombians relied on the Venezuelan San Cristóbal road to send their cattle to Cúcuta.

Political responsibility for administering the Llanos frontier alternated between the nation and the departments. The national territorial system developed by the Radicals in 1868 suffered a setback during Regeneration, but later emerged as a precedent for the Intendancy of Meta and the Comisaría Especial of Arauca. Regardless of the system imposed, political power within the regions was concentrated in the governor, prefect, intendant, or comisario, who, in the absence of functional municipal government, ruled as a quasi-dictator. After 1910, in Meta his power was challenged by the Montfort missionaries and in Arauca by the local police chief, but as Miguel Triana observed, even in these cases the authorities had little influence beyond the capitals of the districts. Without an effective military presence, violence was a part of daily life, be it Indian attacks, rustlers, outlaws, or revolutionaries, and the settlers relied on their own resources to protect their lives and property.

By 1930, the religious orders were firmly established in Meta, Casanare, and Arauca, but their role had altered since the War of Independence. The missions, revived briefly in the 1830s and 1840s, suffered a complete eclipse during the Federation Era, to emerge phoenixlike during Regeneration. Bolstered by renewed religious enthusiasm in Europe and granted extensive powers by the Colombian government in the Convenio of 1904, the Montfort Fathers, Lazarists, and Recoletos took control of public education and social services, in addition to civilizing the Indians. In all three regions, the priests were concentrated in the white towns so that very few were actually engaged in the conversion of natives on the cutting edge of the frontier.

Unlike the cattle frontiers of the Argentine pampas and the North American West, ranching in the Llanos did not expand greatly in the nineteenth century. Cattle herds in Casanare and Arauca recovered from the ravages of the War of Independence to reach a total of

109,250 in 1874 and 535,142 by 1936, but the quality of meat remained low. Lack of roads to the west and Venezuelan tariffs in the east hindered the export of animals and hides. While some ranchers in Meta experimented with artificial pasture and cross-breeding, north of the Meta River ganaderos regarded themselves as progressive if they gave salt to their animals. The continued loss of horses to renguera and the destructive practice of sacrificing female cows before they could reproduce further limited the growth of the industry best suited to the tropical environment.

After 1860, the depressed economy was occasionally relieved by a series of boom-and-bust cycles in forest products that linked the Llanos for the first time to the caprices of international trade. The demand for quinine stimulated the exploitation of cinchona trees in the forests of the Territory of San Martín. Francisco Antonio Uribe opened a road across the mountains from Tolima into the Llanos, and hundreds of workers moved into the territory to collect bark. When the market for quinine collapsed, in the 1880s, Uribe's company switched to rubber extraction. Peaking between 1890 and 1920, the rubber boom was concentrated in the Amazon Basin, but it also affected the forested areas of the Llanos, and Orocué and Arauca City became important way stations for the shipment of latex down the Orinoco. The extraction of latex was carried out in the most destructive manner imaginable, and the enslavement of Indian collectors became an international scandal in 1912. The boom in garza feathers, coterminous with the rubber cycle, was equally ruinous in bringing about the near extermination of the birds without producing any solid basis for the development of a regional economy. More encouraging was the emergence of rice as a viable cash crop in the Intendancy of Meta, after 1910. Easily grown by small and large farmers, and competitive in quality and price despite high transportation costs, rice demonstrated that the Llanos could supply food to the enormous market in Bogotá. After the paving of the highway in the 1930s, more and more commodities grown in Meta would find their way to the altiplano.

If the Llanos frontier was not static between 1830 and 1930, what was its relationship to the heartland? Historians have generally argued that the plains have played only a minor role in Colombian history, yet this study has shown that the frontier was not divorced from national developments. In 1830, Juan Nepomuceno Moreno led an army from Pore to Tunja and Bogotá to unseat the dictatorship of Rafael Urdaneta. President Santander boldly challenged the Vatican when he exercised the patronato to create an auxiliary bishop to restore the missions in the Llanos in 1833. Llaneros formed an important contingent in the rebel army during the Guerra de los Supremos. The Territory of San Martín attracted the attention of such influential Radicals as President Santos Gutiérrez, Salvador Camacho Roldán, and Felipe Pérez. Fighting occurred in San Martín and Casanare during the Civil War of 1895, which proved to be a kind of dress rehearsal for the War of the Thousand Days. Gabriel Vargas Santos, Supreme Director of Liberal forces in that conflict, spent much of his life in Casanare and was regarded by all as a Llanero, although he was a native of Santander. Rebels controlled most of the Llanos throughout the conflict, and Uribe Uribe's failure to replicate Bolívar's Liberation Campaign by marching his army through Casanare and up the cordillera in 1901 was a major factor in the eventual Liberal defeat. Humberto Gómez's revolt in December 1916 and the subsequent Arauca Affair posed a serious crisis for the regime of José Vicente Concha, and provided an opportunity for Enrique Olaya Herrera to gain prestige as an outspoken critic of the government. Last, but not least, Casanare provided the setting and inspiration for Rivera's *La Vorágine*, the most important novel written by a Colombian in the early twentieth century.

The attitude of the highland administrations toward the Llanos frontier ranged from the intensive engagement of the Radicals to the total neglect of Rafael Reyes, but the large number of decrees, laws, and development schemes that legislators debated and adopted strangely had little effect. Most of them failed because Colombia's resources were limited, and it was more vital to national interests to invest these resources in the interior provinces. They also failed because the legislators, beguiled by the widely held myth that the Llanos were a region of untold wealth that within a few years would become the heartland of Colombian prosperity, underestimated the obstacles presented by the tropical environment. Typical is the following statement, taken from a Senate report of September 29, 1892:

The vast and rich eastern region of the Republic known by the name of the Llanos of Casanare and San Martín, by its topography, by the fertility of its soil, and by the abundance and wealth of its natural products is called to be in the more or less distant future, the center of a civilization more advanced perhaps than that which the now occupied interior regions will reach.[1]

One of the most striking impressions left by a review of the nineteenth-century sources is the counterpoint between the overblown rhetoric of Congress, such as the example shown above, and the desperate pleas for assistance from local Llanero officials, municipios, and missionaries who, observing the misery around them, cried out for relief.

For all its shortcomings, national policy toward the frontier between 1830 and 1930 laid a foundation upon which a more rational system of territorial rule could be built, and if the myths of the Romantic Llanero, the Devourer of Men, and the Eastern Lands of Promise retarded progress, they also exerted a compelling fascination for Colombians rash enough to travel to the plains. In 1934, the influential Liberal writer Luis Eduardo Nieto Caballero, returned from a trip by airplane through Meta, Arauca, and Casanare, to write:

The attraction of the Llanos is irresistible. . . . The Llanero is perhaps the only Colombian who rarely complains. Badly dressed, badly fed, with rustic shelter, exposed to the elements, fighting at times with wild animals, frequently alone, absolutely alone, like a point in the immensity, it is clear that he is satisfied . . . I felt the mysterious call of the Llanos, and I understand, exalt and envy the life of the Llanero.[2]

Between 1934 and 1938 another Liberal, President Alfonso López Pumarejo, would feel this call and, in responding to it, enact extensive reforms that would usher Colombia and its eastern frontier into a new era.

Abbreviations

AC	Archivo del Congreso, Bogotá.
ADB	Archivo Departamental de Boyacá, Tunja.
AHN	Archivo Histórico Nacional, Bogotá.
AS	*Archivo Santander*, 24 vols. (Bogotá, 1913–32).
BHA	*Boletín de Historia y Antigüedades*
CHLA	*The Cambridge History of Latin America*, ed. Leslie Bethell, 5 vols. (Cambridge, 1984–86).
HAHR	*Hispanic American Historical Review.*
MANUAL	*Manual de historia de Colombia*, 3 vols. (Bogotá, 1978–80).
SUCESOS	*Sucesos colombianos 1900–1924.* ed. Jorge Villegas and José Yunis. (Medellín, 1976).

Notes

Chapter 1

1. Robert C. West, "The Geography of Colombia," in A. Curtis Wilgus, ed., *The Caribbean: Contemporary Colombia* (Gainesville, 1962), 3–4.

2. John Lynch, *The Spanish-American Revolutions, 1808–1824*, 2d ed. (New York, 1973), 229.

3. Frank Safford, *The Ideal of the Practical: Colombia's Struggle to Form a Technical Elite* (Austin, 1975), 25.

4. Ibid.; Helen Delpar, *Red against Blue: The Liberal Party in Colombian Politics, 1863–1899* (University, Ala., 1981), 14. In *Colombia: A Commercial and Industrial Handbook* (Washington, D.C., 1921), U.S. Trade Commissioner P. L. Bell warned potential investors that the trip from the coast to Bogotá still took from eight days to a month for travelers and four or even five months for freight (p. 244).

5. Lynch, *Spanish-American Revolutions*, 229; Safford, *Ideal of the Practical*, 26.

6. Robert L. Gilmore, "Colombia, The National Period," in Wilgus, *Caribbean*, 76–81; Delpar, *Red against Blue*, 3. An excellent analysis of regional conflicts in the early national period is María Teresa Uribe de Hincapié and Jesús María Alvarez, *Poderes y regiones en la constitución de la nación colombiana, 1810–1850* (Medellín, 1987).

7. Miguel Izard, "Ni cuatreros, ni montoneros, llaneros," *Boletín Americanista* (Barcelona) 13:31 (1981), 86.

8. Frederico Brito Figueroa, *La estructura económica de Venezuela colonial* (Caracas, 1978), 196.

9. C. Langdon White, "Cattle Raising: A Way of Life in the Venezuelan Llanos," *Scientific Monthly* 83 (September, 1956), 122.

10. The Catalan historian Miguel Izard has written extensively on the Venezuelan Llanos. In addition to "Ni cuatreros, ni montoneros," cited above, his publications include *El miedo a la revolución: La lucha por la libertad en Venezuela (1777–1830)* (Madrid, 1979); "Tanto pelear para terminar conversando, el caudillismo en Venezuela," *Nova Americana* (Turin, 1979), 37–81; and "Oligarcas, temblad, Viva la libertad, los llaneros del Apure y la guerra federal," *Boletín Americanista* (Barcelona) 14:32 (1982):227–77. Major works by Venezuelans include J. A. de Armas Chitty, *Tucupido: Formación de un pueblo del llano* (Caracas, 1961); Marco-Aurelio Vila, *Por los espacios llaneros* (Caracas, 1967); Rafael Bolívar Coronado, *El llanero: Estudio de sociología venezolano* (Madrid, 1919); Germán Carrera Damas, *Boves, Aspectos socio-económicos de su acción histórica* (Caracas, 1968). An excellent study by an American scholar is Robert Paul Mathews, *Violencia rural en Venezuela, 1840–1858: Antecedentes socioeconómicos de la guerra federal* (Caracas, 1977).

11. Humberto Plazas Olarte, *Los territorios nacionales* (Bogotá, 1944), 188–392; Juan Medina R., *Geografía económica de Colombia: III*–Boyacá (Bogotá, 1937), 27–31. The tallest peaks in the Sierra Nevada del Cocuy reach an altitude of 5,360 meters.

12. Ernesto Guhl, *Colombia: Bosquejo de su geografía tropical*, 2 vols. (Bogotá, 1976), 1:210.

13. Nancy C. Morey, "Ethnohistory of the Colombian and Venezuelan Llanos," (Ph.D. diss., University of Utah, 1975), 304.

14. Nancy C. Morey and Robert V. Morey, "Relaciones comerciales en el pasado en los llanos de Colombia y Venezuela," *Montalbán* (Caracas) 4 (1975): 534.

15. Robert Morey, "Ecology and Culture Change among the Colombian Guahibo," (Ph.D. diss. University of Pittsburgh, 1977), 42.

16. José Pérez Gómez, *Apuntes históricos de las misiones agustinianas en Colombia* (Bogotá, 1924), 123–26.

17. Marcelino Ganuza, *Monografía de las misiones vivas de agustinos recoletos (candelarios) en Colombia*, 3 vols. (Bogotá, 1954), 1:176–78.

18. Juan M. Pacheco, *Los jesuítas en Colombia*, 2 vols. (Bogotá, 1959–62), 2:346; Jane M. Rausch, *A Tropical Plains Frontier: The Llanos of Colombia 1531–1831* (Albuquerque, 1984), 121.

19. The Recoletos were a branch of the Augustinians founded in New Granada in 1604, who are sometimes called Candelarios. Rausch, *Tropical Plains Frontier*, 121.

20. Archivo Histórico Nacional, Bogotá (hereafter cited as AHN), José Caicedo, Provincia de los Llanos: Padrón formado en el año de 1778. Morcote, October 14, 1778.

21. Morey, "Ecology and Culture Change" 42; Paul Kirchoff, "Food-Gathering Tribes of the Venezuelan Llanos," in Julian E. Steward, ed., *Handbook of South American Indians* (Washington, 1946–50), 447; N. Morey, "Ethnohistory," 235.

22. Manuel Zapata Olivella, *El hombre colombiano* (Bogotá, 1974), 356–60.

23. *Gaceta de Nueva Granada*, January 29, 1832.

24. *Gaceta de Nueva Granada*, March 25, 1832; José Miguel Pinto, "División política de la República de Colombia de 1819 á 1905," *Boletín de Historia y Antigüedades* (hereafter cited as BHA) 5:52 (January 1908):241.

25. Fernando Gómez, "Los censos en Colombia antes de 1905," in Miguel Urrutia and Mario Arrubla, *Compendio de estadísticas históricas de Colombia* (Bogotá, 1970), 21; Medina R., *Geografía económica*, 123. Gómez reprints the seven official censuses taken between 1776 and 1870, while Medina R. breaks down the 1835 census in Casanare by cantons. Jorge Orlando Melo warns that all of the nineteenth-century censuses had wide margins of error due to ineffective state bureaucracy, manipulation by political interests, insufficient functionaries to carry out the census in distant places, disorders caused by civil struggles, and the unwillingness of some inhabitants to be counted for fear of recruitment or new taxes. The census of 1825 is widely believed to be undercounted and that of 1864 was also seriously flawed. Those of 1835, 1843, 1851, and 1870, for all their defects, at least give a gross approximation of population figures. See Melo's essay, "La evolución económica de Colombia, 1830–1900," in *Manual de historia de Colombia* (hereafter cited as MANUAL) (Bogotá, 1979), 2:137–44.

26. AHN, Gobernación de Casanare (hereafter cited as GC), vol. 16, fol. 17.

27. AHN, GC, vol. 16, fol. 225.

28. Delpar, *Red against Blue*, 33.

29. Medina R., *Geografía económica*, 30–31.

30. Felipe Pérez, *Geografía general física y política de los Estados Unidos de Colombia* (Bogotá, 1863; 1883), 2:296–97.

31. *El Nuevo Tiempo* (Bogotá), May 29, 1917.

32. N. Morey, "Ethnohistory," 34–37; Ganuza, *Monografía de las misiones vivas*, 2:99.

33. Rogerio Guáqueta Gallardo, "La Fundación de Arauca," *Comité Bicentenario de Arauca* (Bogotá, January 1976), 14–15.

34. Roberto M. Tisnes J., *Fray Ignacio Mariño, O.P.* (Bogotá, 1963), 95.

35. Juan Nepomuceno Moreno to Santander, Pore, January 19, 1820, *Archivo Santander* (Bogotá, 1913–32) (hereafter cited as AS), 4:64–66; AHN, GC, vol. 16, fol. 225.

36. Ernesto Camejo, *Breves apuntaciones sobre Arauca* (Bogotá, 1940), 23–24; Medina R., *Geografía económica*, 123.

37. F. O. Martin, "Explorations in Colombia," *The Geographical Review* 19 (1929), 629.

38. Ibid., 631–33. The Colombia government has declared La Macarena a national park, but in the last twenty years it has been invaded by thousands of colonos searching for land and is presently dominated by the country's largest guerrilla organization, the Colombian Revolutionary Armed Forces, or FARC. See Alan Weisman, "Dangerous Days in the Macarena," *New York Times Magazine*, April 23, 1989.

39. F. J. Vergara y Velasco, *Nueva geografía de Colombia* (Bogotá, 1901–2), 687; Brunnschweiler, *Llanos Frontier of Colombia*, 5–8.

40. Platt, "Opportunities for Agricultural Colonization," 89.

41. Pedro Aguado, *Recopilación historial* (Bogotá, 1956), 569–81.

42. Basilio Vicente de Oviedo, *Cualidades y riquezas del Nuevo Reino de Granada* (Bogotá, 1930), 233.

43. "Noticia positiva sobre el curso y navegación del río Ariari, ya solo, ya incorporado con el Guayabero," in Antonio B. Cuervo, ed., *Colección de documentos inéditos*, 4 vols. (Bogotá, 1891–1894), 3:107.

44. Alonso de Zamora, O.P., *Historia de la Provincia de San Antonio del Nuevo Reino de Granada* (Caracas, 1930), 381–83.

45. Oviedo, *Cualidades y riquezas*, 235.

46. Gregorio Arcila Robledo, O.F.M., *Las misiones franciscanas en Colombia* (Bogotá, 1950), 259–61; Germán Colmenares, *Las haciendas de los jesuítas en el Nuevo Reino de Granada* (Bogotá, 1969), 127.

47. Rausch, *Tropical Plains Frontier*, 113–14.

48. Oswaldo Díaz Díaz, *La reconquista española*, 2 vols. (Bogotá, 1964–1967), 2:117.

49. David Bushnell, "Elecciones presidenciales colombianas 1825–1856," in Urrutia and Arrubla, *Compendio de estadísticas*, 223.

50. Feliciano Montenegro Colón, *Geografía general*, 4 vols. (Caracas, 1834), 3:550; AHN. Gobernación de Bogotá (hereafter cited as GB), vol. 3, fol. 844.

51. *El Constitucional de Cundinamarca*, September 15, 1832.

52. *El Constitucional de Cundinamarca*, September 22, 1833.

53. John Blydenstein, "Tropical Savanna Vegetation of the Llanos of Colombia," *Ecology* 48 (Winter 1967), 13.

54. Agustín Codazzi, *Geografía física i política de los provincias de la Nueva Granada por la Comisión Corográfica bajo la dirección de Agustín Codazzi*, 4 vols. (Bogotá, 1859), 3:377–79.

55. In *Death by Migration: Europe's Encounter with the Tropical World in the Nineteenth Century* (New York, 1989), Philip D. Curtin notes that the European scientific community divided into two camps to explain the causes of certain tropical diseases. The "contagionists," a minority, believed that cholera and yellow fever were transmitted from one person to another like smallpox and syphilis. The "anticontagionists" argued that epidemics grew out of local conditions of a miasmatic nature. For example, a Dr. Inglis who prepared a sanitary report for Madras, India, in 1863, declared that cholera was caused by "peculiar physical and atmospherical states operating on the decomposing vegetable and organic products at the low fluvial level described, and the sudden cessation, to removal of all fermenting elements requiring meterological conditions for their development" (p. 75). Judging by his description of the causes of disease in the Llanos, Codazzi adhered to the "anticontagionist" school of thought.

Chapter 2

1. Luis Ospina Vásquez, *Industría y protección en Colombia 1810–1930* (Medellín, 1955), 195.

2. "Professional Notes," *Hispanic American Historical Review* (hereafter cited as HAHR) 47:2 (May 1967): 318; Safford, *Ideal of the Practical*, 13.

3. Gilmore, "Colombia," 76.

4. Ibid.

5. Fernando Díaz Díaz, "Estado, iglesia y desamortización," in MANUAL, 2:419.

6. Ibid., 428.

7. David Bushnell, *The Santander Regime in Gran Colombia* (Newark, 1954), 222.

8. J. Lloyd Mecham, *Church and State in Latin America*, rev. ed. (Chapel Hill, 1966), 92.

9. José Manuel Restrepo, *Exposición que el secretario de estado del despacho del interior de la república de Colombia hizo al congreso de 1824* (Bogotá, 1827), 14–15.

10. *Gaceta de Colombia*, July 16, 1826; Bushnell, *Santander Regime*, 179.

11. Santander to President of the Cámara de Representantes, Bogotá, July 11, 1823, *AS*, 4:206.

12. The Jansenists were Catholics, who believed that man attains eternal salvation only if God predestines him for it and that God's gift of grace is irrespec-

tive of any good works that many may do. See Stephen Neill, *History of Christian Missions* (Baltimore, 1964), 207.

13. Kenneth S. Latourette, *The Great Century*, vol. 5 of *A History of the Expansion of Christianity*, 7 vols. (New York, 1943), 71.

14. Ganuza, *Monografía de las misiones vivas*, 2:257.

15. Ibid., 2:265–66.

16. David Bushnell, "The Last Dictatorship: Betrayal or Consummation?," HAHR, 63:1 (February 1983): 83; *Codificación national de todas las leyes de Colombia desde el año de 1821* (hereafter cited as *Cod. nac.*), 32 vols. (Bogotá, 1924), 3:384–88.

17. José Manuel Restrepo, *Historia de la revolución de la República de Colombia en la América Meridional*, 6 vols. (Medellín, 1974), 6:317.

18. Ganuza, *Monografía de las misiones vivas*, 2:260–61.

19. Mecham, *Church and State*, 115.

20. Alvaro Tirado Mejía, "El estado y la política en el siglo xix," in MANUAL, 2:332–33.

21. Mecham, *Church and State*, 116.

22. Díaz Díaz, "Estado," 431.

23. Mecham, *Church and State*, 78, 117–18.

24. AHN, GC, vol. 15, fol. 80.

25. AHN, GC, vol. 15, fol. 879. Moreno was president of the legislature of Casanare at this time.

26. *Gaceta de Colombia*, July 16, 1826; Bushnell, *Santander Regime*, 179. The *Gaceta de Colombia* praised Córdoba for his effort, but afterward the towns seem to have disappeared, for there is no further mention of them.

27. AHN, GC, vol. 15, fol. 112.

28. AHN, GC, vol. 15, fol. 111; *Gaceta de la Nueva Granada*, January 6, 1833. On July 22, 1833, the secretary denied a third proposal to resettle the Meta missions, which was put forward by Raimundo Melgarejo on the grounds that he had already assigned the towns to Gallardo. See AHN, GC, vol. 15, fol. 378.

29. AHN, GC, vol. 15, fol. 108.

30. AHN, GC, vol. 15, fol. 285; *Gaceta de la Nueva Granada*, March 10, 1833.

31. AHN, GC, vol. 15, fol. 879.

32. *Gaceta de la Nueva Granada*, May 5, 1833; Mecham, *Church and State*, 116; *Cod. nac.* 5:8; José Restrepo Posada, *Arquidiócesis de Bogotá; datos biográficos de sus prelados, 1564–1891 y cabildo eclesiástico*, 4 vols. (Bogotá, 1961–1961), 2:346.

33. *Cod. nac.*, 5:10–12.

34. *Gaceta de la Nueva Granada*, March 18, 1832.

35. *Gaceta de la Nueva Granada*, October 11, 1835. A *millar* is a measure of cacao varying between 3½ and 4 pounds. An *arroba* is a measure of weight equal to about 25 pounds.

36. El Arzobispo de Calidonia to Santander, Sogamoso, November 24, 1834, *AS* 21, 103–4; AHN, Curas y Obispos (hereafter cited as CyO), vol. 2, fol. 709.

37. *Gaceta de la Nueva Granada*, June 28, 1835; December 6, 1835.

38. AHN, CyO, vol. 2, fol. 709.

39. Gustavo Arboleda, *Historia contemporánea de Colombia*, 3 vols., 2d ed. (Cali, 1933), 1:316. Chaves continued to be bishop *in partibus* of Calidonia and ended his days in the old convent of San Francisco de Bogotá. Restrepo Posada, *Arquidiócesis de Bogotá*, 2:72.

40. *Gaceta de la Nueva Granada*, November 13, 1836; AHN, CyO, vol. 2, fol. 711.

41. AHN, GC, vol. 16, fol. 513.

42. *Gaceta de la Nueva Granada*, November 18, 1837.

43. AHN, GC, vol. 15, fol. 185.

44. *Cod. nac.*, 7:621–22; *Gaceta de la Nueva Granada*, August 1, 1841.

45. *Gaceta de la Nueva Granada*, March 22, 1834.

46. Archivo del Congreso, Bogotá (hereafter cited as AC), Cámara 1835, Proyectos pendientes, vol. 4, fol. 54, 55.

47. Andrés Mesanza, *Apuntes y documentos sobre la orden dominicana en Colombia (de 1680 a 1930): apuntes o narración* (Caracas, 1929), 145.

48. *Gaceta de la Nueva Granada*, March 3, 1839.

49. Ganuza, *Monografía de las misiones vivas*, 2:287–93.

50. AHN, GC, vol. 16, fols. 792–96.

51. AHN, GB, vol. 3, vol. 140.

52. *El Constitucional de Cundinamarca*, February 18, 1837.

53. *Cod. nac.*, 7:575; *Gaceta de la Nueva Granada*, April 15, 1838.

54. AHN, GB, vol. 6, fol. 606.

55. AHN, GB, vol. 9, fol. 229; Ospina Vásquez, *Industria y protección*, 143. In his annual report of 1839, Secretary of State Pedro Herrán recommended that the canton of San Martín, the canton of Bocas del Toro in Veraguas and the island of Gorgona in the Province of Buenaventura be designated as places where vagrants apprehended in the rest of the republic might be sent. Herrán argued that in finding it difficult to flee, the vagrants would have to work to survive and would benefit those three regions by populating them. Nothing came of this proposal. See P. A. Herrán, *Exposición del secretario de estado*, Bogotá, March 2, 1839.

56. Jesús María Henao and Gerardo Arrubla, *Historia de Colombia*, 5th ed. (Bogotá, 1929), 602.

57. José Manuel Restrepo, *Historia de la Nueva Granada*, 2 vols. (Bogotá 1952–1963), 1:204.

58. Carlos Restrepo Canal, *La Nueva Granada*, 2 vols. (Bogotá, 1971), 2:120.

59. *Gaceta de la Nueva Granada*, February 14, 1841.

60. Restrepo Canal, *La Nueva Granada*, 2:141; Restrepo, *Historia de la Nueva Granada*, 1:215; *Gaceta de la Nueva Granada*, January 22, 1843.

61. William Marian Gibson, *The Constitutions of Colombia* (Durham, N.C., 1948), 159. Gibson writes that the Conservatives were so intent on extirpating federalism "that their zeal prompted them to include in the Constitution of 1843 the utterly unenforceable provision that 'Senators and Representatives represent the Nation and not the Provinces in which they are chosen' (Art. 62)."

62. Robert L. Gilmore, "New Granada's Socialist Mirage," HAHR 36:2 (May 1956): 191–92.

63. After the Constitution of 1843 was promulgated, the portfolios of secretary of the interior and secretary of foreign relations were separated. Ospina Rodríguez was secretary of state for interior and foreign relations until 1844, when he became simply secretary of state for the interior.

64. Gilmore, "New Granada's Socialist Mirage," 192.

65. Ibid. See also Henao and Arrubla, *Historia de Colombia*, 614–15.

66. Mariano Ospina, *Exposición que el secretario de estado . . . dirije al Congreso Constitucional el año de 1842* (Bogotá, 1842), 67.

67. *Cod. nac.* 9:344, 348; J. J. Borda, *Historia de la Compañía de Jesús*, 2 vols. (Paris, 1870), 2:173–79.

68. The two relevant articles in the Constitution of 1843 were Article 15–"It is also the duty of the government to protect the exercise of the Roman Catholic Apostolic religion for the New Granadans"—and Article 16–"The Roman Catholic Apostolic religion is the only cult which the republic supports and maintains." Gibson, *Constitutions of Colombia*, 613.

69. Tirado Mejía, "El estado y la política," 359.

70. *Gaceta de la Nueva Granada*, October 6, 1844; Daniel Restrepo, *La Compañía de Jesús en Colombia* (Bogotá, 1940), 162–65.

71. Mecham, *Church and State*, 120.

72. Restrepo, *La Compañía de Jesús*, 400–2.

73. J. León Helguera, "The First Mosquera Administration in New Granada, 1845–1849" (Ph.D. diss., University of North Carolina, 1958), 220.

74. Ibid., 225.

75. *Gaceta de la Nueva Granada*, March 18, 1844; Restrepo Canal, *La Nueva Granada*, 2:416.

76. Gibson, *Constitutions of Colombia*, 185–86.

77. *Gaceta de la Nueva Granada*, March 18, 1844.

78. *El Constitucional de Cundinamarca*, January 19, 1845.

79. Ibid. Acevedo's allegation that the Indians were cannibalistic should be regarded as rhetorical flourish. There is no evidence that the Llanos Indians engaged in this practice.

80. The Territory of Guanacas included the region known as "Tierradentro," formerly divided between the Provinces of Neiva and Popayán. The island of San Andrés was formerly a canton in the Province of Cartagena, and Raposo had been part of the Province of Buenaventura. *Cod. nac.* 13:68 and 14:49; Helguera, "First Mosquera Administration," 74, 105.

81. *Gaceta de la Nueva Granada*, March 25, 1847; *Gaceta Oficial*, May 4, 1848.

82. *Gaceta Oficial*, May 4, 1848.

83. *Gaceta de la Nueva Granada*, December 21, 1845.

84. Ganuza, *Monografía de las misiones vivas*, 2:315–21.

85. Ibid., 2:325.

86. *Gaceta Oficial*, May 4, 1848.

87. For an excellent summary of the secularization process in northern Mexico, see David Weber, *The Mexican Frontier, 1821–1846: The American Southwest under Mexico* (Albuquerque, 1982), 43–68.

88. *Gaceta Oficial*, April 5, 1850.

Chapter 3

1. Safford, *Ideal of the Practical*, 43.
2. Charles W. Bergquist, *Coffee and Conflict in Colombia, 1886–1910* (Durham, 1978), 7. Although Bergquist concedes that a "fraction of the Conservative party" shared the values of the Liberals, other historians have rejected his economic interpretation of party conflict as overly simplistic. See Delpar, *Red against Blue*, 158–59.
3. Bergquist, *Coffee and Conflict*, 11–12.
4. Delpar, *Red against Blue*, 8.
5. Bergquist, Coffee and Conflict, 9.
6. Luis Eduardo Nieto Arteta, *Economía y cultura en la historia de Colombia* (Bogotá, 1941), 280. Cinchona is a genus of evergreen trees and shrubs of the madder family, and about seventy different species are native to the Andes from Colombia to Peru. The bark of several species is the source of a bitter alkaloid drug known as quinine. In pre-Columbian times, the Peruvian Indians were aware of the bark's medicinal qualities, and it was first introduced in Europe in 1638 by the Condesa Cinchón, wife of a Spanish viceroy of Peru, who used it to cure herself of malaria. The Jesuits propagated the bark in the form of powders, extracts, and infusions, but for many years conservative medical authorities opposed quinine treatment for malaria. After 1820, when pure quinine could be isolated from the bark, its use rapidly gained favor. Today, it has largely been replaced by synthetic compounds such as Atabrine.
7. Ibid.
8. Safford, *Ideal of the Practical*, 43, 188–92. For an excellent comprehensive study of Colombia's economy in the nineteenth century, see José Antonio Ocampo, *Colombia y la economía mundial, 1830–1910* (Bogotá, 1984).
9. Julio Londoño, *Integración del territorio colombiano* (Bogotá, 1967), 289–91.
10. Julio Londoño, ed., *Albúm de la comisión corográfica* (Bogotá, 1953), 10; Safford, *Ideal of the Practical*, 126. Congress created five new provinces in the 1840s—Túquerres and Barbacoas in 1846; Tundama, Chiriquí, and Ocaña in 1849—to bring the total to twenty-five.
11. Between 1855 and 1857, New Granada consolidated its twenty-five provinces into eight states: Panama, Antioquia, Santander, Cauca, Cundinamarca, Boyacá, Bolívar, and Magdalena.
12. Londoño, *Albúm*, 12–13.
13. Ibid., 20.
14. Codazzi, *Geografía física*, 3:376–86.
15. *Gaceta Oficial*, February 4, 1852; Gómez, "Los censos en Colombia," 18–30.
16. Mathews, *Violencia rural en Venezuela*, 68, n. 77.
17. José Manuel Restrepo. *Esposición del secretario del estado*, February 25, 1834; *Gaceta de la Nueva Granada*, April 10, 1835, January 1, 1837; AHN, GC, vol. 14, fol. 620.
18. Pérez, *Geografía general*, 2:302–5.
19. *Gaceta Oficial*, November 16, 1852.

20. *Gaceta de la Nueva Granada*, May 8, November 26, 1843; AHN, GC, vol. 19, fol. 436.

21. *Gaceta Oficial*, November 19, 1852; November 10, 1850; April 22, September 23, 1849. See other descriptions of Moreno in Daniel Delgado, *Excursiones por Casanare* (Bogotá, 1910), 30; and Hiram Bingham, *Journal of an Expedition across Venezuela and Colombia* (New Haven, 1909), 159.

22. *Gaceta Oficial*, December 16, 1849. The Province of Tunja cast ninety votes for Cuervo and sixty-three votes for López in the 1848 election.

23. Enrique Ortega Ricaurte, *Villavicencio: 1842–1942: Monografía histórica* (Bogotá, 1943), 101–4. To check Melo sympathizers in various parts of the province, Colonel Melgarejo recruited former Venezuelan soldiers into his army, even though they did not have proper naturalization papers. Vice President Manuel Mallarino, in 1855, endorsed this action and granted naturalization status to three of these soldiers in gratitude for their services. AHN, GC, vol. 20, fols. 356–57.

24. In his analysis of the election of 1856, Bushnell notes that voter participation was highest in Tunja (71 percent), followed by Casanare (66 percent), basing his calculations on the population figures reported in the 1851 census. Given the thin and widely dispersed population of Casanare, its high voter turnout is particularly implausible unless the census data had been undercounted. Bushnell concludes that if fraud was a factor, both Liberal and Conservative candidates benefited, and fraud was not a dominant characteristic of the electoral process as a whole. David Bushnell, "Voter Participation in the Colombian Election of 1856," HAHR, 51:2 (May 1971):244–45.

25. When abolition was approved on May 21, 1851, there were only two black slaves in the entire province of Casanare. AHN, GC, vol. 19, fol. 914.

26. AHN, GC, vol. 18, fol. 918–25.

27. AHN, GC, vol. 18, fol. 700–714.

28. Safford, *Ideal of the Practical*, 136; Ospina Vásquez, *Industria y protección*, 197; Margarita González, "Las rentas del estado," in MANUAL 2:408.

29. *Gaceta Oficial*, November 19, 1852.

30. AHN, GC, vol. 19, fol. 127.

31. *Gaceta Oficial*, November 19, 1852.

32. Mecham, *Church and State*, 121. Mosquera died in Marseilles, France, on December 10, 1853. Mecham adds that he "was unquestionably one of the outstanding prelates of Latin America and his loss to New Granada, not alone to the Church of that republic, was irreparable."

33. Ibid., 123.

34. AHN, GC., vol. 18, fol. 848.

35. *Cod. nac.*, 8:251–53.

36. AHN, GC, vol. 14, fol. 179.

37. Eugenio Ayape, "Misiones de Casanare," BHA 36 (1949):784; Ganuza, *Monografía de las misiones vivas*, 2:340–46.

38. Ganuza, *Monografía de las misiones vivas*, 2:350–54; Restrepo Posada, *Arquidiócesis de Bogotá*, 2:382–84.

39. Daniel Valois Arce, *Reseña histórica sobre los límites de Colombia y Venezuela* (Medellín, 1970), 32.

40. Mathews, *Violencia rural en Venezuela*, 83.

41. Ibid., 84–85.

42. José Antonio Páez, *Autobiografía del General Páez*, 2 vols. (Caracas, 1975), 2:284.

43. Laureano Vallenilla Lanz, *Cesarismo democrático*, 4th ed. (Caracas, 1961), 118–21; Mathews, *Violencia rural en Venezuela*, 84.

44. AHN, GC, vol. 17, fol. 271.

45. *Gaceta de la Nueva Granada*, November 24, 1839; Restrepo, *Historia de la Nueva Granada*, 1:151; Páez, *Autobiografía*, 2:285.

46. Restrepo, *Historia de la Nueva Granada*, 1:211; *Gaceta de la Nueva Granada*, February 14, 1841.

47. AHN, GC, vol. 19, fol. 545.

48. Pérez, *Geografía general*, 2:338.

49. AHN, GC, vol. 19, fol. 627.

50. Mathews, *Violencia rural en Venezuela*, 88, 176.

51. AHN, GC, vol. 14, fol. 360.

52. AHN, GC, vol. 14, fol. 368.

53. *Gaceta Oficial*, April 24, 1852; Joaquín Díaz Escobar, *Bosquejo estadístico de la región oriental de Colombia* (Bogotá, 1879), 9–10.

54. Rafael Gómez Picón, *Orinoco, río de libertad* (Madrid, 1953), 453.

55. Valois Arce, *Reseña histórica*, 45.

56. *Gaceta Oficial*, June 17, 1857.

57. Delpar, *Red against Blue*, 33.

58. AC, Senado (1869), vol. 4, fol. 210.

59. AHN, GB, vol. 2, fol. 360.

60. *El Constitucional de Cundinamarca*, January 19, 1845; Rufino Gutiérrez, *Monografías*, 2 vols. (Bogotá, 1920, 1921), 1:60; Joaquín Paredes Cruz, *Departamento del Meta* (Villavicencio, 1961), 131.

61. *El Constitucional de Cundinamarca*, January 19, 1845.

62. *Gaceta de la Nueva Granada*, May 17, 1846. A *fanegada* is a land measure equal to about 1.6 acres.

63. Ortega Ricaurte, *Villavicencio*, 82.

64. *Gaceta Oficial*, June 23, 1850.

65. Ortega Ricaurte, *Villavicencio*, 83. At the same time, the legislature erected Cumaral into a *distrito parroquial* and renamed it Serviez.

66. *El Constitucional de Cundinamarca*, August 26, 1852.

67. Ortega Ricaurte, *Villavicencio* 96–98; Ramón Guerra Azuola, "Apuntamientos de Viaje," BHA 4:43 (January 1907): 424; *El Constitucional de Cundinamarca*, June 26, 1852.

68. For example, in 1843 the vecinos of Cáqueza contributed 206 pesos to improve the road. AHN, GB, vol. 11, fol. 426.

69. *El Constitucional de Cundinamarca*, October 30, 1852.

70. At Guerra Azuola's death, his heirs found among his papers an album containing maps, illustrations, and accounts of his travels through New Granada between 1853 and 1860, including a report of his participation in the civil war of 1860 as aide-de-camp to Conservative General Joaquín Paris. The album was presented to the Academia Nacional de Historia and published in installments in the

Boletín de Historia y Antigüedades, 1906–1907. The section dealing with his trip to the Meta River appeared in BHA 4:43 (January 1907):415–30.

71. Guerra Azuola, "Apuntamientos de Viaje," 416. A league is a measure of distance equal to 3.5 miles.

72. Ibid., 417.

73. Ibid., 419.

74. Ibid., 421.

75. Ibid., 420–21.

76. Codazzi, *Geografía física,* 3:396.

77. Ibid., 449.

78. Marco Palacios, *Coffee in Colombia, 1850–1970* (Cambridge, Engl., 1980), 29.

79. Delpar, *Red against Blue,* 49–50.

80. Miguel Triana, *Al Meta* (Bogotá, 1913), 123.

81. *Eco de Oriente* (Villavicencio), October 15, 1918; "Los colonizadores del Llano," *Revista Pan,* no. 15 (Bogotá, 1942), 149.

82. Joaquín Ospina, *Diccionario biográfico y bibliográfico de Colombia,* 3 vols. (Bogotá, 1939), 3:421–22; Raquel Angel de Flórez, *Conozcamos el Departamento de Meta,* 3 vols. (Bogotá, 1962–63), 2:73–75; Luis de Greiff, *Semblanzas y comentarios* (Bogotá, 1942), 107–12.

83. Emiliano Restrepo, *Una excursión al territorio de San Martín* (Bogotá, 1957), 9.

84. *Diario Oficial,* May 17, 1870; Martin, "Exploration in Colombia," 626.

85. Catherine LeGrand, *Frontier Expansion and Peasant Protest in Colombia, 1830–1936* (Albuquerque, 1985), xvi.

Chapter 4

1. José de la Vega, *La federación en Colombia: 1810–1912* (Madrid, 1916), 256.

2. Other historians, besides de la Vega, who minimize the achievements of the Federation Era are Henao and Arrubla, *Historia de Colombia;* and Nieto Arteta, *Economía y cultura.* Antonio Pérez Aguirre, *Los radicales y la regeneración* (Bogotá, 1941); and Eduardo Rodríquez Piñeres, *El olimpo radical* (Bogotá, 1950), offer a more positive view. Jaime Jaramillo Uribe gives a succinct summary of the debate in his "Etapas y sentido de la historia de Colombia," in Mario Arrubla, et al., *Colombia Hoy,* 10th ed. (Bogotá, 1985), 48–49.

3. Gibson, *Constitutions of Colombia,* 273–96; Delpar, *Red against Blue,* 13.

4. Miguel Puentes, *Historia del partido liberal colombiano,* 2d ed. (Bogotá, 1961), 237.

5. Gibson, *Constitutions of Colombia,* 292–93. As discussed in chapter 2, the Constitution of 1843 was the first charter that envisioned the establishment of national territories in regions thinly populated and separated by great distances from Bogotá. Although Article 47 of the Constitution of 1853 stated that "the territorial division of Goajira, Caquetá and others not inhabited by civilized persons may be organized and governed by special laws," no futher steps were taken

until after the promulgation of the Constitution of 1863. See Plazas Olarte, *Los territorios nacionales*, 131–35.

6. The Territory of Bolívar, not to be confused with the State of Bolívar, was carved out of the southwest portion of the State of Santander and included all of the region of Carare and part of Opón. The principal towns at the time were Bolívar and Landázuri. Manuel A. Zamora, *Guía de Colombia* (Bogotá, 1907), 57; Anibal Galindo, *Estadística de Colombia* (Bogotá, February 1876), 104–12.

7. *Cod. nac.* 23:375–81.

8. Ibid. 23:414–25.

9. *Diario Oficial*, February 1, 1870.

10. *Memoria del Ministerio del Gobierno* (hereafter cited as MMG), 1874, 51.

11. MMG, 1881, 78. In *Rafael Núñez and the Politics of Colombian Regionalism, 1863–1886* (Baton Rouge, 1985), James Park points out that the Radicals who dominated the national government between 1867 and 1877 represented Cundinamarca, Boyacá, and Santander and that these states received the lion's share of economic attention in that period. This factor may also explain the preferential treatment given to the eastern frontier vis-à-vis the other territories (p. 33).

12. Among them were Carlos V. Michelsen, Nicolas Pardo, Antonio Muñoz, Ernst Röthlisberger, Edouard André, Alfred Hettner, and Emiliano Restrepo.

13. *Cod. nac.* 21:104.

14. *Memoria del Ministerio de Hacienda y Fomento* (hereafter cited as MMHF), 1869–70, 53.

15. *Diario Oficial*, March 14, 1871.

16. *Diario Oficial*, January 13, 1870; March 6, 1871.

17. The original specifications for the bridge were drawn up by a North American engineer named Hurbult, who was the son of the U.S. minister to Bogotá in 1869. Albelardo Ramos, "Puente de Fierro sobre el Río Negro," *Anales de Ingeniería* (Bogotá), no. 9 (April 1, 1888), 258.

18. Nicolas Pardo, *Correría de Bogotá al Territorio de San Martín* (Bogotá, 1875), 4–12.

19. *Memoria del Ministerio de Fomento* (hereafter cited as MMF), 1881, 37–38.

20. MMF, 1884, 76.

21. Ibid.

22. According to Safford, the Colombian engineering society in Bogotá blamed the collapse of the bridge on the errors of Hurbult, who designed it, rather than González Vásquez, who erected it. Another article in the *Anales de ingeniería* suggested that the fiasco was caused by the vibrations set up by the passage of a disorderly herd of cattle (*Ideal of the Practical*, 221). When Miguel Triana passed by the ruined bridge in 1912 he was told that players of *tejo*—a game something like horseshoes and played widely in Colombia—had taken the screws out of the columns that supported the bridge to use as quoits, weakening the structure so that when cattle passed over it, it collapsed (*Al Meta*, 22).

23. Ernst Röthlisberger, *El Dorado* (Bogotá, 1963), 228–29.

24. *Informe*, Prefect of San Martín, 1875, in MMG, 1876, 9; *Informe*, Prefect of San Martín, 1879, in MMG, 1880, 86.

25. *Diario Oficial*, May 17, 1870. In January 1871, Carlos U. Michelsen and A. Saénz rode along the Colombia–Uribe trail and were favorably impressed. See their *Informe de los exploradores del Territorio de San Martín, exposición nacional*, July 20, 1871 (Bogotá, 1871).

26. *Diario Oficial*, April 30, 1874; *Informe*, Prefect of Casanare, 1877, in MMG, 1878, 98.

27. Alfred Hettner, *Viajes por los Andes Colombianos 1882–1884*, trans. Heinrich Henk (Bogotá, 1976), 317–18.

28. Julio Londoño Paredes, *Derecho territorial de Colombia* (Bogotá, 1973), 72–73.

29. Valois Arce, *Reseña histórica*, 50–53.

30. MMF, 1881, 55; MMF, Bogotá, 1882, 27.

31. MMHF, 1871, 150.

32. "Los colonizadores del Llano," 150.

33. Valois Arce, *Reseña histórica*, 81.

34. José Bonnet, *Comercio oriental por el Río Meta* (Bogotá, 1884), 10.

35. *Anales del Senado*, Series 2, no. 107, August 7, 1884.

36. *El Diario Nacional* (Bogotá), February 10, 1917.

37. Safford, *Ideal of the Practical*, 42.

38. Salvador Camacho Roldán, *Escritos varios*, 3 vols. (Bogotá, 1893), 2:259–62.

39. Ibid., 2:263–69.

40. *Cod. nac.* 25:450–54.

41. MMHF, 1874, 69.

42. José Francisco Bayón, *Inmigración a los Llanos de Casanare y San Martín* (Bogotá, 1881).

43. In 1882, Felipe Pérez wrote, "We must not expect that people from the Andes will come to the Llanos knowing they will die of fevers as soon as they arrive. . . . The immigrants will have to be Venezuelans, savages, or Africans who will dominate the plains whose rough grasses sicken large numbers of animals that try to eat them." *Geografía general*, 304.

44. Camejo, *Breves apuntaciones*, 24.

45. *El Propagador* (Nunchía), April 26, 1918, 102.

46. *Informe*, Prefect of Casanare, 1872, in MMG, 1873, 16; Díaz Escobar, *Bosquejo estadístico*, 39.

47. Camejo, *Breves apuntaciones*, 92, 40.

48. Delgado, *Excursiones por Casanare*, 83.

49. *Informe*, Prefect of San Martín, 1875, in MMG, 1876, 15.

50. Hetter, *Viajes*, 279.

51. Camacho Roldán, "La región oriental," in *Escritos varios*, 3:647–54.

52. Anibal Galindo, *Anuario estadístico de Colombia, 1876* (Bogotá, 1876), 20.

53. *Informe presentado por la Comisión Militar a cargo del General Rafael Ortiz* (Bogotá, 1888), 10–12.

54. Catherine LeGrand, "Labor Acquisition and Social Conflict on the Colombian Frontier, 1850–1936," *Journal of Latin American Studies* 16 (May 1984), 37–38, n. 25.

55. William Paul McGreevey, *An Economic History of Colombia, 1845–1930* (Cambridge, Engl. 1971), 129.

56. *Cod. nac.* 23:414–25.

57. Pérez, *Geografía general*, 332–33.

58. *Cod. nac.* 27:119–22.

59. *Informe*, Prefect of Casanare, 1880 in MMG, 1881, 96.

60. LeGrand, *Frontier Expansion*, 213, footnote 38.

61. *Informe*, Prefect of Casanare, 1882, in MMG, 1883, 23–24.

62. Restrepo, *Una excursión al territorio*, 111.

63. Ibid., 179–82.

64. Ibid., 42; Gutiérrez, *Monografías*, 1:62; *Eco de Oriente* (Villavicencio), October 15, 1918. LeGrand notes that the dispute over the Apiay community was not unique, since hacendados wishing to expand their domain often resorted to partition suits (*juicios de partición*). Partition suits were initiated by a number of joint tenants (*comuneros*) who owned a tract of land in common (an *indiviso*) as the consequence of a land grant, inheritance, or the purchase of shares. The object of the suit was to divide the property legally and to mark the individual portions of each part-owner. *Frontier Expansion*, 54.

65. Restrepo, *Una excursión al territorio*, 174–75.

66. *Informe presentado*, 9–11. "List of Public Land Grants, 1828–1931," in *Memoria del Ministro de Industrias al Congreso Nacional en las sesiones ordinarias de 1931*, vol. 5, 321, 355.

67. "List of Public Land Grants," 326–27.

68. *Cod. nac.* 23:381–82.

69. *Cod. nac.* 25:61–63.

70. *Cod. nac.* 27:36–40.

71. *Cod. nac.* 27:134–38.

72. *Informe*, Prefect of San Martín, 1875, in MMG, 1876, 10; *Informe*, Prefect of San Martín, 1876, in MMG, 1877, 20.

73. *Informe*, Prefect of Casanare, 1872, in MMG, 1873, 15–16.

74. *Informe*, Prefect of Casanare, 1875, in MMG, 1876, 8.

75. Informe, Prefect of Casanare, 1882, in MMG, 1883, 24–25.

76. Gutiérrez, *Monografías*, 61; Ganuza, *Monografía de las misiones vivas*, 2:373.

77. Ganuza, *Monografía de las misiones vivas*, 2:374.

78. Röthlisberger, *El Dorado*, 322.

79. Restrepo Posada, *Arquidiócesis de Bogotá*, 3:337–38.

80. Ibid., 3:404.

81. Ganuza, *Monografía de las misiones vivas*, 2:404.

82. Andrés Mesanza, "Nota biográfico," in Fr. José de Calasanz Vela, *Desde Villavicencio hasta San Fernando de Atabapo. Tirada aparte de America Española* (Cartagena) 2 (1935), 225–26. See also Jane M. Rausch, "José de Calasanz Vela: Frontier Priest," in Judith Ewell and William H. Beezley, *The Human Tradition in Latin America: The Nineteenth Century* (Wilmington, Del., 1989), 141–60.

83. Röthlisberger, *El Dorado*, 250.

84. Gutiérrez, *Monografías*, 61.

85. José de Calasanz Vela, "Visita de las poblaciones del Meta," *Anales religiosos* (Bogotá), 1 (1884), 351–53.

86. Vela, *Desde Villavicencio*.

87. *Cod. nac.* 27:36–40.

88. Galindo, *Anuario estadístico*, 1876, 214–15.

89. Röthlisberger, *El Dorado*, 237; Hettner, *Viajes*, 285.

90. *Diario Oficial*, December 21, 1868.

91. *Informe*, Prefect of San Martín, 1875, in MMG, 1876, 16–17.

92. Gutiérrez, *Monografías*, 64.

93. Informe, Prefect of Casanare, 1882, in MMG, 1883, 166.

94. MMG, 1882, 78.

95. *Informe*, Prefect of San Martín, 1873, in MMG, 1874, 3.

96. MMG, 1884, 43. Law 78 of May 23, 1873, attempted to control this tendency by prohibiting anyone from being elected a deputy or commissioner while serving as a prefect of a national territory. It also prohibited the president from appointing a sitting senator, representative, deputy, or commissioner as prefect. *Cod. nac.* 26:450.

97. Pérez, *Geografía general*, 321.

98. *Informe*, Prefect of Casanare, 1872, in MMG, 1873, 4.

99. Ibid.

100. MMG, 1882, 77–78.

101. *Informe*, Prefect of Casanare, 1874, in MMG, 1875, 10; *Informe*, Prefect of Casanare, 1877, in MMG, 1878, 96.

102. *Informe*, Prefect of San Martín, 1879, in MMG, 1879, 78.

103. *Informe*, Prefect of Casanare, 1877, in MMG, 1878, 102.

104. *Informe*, Prefect of Casanare, 1882, in MMG, 1883, 169.

105. *Informe*, Prefect of San Martín, 1875, in MMG, 1876, 4.

106. *Informe*, Prefect of San Martín, 1879, in MMG, 1879, 75.

107. *Informe*, Prefect of Casanare, 1872, in MMG, 1873, 7.

108. *Informe*, Prefect of Casanare, 1882, in MMG, 1883, 162.

109. *Informe*, Prefect of Casanare, 1872, in MMG, 1873, 6.

110. *Diario Oficial*, September 1, 1869.

111. *Informe*, Prefect of Casanare, 1874, in MMG, 1875, 4.

112. *Informe*, Prefect of Casanare, 1872, in MMG, 1873, 12; *Informe*, Prefect of San Martín, 4.

113. *Cod. nac.* 24:362; Pérez, *Geografía general*, 321. The National University was founded in 1868.

114. *Informe*, Prefect of Casanare, 1882, in MMG, 1883, 173.

115. *Informe*, Prefect of San Martín, 1882, in MMG, 1882, 101.

116. *Informe*, Prefect of San Martín, 1875, in MMG, 1876, 7–8.

117. AC, Senado, "Proyectos Negados," 1880, vol. 5, fol. 20.

118. Díaz Escobar, *Bosquejo estadístico*, 30. In explaining the causes of disease in Casanare, Díaz Escobar, like Codazzi, belonged to the "anticontagionist" school of thought. See chapter 3, n. 53.

119. Ibid., iv.

120. *Cod. nac.* 29:393–94.

121. AC, Senado, "Proyectos Negados," 1880, vol. 5, fol. 20.
122. MMG, 1879, 78.
123. Röthlisberger, *El Dorado*, 321–22.
124. Antonio Pérez Aguirre, *Los radicales y la regeneración* (Bogotá, 1941), 143.
125. A more complete description of these developments can be found in Delpar, *Red against Blue*, 133–57.
126. Quoted by José Araujo, in MMG, 1881, 33–34.
127. MMG, 1881, 37.
128. MMG, 1882, 77–78.
129. Pérez, *Geografía general*, 327.
130. MMG, 1884, 43.
131. *Cod. nac.* 31:105–6; *Anales del Senado*, May 17, 1884, 323; Gibson, *Constitutions of Colombia*, 314.
132. The Great Northern Railway was intended to link Bogotá with the lower Magdalena River by way of Boyacá and Santander. This ambitious construction project received lavish financial support during the presidencies of Manuel Murillo Toro and Santiago Pérez, but after 1878 was abandoned as too costly by Julian Trujillo. See Delpar, *Red against Blue*, 112–22.
133. MMG, 1881, 45.

Chapter 5

1. Park, *Rafael Núñez*, 269; Malcolm Deas, "Colombia, Ecuador and Venezuela, c. 1880–1930," in *The Cambridge History of Latin America* (hereafter cited CHLA), ed. Leslie Bethell, 5 vols. (Cambridge, 1986), 5:645. In 1986, the Banco de la República celebrated the one-hundredth anniversary of the Constitution of 1886 by underwriting a number of special publications, including *Colombia 1886: programa centenario de la constitución* (Bogotá, 1986), which includes short essays on many facets of Colombian life in 1886.
2. Park, *Rafael Núñez*, 189.
3. Plazas Olarte, *Los territorios nacionales*, 138.
4. *El Boyacense* (Tunja), July 10, 1890.
5. *Informe*, Prefect of Casanare, 1889, in *El Boyacense* (Tunja), April 5, 1889; *Informe*, Prefect of Casanare, 1890, in *El Boyacense* (Tunja), July 10, 1890.
6. *Ordenanzas expedidas por la asamblea departamental de Boyacá en sus sesiones de 1892* (Tunja, 1892), 82, 89; *Gaceta de Cundinamarca*, July 28, 1892.
7. AC, Cámara, "Asuntos Despachados," vol. 10, fol. 34.
8. "Laudo en la cuestión de límites entre la república de Colombia y los Estados Unidos de Venezuela," Madrid, March 16, 1891. Valois Arce reprints the entire text of this document in *Reseña histórica*, 69–72.
9. *Informe presentado*, 14.
10. Ibid., 12.
11. The manuscript of Vela's report is located in the Fondo Marco Fidel Suárez, in the Biblioteca Nacional. In 1988, the Fondo Cultural Cafetero commissioned anthropologist Alfredo Molano to retrace Vela's voyage, keeping a diary such as the Dominican had done one hundred years before. It then published a

new edition of *Desde VIllavicencio hasta San Fernando de Atabapo*, together with Molano's account under the title *Dos viajes por la orinoquia colombiana, 1889–1988* (Bogotá, 1988). For my research, however, I used the older edition published in installments in *América Española* (Cartagena), 2:225–40, 353–77 (1935); 3:150–78, 210–39, 304–24 (1936).

12. Vela, *Desde Villavicencio*, 3:212.

13. Ibid., 3:322–24.

14. *Anales del Senado*, September 29, 1892, 167.

15. *Diario Oficial*, October 1, 1892.

16. *Diario Oficial*, January 27, 1893.

17. *Diario Oficial*, September 6, 1897.

18. *Informe*, Prefect of Casanare, 1889, in *El Boyacense* (Tunja), April 5, 1889.

19. Ibid.

20. Jorge Brisson, *Casanare* (Bogotá, 1896), 43.

21. AHN, Ministerio de Gobierno (hereafter cited as MG), vol. 48, fol. 458.

22. AHN, MG, vol. 48, fol. 460.

23. AHN, MG, vol. 50, fol. 208.

24. *Informe*, Prefect of Casanare, 1898, in MMG 1898, 51.

25. Rafael Núñez was elected president for a six-year term in 1886, but he served for only about a year, departing for Cartagena in 1888 and leaving the government in the hands of the presidential designate, Carlos Holguín. While in retirement, he made his views known in Bogotá by means of telegrams and newspaper articles. In 1891, he was elected to another six-year term, but remained in Cartagena while Vice President Miguel Antonio Caro acted as chief executive. He was preparing to return to Bogotá when he died on September 18, 1894.

26. *Memorias del Ministerio de Justicia* (hereafter cited as MMJ), 1894, lxxx.

27. *Diario Oficial*, February 3, 1884.

28. MMF, 1890, xxii; *El Boyacense* (Tunja), April 6, 1893.

29. Mecham, *Church and State*, 126.

30. MMF, 1890, xxii.

31. The jurisdiction of the Roman Catholic church is organized in dioceses that are headed by bishops, but in practice, not all episcopal jurisdictions are dioceses and not all bishops have territories. Missionary territories which are subject to the Congregation of the Propagation of the Faith are territorially divided, but their officers are called vicars apostolic or prefects apostolic, according to the size and population of the territory. The vicariate is organized with the intention that it should grow to diocesan stature. One important difference between it and the diocese is that the pope can limit the powers of the vicar or prefect, who is in all other respects the effective bishop of his territory. The pope cannot limit the jurisdiction of a diocesan bishop. See John L. McKenzie, *The Roman Catholic Church* (New York, 1969), 40.

32. Ganuza, *Monografía de las misiones vivas*, 3:99–109.

33. Ibid., 3:143.

34. Ibid., 3:273. The Hermanas de la Caridad or Dominican Sisters of Charity of the Presentation of the Blessed Virgin belonged to a Dominican order founded in Tours, France, in 1697. The first sisters arrived in Bogotá in 1873 at

the invitation of Archbishop Vicente Arbeláez. By the 1920s they had established nearly seventy houses devoted to the work of the order: primary and secondary education, hospitals, asylums, and orphanages. See Henao and Arrubla, *Historia de Colombia*, 742.

35. Ibid., 3:358. In addition to Ganuza's three-volume history and the *Ensayo de gramática hispano-goahiva*, compiled in 1895 by Manuel Fernández and Marcos Bartolomé, three other Recoletos published works related to their experiences in Casanare. These were Santiago Matute, *Los padres Candelarios en Colombia o Apuntes para la historia*, 6 vols. (Bogotá, 1897–1903); Nicolás Casas y Conde, *Los hechos de la revolución en las misiones de Casanare* (Bogotá, 1900); and three books by Pedro Fabo—*Restauración de la Provincia de la Candelario* (Bogotá, 1911); *Idiomas y etnografía de la región oriental de Colombia* (Barcelona, 1911); and *El Dr. Navascués: Novela de costumbres casanareños* (Bogotá, 1904).

36. José Joaquín Ortega Torres, *La obra salesiana en Colombia: los primeros cincuenta años, 1890–1940* (Bogotá, 1941), 6, 144.

37. Carlos Cuervo Márquez, "El Llano" in Restrepo, *Una excursión al territorio*, 326.

38. Vela was buried under the main altar of the church in Uribe, and the tomb was marked by a marble stone inscribed: "Fr. José C. Vela was born August 27, 1840. He received Holy Orders on September 28, 1870. He served disinterestedly the parishes of the Llanos of San Martín for twenty-four years. R.I.P." This stone can now be seen in the principal cemetery of Villavicencio, where it was moved along with Vela's remains in the 1950s by Colombian authorities during La Violencia.

39. Ortega Torres, *La obra salesiana en Colombia*, 166–68.

40. Ibid., 191.

41. José Joaquín Ortega Torres, *La obra salesiana en los lazaretos* (Bogotá, 1938), 148.

42. Ortega Torres, *La obra salesiana en Colombia*, 195.

43. *Informe*, Intendant of San Martín, 1898, in MMG, 1898, 5.

44. Valois Arce, *Reseña histórica*, 79–88.

45. *Diario Oficial*, January 16, 1891.

46. Brisson, *Casanare*, 130–31.

47. AHN, MG, vol. 47, fols. 110, 111.

48. Gómez Picón, *Orinoco*, 455.

49. Brisson, *Casanare*, 205–6; *Informe*, Intendant of Casanare, 1898, in MMG, 1989, 46–50.

50. Brisson, *Casanre*, 154, 305; Ortega Ricuarte, *Villavicencio*, 128.

51. *Informe*, Intendant of Casanare, 1904, in MMG, 1904, 148; AHN, Baldíos, vol. 18, fol. 397; vol. 19, fol. 235; *Informe*, Intendant of Casanare, 1898, in MMG, 1898, 46–50.

52. In February 1923, the Ministry of Public Works signed a contract with José Nieto, by which the latter promised to establish navigation of the Meta and adjoining rivers with ships with a capacity of three to five tons run by competent people. There is no evidence that Nieto was able to fulfill this commitment. See *El Espectador*, February 11, 1923.

53. Safford, *Ideal of the Practical*, 189.

54. Juan de Dios Tavera B., *Eco de Oriente* (Bogotá, 1879), 1–11; Safford, *Ideal of the Practical*, 191.

55. AC, Cámara, "Asuntos Despachados," vol. 11, fol. 155.

56. AC, Cámara, "Asuntos Despachados," vol. 11, fol. 153.

57. Peregrino Ossa V., *Geografía de la intendencia nacional del Meta* (Bogotá, 1937), 81.

58. MMF, 1890, xxiv.

59. Brisson, *Casanare*, 309. After submitting his report, Brisson continued to travel through Casanare, and in one instance, he served as a member of a judicial inquiry that was investigating the suspicious drowning of the alcalde of Trinidad, Luis María Hernández. In 1896, he published his observations from these excursions in the book cited above, which he optimistically dedicated to "His excellency sr. don M.A. Caro, illustrious initiator and protector of the progress and development of Casanare."

60. MMG, 1898, lvi.

61. Bergquist, *Coffee and Conflict*, 22. For a discussion of the cycles of quinine production see José Antonio Ocampo, *Colombia y la economía mundial 1830–1910* (Bogotá, 1984), 271–82.

62. Restrepo, *Una excursión al territorio*, 115; Flórez, *Conozcamos*, 75.

63. René de la Pedraja Tomán, *Los llanos: colonización y economía* (Bogotá, CEDE Documento 072, June 1984), 56.

64. Ibid., 55.

65. Ibid., 34. The sources for cattle censuses cited by de la Pedraja are as follows: 1825—*Gaceta de Colombia*, August 5, 1827; 1856—"Mapa corográfico de la provincia de Casanare. Levantado de orden del gobierno por el general Agustín Codazzi 1856" in AHYN, Sección Mapoteca No. 6, Mapa No. 14 V.C. 522; 1874—Oficina de Estadística Nacional, *Anuario estadístico de Colombia* (Bogotá, 1875), 131.

66. Ibid., 36–37; Restrepo, *Una excursión al territorio*, 155–59.

67. Delgado, *Excursiones por Casanare*, 101–2, 218.

68. de la Pedraja Tomán, *Los llanos*, 35.

69. John Rouse, *The Criollo: Spanish Cattle in the Americans* (Norman, Okla., 1977), 164.

70. de la Pedraja Tomán, *Los llanos*, 36.

71. Ortega Ricaurte, *Villavicencio*, 111.

72. de la Pedraja Tomán, *Los llanos*, 61.

73. Ocampo, *Colombia*, 376–89; Rollie E. Poppino, *Brazil: The Land and People*, 2d ed. (New York, 1973), 143.

74. Ocampo; *Colombia*, 381.

75. Restrepo, *Una excursión al territorio*, 213.

76. *Gaceta de Cundinamarca*, December 24, 1886; *Informe*, Intendant of San Martín, 1898, in MMG, 1898, 3.

77. *Gaceta de Cundinamarca*, June 7, August 16, and October 18, 1887. One of these grants was awarded jointly to Emiliano Restrepo and Manuel Restrepo H.

78. *Memoria del Ministro de Industrias*, vol. 5, 326–28.

79. de la Pedraja Tomán, *Los llanos*, 63.

80. AHN, Baldíon, vol. 8, fol. 71.
81. AHN, Baldíos, vol. 18, fol. 364.
82. Ocampo, *Colombia*, 388.
83. "Los colonizadores del Llano," 172.
84. AHN, MG, vol. 47, fol. 512.
85. *Informe*, Intendant of San Martín, 1898, in MMG, 1898, 12.
86. Ortega Torres, *La obra salesiana en Colombia*, 222–23.
87. Ibid., 225.
88. *Informe*, Intendant of San Martín, 1898, in MMG, 1898, 12.
89. Nohora Beatriz Guzmán Ramírez, "La expansión de la frontera económica en el pie de monte llanero, 1856–1904; el caso de Medina," in *Los Llanos: Una historia sin fronteras, 1° Simposio de Historia de los Llanos Colombo-Venezolanos* (Bogotá, 1988), 460.
90. AHN, MG, vol. 47, fol. 513.
91. AHN, Ministerio de Hacienda, vol. 15, fol. 354.
92. *Informe*, Intendant of San Martín, 1898, in MMG, 1898, 6.
93. AHN, Baldíos, vol. 12, fol. 8–9; vol. 18, fol. 1.
94. AHN, Baldíos, vol. 10, fol. 174.
95. *Eco de Oriente* (Villavicencio), October 15, 1918.
96. de la Pedraja Tomán, *Los llanos*, 21.
97. AHN, Baldíos, vol. 16, fol. 58; vol. 18, fol. 372.
98. AHN, MG, vol. 47, fol. 43. The term *montaña* was used in the Llanos to mean an impenetrable forest. H. J. Mozans, who traveled down the Orinoco and up the Meta to get to Bogotá in 1907, discovered what was meant by *montaña* when his party left the Humea River to begin the overland journey to Villavicencio by mule and horseback. He wrote: "During the first hour after starting we had to struggle through what the natives call the *montaña*. It had nothing mountainous about it, as the name would seem to indicate, but was a dark, nearly impervious wood, almost at a level with the waters of the Humea. In the dry season, I doubt not, the path through this forest would present no difficulty, but during the rainy season it was next to impassable. Everywhere there was deep, sticky mud and deeper pools and dirty stagnant water. Often our horses sank to the saddle-girths in the tenacious slime, and it was only by the greatest effort that they were able to extricate themselves. At times, where the mud and water were unusually deep we were forced for short stretches, to make our way through pathless forest. Then every step was impeded by branches and lianas and progress was next to impossible. Finally, with great difficulty for the animals and not a little danger to ourselves, we succeeded in effecting our exit from this terrible *montaña*, and before we were aware of it, we found ourselves on high and dry ground on the edge of a beautiful, smiling prairie of apparently limitless extent." *Up the Orinoco and Down the Magdalena* (New York, 1910), 201.
99. AHN, MG, vol. 48, fol. 378.
100. AHAN, MG, vol. 48, fol. 420.
101. AHN, MG, vol. 46, fol. 460.
102. AHN, MG, vol. 46, fol. 464.
103. *Informe*, Intendant of Casanare, 1898, in MMG, 1898, 36.
104. AHN, MG, vol. 53, fol. 755–56.

105. AHN, MG, vol. 45. fol. 500.
106. *Informe*, Intendant of San Martín, 1898, in MMG, 1898, 6.
107. Deas, "Colombia, Ecuador and Venezuela," 647.
108. AHN, MG, vol. 47, fol. 406.
109. AHN, MG, vol. 48, fol. 314.
110. Bergquist, *Coffee and Conflict*, 48–49.
111. There is no systematic account of the civil war of 1895 in the Llanos. This information is pieced together from Recoleto accounts in Ganuza, *Monografía de las misiones vivas*, 3:282–94.
112. AHN, MG, vol. 49, fols. 376–89, 438–50.
113. AHN, MG, vol. 49, fol. 418.
114. AHN, MG, vol. 49, fols. 548–49.
115. AHN, MG, vol. 49, fols. 391, 396.
116. AHN, MG, vol. 50, fol. 324; vol. 51, fol. 690.
117. AHN, MG, vol. 50, fol. 889.
118. MMG, 1898, 54.

Chapter 6

1. The best account of this period is Bergquist's *Coffee and Conflict*. For general surveys, see Deas, "Colombia, Ecuador and Venezuela"; Darío Mesa, "La Vida Política después de Panama," in MANUAL, 3:83–176; and Javier Ocampo López, *Historia básica de Colombia* (Bogotá, 1987), 257–72.
2. Delpar, *Red against Blue*, 158.
3. Deas, "Colombia, Ecuador and Venezuela," 647. There is considerable debate about the causes of the war. Bergquist argues that the unhappiness of Liberals and Conservatives was linked to the export–import sector, which opposed Regeneration mainly because of its statist economic policies and reliance on paper money, while Helen Delpar, among others, reaffirms the traditionally cited factors of Conservative exclusion of Liberals from public office, the onset of economic depression caused by a drop in coffee prices in 1896, the emergence of Rafael Uribe Uribe as a charismatic leader for those who favored war, and the installation of Cipriano Castro as president of Venezuela, who was sympathetic to the cause of the Colombian Liberals. See *Red against Blue*, 158–84.
4. Bergquist, *Coffee and Conflict*, 149.
5. Puentes, *Historia del partido liberal*, 486.
6. Quoted by Gonzalo España in *La guerra civil de 1885: Núñez y la derrota del radicalismo* (Bogotá, 1985), 111.
7. Brisson, *Casanare*, 67.
8. AHN, MG, vol. 53, fol. 543.
9. Delpar, *Red against Blue*, 178.
10. Pedro Fabo, *Liberaladas de una revolución* (Pamplona, 1914), 12–18; Casas y Conde, *Los hechos de la revolución*, 12.
11. AHN, MG, vol. 54, fol. 794; Ortega Torres, *La obra salesiana en Colombia*, 352.
12. Gonzalo Paris Lozano, *Guerrilleros del Tolima* (Bogotá, 1984), 35.

13. Bergquist, *Coffee and Conflict*, 163; Ospina, *Diccionario biográfico*, 3:537–38. The *Código de Maceo* is reprinted by Jorge Villegas and José Yunis, in *La guerra de los mil días* (Bogotá, 1978), 196–99.

14. Paris Lozano, *Guerrilleros del Tolima*, 36–37.

15. Quoted by Puentes, in *Historia del partido liberal*, 486.

16. Joaquín Tamayo, *La revolución de 1899* (Bogotá, 1975), 66.

17. Quoted by Guillermo Plazas Olarte, in *La guerra civil de los mil días* (Tunja, 1985), 175.

18. Tamayo, *La revolución de 1899*, 69.

19. Quoted by Rafael Serrano Camargo, in *El general Uribe* (Bogotá, 1976), 154.

20. Bergquist, *Coffee and Conflict*, 149.

21. Plazas Olarte, *La guerra civil*, 128.

22. Vincent Dunlap, "Tragedy of a Colombian Martyr: Rafael Uribe Uribe and the Liberal Party, 1896–1914" (Ph.D. diss., University of North Carolina, 1979), 162–63.

23. Bergquist, *Coffee and Conflict*, 163.

24. Charles W. Bergquist, "Coffee and Coffee in Colombia, 1886–1904: Origins and Outcome of the War of the Thousand Days," (Ph.D. diss., Stanford University, 1973), 316.

25. Tulio Arbeláez, *Episodios de la guerra de 1899–1903: campañas del general Cesáreo Pulido por su primer ayudante general* (Manizales, 1904), 6–32.

26. Ibid., 32.

27. Ibid., 35.

28. Dunlap, "Tragedy of a Colombian Martyr," 177; Serrano Camargo, *El General Uribe*, 199.

29. Rafael Uribe Uribe, *Documentos políticos y militares*, 4 vols. (Medellín, 1982), 4:325.

30. Plazas Olarte, *La guerra civil*, 160–61; Serrano Camargo, *El General Uribe*, 202.

31. Serrano Camargo, *El General Uribe*, 204–206; Tamayo, *La revolución de 1899*, 179–80; Uribe Uribe, *Documentos políticos*, 4:334–42.

32. Uribe Uribe, *Documentos políticos*, 4:343–44.

33. Ibid., 4:345–47.

34. The bitterness that each man felt for the other is well expressed in the tracts that they published after the war—*La razón de mi dicho* (Bogotá, 1904), by Vargas Santos; and *Querello* (Bogotá, 1904), by Uribe Uribe. One senses that Uribe Uribe's dislike for Vargas Santos was tinged with an antipathy against Llaneros. In a letter to A. J. Restrepo, written in Port-of-Spain, Trinidad, in May 1902, he described the Supreme Director in the following terms:

A grandfather of short stature, sanguineous and chubby; of habits so methodic, that he has to eat and sleep at certain hours, and if not, he is annoyed; a sworn enemy of the cold country and of sleepless nights; tireless as an *ombre* [Spanish card game] player; a friend of funny anecdotes and tertulias; dominated by a traditional physical and mental laziness, his spirit, like his body is pleased by swinging voluptuously and slowly in the hammock; and as a hotlander and Llanero, he is fatalistic, lax and apathetic. Quoted by Dunlap, "Tragedy of a Colombian Martyr," 179–80.

35. Bergquist, *Coffee and Conflict*, 186–87.

36. Ibid., 185; Arbeláez, *Episodios de la guerra*, 37–38.

37. *Informe*, Intendant of Casanare, 1904, in MMG, 1904, 142.

38. Ibid., 143. Amézquita's *Informe* is the only account I have been able to locate that discusses events in Casanare after May 1902.

39. An editorial in the Bogotá periodical *La Opinión*, on October 18, 1900, marked the first anniversary of the outbreak of the War of the Thousand Days with wry humor, by stating: "In one century we have suffered three international wars, fourteen general revolutions and ten partial revolutions and 300,000 Colombians have died. Unfortunately our national sport is war, just as England has horses and Spain bull fights." Cited in Jorge Villegas and José Yunis, eds., *Sucesos colombianos 1900–1924* (Medellín, 1976) (hereafter cited as SUCESOS), 15.

40. *El Nuevo Tiempo* (Bogotá), June 25, 1903 as cited in SUCESOS, 50. Bergquist notes that historians usually place the war's casualties at 100,000 deaths but adds that this figure "is no more than a guess." (p. 133).

41. Bergquist, *Coffee and Conflict*, 165.

42. *El Nuevo Tiempo*, on October 31, 1903, reported that there were rumors that separatists in Boyacá wanted to annex themselves to Venezuela. On March 15, 1904, it noted: "It is said and repeated with insistence that there are tendencies toward succession in Cauca, Antioquia and even in other sections of Colombia" (as cited in SUCESOS, 59, 70). Amézquita, in his informe of 1904, discounted the rumors that Casanare would secede and join Venezuela, "notwithstanding the scorn that the national government has for this region" (p. 143).

43. AHN, MG, vol. 54, fols. 799–801.

44. AC, Senado 1904, "Proyetos originarios en la Cámara," vol. 1, fols. 173–211.

45. MMG, 1904, 42.

46. AHN, MG, vol. 54, fol. 803.

47. Flórez, *Conozcamos*, 77.

48. "Los colonizadores del Llano," 149.

49. *Informe*, Intendant of Casanare, 1904, in MMG, 1904, p. 149.

50. Valois Arce, *Reseña histórica*, 90; AHN, MG, vol. 55, vol. 676; MMG, 1922, xlviii.

51. AHN, MG, vol. 454, fols. 545–51.

52. Casas y Conde, *Los hechos de la revolución*, 38. Fabo, in *Liberaladas de una revolución*, also recounts these events.

53. L. E. Nieto Caballero, among others, disputed the Recoletos' accounts of the rebels' behavior. In an article published in *La Linterna* (Tunja), July 10, 1914, he wrote, "In Casanare in 1900 the missionaries suffered a lamentable fate due to the persecutions of some revolutionaries, but far from this being the norm, they were an isolated case which escaped the vigilance and instruction of the Jefes of the revolution."

54. *Informe*, Intendant of Casanare, 1904, in MMG, 1904, 145.

55. Delgado, *Excursiones por Casanare*, 206–15.
56. Ortega Torres, *La obra salesiana en Colombia*, 299–300.
57. Ibid., 353.
58. Plazas Olarte, *Los territorios nacionales*, 147–48.
59. MMG, 1904, 210–27. In 1908, Delgado estimated the population of Casanare at sixteen thousand whites and Indians. See *Excursiones por Casanare*, 5.
60. *Informe*, Intendant of San Martín, 1904, in MMR, 1904, 159.
61. Bergquist, *Coffee and Conflict*, 223; Henao and Arrubla, *Historia de Colombia*, 763.
62. J. Fred Rippy, "The Dictators of Colombia and Venezuela," in A. Curtis Wilgus, *South American Dictators* (New York, 1963), 387; Eduardo Lemaitre, *Rafael Reyes: biografía de un gran colombiano*, 3d ed. (Bogotá, 1967), 269.
63. Mesa, "La Vida Política," 96.
64. Ibid., 117. Rippy, "Dictators of Colombia and Venezuela," 390. Reyes's other works were: *Viaje a España y Portugal* (Madrid, 1912); *The Two Americas* (New York, 1914) and *Notas de un viaje de Bogotá a la Patagonia y Tierra del Fuego* (Bogotá, 1917).
65. Bergquist, *Coffee and Conflict*, 242–46.
66. Henao and Arrubla, *Historia de Colombia*, 765. Bergquist offers a good but brief survey of the Reyes years. The best biography is the already cited *Rafael Reyes*, by Lemaitre. Two other flattering portrayals are by Baldomero Sanín Cano, "Administración Reyes" in his *Escritos* (Bogotá, 1977), 65–105; and José María Cordobés Moure, "Reminiscencias: Rafael Reyes Prieto," in BHA 4:44 (1907):449–509. None of these studies devote attention to events in the Llanos.
67. Cordobés Moure, "Reminiscencias," 456–62; Rippy, "Dictators of Colombia and Venezuela," 384–85.
68. Cited by Ricardo Sánchez Ramírez in *La reconstrucción nacional: estudio de la administración de Excmo. sr. gen. D. Rafael Reyes* (Bogotá, 1908), vi–vii. This volume contains the official *memorias* presented by Reyes' cabinet ministers.
69. Ocampo, *Colombia*, 384–86.
70. Luis Martín, *The Kingdom of the Sun* (New York, 1974), 241–42.
71. Valois Arce, *Reseña histórica*, 92–93.
72. Mecham, *Church and State*, 133; Antonio José Uribe, *Anales diplomáticos y consulares de Colombia*, 6 vols. (Bogotá, 1920), 6:432–39.
73. Delgado, *Excursiones por Casanare*, 14.
74. Nicolás Casas y Conde, *Colonización de Casanare* (Bogotá, 1905).
75. Gonzalo Uribe Villegas, *Los arzobispos y obispos colombianos desde el tiempo de la colonia hasta nuestros días* (Bogotá, 1918), 44.
76. Fabo, *Restauración*, 260.
77. Delgado, *Excursiones por Casanare*, 14.
78. Ibid., 206.
79. Ibid., 209.
80. Ortega Torres, *La obra salesiana en Colombia*, 354; *Bodas de plata misionales de la Compañía de María en Colombia: 1904–1929* (Villavicencio, 1929), 116; Flórez, *Conozcamos*, 104.
81. *Bodas de plata*, 112.
82. MMG, 1910, 19; Paredes Cruz, *Departamento del Meta*, 195; Oscar

Alfonso Pabón Monroy, "Restrepo," in *Trocha* (Villavicencio), no. 168 (December 1989), 18–19.

83. *El Nuevo Tiempo*, February 4, 1905, as cited in SUCESOS, 79–80.
84. Lemaitre, *Rafael Reyes*, 296. See also Ramón P. de Hoyos, *Reviviendo la historia* (Cartagena, 1945).
85. Ibid., 297.
86. Pinto, "División política," 244.
87. Londoño, *Integración*, 340–42.
88. Bergquist, *Coffee and Conflict*, 226.
89. *Diario Oficial*, February 11, 1905.
90. *Diario Oficial*, March 16, 1906.
91. Diario Oficial, July 17, 1907; MMG, 1922, lxix–lxxii.
92. Sánchez Ramírez, *La reconstrución nacional*, 25.
93. MMG, 1922, lxix.

Chapter 7

1. Christopher Abel, *Política, iglesia y partidos en Colombia* (Bogotá, 1987), 19. Good summaries of this era can be found in Deas, "Colombia, Ecuador and Venezuela," 641–84; Mesa, "La vida política," 33–178; and Jorge Orlando Melo, "La república conservadora," in *Colombia: Hoy*, 9th ed. (Bogotá, 1985), 52–101.
2. Abel, *Política*, 75–76. Abel is citing here Eduardo Rodríquez Piñerez, who wrote in 1918 that Colombia might be compared to the Austro-Hungarian Empire, in that it was not a country (*país*) but an administration (*administración*)." See his *Por tierras hermanas de Bogotá por Quito a la frontera del sur. Impresiones de un viaje* (Bogotá, 1918), 37; Londoño, *Integración*, 346–47; *Diario Oficial*, December 16, 1909.
3. Abel, *Política*, 319.
4. Deas, "Colombia, Ecuador and Venezuela," 650–51.
5. John Lynch, "The Catholic Church in Latin America, 1830–1930," in CHLA, 4:526.
6. Abel, *Política*, 34, 83.
7. Deas, "Colombia, Ecuador and Venezuela," 658.
8. LeGrand, *Frontier Expansion*, 92–93. See Carlos Uribe Celis, *Los años veinte en Colombia: ideología y cultura* (Bogotá, 1984), for an excellent social history of the 1920s.
9. MMG, 1910, 11.
10. Archivo Departamental de Boyacá (hereafter cited as ADB), *Informe del Gobernador de Boyacá a la Asemblea Departamental en sus sessiones ordinarias, 1911* (hereafter cited as Informe, Governor of Boyacá), 4.
11. Plazas Olarte, *Los territorios nacionales*, 153–55.
12. Londoño, *Integración*, 347.
13. AC, Senado 1913, vol. 3, fol. 8.
14. *Mensaje del Presidente*, José Vicente Concha, 1915, 22.
15. *Mensaje del Presidente*, Pedro Nel Ospina, 1923, 20.
16. Plazas Olarte, *Los territorios nacionales*, 156.

17. *Historia de las leyes expedidas por el congreso en el año de 1926*, 2 vols. (Bogotá, 1927), 2:482.

18. Plazas Olarte, *Los territorios nacionales*, 158.

19. Uribe, *Anales diplomáticos*, 6:432–39.

20. Martín, *Kingdom of the Sun*, 240–41; Victor Daniel Bonilla, *Servants of God or Masters of Men?* (Middlesex, 1972), 97.

21. *Conferencias episcopales de Colombia*, vol. 1 (1908–1953) (Bogotá, 1956), 263–66.

22. Abel, *Política*, 43; Antonio José Uribe, *La reforma administrativa* (Bogotá, 1917), 575. A copy of the Convenio of 1902, as it was renewed in 1928, is in Plazas Olarte, *Los territorios nacionales*, 241–44.

23. *Informe*, Intendant of Meta, 1928, in MMG, 1928, 499; MMG, 1921, 217.

24. Triana, *Al Meta*, 40. The two circuits were combined in the 1920s, with a single magistrate from the Bogotá judicial district residing in Villavicencio. However, the corregimiento of Uribe was part of the judicial district of Neiva. See, *Informe*, Intendant of Meta, 1928, in MMG, 1928, 402.

25. Triana, *Al Meta*, 40.

26. A complete list of the intendants of Meta and their terms of office can be found in Paredes Cruz, *Departamento del Meta*, 43–45.

27. *Informe*, Intendant of Meta, 1916, in MMG, 1916, 538; *Informe*, Intendant of Meta, 1917, in MMG, 1917, 273; *Informe*, Intendant of Meta, 1926, in MMG, 1926, 64.

28. Triana, *Al Meta*, 38.

29. *Informe*, Intendant of Meta, 1915, in MMG, 1915, 208.

30. *Informe*, Intendant of Meta, 1913, in MMG, 1913, 75.

31. Triana, *Al Meta*, 44.

32. *Informe*, Intendant of Meta, 1925, in MMG, 1925, 34.

33. *Informe*, Intendant of Meta, 1924, in MMG, 1924, 168.

34. *Informe*, Intendant of Meta, 1928, in MMG, 1928, 401.

35. This information has been gathered from several reports included in *Bodas de plata*.

36. Triana, *Al Meta*, 41.

37. Hamilton Rice, "Further Explorations in the Northwest Amazon Basin," *Geographical Journal* 44, 2 (August 1914):140. The Englishman Francis Trevelyan Buckland (1826–80) wrote about natural science for the general public. His book *Curiosities of Natural History* (New York, 1859) was widely read and included such topics as "A Hunt in a Horse-Pond," "Bats," and "The Cobra de Capello."

38. Maurice Dieres Monplaisir and Gabriel Capdeville, *Las misiones católicas en Colombia: informes de los años 1919, 1920, 1921, 1922, 1923* (Bogotá, 1921–1922), 76.

39. *Eco de Oriente* (Villavicencio), January 26, 1919.

40. Ibid., May 18, 1919.

41. Ibid., November 30, 1916.

42. Ibid., September 2, 1917; *El Diario Nacional*, September 20, 1917.

43. Raquel Angel de Flórez interviewed Padre Mauricio, when she was

gathering material for her history of the Department of Meta. When she mentioned his noticeable French accent, he curtly responded, "Why do you say that my accent is markedly French if I am sure that now it is completely llanero?" Flórez wrote, "Intelligent, energetic, frank, psychologist and honest, he himself told us, 'My tongue stings!'" *Conozcamos*, 2:72.

44. *El Tiempo*, April 25, 1923.

45. Ibid.

46. *El Diario Nacional*, February 15, 1919.

47. *El Tiempo*, May 8, 1923.

48. Ibid.

49. *El Tiempo*, December 1923, as cited in SUCESOS, 432.

50. *El Tiempo*, May 8, 1923; *El Espectador*, April 25, 1923.

51. *El Espectador*, June 21, 1923; *Informe*, Intendant of Meta, 1924 in MMG, 1924, 158.

52. *El Tiempo*, May 8, 1923.

53. *El Tiempo*, May 8, 1923 as cited in SUCESOS, 450–51.

54. *El Tiempo*, May 15, 1923; *El Espectador*, May 21, 1923.

55. Luis Eduardo Nieto Caballero met Montplaisir in 1931, while he was touring the Orinoco Region, and profiled his complex personality with the following words: "He is an interesting man. Extremely energetic, and fond of science, he has a printing press, laboratory, a meteorological observatory; he studies insects, examines plants, experiments with different crops; publishes a periodical, attacks Liberalism, directs the Conservative Party, organizes the elections, leads processions, smokes tobacco from morning until night; has a music band; visits schools, is affable when he wants to be, but is generally gruff, an enemy of bathing and other concupiscences; very short with visitors, ascetic in his lifestyle; concerned about aviation, the progress of the region and the church, to which he adds each year a thousand bricks. It is one of those edifices that one begins realizing that it will never be finished . . . I have only excellent memories of him not withstanding that I consider his work as a missionary incompatible (*muy poco de acuerdo*) not only with the needs of the Llano but also with its promises." *Vuelo al Orinoco* (Bogotá, 1935), 245–49.

56. *Mensaje del Presidente*, Carlos E. Restrepo, 1914, 59.

57. *Informe del Vicariato Apostólico de los Llanos de San Martín*, José María Guiot, August 20, 1916, 165; *Informe del Provicario Apostólico*, Gabriel Capdeville, February 2, 1918, 51.

58. *Informe*, Intendant of Meta, 1920, in MMG, 1920, 22.

59. *Informe*, Intendant of Meta, 1928, in MMG, 1928, 414.

60. *Bodas de plata*, 128.

61. Ibid., 137; *Informe*, Intendant of Meta, 1928, 494–95.

62. *Informe*, Intendant of Meta, 1928, in MMG, 1928, 408; *Informe*, Intendant of Meta, 1926, in MMG, 1926, 79.

63. *Informe*, Intendant of Meta, 1928, in MMG, 1928, 410.

64. Triana, *Al Meta*, 42.

65. Rice, "Further Explorations," 140.

66. *Informe*, Intendant of Meta, 1913, in MMG, 1913, 84–86.

67. Raymond B. Fosdick, *The Story of the Rockefeller Foundation* (New York, 1952), 31.

68. *Informe*, Intendant of Meta, 1917, in MMG, 1917, 277.

69. *Informe*, Intendant of Meta, 1919, in MMG, 1919, 2:111.

70. *Mensaje del Presidente*, Marco Fidel Suárez, 1920, 67; Kathleen Romoli, *Colombia: Gateway to South America* (Garden City, 1941), 302.

71. *Informe*, Intendant of Meta, 1925, in MMG, 1925, 38–39.

72. *Informe*, Intendant of Meta, 1928, in MMG, 1928, 486; *Informe*, Intendant of Meta, 1931, in MMG, 1931, 89

73. Omar Baquero, *Departamento del Meta: Historia de su integración a la nación 1536–1936*, Thesis, Departamento de Sociología, Universidad Nacional de Colombia, Bogotá, 1986, 94. Baquero concluded that Meta was the fastest growing region in Colombia between 1905 and 1938, based on his analysis of census figures presented by Alberto Pardo Pardo in *Geografía económica y humana de Colombia* (Bogotá, 1972), 61–62.

74. José María Guiot, *Vicariato Apostólica de los Llanos de San Martín*, Villavicencio, August 20, 1916, 170–77; *Bodas de plata*, 104–5.

75. *Bodas de plata*, 106.

76. LeGrand, *Frontier Expansion*, 99.

77. AC, Leyes, 1918, vol. 5, fol. 239.

78. *Informe*, Intendant of Meta, 1920, in MMG, 1920, 29.

79. *Mensaje del Presidente*, Pedro Nel Ospina, 1923, 8.

80. MMG, 1924, 14.

81. *Informe*, Intendant of Meta, 1928, in MMG, 1928, 499; *Informe*, Intendant of Meta, 1932, in MMG, 1932, 106–8.

82. LeGrande, *Frontier Expansion*, 97.

83. Ibid., 99–100.

84. Ibid., 101.

85. *Informe*, Intendant of Meta, 1924, in MMG, 1924, 169.

86. *Informe*, Intendant of Meta, 1927, in MMG, 1927, 76.

87. *Eco de Oriente* (Villavicencio), October 15, 1918; *Informe*, Intendant of Meta, 1928, in MMG, 1928, 479.

88. *Informe*, Intendant of Meta, 1928, in MMG, 1928, 475–77.

89. Peregrino Ossa V., "La ganadería en los llanos orientales," *Revista Nacional de Agricultura* 23:304–5 (September-October 1929), 96.

90. Ibid.

91. *Informe*, Intendant of Meta, 1913, in MMG, 1913; 82; *Informe*, Intendant of Meta, 1925, in MMG, 1925, 50.

92. *Eco de Oriente* (Villavicencio), June 10, 1919.

93. *Informe*, Intendant of Meta, 1925, in MMG, 1925; 41; *El Tiempo*, November 19, 1922.

94. *Informe*, Intendant of Meta, 1921, in MMG, 1921, 558. In July 1916, Francisco Arango U. came to Bogotá to protest an 8 percent tax that the government had just imposed on rubber. He told the editor of *El Diario Nacional* that he believed the tax would cripple rubber collection in Vaupés. See *El Diario Nacional*, July 10, 1916.

95. *Informe*, Intendant of Meta, 1928, in MMG, 1928, 469–71.

96. *El Nuevo Tiempo*, March 21, 1917. In 1891, Antioquia's government signed what proved to be a disastrous contract with Punchard-MacTaggart and Lowther. Not only did the firm fail completely to fulfill its promises to build a railroad, but it involved the department in speculations with bonds outside the country and brought lawsuits against both department and nation. After a long legal battle, a Swiss tribunal decided against Colombia, and the government had to pay a heavy indemnity to Punchard. See Gabriel Poveda Ramos, "Nuestra historia ferroviaría," in *Revista Antioqueña de Economía y Desarrollo 21*, (tercer cuatrimester 1986), 8.

97. AC, Senado "Proyectos," 1916, vol. 2, fol. 244.

98. *Eco de Oriente* (Villavicencio), September 14, 1916.

99. Ibid., September 28, 1919.

100. AC, Senado "Proyectos," 1916, vol. 2, fol. 244.

101. Alfredo Ortega, *Historia de los ferrocarriles colombianos*, 3 vols. (Bogotá, 1932), 3:254–60; Roberto Velandía, *Encyclopedia histórica de Cundinamarca*, 6 vols. (Bogotá, 1979), 1:325; *El Diario Nacional*, March 4, 1917, and March 6, 1917.

102. *El Nuevo Tiempo*, March 21, 1917.

103. *El Diario Nacional*, April 10, 1917.

104. Ibid., April 26, 1917.

105. *Ferrocarril del Meta* (Villavicencio), August 21, 1917.

106. Velandía, *Encyclopedia histórica*, I, 325; Ortega, *Historia de los ferrocarriles*, 3:260. In 1925, another bill was introduced in the Senate which would have authorized the Ministry of Public Works to study once again the feasibility of building a railroad from Bogotá to a port on the Meta. Vecinos from the municipios of Fosca and Choachí signed petitions supporting the plan and urging that the railroad be routed through their communities. The bill failed after passing first debate on October 15, 1925. AC, Senado, 1925, vol. 2, fol. 156.

107. *Memoria del Ministerio de Obras Públicas* (Bogotá, 1936), 78–80.

108. *Informe*, Intendant of Meta, 1925, in MMG, 1925, 41.

109. *Informe*, Intendant of Meta, 1918, in MMG, 1918, 354–55; *Lo que nos contó el abuelito: Villavicencio: 1842–1942* (Villavicencio, 1942), 58.

110. *Informe*, Intendant of Meta, 1933, in MMG, 1933, 67.

111. *Informe*, Intendant of Meta, 1928, in MMG, 1928, 507.

Chapter 8

1. *Informe*, Comisario Especial (hereafter cited as CE) of Arauca, 1921, in MMG, 1921, 560.

2. ADB, *Informe de Provincia de Arauca*, in Informe, Governor of Boyacá, 32–33.

3. Delgado, *Excursiones por Casanare*, 215–16; Triana, *Al Meta*, 152.

4. Jane M. Loy, "Elegance, Ecology and Egrets," *Américas*, 28:10 (October 1976):19–24.

5. Delgado, *Excursiones por Casanare*, 64.

6. *Informe de Provincia de Arauca*, 1911, 33.

7. Ibid.

8. Delgado, *Excursiones por Casanare*, 86.
9. Triana, *Al Meta*, 134.
10. *Informe*, CE of Arauca, 1912, in MMG, 1912, 64.
11. AC, Senado, 1913, vol. 7, fol. 138.
12. Max Carriazo, *Llanos orientales* (Bogotá, 1910), 64–67.
13. ADB, Informe, Governor of Boyacá, 1911, 5; Plazas Olarte, *Los territorios nacionales*, 153.
14. *Mensaje del Gobernador de Boyacá*, 1924 (Tunja, 1924), 23.
15. *Informe*, CE of Arauca, 1920, in MMG, 1920, 87–93.
16. MMG, 1924, 50–51.
17. Camejo, *Breves apuntaciones*, 32–33.
18. *Informe*, CE of Arauca, 1919, in MMG, 1919, II, 260; *Informe*, CE of Arauca, 1932, in MMG, 1932, 159.
19. MMG, 1911, 869; *Informe*, CE of Arauca, 1914, in MMG, 1914, 69–70.
20. MMG, 1916, vi–xii.
21. *Memoria del Ministro de Relaciones Exteriores*, 1916, 88.
22. MMG, 1916, xi–xii.
23. *El Diario Nacional*, July 18, 1916.
24. *El Trabajo* (Cúcuta), February 10, 1917.
25. Interview with Humberto's foster father, Germán Reyes in *El Nuevo Tiempo*, January 13, 1917.
26. Interview with Eduardo Carvajal, *El Nuevo Tiempo*, January 10, 1917.
27. Both Abadía Méndez in MMG, 1917, iv, and Concha in *Exposición del Poder Ejecutivo al congreso de 1917 y documentos sobre los acontecimientos de Arauca* (hereafter cited as *Exposición*) (Bogotá, 1917), 22, find Escallón guilty of indiscretion in sending the largest part of his force to the Llanos. A correspondent from Guasdualito wrote, "General Escallón not only did not continue the work of General Ortiz but paid no attention to the warnings to take adequate precautions." *El Trabajo* (Cúcuta), February 10, 1917.
28. *El Diario Nacional*, February 9, 1917.
29. Telegram: Luis Flórez to Concha, Guasdualito, January 9, 1917, in *Exposición*, 25.
30. *Gil Blas* (Bogotá), February 16, 1917. Romero later denied his involvement in a telegram dated Arauca, March 17, alleging that he had been falsely accused by Marco Torres Elicechea. See *Gil Blas* (Bogotá), April 2, 1917.
31. *El Diario Nacional*, May 29, 1917.
32. *El Espectador*, January 30, 1917; Interview with Zoilo Escallón, in *El Nuevo Tiempo*, May 31, 1917.
33. Telegrams: Santos to Dir. Gen. of the Policia Nac., Pore, January 7, 1917; Suárez to Abadía Méndez, Nunchía, January 8, 1917, *Exposición*, 17–21.
34. *El Diario Nacional*, December 19, 1916.
35. *Exposición*, 8.
36. *El Diario Nacional*, January 11, 1917.
37. Jesús García, "Informe del Jefe Civil y Militar, July 1917" (hereafter cited as IJCM), in *Exposición*, 30.
38. Jesús García R., "Informe a los Ministros de Gobierno y Guerra, June 1, 1917" (hereafter cited as IMGG), in *Exposición*, 47.

39. García, IJCM, 32.

40. Ibid., 36.

41. *Exposición*, 11.

42. Three unusual photographs appeared in *El Trabajo*, on April 14, 1917. Taken in mid-January in Arauca, they showed Humberto Gómez in military uniform as Supreme Jefe of Arauca; Eloy Sánchez, second in command; and Gómez's men passing in review through the Arauca City plaza.

43. *El Nuevo Tiempo*, January 13, 1917; *La Unión Conservadora* (Tunja), February 23, 1917.

44. *El Diario Nacional*, January 9, 10, 12; February 6; March 22, 1917.

45. Interview with Atilio D'Anello, *El Diario Nacional*, May 25 and May 28, 1917.

46. *El Diario Nacional*, July 18, 1917. Valentín Hidalgo described the above execution to the judge at Santa Rosa.

47. *El Diario Nacional*, May 29, 1917.

48. Reprinted in *El Diario Nacional*, July 2, 1917.

49. Reprinted in *El Diario Nacional*, July 17, 1917.

50. García, IMGG, 46; *Anales de la Cámara de Representantes*, December 22, 1917, 465.

51. Proceedings of the Chamber of Representatives as recorded by *El Nuevo Tiempo*. September 9, 1917.

52. *Exposición*, 12–13.

53. *Anales de la Cámara de Representantes*, December 22, 1917, 465.

54. *El Diario Nacional*, September 10, 1917.

55. *Anales de la Cámara de Representantes*, December 22, 1917, 465.

56. *El Diario Nacional*, September 21,1917.

57. *Memoria del Ministro de Relaciones Exteriores*, 1918, 75–76.

58. Ibid. In an interview with the author on February 16, 1976, former Colombian consul and Intendant of Arauca, Sr. Rogerio Guáqueta G., stated that Humberto claimed legal citizenship in Venezuela as well as Colombia, and for this reason he was never handed over to Colombian authorities. He lived in Venezuela until the statute of limitations had expired for his crimes. Then he returned to Cúcuta, where he died in the 1950s.

59. Reprinted in *El Diario Nacional*, July 27, 1917.

60. *Memoria del Ministro de Relaciones Exteriores*, 1917, 132.

61. Valois Acre, *Reseña histórica*, 102.

62. *Informe*, CE of Arauca, 1919, in MMG, 1919, 2:271–73.

63. *Informe*, CE of Arauca, 1923, in MMG, 1923, 222.

64. AC, Senado, 1919, vol. 6, fol. 271; *El Tiempo*, November 16, December 12, 1922; *Informe*, CE of Arauca, 1929, in MMG, 1929, 230.

65. *Informe*, CE of Arauca, 1913, in MMG, 1913, 89–91; *Informe*, CE of Arauca 1919, in MMG, 1919, 269.

66. *Informe*, CE of Arauca, 1914, in MMG, 1914, 64–66.

67. *El Deber* (Tunja), May 13, 1921; *Informe*, CE of Arauca, 1914, in MMG, 1914, 86; Emilio Laquére, *Informe de Prefectura Apostólica, Chita, May 6, 1918*, 33–39.

68. The Daughters of Charity of St. Vincent de Paul first came to Colom-

bia in 1882. Laquére, *Informe de Prefectura Apostólica de Arauca, Chita, May 12, 1920,* 115.

69. Laquére, *Informe de Prefectura Apostólica de Arauca, Chita, May 19, 1917,* 188–89.

70. Laquére, *Informe de Prefectura Apostólica de Arauca, Chita, May 12, 1920,* 120–22.

71. Ibid.

72. In 1922, Laquére reported thirty-one schools with 1,334 in the Apostolic Prefecture, but these figures were greatly out of line with his other reports. The 1926 figures listed here are from the *Informe,* CE of Arauca, 1926, in MMG, 1926, 93. See also Laquére, *Informe de Prefectura Apostólica de Arauca, May 19, 1922,* 116.

73. *Informe,* CE of Arauca, 1920, in MMG, 1920, 91; *Informe,* CE of Arauca, 1926, in MMG, 1926, 95; *Informe de Prefectura Apostólica de Arauca, May 19, 1922,* 59–62.

74. MMG, 1912, 58; *Informe,* CE of Arauca, 1914, in MMG, 1914, 61; *El Nuevo Tiempo,* July 21, 1917; *La Unión Conservadora* (Tunja), July 1917.

75. *El Nuevo Tiempo,* July 24, 1917.

76. *Informe,* CE of Arauca, 1919, in MMG, 2, 1919, 265; *Informe,* CE of Arauca, 1932, in MMG, 1932, 175.

77. AC, Senado, 1912, vol. 7, fol. 389; Carlos E. Restrepo, *Mensaje del Presidente, 1914,* 67.

78. Marco Fidel Suárez, *Mensaje del Presidente, 1920,* 24; *El Trabajo* (Cúcuta), May 17, 1917; *Informe,* CE of Arauca, 1926, in MMG, 1926, 98; *Informe,* CE of Arauca, 1919, in MMG, 1919, 266; *El Araucano* (Arauca City) no. 3 February 4, 1934.

79. *Informe,* CE of Arauca, 1929, in MMG, 1929, 226–31.

80. *Informe,* CE of Arauca, 1918, in MMG, 1918, 360.

81. Antonio Olivares, O.F.M., *Las ciconiiformes colombianas* (Bogotá, 1973), 61.

82. Rómulo Gallegos, *Dōna Bárbara,* trans. Robert Malloy (New York, 1948), 292.

83. Ibid., 293.

84. Ibid.

85. Carriazo, *Llanos orientales,* 20.

86. Ibid., 20–25.

87. Ibid.

88. *Informe,* CE of Arauca, 1919, in MMG, 1919, 4; Camejo, *Breves apuntaciones,* 36–37.

89. James Laver, *Taste and Fashion: From the French Revolution to the Present Day* (London, 1946), 123, 99; *Informe,* CE of Arauca, 1926, in MMG, 1926, 106.

90. Camejo, *Breves apuntaciones,* 37. See also Jane M. Loy, "Elegance, Ecology and Egrets," *Américas* 28:10(October 1976), 19–24.

91. *Informe,* CE of Arauca, 1926, in MMG, 1926, 105.

92. Ibid.

93. Peregrino Ossa V., "La ganadería en los llanos orientales," *Revista Nacional de Agricultura,* 23:303–4 (September-October 1929), 101–3.

94. Pantaleón Cortés, "La llanura de Arauca," *Revista Nacional de Agricultura,* 16:211–12 (January-February 1922), 195–99.

95. *Informe,* CE of Arauca, 1931, in MMG, 1931, 136; *El Araucano* (Arauca City), September 22 and 29, 1935.

96. *El Tiempo,* June 11, 1917.

97. *El Trabajo* (Cúcuta), October 21, 1917. See also AC, Cámara, 1917, vol. 7, fol. 235; and *Informe,* CE of Arauca, 1919, in MMG, 1919, 2, 267.

98. *La Linterna* (Tunja), January 18, 1918.

99. *La Unión Conservadora* (Tunja), March 22, 1918; Henao and Arrubla, *Historia de Colombia,* 842. A third candidate, José María Lombana, running as a Radical, polled 71 votes from Casanare, 0 from Arauca, and 24,041 nationally.

100. Alfredo Carvajal Sinisterra, "El petroleo del Llano," in *Llanos de Colombia* (Bogotá, 1986), 182.

Chapter 9

1. For example, the Fiscal Inspector, in his report of March 1918, recommended that Casanare be given special legislation or be made a national intendency because of its lack of revenues and the uniqueness of its customs. No action was taken on this recommendation. *El Boyacense,* April 9, 1918.

2. Medina R., *Geografía económica de Colombia,* 211–12.

3. The 1918 census figures for the municipios in Boyacá and Casanare are found in Medina R., *Geografía económica de Colombia,* 155–60.

4. *Informe,* Prefect of Casanare 1932, in *Mensaje del Gobernador de Boyacá a la Asamblea Departamental de 1932* (hereafter cited as MGB), 7–9.

5. Delgado, *Excursiones,* 16–19. On the *rosca* headed by Perdomo, see the exchange of letters in *La Linterna* (Tunja), April 28, June 9, July 28, and August 18, 1916, and *La Unión Conservadora* (Tunja), February 23, 1917. Támara had been capital in the nineteenth century on two previous occasions, 1842–43 and 1891–95.

6. Bingham, *Journal of an Expedition,* 178.

7. *Informe,* Prefect of Casanare 1923, in MGB, 1924, 5.

8. Triana, *Al Meta,* 206

9. Mozans, *Up the Orinoco,* 173.

10. *Informe,* Prefect of Casanare, 1928, in MGB, 1929, 74.

11. Gibson, *Constitutions of Colombia,* 343–45.

12. *Informe,* Prefect of Casanare 1929, in MGB, 1930, 17.

13. Plazas Olarte, *Los territorios nacionales,* 211.

14. Jesús García R., *Mensaje del Gobernador de Boyacá,* March 1, 1920, 10–13.

15. *Informe,* Prefect of Casanare 1938, in *Informe del Secretario de Goberno al Señor Gobernador del Departament* (hereafter cited as ISG), 1939, 57.

16. *Informe,* Prefect of Casanare, 1932, in MGB, 1932, 15.

17. *Informe,* Prefect of Casanare, 1923, in ISG, 1924, 4–10.

18. *Informe,* Prefect of Olmedilla, 1921, in MGB, 1921, 90.

19. *Informe,* Prefect of Nunchía, 1915, in MGB, 1916, 52.

20. *Informe,* Prefect of Nunchía, 1911, in MGB, 1911, 28–29.
21. *Ordenanzas expedidas por la Asamblea de Boyacá* (Tunja, 1911), 24–26; *Informe,* Prefect of Nunchía, 1914, in MGB, 1915, 52.
22. Medina R., *Geografía económica de Colombia,* 439–40.
23. *Informe,* Prefect of Casanare, 1929, in MGB, 1930, 21.
24. Plazas Olarte, *Los territorios nacionales,* 157; *Informe,* Prefect of Casanare, 1931, in MGB, 1931, 71.
25. *Informe,* Prefect of Casanare, 1923, in MSG 1924, 4; Medina R., *Geografía económica de Colombia,* 370. When Casanare became a national intendancy in 1972, Yopal was designated as its capital.
26. *Informe,* Prefect of Nunchía, 1914, in MGB, 1915, 50–52.
27. *Informe,* Prefect of Casanare, 1935, in ISG, 1935, 48–50.
28. *Informe,* Prefect of Casanare, 1921, in MGB, 1922, 11.
29. AC, Senado, 1920, vol. 8, fol. 353; Ley, 1929, vol. 1, fol. 220.
30. *Exposición,* 20.
31. Ibid., 25–26.
32. Ibid., 11.
33. *El Espectador,* January 18, 1917.
34. *La Unión Conservador* (Tunja), February 23, 1917.
35. *La Unión Conservador* (Tunja), April 13, 1917. Regretably, the Santos–Perdomo debate must be traced through *La Unión Conservador,* since the 1917 issues of *La Linterna* are missing from the Biblioteca Nacional collection, and I was unable to consult them in Tunja. A compilation of Santos's writings, *Danza de las horas* (Bogotá, 1969) includes some articles written in 1917.
36. *Informe,* Prefect of Nunchía, 1914, in MGB, 1915, 52; *Informe,* Prefect of Nunchía, 1915, in MGB, 1916, 35.
37. *Informe,* Prefect of Casanare, 1919, in MGB, 1920, 49–51; *Informe,* Prefect of Olmedilla, January 15, 1921, in MGB, 1921, 89; *Informe,* Prefect of Olmedilla, November 30, 1921, in MGB, 1922, 35.
38. Nicolas García Samudio, MGB, 1928, 5–6; *Informe,* Prefect of Casanare, 1929, in MGB, 1930, 14–15.
39. *Informe,* Prefect of Casanare, 1931, in MGB, 1931, 66.
40. *Informe,* Prefect of Nunchía, 1914, in MGB, 1915, 56.
41. *El Deber* (Tunja), May 13, 1921; *Revista de Misiones* 7:77 (October 1931,):449; *Revista de Misiones* 4:36 (May 1928):198–206.
42. Casanare, Vicariato Apostólico de Casanare, *Informe del Reverendo Padre Vicario Apostólico de Casanare,* 1919, 1920, Convento del Desierto, June 28, 1920, 104.
43. Ibid., 103; *Informe del Vicario Apostólico de Casanare,* Támara, January 29, 1921, 26; *Revista de Misiones* 4:36 (May 1928):198–206.
44. *Revista de Misiones* 7:77 (October 1931):446–451.
45. *Informe,* Prefect of Casanare, 1932, in MGB, 1932, 17.
46. Eugenio Ayape, "Misiones de Casanare," BHA 28:323–24 (September-October 1941):798; *Informe,* Prefect of Casanare, 1919, in MGB, 1920, 49–51; *Informe,* Prefect of Casanare, 1928, in MGB, 1929, 71–75.
47. *Revista de Misiones* 7:77 (October 1931), 447.
48. *La Linterna* (Tunja), March 17, 1916.

49. *Informe*, Prefect of Casanare 1935, in ISB, 1935, 46.

50. *Revista de Misiones* 7:77 (October 1931):446–51.

51. *Informe*, Prefect of Nuncía, 1916, in MGB, 1917, 36; *Informe*, Prefect of Casanare, 1938, in ISB, 1939, 74; *El Propagador* (Támara) 3:28, February 25, 1920; 3:31, June 25, 1920.

52. *Informe*, Prefect of Casanare, 1923, in MGB, 1924, 6.

53. *Informe*, Prefect of Casanare, 1932, in MGB, 1932, 19.

54. *La Linterna*, (Tunja), April 14, 1916.

55. *Informe*, Prefect of Casanare, 1928, in MGB, 1929, 72–73; *Informe*, Prefect of Casanare, 1929, in MGB, 1930, 27.

56. AHN, Ministerio de Industrias (hereafter cited as MI), *Correspondencia de Baldíos*, vol. 41, fol. 344.

57. AHN, MI, *Correspondencia de Baldíos*, vol. 50, fol. 428; vol. 55, fol. 165; vol. 58, fol. 461.

58. AHN, MI, *Correspondencia de Baldíos*, vol. 65, fols. 290, 296, 298.

59. *Informe*, Prefect of Casanare, 1929, in MGB, 1930, 24.

60. Eduardo Neale-Silva, *Horizonte humano: vida de José Eustasio Rivera*, 2d ed. (México, 1986), 139–40.

61. Conrado Zuluaga Osorio, *José Eustasio Rivera 1888–1988* (Bogotá, 1988), 99–101.

62. Neale-Silva, *Horizonte humano*, 131.

63. Ibid.

64. Ibid., 151.

65. Roberto Simón Crespi, "*La Vorágine:* Cincuenta Años Después," in Montserrat Ordóñez, *La Vorágine: Textos críticos* (Bogotá, 1987), 423.

66. Jean Franco, *The Modern Culture of Latin America* (Middlesex, Engl., 1970), 100.

67. A representative collection of these reviews can be found in *La Vorágine: Textos críticos*, ed. Montserrat Ordóñez Vila, cited above.

68. José María Samper, *Ensayo sobre las revoluciones políticas y la condición social de las repúblicas colombianas* (Paris, 1861), 91. It should be noted that beginning with Samper, costumbrista descriptions ignored the women of the Llanos, about whom almost nothing was written.

69. Ibid., 93.

70. Vergara y Velasco, *Nueva geografía de Colombia*, 683.

71. Ibid., 685–87.

72. José María Vergara y Vergara, *Historia de la literatura en Nueva Granada* (Bogotá, 1902).

73. Brisson, *Casanare*, vi.

74. Mozans, *Up the Orinoco and Down the Magdalena*, 202.

75. Ibid., 205.

76. Ibid., 130.

77. Phanor James Eder, *Colombia* (New York, 1913), 235. Writing in the same year, Miguel Triana, in *Al Meta*, also argued that the "centaur of old was disappearing in the Llanos," but he was referring to the Intendency of Meta and attributed the phenomenon to the influence of the press, telegraph, railroad, steamboat, and colonization from the highlands (p. 124).

78. Bingham, *Journal of an Expedition*, 113.

79. Vargas Vergara, cited by Eder, *Colombia*, 232.

80. The first novel about Casanare was *El doctor Navascués*, by Recoleto missionary Pedro Fabo. Fabo published the bok in Bogotá in 1904. A costumbrista work, it received mixed reviews and failed to attract much popular attention.

81. Simón Crespi, "*La Vorágine:* Cincuenta Años Después," 423.

82. José Eustasio Rivera, *The Vortex*, trans. Earle K. James (New York, 1935), 26.

83. Ibid., 99.

84. Ibid., 149.

85. Eduardo Zuleta Angel, *El Presidente López* (Medellín, 1966), 225–26.

86. "Los colonizadores del Llano," 145.

Conclusion

1. *Anales del Senado*, September 29, 1892, 167.

2. Luis Eduardo Nieto Caballero, *Vuelo al Orinoco* (Bogotá, 1935), 124–28.

Glossary

Two excellent guides of llanero vocabulary are María Teresa Cobos, "Del habla popular en el llano," *Boletín Cultural y Bibliográfico* (1966), 949–81; and "Vocabulario del Llanero," in Miguel Angel Martín, *Del folclor llanero* (Villavicencio, 1982), 180–208.

Aduana. Customs house.

Alpargatas. Sandals.

Arroba. Unit of weight, equivalent to about twenty-five pounds.

Baldíos. Public-domain land, ownership of which is vested in the nation.

Baquiano. Individual who knows the Llanos well.

Bayetón. Large woolen poncho.

Bongo. Dugout canoe fashioned from a single tree trunk, usually with a capacity for five or six persons.

Cachaco. Bogotano.

Caimán. Alligator.

Camino de herradura. Mule path.

Camino de rueda. Cart road.

Campesino. Peasant.

Caño. Narrow waterway originating in the Llanos, which moves with little velocity.

Capitanía. Unit of Indians ranging from 100 to 700 members, loyal to a single chief.

Carga. Unit of measure, equivalent to about six bushels.

Casa cural. Priest's house.

Casa municipal. Town hall.

Caserío. Small village.

Chucherías. Gewgaws.

Colono. Individual who farms or grazes cattle on public lands with no legal title to the territory.

Comisión. Posse.

Conuco. Garden plot.

Costumbrismo. Literary genre typified by an emphasis on aspects of local color and the customs of a specific region or locale.

Degüello. Slaughter; also, a tax on slaughtered animals.

Doctrina. Curacy.

Estero. Low, flooded area.

Fanegada. Land measure, equivalent to about 1.6 acres.

Fundación. Ranch with less than one thousand cattle.

Gamonal. Oppressive large landowner and local boss.

Ganadero. Cattleman, rancher.

Garza. Heron.

Hato. Ranch with more than one thousand cattle.

Jefe político. Chief administrative officer of a cantón.

Legua. League. A measure of distance equal to three and one-half miles.

Libra. Pound.

Millar. Measure of cacao, varying between 3.5 and 4 pounds.

Novillo. Young bull.

Palenque. Fortified hamlet.

Páramo. High-mountain, treeless plateau.

Párroco. Parish priest.

Peaje. Road toll.

Petaca. Trunk.

Quebrada. Gorge.

Ramal. Mountain spur.

Reducción. Settlement of Indians converted to Christianity.

Reducir. To bring Indians into submission.

Renguera. Rabieslike disease transmitted to cattle and horses by vampire bats.

Resguardo. Squadron of police or soldiers.

Savanas cautivas. Plains populated with cattle, free of forests.

Vara. Measure of length, equivalent to about thirty-three inches.

Bibliography

Archival Materials

ARCHIVO HISTÓRICO NACIONAL, BOGOTÁ

Established in 1868, this archive is a major repository for manuscripts from the sixteenth through the nineteenth centuries. The Sección de la República has a substantial amount of material concerning the Llanos. The documents are bound into volumes arranged in *fondos*, or collections, according to subject matter. Each document is indicated by fondo, volume, and folio number. The following fondos proved to be of greatest value:

Baldíos (1879–1898)
Curas y Obispos (1836–1857)
Gobernación de Bogotá (1832–1857)
Gobernación de Casanare (1836–1857)
Ministerio de Gobierno (1879–1898)
Ministerio de Hacienda (1879–1898)

ARCHIVO DEL CONGRESO, BOGOTÁ

This archive contains manuscripts concerning the activities of the Colombian Congress from 1819 to the present. The materials for each year are divided into three categories—Senado, Cámara, and Leyes—and are bound into separate volumes under the headings of Proyectos Pendientes, Peticiones, Informes de Comisión, etc. In 1937, Ernesto Esguerra Serrano published a two-volume *Indice general alfabético del Archivo del Congreso*. Using this index as a guide, I sampled, more or less at random, volumes with information concerning the Llanos between 1837 and 1927.

Published Documents

Two important categories of documents concerning the history of the Llanos are those published by the government and those concerning the church. Government documents include decrees and laws, presidential messages, *memorias* of ministers, congressional records, official newspapers, and censuses. By far the most useful sources for this study were the annual reports of the governors, intendants, prefects, and comisarios who administered Meta, Casanare, and Arauca between 1830 and 1930. These *informes* were published with the *memorias* of the secretaries or ministers of government, or, in the case of Casanare after 1909, with the annual messages of the governor of Boyacá. Church documents include accounts written by missionaries, histories of religious orders, annual reports of apostolic vicars and prefects, and official newspapers.

Most of these documents can be found at one of the three libraries in Bogotá. The Biblioteca del Ministerio de Gobierno has a complete collection of national and departmental laws and official newspapers. The Biblioteca Nacional has copies of everything listed above, but the catalogue is incomplete and dedicated persistence is necessary to locate the needed document. The holdings of the Biblioteca Luis Angel Arango are not as extensive, especially for the nineteenth century, but its catalogue is up to date and materials are easily consulted there.

The Archivo Departamental de Boyacá, located in the Casa de Don Juan de Castellanos in Tunja, has copies of departmental *ordenanzas* and decrees; *El Boyacense*, the official newspaper; and a complete collection of the annual *mensajes* of the governors.

I. GOVERNMENT DOCUMENTS

Archivo Santander, 24 vols. Bogotá, 1913–32.

Boyacá. *Informes del Gobernador*, 1905–36.

———. *Ordenanzas expedidas por la aseamblea departamental de Boyacá en sus sesiones de 1892*. Tunja, 1892.

Codazzi, Agustín. *Geografía física i política de las provincias de la Nueva Granada*. Publicaciones del Banco de la República, Archivo de la Economía Nacional, no. 24. Bogotá, 1959.

Codificación nacional de todas las leyes de Colombia desde el año de 1821. 34 vols. Bogotá, 1924–55.

Colombia. Comisión Militar. *Informe presentado por la Comisión militar a cargo de General Rafael Ortiz*. Bogotá, 1888.

———. *Exposición del Poder Ejecutivo al Congreso de 1917 y documentos sobre los acontecimientos de Arauca*. Bogotá, 1917.

———. *Historia de las leyes*. 14 vols. Bogotá, 1926–40.

———. Ministerio de Fomento. *Memorias*, 1880–94.

———. Ministerio de Gobierno. *Memorias*, 1823–1936.

———. Ministerio de Gobierno. División territorial. *Leyes, Decretos y documentos*. Bogotá, 1908.

———. Ministerio de Guerra. *Memorias*, 1917–21.

———. Ministerio de Hacienda. *Memorias*, 1833–83.

———. Ministerio de Industrias. *Memorias*, 1931.

———. Ministerio de Justicia. *Memorias*, 1894.

———. Ministerio de Relaciones Exteriores. *Memorias*, 1911–23.

———. Presidente. *Mensajes presidenciales*, 1832–1923.

Cuervo, Antonio B., comp. *Colección de documentos inéditos sobre la geografía y la historia de Colombia*. 4 vols. Bogotá, 1891–1894.

Galindo, Anibal. *Anuario estadístico de Colombia, 1876*. Bogotá, 1876.

Gibson, William Marion. *The Constitutions of Colombia*. Durham, 1948.

Gutiérrez, Rufino. *Monografías*. Bogotá, 1920.

Ortega Díaz, Alfredo. *Ferrocarriles colombianos: Legislación ferroviaria*. Bogotá, 1949.

Sánchez Ramírez, Ricardo. *La reconstrucción nacional*. Bogotá, 1908.

Uribe, José Antonio. *Anales diplomáticos y consulares de Colombia*, 6 vols. Bogotá, 1920.

———. *La reforma administrativa*. Bogotá, 1917.

Official Newspapers

Boyacá. *El Boyacense*, 1865–92.

Colombia. Cámara de Representantes. *Anales*, 1882–1930.

———. Senado. *Anales del Senado*, 1883–1930.

———. República. *Gaceta de Colombia*, 1821–1832.

———. ———. *Gaceta de la Nueva Granada*, 1832–1847.

———. ———. *Gaceta Oficial*, 1848–61.

———. ———. *Diario Oficial*, 1864–98.

Cundinamarca. *El Constitutional de Cundinamarca*, 1851–1852, 1857–1868.

———. *El Neo-Granadino*, 1848–1857.

———. *Diario de Cundinamarca*, 1869–1890.

———. *Gaceta de Cundinamarca*, 1889–1890.

Meta. *Gaceta del Meta*, 1917–1918.

2. CHURCH DOCUMENTS

Arcila Robledo, Gregorio. *Las misiones franciscanas en Colombia*. Bogotá, 1910.

Bodas de plata misionales de la compañía de María en Colombia, 1904–1929. Villavicencio, 1929.

Casas y Conde, Nicolás. *Colonización de Casanare*. Bogotá, 1905.

———. *Hechos de la revolución de las misiones de Casanare*. Bogotá, 1900.

Conferencias episcopales de Colombia. Tomo 1. 1908–53. Bogotá, 1956.

Delgado, Daniel. *Excursiones por Casanare*. Bogotá, 1910.

Fabo, Pedro. *Restauración de la provincia de la Candelaria*. Bogotá, 1911.

———. *Liberaladas de una revolución*. Pamplona, 1914.

Ganuza, Marcelino. *Monografía de las misiones vivas de agustinos recoletos (candelarios) en Colombia*. 3 vols. Bogotá, 1921.

Matute, Santiago. *Los padres candelarios en Colombia o apuntes para la historia*. 6 vols. Bogotá, 1897–1903.

Mesanza, Andrés. *Apuntes y documentos sobre la orden dominicana de Colombia (de 1680 a 1930): apuntes o narración.* Caracas, 1929.

Prefectura Apostólica de Arauca. *Informe del Prefecto Apostólico,* 1917–22.

Ortega Torres, José Joaquín. *La obra salesiana en Colombia: Los primeros cincuenta años: 1890–1940.* Bogotá, 1941.

———. *La obra salesiana en los lazaretos.* Bogotá, 1938.

Oviedo, Basilio Vincente de. *Cualidades y riquezas del Nuevo Reino de Granada.* Bogotá, 1930.

Pérez Gómez, José. *Apuntes históricos de las misiones agustinianas en Colombia.* Bogotá, 1924.

Restrepo Posada, José. *Arquidiócesis de Bogotá: Datos biográficos de sus prelados, 1564–1891 y cabildo eclesiástico.* 4 vols. Bogotá, 1961–1971.

Vela, José de Calasanz. "Visita a las Misiones del Meta," *Anales Religiosos* (Bogotá), 1 (1884), 351–53.

Vicariato Apostólico de Casanare. *Informe del Vicario Apostólico,* 1917–1921.

Vicariato Apostólico de San Martín. *Informe del Vicario Apostólico,* 1916–1922.

Zamora, Alonso de. *Historia de la Provincia de San Antonio del Nuevo Reino de Granada.* Caracas, 1930.

Official Newspapers

Bogotá. *Anales Religiosos,* 1883–86.
Támara. *El Propagador,* 1917–21.
Villavicencio. *Eco de Oriente,* 1916–20.

3. NONOFFICIAL NEWSPAPERS

Bogotá: *El Agricultor,* 1881.
        El Diario Nacional, 1916–1919.
        El Espectador, 1917.
        Gil Blas, 1917.
        El Nuevo Tiempo, 1902–1932.
Arauca: *El Araucano,* 1934–36.
Cúcuta: *La Tarde,* 1919.
        El Trabajo, 1917–1918.
Tunja: *Boyacá Liberal,* 1921–1922.
        El Deber, 1918–1921.
        La Linterna, 1900–1917, 1918, 1920.
        Repertorio Boyacense, 1920–1930.
        La Unión Conservadora, 1917–1918.
Villavicencio: *Ferrocarril del Meta,* 1917.

4. CHRONICLES, DIARIES, MEMOIRS, AND TRAVEL ACCOUNTS

Aguado, Pedro de. *Recopilación historial.* 4 vols. Bogotá, 1956.

Arbeláez, Tulio. *Episodios de la guerra de 1899–1903: Campañas del general Cesáreo Pulido por su primer ayudante general.* Manizales, 1904.

Bayón, José Francisco. *Inmigración a los llanos de Casanare y San Martín.* Chocontá, 1881.

Bingham, Hiram. *Journal of an Expedition across Venezuela and Colombia.* New Haven, 1909.

Bonnet, José. *Comercio oriental por el río Meta.* Bogotá, 1884.

Brisson, Jorge. *Casanare.* Bogotá, 1896.

Camacho Roldán, Salvador. *Escritos varios.* 3 vols. Bogotá, 1983.

Carriazo, Max. *Llanos Orientales.* Bogotá, 1910.

Cordobés Moure, José María, "Reminiscencias: Rafael Reyes Prieto." BHA 4:44 (1907): 449–509.

Cuervo Márquez, Carlos. *El Llano.* Banco de la República: Archivo de la Economía Nacional. Vol. 7. Bogotá, 1955.

Díaz Escobar, Joaquín. *Región Oriental de Colombia.* Bogotá, 1879.

Díos Tavera, Juan de. *Eco de Oriente.* Bogotá, 1879.

Eder, Phanor James. *Colombia.* New York, 1913.

Guerra Azuola, Ramón. "Apuntamientos de Viaje." BHA 4:38 (August 1906): 65–72; 43 (January 1907): 415–31.

Hettner, Alfred. *Viajes por los Andes Colombianos (1882–1884),* trans. Heinrich Henk. Bogotá, 1976.

Michelsen U., Carlos, and A. Saénz. *Informe de los exploradores del territorio de San Martín.* Bogotá, 1871.

Mozans, H. J. *Up the Orinoco and Down the Magdalena.* New York, 1910.

Nieto Caballero, Luis Eduardo. *Vuelo al orinoco.* Bogotá, 1935.

Páez, José Antonio. *Autobiografía del General Páez.* 2 vols. Caracas, 1975.

Pardo, Nicolás. *Correría de Bogotá al territorio de San Martín.* Bogotá, 1875.

Por el oriente colombiano: Navegación del Meta y su vía directa a más corto. Bogotá, 1924.

Reclus, Eliseo. *Colombia,* trans. F. J. Vergara y Velasco. Bogotá, 1958.

Restrepo, Emiliano. *Una excursión al territorio de San Martín.* Bogotá, 1957.

Reyes, Rafael. *Escritos varios.* Bogotá, 1920.

Röthlisberger, Ernst. *El Dorado.* Bogotá, 1963.

Rozo M., Darío. "Viaje por la región de Casanare." *Revista Geográfica de Colombia,* no. 8 (August 1939): 20–28.

Sanín Cano, Baldomero. *Escritos.* Bogotá, 1977.

Santos, Enrique. *Danza de las horas.* Bogotá, 1969.

Triana, Miguel. *Al Meta.* Bogotá, 1913.

Uribe Uribe, Rafael. *Documentos políticos y militares.* 4 vols. Medellín, 1982.

Vargas Santos, Gabriel. *La razón de mi dicho.* Bogotá, 1904.

Vela, José de Calasanz. *Desde Villavicencio hasta San Fernando de Atabapo. América Española* (Cartagena), 2 (1935): 225–40, 353–77; 3 (1936): 150–78, 210–39, 304–24.

———. *Dos viajes por la orinoquia colombiana: 1889–1988.* Bogotá, 1988.

Zuleta Angel, Eduardo. *El Presidente López.* Medellín, 1966.

5. ATLASES, GEOGRAPHIES, AND BIOGRAPHICAL DICTIONARIES

Acevedo Latorre, Eduardo. *Diccionario geográfico de Colombia.* 2 vols. Bogotá, 1971.

Codazzi, Agustín. *Atlas geográfico é histórico de la república de Colombia.* Paris, 1889.

Díaz Lemos, Angel M. *Compendio de geografía de la república de Colombia.* 6th ed. Barcelona, 1907.

Londoño, Julio. *Album de la Comisión Corográfica.* Bogotá, 1953.
Medina R., Juan. *Geografía económica de Colombia. 3: Boyacá.* Bogotá, 1936.
Montenegro Colón, Feliciano. *Geografía general.* 4 vols. Caracas, 1834.
Ospina, Joaquín. *Diccionario biográfico y bibliográfico de Colombia.* 3 vols. Bogotá, 1937.
Ossa V., Peregrino. *Geografía de la intendencia nacional del Meta.* Bogotá, 1937.
Pérez, Felipe. *Geografía general, física y política de los Estados Unidos de Colombia.* Bogotá, 1883.
Vergara y Velasco, F. J. *Nueva geografía de Colombia.* Bogotá, 1901–1902.
Zamora, Manuel M. *Guía de la República de Colombia.* Bogotá, 1907.

6. THESES AND DISSERTATIONS

Baquero, Omar. "Departamento del Meta: Historia de su integración a la nación—1536–1936." Thesis, Departamento de Sociología, Universidad Nacional–Bogotá, 1986.
Bergquist, Charles W. "Coffee and Conflict in Colombia, 1886–1904: Origins and Outcome of the War of the Thousand Days." Ph.D. dissertation, Stanford University, 1973.
Dunlap, Vincent Baillie. "Tragedy of a Colombian Martyr: Rafael Uribe Uribe and the Liberal Party, 1896–1914." Ph.D. dissertation, University of North Carolina, 1979.
Helguera, José León. "The First Mosquera Administration in New Granada, 1845–49." Ph.D. dissertation, University of North Carolina, 1958.
Morey, Nancy Kathleen Creswick. "Ethnohistory of the Colombian and Venezuelan Llanos." Ph.D. dissertation, University of Utah, 1975.
Morey, Robert. "Ecology and Culture Change among the Colombian Guahibo." Ph.D. dissertation, University of Pittsburgh, 1970.

7. BOOKS

Abel, Christopher. *Política, iglesia y partidos en Colombia, 1886–1953.* Bogotá, 1987.
Arboleda, Gustavo. *Historia contemporánea de Colombia.* 3 vols. 2d ed. Cali, 1933.
Armas Chitty, José Antonio. *Tucupido: Formación de un pueblo del llano.* Caracas, 1961.
Banco de la República. *Colombia 1886: Programa centenario de la constitución.* Bogotá, 1986.
Bell, P. L. *Colombia: A Commercial and Industrial Handbook.* Washington, D.C., 1921.
Bergquist, Charles. *Coffee and Conflict in Colombia, 1886–1910.* Durham, 1978.
Bolívar Coronado, Rafael. *El llanero: Estudio de sociología venezolano.* Madrid, 1919.
Bonilla, Victor Daniel. *Servants of God or Masters of Men? The Story of a Capuchin Mission in Amazonia.* London, 1972.
Bowman, Isaiah. *Limits of Land Settlement.* New York, 1937.
Brito Figueroa, Frederico. *La estructura económica de Venezuela colonial.* 2d ed. Caracas, 1978.

Brunnschweiler, Dieter. *The Llanos Frontier of Colombia: Environment and Changing Land Use in Meta*. East Lansing, Mich., 1972.

Bushnell, David. *The Santander Regime in Gran Colombia*. Newark, 1954.

Camejo, Ernesto. *Breves apuntaciones sobre Arauca*. Bogotá, 1940.

Carrera Damas, Germán. *Boves: Aspectos socio-económicos de su acción histórica*. Caracas, 1968.

Collier, Richard. *The River that God Forgot*. London, 1968.

Colmenares, German. *Las haciendas de los jesuítas en el Nuevo Reino de Granada*. Bogotá, 1969.

Curtin, Philip D. *Death by Migration: Europe's Encounter with the Tropical World in the Nineteenth Century*. New York, 1989.

de Greiff, Luis. *Semblanzas y comentarios*. Bogotá, 1942.

de Hoyos, Ramón P. *Reviviendo la historia*. Cartagena, 1945.

de la Pedraja Tomán, Rene. *Los llanos: Colonización y economía*. Bogotá: CEDE: Universidad de los Andes. 1984.

de la Vega, José. *La federación en Colombia, 1810–1912*. Madrid, 1916.

Delpar, Helen. *Red against Blue: The Liberal Party in Colombian Politics, 1863–1899*. University, 1981.

Díaz Díaz, Oswaldo. *La reconquista española*. 2 vols. Bogotá, 1964–1967.

España, Gonzalo. *La guerra civil de 1885: Núñez y la derrota del radicalismo*. Bogotá, 1985.

Fabo, Pedro. *Idiomas y etnografía de la región oriental de Colombia*. Barcelona, 1911.

———. *El Dr. Navascués. Novela de costumbres casanareñas*. Bogotá, 1904.

Flórez, Raquel Angel de. *Conozcamos el departamento del Meta*. 3 vols. Bogotá, 1962–1963.

Flórez, Isaac. *Enfermedades dominantes en los llanos de la región oriental de Colombia*. Villavicencio, 1919.

Fosdick, Raymond B. *The Story of the Rockefeller Foundation*. New York, 1952.

Franco, Jean. *The Modern Culture of Latin America*. Rev. ed. Middlesex, 1970.

Gallegos, Rómulo. *Doña Bárbara*. Trans. Robert Malloy. New York, 1948.

Gast Galvis, Augusto. *Historia de la fiebre amarilla en Colombia*. Bogotá, 1982.

Gómez Picón, Rafael. *Orinoco, río de libertad*. Madrid, 1953.

Hardenburg, W. E. *The Putumayo: The Devil's Paradise*. London, 1912.

Henao, Jesús María, and Gerardo Arrubla. *Historia de Colombia*. 5th ed. Bogotá, 1929.

Hennessey, Alistair. *The Frontier in Latin American History*. Albuquerque, 1978.

Izard, Miguel. *El miedo a la revolución: La lucha por la libertad en Venezuela (1777–1830)*. Madrid, 1979.

Lamar, Howard, and Leonard Thompson, eds. *The Frontier in History: North America and Southern Africa Compared*. New Haven, 1981.

Latourette, Kenneth S. *The Great Century: The Americas, Australasia and Africa*. Vol. 5 of *A History of the Expansion of Christianity*. 7 vols. New York, 1943.

Lavar, James. *Taste and Fashion: From the French Revolution to the Present Day*. 2d ed. London, 1946.

LeGrand, Catherine. *Frontier Expansion and Peasant Protest in Colombia, 1830–1936*. Albuquerque, 1986.

Lemaitre, Eduardo. *Rafael Reyes: Biografía de un gran colombiano*. 3d ed. Bogotá, 1967.

Londoño, Julio. *Integración del territorio colombiano.* Bogotá, 1967.
————. *Derecho territorial de Colombia.* Bogotá, 1973.
Lynch, John. *The Spanish-American Revolutions, 1808–1826.* New York, 1973.
Martín, Luis. *The Kingdom of the Sun.* New York, 1974.
Martín, Miguel Angel. *Del folclor llanero.* Villavicencio, 1982.
Mathews, Robert Paul. *Violencia rural en Venezuela 1840–1858: Antecedentes socio-económicos de la guerra federal.* Caracas, 1977.
McGreevey, William Paul. *An Economic History of Colombia, 1845–1930.* Cambridge, England, 1971.
Mecham, J. Lloyd. *Church and State in Latin America.* Rev. ed. Chapel Hill, 1966.
McKenzie, John L. *The Roman Catholic Church.* New York, 1969.
Neal-Silva, Eduardo. *Horizonte humano: Vida de José Eustasio Rivera.* 2d ed. Mexico, 1986.
Neill, Stephen. *History of Christian Missions.* Baltimore, 1964.
Nieto Arteta, Luis Eduardo. *Economía y cultura en la historia de Colombia.* Bogotá, 1941.
Ocampo, José Antonio. *Colombia y la economía mundial, 1830–1910.* Bogotá, 1984.
Ocampo López, Javier. *Historia básica de Colombia.* Bogotá, 1987.
————. *Historia del pueblo boyacense.* Tunja, 1983.
Olivares, Antonio. *Las ciconiiformes colombianas.* Bogotá, 1973.
Ordoñez Vila, Montserrat. *La vorágine: Textos críticos.* Bogotá, 1932.
Ortega Díaz, Alfredo. *Ferrocarriles colombianos: Resumen histórico.* 2 vols. Bogotá, 1923.
————. *Historia de los ferrocarriles colombianos.* 3 vols. Bogotá, 1932.
Ortega Ricaurte, Enrique. *Villavicencio: 1842–1942: Monografía histórica.* Bogotá, 1943.
Ospina Vásquez, Luis. *Industria y protección en Colombia 1810–1930.* Medellín, 1955.
Pacheco, Juan M. *Los jesuítas en Colombia.* 2 vols. Bogotá, 1959–1962.
Palacios, Marco. *Coffee in Colombia (1850–1970): An Economic, Social and Political History.* Cambridge, England, 1980.
Paredes Cruz, Joaquín. *Departamento del Meta.* Villavicencio, 1961.
Paris Lozano, Gonzalo. *Guerrilleros del Tolima.* Bogotá, 1984.
Park, James. *Rafael Núñez and the Politics of Colombian Regionalism, 1863–1886.* Baton Rouge, 1985.
Pérez Aguirre, Antonio. *Los radicales y la regeneración.* Bogotá, 1941.
Perico Ramírez, Mario. *Reyes: De cauchero a dictador.* Tunja, 1974.
Plazas Olarte, Guillermo. *La guerra civil de los mil días: Estudio militar.* Tunja, 1985.
Plazas Olarte, Humberto. *Los territorios nacionales.* Bogotá, 1944.
Poppino, Rollie E. *Brazil: The Land and the People.* 2d ed. New York, 1973.
Puentes, Milton. *Historia del partido liberal colombiano.* 2d ed. Bogotá, 1961.
Rausch, Jane M. *A Tropical Plains Frontier: The Llanos of Colombia, 1531–1831.* Albuquerque, 1984.
Restrepo, Daniel. *La Compañía de Jesús en Colombia.* Bogotá, 1940.
Restrepo, José Manuel. *Historia de la Nueva Granada.* 2 vols. Bogotá, 1952.
————. *Historia de la revolución de la república de Colombia en la América meridional.* 8 vols. Bogotá, 1942–1950.

Restrepo Canal, Carlos. *La Nueva Granada.* 2 vols. Bogotá, 1971–1975.

Rivera, José Eustasio. *La Vorágine.* Trans. Earle K. James. New York, 1935.

Rodríguez Piñeres, Eduardo. *El olimpo radical.* Bogotá, 1950.

Rojas P., Daniel, and Marco Tulio Torres. *Lo que nos contó el abuelito.* Villavicencio, 1942.

Romoli, Kathleen. *Colombia: Gateway to South America.* New York, 1941.

Rouse, John. *The Criollo: Spanish Cattle in the Americas.* Norman, 1977.

Safford, Frank. *The Ideal of the Practical: Colombia's Struggle to Form a Technical Elite.* Austin, 1976.

Samper, José M. *Ensayo sobre las revoluciones políticas y la condición social de los repúblicas colombianas (hispano-amercanas).* Paris, 1861.

Serrano Camargo, Rafael. *El General Uribe.* Bogotá, 1978.

Tamayo, Joaquín. *La revolución de 1899.* Bogotá, 1975.

Taylor, George Rogers. *The Turner Thesis Concerning the Role of the Frontier in American History.* 3d ed. Boston, 1977.

Tisnes J., Roberto María. *Fray Ignacio Mariño, OP: Capellán general del ejército libertador.* Bogotá, 1963.

Uribe Celis, Carlos. *Los años veinte en Colombia: Ideología y cultura.* Bogotá, 1985.

Uribe de Hincapié, María Teresa, and Jesús María Alvarez. *Poderes y regiones en la constitución de la nación colombiana, 1810–1850.* Medellín, 1987.

Vallenilla Lanz, Laureano. *Cesarismo democrático.* 4th ed. Caracas, 1961.

Valois Arce, Daniel. *Reseña histórica sobre los límites entre Colombia y Venezuela.* Medellín, 1970.

Velandía, Roberto. *Encyclopedia histórica de Cundinamarca.* 6 vols. Bogotá, 1979.

Vila, Marco Aurelio. *Por los espacios llaneros.* Caracas, 1967.

Villegas, Jorge, and José Yunis. *La guerra de los mil días.* Bogotá, 1978.

———. *Sucesos colombianos: 1900–1924.* Medellín, 1976.

Weber, David. *The Mexican Frontier 1821–1846: The American Southwest under Mexico.* Albuquerque, 1982.

Zapata Olivella, Manuel. *El hombre colombiano.* Bogotá, 1974.

Zuluaga Osorio, Conrado, ed. *José Eustasio Rivera 1888–1988.* Bogotá, 1988.

8. ARTICLES

Ayape, Eugenio. "Misiones de Casanare." BHA 28:323–24 (September-October 1941): 769–98; 36:420–22 (October-December 1949): 650–80.

Bates, Marston. "Climate and Vegetation in the Villavicencio Region of Eastern Colombia." *Geographical Review* 38 (October 1948): 555–74.

Blydenstein, John. "Tropical Savanna Vegetation of the Llanos of Colombia." *Ecology* 48:1 (Winter 1967): 1–14.

Bushnell, David. "Elecciones presidenciales colombianos 1825–1856." In Miguel Urrutia and Mario Arrubla, *Compendio de estadísticas históricas de Colombia,* 219–314. Bogotá, 1970.

———. "The Last Dictatorship: Betrayal or Consummation?" HAHR 63:1 (February 1983): 65–105.

———. "Voter Participation in the Colombian Election of 1856." HAHR 51:2 (May 1971): 237–49.

Carvajal Sinisterra, Alfredo. "El petroleo del llano." In *Llanos de Colombia,* 178–86. Bogotá, 1986.

Cortés, Pantaleón. "La llanura de Arauca." *Revista Nacional de Agricultura* 16:211–12 (January-February 1922): 193–99.

Crist, Raymond E. "Fixed Physical Boundaries and Dynamic Cultural Frontiers: A Contrast." *American Journal of Economics and Sociology* 12:2 (April 1953): 221–30.

————. and Ernesto Guhl. "Pioneer Settlement in Eastern Colombia." *Annual Report 1956,* Smithsonian Institution, Washington, 391–414.

Deas, Malcolm. "Colombia, Ecuador and Venezuela, c. 1880–1930." In CHLA 5:641–82.

Díaz Díaz, Fernando. "Estado, iglesia y desamortización." In MANUAL 2:411–42.

Gilmore, Robert. "Colombia: The National Period." In A. Curtis Wilgus, ed., *The Caribbean: Contemporary Colombia,* 75–86. Gainesville, 1962.

————. "Nueva Granada's Socialist Mirage." HAHR 36:2 (May 1956): 190–210.

Gómez, Fernando. "Los censos en Colombia antes de 1905." In Miguel Urrutia and Mario Arrubla, *Compendio de estadísticas históricas de Colombia,* 9–30. Bogotá, 1970.

González, Margarita. "Las rentas del estado." In MANUAL 2:387–410.

Guáqueta Gallardo, Rogerio. "La fundación de Arauca." *Comité Bicentenario de Arauca.* Bogotá, January 1976.

Gúzman Ramírez, Nohora. "La expansión de la frontera económica en el pie de monte llanero, 1856–1904: El caso de Medina." In *Los llanos: una historia sin fronteras.* 1st Simposio de Historia de los Llanos Colombó-Venezolanos, 459–68. Bogotá, 1988.

Izard, Miguel. "Ni cuatreros, ni montoneros, llaneros." *Boletín Americanista* (Barcelona) 13 (1981): 83–142.

————. "Tanto pelear para terminar conversando, el caudillismo en Venezuela." *Nova Americana* (Turin) 2 (1979): 37–81.

Jaramillo Uribe, Jaime. "Etapas y sentido de la historia de Colombia." In Mario Arrubla, et al., *Colombia hoy,* 10th ed., 15–51. Bogotá, 1985.

Kirchhoff, Paul. "Food-gathering tribes of the Venezuelan Llanos." In Julian Steward, ed., *Handbook of South American Indians,* vol. 4, *The Circum-Caribbean Tribes,* 445–68. New York, 1963.

LeGrand, Catherine. "Labor Acquisition and Social Conflict on the Colombian Frontier, 1850–1936." *Journal of Latin American Studies* 16:1 (May 1984): 27–49.

"Los colonizadores del Llano." *Revista Pan* (Bogotá) 15 (August 1937): 145–50ff.

Loy, Jane M. "Elegance, Ecology and Egrets." *Américas* 28:10 (October 1976): 19–24.

————. "Rebellion in the Colombian Llanos: The Arauca Affair of 1917." *The Americas* 34:4 (April 1978): 502–31.

Lynch, John. "The Catholic Church in Latin America, 1830–1930." In CHLA 4:527–95.

Martin, F. O. "Exploration in Colombia." *Geographical Review* 19 (1929): 621–37.

Melo, Jorge Orlando. "La evolución económica de Colombia, 1830–1900." In MANUAL 2:135–207.

————. "La república conservadora (1880–1930." In Mario Arrubla, et al., *Colombia hoy,* 10th ed., 52–101. Bogotá, 1978.

Mesa, Darío. "La vida política después de Panamá." In MANUAL 3:83–176.

Morey, Nancy C., and Robert V. Morey. "Relaciones commerciales en el pasado en los llanos de Colombia y Venezuela." *Montalban* (Caracas) 4 (1975): 5–36.

Ortiz Gómez, Francisco, and Helena Pardilla Rueda, "Indígenas de los Llanos Orientales." In Instituto Colombiano de Antropología, *Introducción a la Colombia amerindia*, 83–95. Bogotá, 1987.

Ossa V., Peregrino. "La ganadería en los llanos orientales." *Revista Nacional de Agricultura* 23:303–4 (September-October 1929): 96–103.

Pabón Monroy, Oscar Alfonso. "Restrepo." *Trocha* (Villavicencio) 168 (December 1989): 18–19.

Parsons, James J. "Europeanization of the Savanna Lands of Northern South America." In David R. Harris, ed., *Human Ecology in Savanna Environments*, 267–89. London, 1980.

Pinto, José Miguel. "División política de la República de Colombia de 1819 a 1905." BHA 5:52 (January 1908): 240–44.

———. "División política del Departamento de Boyacá de 1821 a 1905." BHA 6:69 (February 1911): 578–81.

Platt, Raye. "Opportunities for Agricultural Colonization in the Eastern Border Valleys of the Andes." In *Pioneer Settlement*, American Geographical Society Special Publication 14, 80–107. New York, 1932.

Poveda Ramos, Gabriel. "Nuestra historia ferroviaria." *Revista Antioqueña de Economía y Desarrollo* (Medellín) 21:3 (1986): 6–19.

Ramos, Abelardo. "Puente de fierro sobre el Río Negro." *Anales de Ingeniería* 1:9 (April 1888): 257–60.

Rausch, Jane M. "José de Calasanz Vela: Frontier Priest." In Judith Ewell and William H. Beezley, eds., *The Human Tradition in Latin America: The Nineteenth Century*, 141–60. Wilmington, Del., 1989.

Rice, Hamilton. "Further Explorations in the Northwest Amazon Basin." *Geographical Journal* 44:2 (August 1914): 137–68.

Rippy, J. Fred. "Dawn of the Railroad Era in Colombia," HAHR 23:4 (November 1943): 650–63

———. "The Dictators of Colombia and Venezuela." In A. Curtis Wilgus, ed., *South American Dictators*, 367–90. New York, 1963.

Simón Crespi, Roberto. "*La Vorágine:* Cincuenta años después." In Montserrat Ordoñez Vila, *La Vorágine: Textos Críticos*, 417–29. Bogotá, 1987.

Trirado Mejía, Alvaro. "El estado y la política en el siglo XIX." In MANUAL 2:327–84.

Vargas Vergara, J. M. "Región oriental de Colombia." *Revista del Ministerio de Obras Públicas* 4:2 (1909): 119–22; 3:182–88; 6:394–96; 7:473–76.

Weisman, Alan. "Dangerous Days in the Macarena." *The New York Times Magazine* (April 23, 1989): 40–48.

West, Robert C. "The Geography of Colombia." In A. Curtis Wilgus, ed., *The Caribbean: Contemporary Colombia*, 3–21. Gainesville, 1962.

White, C. Langdon. "Cattle Raising: A Way of life in the Venezuelan Llanos." *The Scientific Monthly* 83 (September 1956): 122–29.

Index

Moreno, Ezequiel, 149–50
Moreno, J. Trinidad, 107, 116, 121, 123–24
Moreno, Juan Nepomuceno, 12, 16, 29, 31, 36, 332
Moreno, Lisandro A., 126, 168
Moreno (town), 66
Morillo, Pablo, 21
Morillo Toro, Manuel, 67
Morón, Eugenio, 210–11
Mosquera, Joaquín, 30
Mosquera, Manuel José, 30, 43, 45, 53, 69

Mosquera, Tomás Cipriano, 30, 45–46, 62, 67; anticleric actions, 116, 149; Liberal tendencies of, 48–49; return to power, 77, 83; scientific progress under, 64; siezed power, 69
Motto, Alejandro, 310
Moyano, Heliodoro, 235
Mozans, H. J., 300, 323–24
Muñoz, Cornelio, 72, 74
Murillo Toro, Manuel, 89, 95–96, 116
Mutis, Jerónimo, 241, 248, 255, 286

National Junta on Missions, 229–30
Neale-Silva, Eduardo, 320
Neira, Juan José, 45
Neira, Ramón, 186
New Granada (1832–1857), 1–23; heartland of, 1–3; exports, 63; Indians in, 38–40; missionary reprise, 29–55; regionalism dominant in, 3
Nieto, José, 319–20
Nieto, Luis, 270
Nieto, Manuel José, 309
Nieto Caballero, Luis Eduardo, 334
Norzagaray, Leonidas, 146
Novoa, Aristides, 180, 237–41, 285, 292
Novoa L., Jorge, 172, 175
Nueva geografía de Colombia (Vergara y Velasco), 322

Nuevos jéneros i especies de plantas..., 64
El Nuevo Tiempo, 265, 275, 277
Nunchía (town), 10, 298–300, 303
Núñez, Rafael, 137–39, 157, 181; president of Bolívar, 129–30; reconciliation with church, 148–49; mentioned, 67, 87, 97, 102, 145, 147, 206, 256

Obando, José María, 45, 67, 83
La obra salesiana en Colombia (Ortega Torres), 153
Obregón, Gregorio, 93
Oca, Monte de, 270
Olarte Camacho, Francisco, 259
Olaya Herrera, Enrique, 223, 275, 278, 329, 333
O'Leary, Carlos, 100
O'Leary, Simón, 97
Olmena, Esteban, 38
Ordóñez, Antonio, 207
Ordóñez, Nepomuceno, 33
Orinoco River, 5, 10, 17
Orinoco (ship), 76
Orocué: in 1918, 300–301; river commerce and, 155–56
Oropeza, José María, 313
Oropeza, Josefa, 320
Oropeza, Ramón, 319
Ortega Torres, José Joaquín, 153
Ortiz, Daniel, 267–68, 272
Ortiz, Juan de Dios, 172
Ortiz, Rafael, 104, 109, 140–41, 159, 174, 202
Osorio, Alejandro, 49, 52, 54
Osorio, Ignacio, 79
Osorio, José, 239
Ospina, Luna, 250
Ospina, Manuel, 67
Ospina, Pedro Nel, 223–24, 228, 248, 266
Ospina Camacho, Mariano, 186–87, 189, 198–99
Ospina Chaves, Mariano, 197
Ospina Rodríquez, Mariano, 47–48, 50–52, 62, 69, 76

About the Book and the Author

The Llanos Frontier in Colombian History, 1830–1930
Jane M. Rausch

The Llanos Orientales of Colombia, the eastern fifth of the country, is one of the little-known frontier regions of South America. Because the Llanos have attracted little scholarly interest, the region is assumed to be unimportant; but Rausch carefully reconstructs for the first time in English the many ways in which the Llanos have played a far greater role in the evolution of Colombia than previously recognized.

In 1830 an army from the Llanos unseated the dictatorship of Rafael Urdaneta. Additionally, men from the Llanos formed key contingents in the numerous wars and rebellions that shook the country in the nineteenth and early twentieth century. These protests were born, in part, out of frustration over the region's unrealized potential, particularly the inability of the central government to administer the region and integrate it economically into the nation. Indicative of the political chaos was the absence of an effective military presence, without which violence became a part of everyday life, whether it came in Indian attacks or marauding by rustlers, outlaws, and revolutionaries.

Jane M. Rausch, professor of history at the University of Massachusetts, has written extensively on Colombia's history. Her study of the Llanos during the colonial period is presented in *A Tropical Plains Frontier: The Llanos of Colombia, 1531–1831* (UNM Press, 1984).